Memories of Revolt

Memories of Revolt

*The 1936–1939 Rebellion
and the Palestinian National Past*

Ted Swedenburg

 University of Minnesota Press

Minneapolis

London

Published by the University of Minnesota Press
111 Third Avenue South, Suite 290, Minneapolis, MN 55401-2520
http://www.upress.umn.edu
Printed in the United States of America on acid-free paper

Second Printing 1998

Library of Congress Cataloging-in-Publication Data

Swedenburg, Ted.
    Memories of revolt : the 1936–1939 rebellion and the Palestinian
national past / Ted Swedenburg.
        p.   cm.
    Includes bibliographical references and index.
    ISBN 0-8166-2164-0 (hc). — ISBN 0-8166-2165-9 (pb)
    1. Palestine—History—Arab rebellion, 1936–1939.   2. Palestinian
Arabs—Interviews.   I. Title.
    DS126.S88   1995
    956.94'04—dc20   95-19977

To the memory of Bertha Swanson Swedenburg

Contents

Glossary

damm: blood; an affair involving homicide

diwân: sitting room

fasâ'il al-salâm: peace bands; the counterrevolutionary bands organized to fight the rebels in 1938–39

faza': alert, call to arms

hamûla (pl. *hamâ'il*): patronymic group in which membership is expressed in a patrilineal idiom

hatta (pl. *hattât*): headcovering worn by Palestinian peasants; adopted as distinctive headdress of the rebels of 1936–39; today, a Palestinian national signifier. Also known as the *kûfîya.*

hijâb (pl., *hujub*): headcovering worn by women as a sign of their modesty and propriety; also known in Palestine as the *mandîl*

hilf: confederation of peasant *hamâ'il,* often including Bedouin tribes

hizb: group or faction; political party

irhâbîyîn: terrorists

khâ'in (pl. *khuwwan*): traitor

kûfîya (pl. *kûfîyât*): see *hatta*

majlisî: a supporter of the national movement; literally, a councilist, that is, a follower of Grand Mufti Hâjj Amîn al-Husaynî, head of the Supreme Muslim Council (*majlis*) and leader of the national movement in the 1930s

mandîl (pl. *manâdîl*): see *hijâb*

mujâhid (*mujâhidîn*): freedom fighter

mujrimîn: criminals

mukhtâr (pl. *makhâtîr*): village headman

mu'ârida: opposition; refers here to the Nashâshîbî-led opposition to the national movement that arose in the course of the revolt

nakba: disaster; the disaster of 1947–48 in which 770,000 Arab refugees were expelled from Palestine

qâ'id (pl. *quwwâd*): commander

qâ'id fasîl (pl. *quwwâd fasâ'il*): rebel band commander

qumbâz: the "traditional" dress worn by an elderly male Palestinian peasant

shabâb: young men; term used to refer to youths involved in confrontations with soldiers in both the 1936–39 revolt and the intifada

shahîd: martyr

simsâr (pl., *samâsira*): land dealer; implies someone who sold land to the Zionists

sûq: market

taqsîm: partition (of Palestine)

tawq: search-and-encirclement operation mounted by the British army

tawsha: fight, brawl

thawra: revolt; often used in reference to the 1936–39 rebellion

thâ'ir (pl. *thuwwâr*): rebel, revolutionary

watan: nation; homeland

watanî: nationalist

za'îm (pl. *zu'âmâ'*): a leader from the urban notable class

Acknowledgments

It can hardly be claimed that this book is the product of my individual efforts, as so many people have helped make it possible.

First I must gratefully acknowledge my parents, Romain Swedenburg and the late Bertha Swedenburg, and my brother Ray, who first took me to Palestine/Israel and have been unstinting in their support for my continuing ventures in this troubled field. Thanks as well to my stepmother, Juanita Swedenburg, for her warm encouragement.

At the University of Texas (UT) at Austin, I had the special fortune of belonging to a lively, argumentative, and stimulating study group that included Mariana Adler, James Brow, Amy Burce, Mary Crain, Doug Foley, Terry Greenwood, Joan Gross, David Knowlton, Kristin Koptiuch, José Limón, David McMurray, Forrest Pyle, Hilary Radner, Jennifer Sharpe, Kate Sullivan, and Mike Woost. Our collective conversations and discussions were invaluable in helping me work out many of the theories and ideas that have produced this project. The teaching and encouragement of Peter Gran and Gayatri Spivak at UT were also inspirational. Ella Gant and Lee Taylor also helped in special ways during my days in Austin.

Many people assisted me in special ways while I was doing fieldwork in Palestine/Israel in 1984–85, and I cannot begin to thank them enough: the family of Sonia Nimr, Sami Kilani and his entire family, Yaqub and Hanan Hijazi, Bulus Bulus, Musaddaq al-Masri, Muhammad Shadid, Assia Habash (Imm Samaan), Salim Tamari, Amal Nashashibi, Suad Amari, Philip and Maha Davies, John Viste, Tom Ricks, George Bisharat, Penny Johnson, Raja

Shehadeh, Joost Hiltermann, Hisham Dais, Walid Nazzal, Jan and Samir Abu Shakra, Nazim Shraydi, Adnan Sabbagh, Hussein Bargouti, Marty Rosenbluth, and Fahmi Abbushi. Anita Vitullo and Samaan, Rasha, and Jumana Khoury deserve special thanks for their steady support, encouragement, and warm hospitality. There are many others in villages who assisted in various ways who are best left unidentified. And above all, the men and women we interviewed warrant my special gratitude for their cordiality and tolerance of our imposing questions.

A number of people are to be thanked for assisting me in significant ways while I did archival work in England in 1984 and 1985: Peter, Colleen, and Steven Sharpe; Fuad and Pamela Bishti; Anis Barghuthi; and Adel Samara.

The following persons read various portions, bits, and versions of this manuscript and made important comments, contributions, and suggestions: Clarissa Bencomo, Ruth Frankenberg, Akhil Gupta, Barbara Harlow, Jane Henrici, Paul Keyes, Smadar Lavie, Kristin Koptiuch, Joan Mandell, Lata Mani, David McMurray, Fred Pfeil, Jay O'Brien, Martina Rieker, Rosemary Sayigh, Jennifer Sharpe, Nick Siegel, and Mike Woost. Lila Abu-Lughod, George Marcus, and Julie Peteet also gave me detailed and insightful comments that proved invaluable as I finished the manuscript. Makram Copty assisted me in translating several interviews. Thanks as well to Nadia Abu El-Haj for providing useful sources on Israeli archaeology; to Ellen Fleischmann for sources and discussions on Palestinian women; to Karen Buckley, who kindly gave me access to transcripts of interviews she conducted with Palestinian refugees in Damascus; and to Salih 'Abd al-Jawwad for stimulating my thinking on the issue of collaboration. Anton Shammas also deserves a word of thanks for his encouragement.

In Seattle, I was fortunate to have emotional and intellectual support from a number of friends during a trying time: Steve Shaviro, Jeff Peck, Michael Siever, Jere Bacharach, Resat and Kathy Kasaba, Akhil Gupta, David McMurray, Joan Gross, Lee Taylor, Purnima Mankekar, Ali Ahmida, Lata Mani, Ruth Frankenberg, Valentine Daniel, Sandra Campbell, Ashutosh Chilkoti, Janet Fryberger, Dana Bates, Fred Pfeil, Ann Augustine, Charlie Hale, Carter Bentley, Jeff Olson, and Teresa Truax.

Special appreciation is due to James Brow, a careful reader and a great teacher, and especially to Robert Fernea, for his unflagging and invaluable sustenance, encouragement, accessibility and—most important—his warm friendship. I also received crucial suggestions and support from the other members of my dissertation committee: Barbara Harlow, José Limón, and Philip Khoury.

I have also had the good fortune to work with a marvelous editor, Janaki Bakhle, without whose encouraging words, gentle prodding, and wonderful enthusiasm I would not have brought this project to completion.

Grants from the Social Science Research Council and the Graduate School, University of Texas at Austin, enabled me to carry out my fieldwork and archival research in 1984–85. Subsequent work has been supported by the American Council of Learned Societies, the Social Science Research Council, and the American University in Cairo.

I extend my very special gratitude to Sonia Nimr, with whom I conducted many of the interviews on which this work is based. She was a delightful and stimulating intellectual and research companion and a constant source of inspiration. I have fond memories of our many arguments, discussions, and adventures. This work would never have been possible without her collaboration.

Finally, my undying thanks to Kelley and Evan O'Callaghan, who so graciously put up with the burdens that the writing of this book imposed on our family. I hope it was worth it.

Introduction

Memories of Revolt

Along the Way to the "Field"

Ethnographies conventionally open with the anthropologist's dramatic arrival in a previously unknown territory, his first day in the field, his initial impressions of the natives and their reactions to a new and disorienting presence in their midst. Such a beginning would be impossible here. First, it would depend upon the kind of radical distinction—between the Western "home" and "the field" somewhere "out there"—that now appears theoretically untenable, given our increasing awareness of the significance of transnational forces in the construction of cultures and identities. Second, such a beginning seems particularly inappropriate in light of the West's long-standing interests and entanglements in Palestine, the principal "field" of this study, and because my own relation to the region and people considerably predates my officially sanctioned academic fieldwork. So in lieu of a story of my "first contact" with virgin territory, I trace a genealogy of the involvements and relations with Palestine and its people that developed prior to my entry into "the field."

My early relationship to Palestine/Israel was largely determined by religion. I was raised in a strongly Christian home by a Methodist minister and his devout spouse, and read and studied the Old and New Testaments at church services, in Sunday school, and—after Arthur Godfrey was shut off—virtually every morning over oatmeal or Cheerios. One of the favored texts of my bookwormish childhood was a Bible atlas, which I pored over, locating place-names on the maps that corresponded to stories in scripture. Palestine (the Holy Land, Israel) was hardly "foreign" to me—I was almost as familiar with its geography as with that of any of our fifty states. But I imagined it primarily as a biblical space whose sites held meaning because of events recorded in the Old and New Testaments. I did have a vague notion about its contemporary history, mainly that, after protracted suffering in exile, the Jews had finally "returned" to the Holy Land. I knew this primarily from *The Diary of Anne Frank* and the graphic depictions of her life and the Holocaust in *Life* magazine—a weekly that in the fifties had "the cultural impact of all three television networks rolled into one" (Calvin Trillin, cited by Bryan 1993: 784).

Armed with such prior understandings and having reached the age of twelve, in winter 1961–62 I visited the Holy Land with my family. We spent three weeks in Jordan, primarily in the West Bank, and a week in Israel, including a night at Kibbutz Yohannon. Like most religious pilgrims to Israel/Palestine, the chief aim of our tour was to retrace the steps of Jesus and other biblical fathers. Yet, partly because of luck, partly because of political inclination, we didn't just see a land wholly determined by the Bible. For among my parents' religious convictions was the need for social justice. I did not always appreciate this, especially during the late sixties and early seventies when I so envied those New Left "red diaper babies" raised in bohemian-leftist or Communist households, environments that seemed glamorous and desirable compared with my own blandly liberal whitebread childhood. But I must now credit the ethicopolitical positions of my folks, who took me to listen to the stunning oratory of the Reverend Martin Luther King Jr. and other Southern Christian Leadership Conference (SCLC) leaders at San Francisco's Cow Palace in 1959 and who considered the John Birch Society and the bomb shelter campaign the pinnacles of lunacy. My father used to invite "Freedom Riders" to address his congregation from the pulpit, and he marched in a civil rights demonstration in San Jose. But I also recall that no blacks lived in Los Gatos, that there was only one Jewish kid in our tract-home neighborhood, and that my schoolmates and I habitually referred to Mexican Americans as "spics" and "greasers." Nevertheless, along with my family I was still somewhat predisposed to sympathize when the Arab tour guides in Jordan showing us where Jesus was born and crucified occasionally called attention to the plight of the Palestinians, known then in the West—when mentioned at all—primarily as pitiful "Arab refugees." Perhaps a more important role in raising our awareness of the Palestinian issue was played by our host in Jordan, Stan Remington, an employee of Point Four, the predecessor of USAID.

One gloomy December day Stan bundled us all into his Land Rover. Guided by an American Christian relief worker, we drove over a poorly marked and incredibly bumpy track to a "border village"[1] in the Hebron (al-Khalîl) district called Twaynî. Twaynî's inhabitants, we were dismayed to learn, had lost all their agricultural properties, located in the nearby plains to the west, when the Jewish state was created in 1948. Because they retained their simple dwellings in the highlands, the residents of Twaynî were not classified as "refugees" and—although their means of livelihood had been expropriated—were therefore ineligible for UNRWA relief. Coming straight from a lily-white Beaver Cleaver neighborhood in the Santa Clara Valley, I was astonished and appalled by Twaynî's stark poverty and angered by the world's indifference. My recollection—recently refreshed by my father's slide collection—is of a bleak atmosphere, of rocky hills, earth, and low mud-and-stone houses all hewn from the same monotonous greyish brown materials, unrelieved by the greenery of trees or plants. I picture buzzing flies, scrawny animals, urchins in ragged dress and with unkempt hair, a nursing mother, open running sewage. We hurriedly uttered our salaams and departed Twaynî upon learning that some villagers, ever the hospitable and amiable Arabs despite their destitution, were rounding up some of the stringy chickens we had noticed earlier scrabbling around on the rugged ground so that they could honor us with dinner.

Perhaps I'm still motivated by a desire to repay those generous and impoverished villagers for their offer of roasted *dajâj*. But there were more steps along the way before I realized there was any debt to discharge. In 1964, my father took a job as pastor of the Community Church in Beirut, Lebanon, partly because he and my mother worried that my brother and I would grow up with a distorted, circumscribed, and monotone view of the world if we stayed in suburban California. I was enrolled in the American Community School (ACS), where I tried my best to replicate the "normal" American teenager's experiences by learning to play the guitar, developing a fondness for beer, and participating in ACS's teenage rites of passage, like Sadie Hawkins Day. But "events" (*hawâdith*) sometimes interfered. Along with most other U.S. citizens, I was evacuated from Beirut during the war of June 1967. The pleasures of an unexpected summer in Europe were periodically darkened when I ran into North Americans or Israelis triumphantly celebrating the devastating victory the Jewish state had inflicted upon its Arab neighbors. I was left infuriated and frustrated at the absence of space within which to articulate an opposing viewpoint. For I had already tried to educate myself about the Palestine problem by reading anti-Zionist Jewish authors like Alfred Lilienthal and Rabbi Elmer Berger. So perhaps it is not so curious that in 1968–69, after I finally achieved what I so desired while living in Beirut— to get into a "hip" U.S. college, escape from my parents, dispense with the services of barbers, and join in the cultural politics of "the sixties"—my Lebanon experiences, limited as they were, alienated me from many of my classmates at Swarthmore. I remember one class on religion in which our professor, in the course of a discussion of a text of Thomas Aquinas, explained that Aquinas had got his main arguments from "some Arab philosophers." The class of about two hundred students broke into spontaneous laughter.[2] Even within the New Left and the antiwar movement I felt slightly out of place because of most U.S. progressives' persistent refusal to entertain criticisms of Israel. I recall, for instance, that the celebrated Peoples' Park confrontations in Berkeley had their beginnings in a march commemorating Israel Independence Day. I was delighted, at the end of my freshman year, when my parents took pity and invited me to return "home" and enroll in the American University of Beirut (AUB).

My first days at AUB in fall 1969 were marked by a student strike in solidarity with the Palestinian guerrillas and people who had driven Lebanese intelligence agents and military forces from their refugee camps and installed the rule of the Palestine Liberation Organization (PLO).[3] This event inaugurated a whole new era in Lebanese political life, an era in which the Palestinian resistance movement was a dominant force. Beirut was a vortex of progressive and pro-Palestinian activity, and AUB students were avid participants in the general ferment. I was carried along by the enthusiasm, as Palestinians transformed their image from that of hapless refugees to, depending on your viewpoint, armed revolutionaries or terrorists. I made friends and allies with Palestinians active in student politics and in various factions of the resistance movement, as well as with progressive students from all over the first and third worlds, and participated—insofar as possible for a foreigner—in the student movement. I visited Amman twice in 1970, before the Palestinian defeat of Black September, and met guerrilla leaders, fighters, and activists. I was involved in student work projects at refugee camps in Beirut and Tyre. Some of my friends and acquaintances received military training in the guerrilla movement, and one even successfully hijacked an airplane. Some undertook other crazy, brave, frivolous, sincere, deadly, heroic, and destructive actions, such as are characteristic of periods of social ferment. Several friends and acquaintances variously fell as combatants in battle, were struck dead by sniper fire, or were kidnapped, tortured, and murdered during the early phase of the Lebanese Civil War—mainly at the hands of fascists. Some of my Palestinian friends from the West Bank, who studied at AUB before any four-year colleges were opened in the Occupied Territories, returned home to face arrest and torture at the hands of the occupation forces. Several former Palestinian classmates are now successful professionals (mainly academics) in both the West and the West Bank. A few occupy positions in the PLO (outside Palestine), while others have played roles in recent peace negotiations. As for my own trajectory, the Lebanese Civil War forced me to abandon Beirut for the United States in 1976, but I stayed in touch with the Palestinian "cause" through intermittent solidarity and human rights work before and during my tenure as a graduate student.

The point of this account is to underscore the complex mix of attachments, investments, relations, experiences, emotions, and understandings that already connected me to Palestine before I began "fieldwork." My friendships and experiences from Beirut days and from political work in the United States, moreover, were crucial for my ethnographic research in the West Bank, ensuring support networks and contacts and enabling my understanding of, and capacity to manage, life under military occupation.

Thawra

When I first began to study the history of Palestine, I was interested by what I read about the events of 1936–39. In April 1936, Palestinian Arabs launched a general strike that lasted six months and turned into what became known as *al-thawra al-kubra* (the Great Revolt) of 1936–39, the most significant anticolonial insurgency in the Arab East during the interwar period. The strike began in the wake of a series of incidents initiated by the April 13 murder of two Jews by Arab insurgents. A wave of brutal reprisals and counterreprisals ensued, followed by the government's declaration of a state of emergency. "National committees" sprang up in all the Arab cities and towns and declared a general strike. Palestinian notables followed the wave of popular enthusiasm, and on April 25 the political parties met and established a coordinating body known as the Higher Arab Committee (HAC) headed by the Grand Mufti, Hâjj Amîn al-Husaynî. The HAC, which represented a kind of alliance between traditional notables and emergent middle-class urban radicals, took over the leadership of the strike and articulated its demands: that Great Britain, which occupied Palestine in 1917 and governed it as a mandate from the League of Nations, put an end to Jewish immigration, ban land sales to the Jews, and grant the country its national independence.

Although the insurgency erupted in the urban centers, its focus rapidly shifted to the countryside. In May 1936, peasant guerrilla bands began to mount operations against British forces, primarily in the highlands of Palestine (the central massif—basically the area known today as the West Bank—and the Galilean hills in the north). Although officially under the control of the HAC, the rebel bands operated relatively independently of the urban leaders. Their capacity to threaten the British hold on the country increased markedly by August, in part because Fawzî al-Dîn al-Qâwûqjî, a well-known pan-Arab nationalist of Syrian origin with considerable military experience, entered Palestine and declared himself commander in chief of the rebel forces. The British launched tough military countermeasures and exerted pressure on the HAC by agency of the Arab monarchs of Iraq, Jordan, and Saudi Arabia (nominal heads of independent states who were in fact under close imperial supervision). The HAC called off the general strike and insurrection on October 10, 1936, with the understanding that the Arab kings and princes would intercede with the British government on behalf of the Palestinians and that the government would act in good faith to work out new solutions.

A tense interim period ensued. While Palestinian notables pegged their hopes on a Royal Commission of Inquiry, militants and rebel commanders prepared for a new round of fighting. In July 1937, the Peel Commission issued its report, which recommended the partition of Palestine into Arab and Jewish states. Arab opinion was outraged, especially over the plan's provision for the overwhelmingly Arab Galilee to be included in the Jewish state. In September 1937, the district commissioner for the Galilee, Lewis Andrews, was assassinated by Arab gunmen.[4] The British retaliated by banning the HAC and arresting or deporting hundreds of urban leaders and activists. Others, like the Mufti, who escaped to Lebanon, fled into exile. Although the official national leadership was decimated, the armed revolt was relaunched in fall 1937, its command firmly in the hands of peasant partisans in the countryside.

The second stage of the insurrection reached its apex during summer and fall 1938, when insurgents gained control of the highlands and most Arab urban centers of Palestine. At this point, the rebellion's peasant and lower-class character crystallized, as the rebel command imposed subaltern dress codes on urban residents, declared a moratorium on debts, banned the use of electricity, canceled rents on apartments, and extracted large "contributions" from the wealthy classes, many of whom fled the country. But the apogee was short-lived, and rebel power began to recede in the face of a British counteroffensive and under the pressure of fracturing from within. The British were able to deploy a ground force of some twenty thousand troops, RAF aircraft, superior firepower, armed Zionist auxiliaries, and the classical savagery of colonial counterinsurgency. In addition, they exploited the rebel movement's internal struggles and certain errors—its alienation of the wealthy, the brutalities of particular commanders, abuses in the campaign of assassination of "traitors," and the absence of a centralized rebel command. The British military encouraged and assisted the disaffected notables and their peasant clients, who established local counterrevolutionary "peace bands" and did battle with rebel forces in several areas. The government meanwhile launched a diplomatic offensive, bringing Palestinian Arab and Zionist delegates to London in February 1939 for separate but inconclusive talks. In May 1939 the government issued a White Paper that declared its opposition to Palestine becoming a Jewish state, stated that Jewish immigration would be limited to seventy-five thousand over the next five years and that land sales would be strictly regulated, and affirmed that an independent Palestinian state would be established over the next ten years, with interim steps toward self-government. Although the White Paper did not satisfy the maximal Arab national demands, it amounted to a partial concession to the aims of the rebellion and in particular, a backing off from the partition proposal. Although the official leadership and rebel commanders rejected the White Paper, the Arab population's more favorable disposition toward it took some wind out of the sails of the insurgency.

British military force plus internal crumbling finally brought about the demise of the revolt by September 1939, when war with Germany broke out. The Arab community had suffered nearly 20,000 casualties (5,032 dead, 14,760 wounded), according to Walid Khalidi's estimate (1971: 848–49). Although the crushing of the revolt weakened the national movement and helped prepare the way for the calamities to come, it is nonetheless important to record that, for a time, this largely peasant insurgency had effectively challenged the might of the world's greatest imperial power.[5]

At the time of the revolt, Palestine was the world's second greatest exporter of citrus (in particular, the famous Jaffa orange) after Spain. But it was Palestine's strategic position, astride the path to India, jewel in the imperial crown, that British planners considered of greater significance. During the thirties, colonial strategists viewed Palestine as a future alternative site in which to station troops once the Anglo-Egyptian Treaty (negotiated in

1936) came due for revision in 1955. The road and air routes from Haifa to India via Iraq were viewed as crucial alternatives to the Suez Canal thoroughfare, especially in case of a war over Egypt. Equally important to imperial interests was the pipeline carrying oil from northern Iraq to Haifa, whose refineries furnished fuel to the British fleet in the eastern Mediterranean and the "very large supplies required by the French" allies. Haifa was also the only port in the eastern Mediterranean that could serve as a base for British imperial naval forces.[6] Strategists likewise considered Palestine to be a strategic buffer between Suez and Britain's potential enemies to the north (Germany, the USSR). When Neville Chamberlain signed the September 1938 Munich Agreement, one of his motivations for doing so was surely that it freed up an army division to deploy in the counteroffensive against Palestine's rebellious peasants, who had occupied many urban centers and were threatening British imperial hegemony.

Given Palestine's strategic significance in the thirties for the leading colonial power, I was surprised by the relative dearth of information about this momentous insurgency. The revolt was and continues to be either ignored or denigrated by mainstream Israeli and Western historiography on Palestine. It has likewise received minimal attention from progressive Western scholars. The Western left's political imaginary continues instead to be exercised by the Spanish Civil War, the "epic" struggle against fascism that occurred concurrently with the *thawra* in Palestine. In the thirties Western progressives largely disregarded the Palestinian anticolonial struggle or considered it compromised by "fascist" sympathies;[7] their progeny still treat it with Eurocentric disdain today.[8] Existing sympathetic accounts are unfortunately marred by condescension and disinterest toward the peasantry. Liberal Israeli historian Yehoshuah Porath's monumental study of the Palestinian national movement between 1918 and 1939 (1974; 1977) remains the most comprehensive account of the 1936–39 revolt and demonstrates that the peasantry played a dominant role in the insurgency's leadership. Nonetheless, Porath pays insufficient attention to the Palestinian peasantry's traditions of resistance or its cultural specificities, and he dismisses the *fallâhîn* for failing to throw up a revolutionary (Leninist) leadership and for its inability to articulate a systematic ideology (1977: 265–69). More surprising is Palestinian historiography, which generally romanticizes the peasantry for its bravery and heroism during the revolt but attributes to it a backward political consciousness. This position seems to have served as an alibi for the absence of any serious study of the *fallâhîn*—except as repository of "folklore." A body of scholarship that constitutes a proper social history, that deals seriously with the Palestinian peasantry and views it as an agent, is only just emerging.[9]

These significant silences about the revolt and peasants' role in it, on the part of mainstream as well as progressive sources, prompted me to undertake my study of how the revolt was remembered by some of its peasant protagonists. I start my discussion of the nature of my own project and how it was carried it out with a look at my own contradictory positionings in relation to this subject and to the persons and forces involved in constructing its memories. I digress again through the field of my own memories.

Positionings

My first viewing of Pontecorvo's *Battle of Algiers*—to this day one of a handful of sympathetic cinematic depictions of popular Arab struggles with any currency in the West—was in late 1968, during my freshman year at Swarthmore, at a screening sponsored by the black students' organization at the University of Pennsylvania. The audience was composed chiefly of militant young African Americans. The heat of insurrection permeated the air. Panthers were on the move throughout the urban United States. I eagerly participated in the clamorous cheering for the Algerian masses and the Front de Libération Nationale (FLN) and the jeering at the French army torturers.

But one scene caught me up short, disrupting any sense of easy solidarity with the *mujâhidín*. An unveiled young Algerian with stylish hair, attired in modish skirt and blouse, ventures out of the Algiers casbah and into the European quarter, to endure the taunts and gawks of the male *colons* (compare Fanon 1967: 58–59). She enters a modern café jammed with carefree European teenagers grooving to the rock 'n' roll jangling from a jukebox. The smartly dressed *mujâhida* sits quietly on her stool, sips an espresso, gets up to leave. We notice that her handbag remains under the counter. Moments later, a bomb detonates, killing several teenagers, leaving the rest bleeding and screaming.

As I watched, I could easily picture myself as one of those shredded bodies, my blood and flesh mingling with the burnished chrome and the formica art deco café rubble. For as a teenager in Beirut, I used to frequent similar boîtes, consume Beiruti milkshakes, bop to the Beatles, chase miniskirted girls. The resemblances were uncanny, overwhelming, and scary. My sensation of déjà vu was rooted in the analogies between the neocolonial position of transplanted unitedstatesian teens in mid-sixties Lebanon and that of French youths in late-fifties settler-colonial Algeria. My classmates' fathers and my dad's churchgoers were employed by all the various institutions of the U.S. geopolitical project: ARAMCO, Raytheon, the U.S. Embassy, Tapline, AUB, the Presbyterian and Baptist missions, and—I learned later—the CIA. Beirut was at the center of U.S. neoimperial interests in the Middle East, and a port of call—until 1967—for the Sixth Fleet. (I once spent an afternoon on board a U.S. aircraft carrier anchored in Beirut harbor and met a sailor who told me that some of the jets carried nuclear weapons—a fact well hidden from the Lebanese public.) Just like the *colons* in Algiers, we neo-colonial U.S. teens in Beirut considered ourselves superior to the locals, whom we routinely referred to as "Lebs."

My position as a film viewer at that moment was something like that of the women Freud describes in "A Child Is Being Beaten" (1959). Unlike the ideal, well-oedipalized male, I was momentarily unable to maintain the "proper" fetishistic viewer distance from the scene (Penley 1984: 385) and instead occupied contradictory positions—despite the progressive intentions of the film, which enjoins the viewer to identify with the anticolonial struggle and to reject Western values and privileges. The on-screen bombing brought home the illusory nature of any unproblematic connections or effortless solidarity with the FLN. No hard and fast us-and-them relation was possible—I was not fully an imperialist, but I couldn't go totally over to the insurgent camp, either. "The relationship," as Jacqueline Rose observes of the cinema experience, "between viewer and scene is always one of fracture, partial identification, pleasure and distrust" (1986: 227). Similarly, the relation between the ethnographer/political sympathizer and her beloved object of investigation is equally split and mobile and not simply the product of her own will. Expanding upon Freud's essay, I could say that my own identification with regard to *Battle of Algiers* seemed to include doubly contradictory moments of "masochism" (identification with the "victims"—tortured Algerians *and* blown-up blonde teenagers) as well as "sadism" (identification with the "victimizers"—female bomber *and* French colonel Mathieu).

This contradictory positioning in relationship to these (neo)colonial fields of power was hammered in early in the course of my academic fieldwork. It was November 1984, about a month after my arrival in the West Bank, and shortly after I had established residence in Nablus. I was driving on the main road toward downtown when my Fiat suddenly shuddered under the impact of a heavy blow to its side. An unseen Palestinian youth had darted out of an alley, heaved a large rock, and instantly vanished. He managed to inflict a large dent above the gas cap but failed to shatter the windshield, the usual goal of airborne projectiles in occupied Palestine. The stone-hurler doubtless targeted my car amid the thick traffic because its yellow license plates and my appearance led him to believe I was an Israeli settler. (Although I resided in the West Bank, I had to register my car in Arab East Jerusalem because I held a tourist visa. Unlike the rest of the West Bank, East Jerusalem has been officially annexed to Israel, and therefore the cars of its Arab noncitizen residents sport the yellow license plates of Israel proper. By contrast, blue plates distinguish the vehicles driven by West Bank Palestinians. My yellow plates stood out in Nablus, sixty-three kilometers north of Jerusalem.)

I was so shaken that I was ready to abandon fieldwork, which would require driving my yellow-plated vehicle throughout the territories. Why should *I* be subject to stoning, I wondered, when unlike most other Westerners I saw in the West Bank—settlers, tourists, embassy officials—I was an avowed sympathizer with the Palestinians. My kneejerk response emblematized a reluctance to fully acknowledge my implication in the forces of domination in the West Bank. My Palestinian friends' reactions to the incident underscored their better understanding of my ambiguous position. Since they faced the dangers of violence and harassment virtually every day, they saw my experience as unexceptional, hardly worthy of sympathy since it couldn't compare with being shot, beaten, arrested without charges, tortured, or having one's house blown up for alleged "security" offenses. Like Jean Genet with the fedayeen in Jordan, I was "among [*auprès*]—not with [*avec*]"—the Palestinians of the Occupied Territories (Genet 1989: 3; 1986: 11).

But although I was "among" and not totally "with" them, my friends suggested that I display a *kûfîya* (the celebrated Palestinian headscarf) on the dash of my car and hang another around my neck in order to deter stone-throwers in the future. Accoutred in this manner, I was pretty much guaranteed safe passage as I drove around the West Bank over the next twelve months (I was stoned only once more and suffered no damage). But whenever I spotted an Israeli army checkpoint on the road ahead, I ripped the *kûfîyât* off the dashboard and from around my shoulders and stashed them on the floor. When my Palestinian research partner Sonia Nimr was along, she hid hers as well. The soldiers, taking me for an Israeli Jew or a tourist, usually waved me through, and so, unlike Palestinians in blue-plated cars, I did not have to endure bothersome searches or long traffic lines. So to avoid harassment or delay by the forces of the occupation who tended to regard me as their ally, I was constantly shifting my position on my fieldwork trips between solidarity—symbolic and felt—with the Palestinians and identification with the occupier.

My uses of the *kûfîya* illustrate some of the contradictions of my position. While sympathizing strongly with the struggle against military rule, in the course of my work I found myself continually linked, for reasons beyond my control, with the very forces of domination that I hoped my research and subsequent writing might, in some small way, aid in undoing. Such ambiguities had a significant bearing on my research. I was interested chiefly in how elderly men who fought in the 1936–39 revolt remembered that significant event, and in the relationship of their memories to both standard Israeli historical discourse and official Palestinian nationalist historiography. While my study would be based largely upon interviews with those who fought in the rebellion, I did not assume beforehand that the revolt's "truths" would be revealed by their heretofore-ignored accounts. My aim was not to fill in a "gap" in academic knowledge nor to write a "history" from the point of view of the marginalized, assuming that the facts or data produced during interviews could speak for themselves. My interest was rather in investigating the histories that subjects made of those insurrectionary events, in the constructed nature of their experiences and recollections, in the working-over of memories by dominant historiography and subsequent events, and in the ongoing struggle over this national signifier (see Scott 1992). I was rather more keen on understanding what produced gaps and silences than in filling in all the lacunae in the interests of a more "complete" empirical understanding. My concern therefore was "not [so much] whether facts are real but what the politics of their interpretation and representation are" (Taussig 1987: xiii).

What I found particularly remarkable about the memories of the old people I interviewed was the degree to which their sense of history was overdetermined by the current situation. In particular, popular views tended to be couched within a contemporary nationalist idiom. Under the pressure of Israeli colonial repression, the various strands of popular memory and official Palestinian histories fused into a fairly unified picture. My interviewees' stress on a holistic Palestinian identity and their concerns for authenticity might appear obsessive, xenophobic, or essentialist, but they should be understood as particular responses to the Israeli authorities' efforts to suppress all manifestations of Palestinian nationalism.

The former rebels were aware that Israeli policies aimed not just at forcibly suppressing memories of revolt but at ideologically defacing and denigrating that symbol of national resistance as well. Little wonder that elderly fighters hesitated at revealing everything they knew about the revolt, since their stories would be carried back to the United States. Old Palestinian men were keenly aware that they were engaged in a struggle over the very legitimacy of their national existence, and many felt that to portray their history as fractured might sully a national reputation that was under constant assault. So they usually took care to protect the Palestinian image and to project a history of national unity and propriety. Many accounts were therefore punctuated by significant silences and resistances, by the passing over of issues that might project the "wrong" picture of the 1936–39 revolt and expose the society's fault lines.

My privileged position as investigator enabled me to find cracks in this constructed mnemonic edifice of national unity. By traveling between different sites of memory and locating persons with opposing views and interests, by searching in archives and reading published accounts, I could cross-check data and find different versions of the same story. I was also able to find evidence of a tradition of "negative" class consciousness (Gramsci 1971: 272–73) from old rebels who claimed that the Palestinian urban leadership had been corrupt and timid and that the middle classes were insufficiently active, in contrast to the poor and the peasants who behaved as honorable and militant nationalists. Interviewees often emphasized peasant initiatives and interests, providing views of the revolt that were subtly at odds with official histories, which smoothed over differences in the interests of a nationalist conformity.

By such means I was able to show that any representation of Palestinian society as a timeless presence and of the revolt as a manifestation of national unity was an active reconstruction. But thinking back, the anger of one man who served as an officer in the Palestine police still makes me uncomfortable. This former policeman used to tell his daughter Nuha, whom I had known as a student at AUB, stories about misdeeds and excesses that certain rebel commanders had committed during the revolt. She passed some of these tales along to me during one of our periodic meetings at the West Bank university where she taught. When she told her father she had done so, he exploded: "How can you trust an American?! What do you think he might do with such stories?" This reaction made me question my emphasis on class differences within Palestinian society and my problematizing of the official Palestinian nationalist narrative. Was I simply imposing my own vision of this past, stressing what *I* (and some of my Palestinian friends) desired as a democratically inclined socialist? For I was frequently requested to convey a rather different message. Many of my interlocutors regarded me as a possible relay to U.S. public opinion, as someone who might put forward a positive image of the Palestinians that might help their case. Several people urged me to write about their pressing current problems rather than about the merely "historical" events of the 1930s.

My study of these memories of revolt required an effort to unlearn an academic training in anthropology and history that enjoins one to uncover the objective truth. As Foucault has shown, the project of "making visible" is integrally linked to operations of power and practices of subjection. Surveillance and hierarchical observation are not neutral, objective practices but coercive exercises in disciplinary power (1979: 170–71). The silences, resistances, dissimulations, avoidances, and hedgings about the past that I encountered had a greater "truth" value than supposedly neutral historical facts. This "truth" seemed to originate in an unequal relation of power, between occupier and occupied, between researcher and subject. Furthermore, much of the real "truth" of the old rebels' tendentious memories and active forgettings could be traced back to the United States, underwriter of Israel's efforts to efface all traces of Palestinian nationalism. This led me to resist the disciplinary imperative, that insidious will to truth that insists that ethnographers behave like detectives, ferreting out and rendering visible all "facts" in the name of professional standards. Solidarity requires us to learn from and (to a certain extent) be tactically complicit with the silences and resistances of the people with whom we live and study. So I have tried to convey an understanding of why some Palestinians might feel it necessary to conceal some "truths," to forget others, and to embellish the positive. Positioned as I am, I have felt that at least part of my role was to help develop a plausible narrative within which the Palestinian case might be argued in the West. My narrative here, like all narratives, is necessarily based on its own partial truths and strategic excisions. "All constructed truths are made possible by powerful 'lies' of exclusion and rhetoric" (Clifford 1986: 7).

Because this study occupies these contradictory positions, I suppose it will no doubt dissatisfy those who desire a simple story based on unabashed solidarity and polar oppositions and will displease those who seek disengaged and objective truths. For I argue, on one hand, from a position of solidarity with a Palestinian nationalist representation of the 1936–39 revolt, which marks a moment of closure. On the other hand, I attempt to *situate* the constructed arbitrariness of the case by self-consciously exposing its seams and taking responsibility both for what I choose to reveal and what I assert might need to be provisionally covered over. I have tried to write not from an Olympian location of disinterested and all-seeing objectivity, but from a series of vulnerable, contingent, and situated positions that invite rather than resist contention. Thus my own position is inherently contradictory, caught between Palestinian populist and nationalist imperatives, as well as the necessity to produce some academic "truths."

Multiple Vision

The analysis of the production of a social memory of the 1936–39 revolt also requires the use of a framework that is not limited simply to the "local" setting. Contemporary Palestinian memories of the 1936–39 revolt cannot be understood merely as a local phenomenon, as fully "other" from our (U.S.) experiences, for they are situated within a complex and fractured global discursive field. The revolt is one component in a wider contest in which "our" memories and practices are also variously implicated and crucially engaged, even—perhaps especially—if we simply ignore our involvement.

Recent academic work on history as a cultural construction tends to conceive of memory as a collective project that is crucial to the consolidation or construction of group, community, or national identities.[10] Such antiessentialist works conceptualize memory as a site of hegemonic struggle, as a fluid ideological terrain where differences between dominant and subordinate are played out. They prove invaluable to our efforts to understand the popular dimension of memory, but are nonetheless marred by a tendency to neglect memory's transnational dimension. If we are beginning to recognize the global dimension of economy and culture, we must also reconceptualize memory and history as (partial) transnational constructions. The Palestinian situation requires that we conceive of memory as a multidimensional, displaced, and local-global construction.

At the local level, Palestinian memory is the site of at least two overlapping struggles, the "internal" struggle between Palestinian popular and official nationalist views, and the "inter-national" struggle between Palestinian and Israeli views of the revolt. At the "inter-national" level, the struggle pits repressive Israeli apparatuses—working to erase the monuments of Arab memory from the land and to censor Palestinian historical texts—against Palestinian attempts to create and preserve a national memory through historical institutions, artistic expression, and everyday storytelling. But in a sense, even the Palestinian-Israeli dimension of memory is not, strictly speaking, "local," since both Israelis and Palestinians are connected to important diaspora populations and institutions. Israel's far-flung ideological resources in particular have helped it to win and sustain substantial sympathy in the West, a critical factor in explaining the ongoing military occupation and colonization of Palestinian territories.[11] Local Palestinians likewise depend on the "outside" (especially the PLO) to furnish resources for resistance, such as the elaboration of "official" historical narratives. Essential Palestinian archives, research organizations, publishing houses, and national institutions have been established in Paris, Nicosia, Beirut, Tunis, Kuwait, and Washington, D.C., and Palestinians increasingly argue their historical case in English.[12]

The United States is also a critical site in this struggle. Unwavering U.S. governmental and elite support for Israeli polices has powerfully impinged upon Palestinian memory and is essential to understanding its fragile and fragmented character. Media images of terrorists, stone-throwing youths, biblical Palestine, and the Holocaust, and incessant flows of pro-Israel and anti-Palestinian discourse from the state, media, and academy are some striking instances of U.S. connections to history construction in Israel/Palestine.

The memories of the old people I interviewed were dispersed across and constructed through these interconnected and overlapping fields. They recognized that the struggle over Palestinian identity was not merely a matter of localized dialogue and violence, but also involved powerful international forces (particularly the United States). Thus their memories of revolt possessed a kind of multiple vision or consciousness, as they maneuvered delicately between articulations of the popular and the national. At one level, their memories were situated in a subordinate and partially antagonistic relation to Palestinian nationalist memory; at another, they were *aligned* with nationalist discourse in opposition to Israel's ideological and repressive apparatuses and Israel's international supporters. Through their discussions with me, they attempted at the same time, to appeal to the international community.

My interlocutors' multiple vision represents ways of seeing and remembering with important consequences for critical theory. On the one hand, elderly Palestinians' mode of recollection, which in the interests of nationalism had to posit history as real and authentic, is a caution against dogmatic deconstruction and antiessentialism.[13] On the other, *within* the national framework, their views often participated in internal struggles around issues of class, gender, religion, generation, and region. Such internal heterogeneity, albeit circumscribed by the national imperative, likewise serves as a warning against any "nativist" or "nationalist-absolutist" position regarding the Palestinian past.

At Work in the Field

This study is based largely on archival research in England, Israel, and the United States, and on fieldwork in Israel and the Occupied Territories that was conducted between October 1984 and November 1985. My original fieldwork plan was to be based in a single West Bank village, to focus on memories in that community, and to undertake supplementary studies of nearby villages. But the conditions of the occupation made it very difficult to establish residence in any village, and therefore this line of intensive or "thick" research proved impossible to pursue. So I opted to live in the city of Nablus and began to make contact with former rebels in area villages. Then I learned that Sonia Nimr, a Palestinian history graduate student from the University of Exeter, was already interviewing rebels in the Jinîn area, north of Nablus, for the purposes of an oral history dissertation on the 1936–39 revolt. We met in December 1984 and decided to work together interviewing old *mujâhidîn*. I should note that had it not been for the Palestinian friends I had made at AUB and my subsequent history of political engagement, it is unlikely that Sonia, who had spent three years in an Israeli prison for membership in an "illegal" organization, would have agreed to collaborate with me.

Our joint work, as it turned out, was extremely beneficial for both of us, and we accomplished a great deal more as a team than would have been possible working separately. Sonia's network of contacts was more extensive than my own, in part because she had been collecting names for a longer period, but also because she was a "native." I quickly discovered that our "target" population of old peasant rebels was extremely suspicious of foreigners and strangers; had I not been in Sonia's company, many would never have spoken with me. Her ability to allay the fears and mistrust of reluctant old men, her skill in coaxing them into discussing their revolutionary pasts with outsiders, was critical to the success of our project. Sonia's late grandfather's work as a doctor in Jinîn in the thirties and his reputation throughout north-central Palestine as an honest character who had dared to treat wounded rebels greatly facilitated our entrée into households of revolt veterans. Sonia's ability to handle the many village dialects, which differ markedly from the urban Palestinian dialect with which I was somewhat familiar, was also a great asset—although on occasion even she was stumped by a word or expression peculiar to a particular region. Perhaps my main contribution to the endeavor was the Fiat that I had purchased with my research grant. My car gave us tremendous mobility and flexibility in our work, and for Sonia represented a great improvement over the public transport that she had largely relied on before. Sonia had also found that when she interviewed revolt veterans on her own, they often did not treat her seriously because of her gender. But when former rebels saw that she was accompanied by a *man* who had come "all the way from America," and when she mentioned that *both* of us were about to become "doctors" and planned to write books that would be published in the West, prospective interviewees were usually impressed by the seriousness of the endeavor. (It should be added that no one, in those conservative Palestinian villages, ever raised an objection to the fact that a North American man and a Palestinian woman, married but not to each other, were traveling around together.) Finally both of us benefited from the constant exchange of support, arguments, encouragement, and ideas. We pushed each other to keep going in difficult or trying situations, where on our own we would undoubtedly have given up.

Our aim was to locate and interview as many revolt veterans as we possibly could in villages throughout Israel/Palestine, in particular men who had been local commanders. We also interviewed men who did not fight but had lived through it and were well informed about it, as well as a few relatives of prominent rebel commanders. We also spoke to a few old women, without much success (see chapter 6). We focused our efforts on Palestinian villages in the Jinîn-Nablus-Tûlkarm district (Sonia was living with her family in Jinîn and I lived in Nablus), which encompassed communities in the Israeli "Triangle" (around Tûlkarm) and inside the West Bank. This was the main center of rebel activity during the *thawra,* known by the British as the "Triangle of Fear" or the "Triangle of Terror." In addition we interviewed fighters in Israeli-Palestinian villages of the western Galilee, another important axis of the rebellion. Some interviews were also carried out in the Jerusalem-Ramallah district and the Gaza Strip. The main focus therefore was on recollections of *mujâhidîn* in the rural north, where the armed revolt was most forceful.

The fieldwork, therefore, did not involve an intensive study of one village or even a small group of villages, but instead entailed short stays in a number of communities. We tried to compensate for the lack of in-depth study of any particular community with a breadth of interviews in many villages. Most men were interviewed only once, for between two and four hours, and interview sessions were usually tape-recorded and later transcribed. A few men whom we considered particularly good sources of information, insight, and stories were interviewed two or three times. But often we felt as if we were doing "salvage ethnography," given the advanced age of most of our interviewees. On several occasions, while dashing around trying to locate as many remaining veterans of the *thawra* as possible, we would run into someone who had furnished us names of people to interview. It's too bad you didn't make it to such-and-such village to interview Abû Fûlân, she would say, because he died just last week during the cold snap. So we crossed another name off our list, saddened that an entire generation of fighters was rapidly passing away, untapped as sources for histories of the "Great Revolt." Age also created other problems, in particular poor health, hearing problems, and a scarcity of teeth, which compounded our difficulties in comprehending rural dialects. A few men were approaching senility, so their reminiscences were unreliable or patchy. As we spoke to these elderly villagers, we were often struck by the unequal global access to food, health care, and shelter, one of whose results was that our "target" population enjoyed poorer health and shorter life spans than men of a comparable generation in the United States or Britain.

Besides conducting these interviews, I attempted to investigate (mainly on my own) the broader contexts of the memory of the revolt. I studied official, academic, and oppositional historical narratives (archival and secondary), written in English and Arabic, from Western, Israeli, and Palestinian sources. I also visited historical sites pertinent to this contested history and attended Palestinian events of national significance whenever I was able. In addition, I discussed my project, and the revolt in particular, with anyone who was interested, in order to get a sense of how younger Palestinians remembered the rebellion. In the course of our work together, Sonia and I were invited to give a presentation at Birzeit University, which gave us the chance to discuss our preliminary findings with Palestinian academics.

Synopsis

Chapter 1 provides an overview of the struggle over the Palestinian national past under colonial conditions, investigating how Israeli rule and particularly military occupation endanger Palestinian popular memories and how those memories are complex means of resistance, differently oppositional to both official Israeli as well as Palestinian memory. I focus in particular on the contradictory interpretations of two key signifiers, Shaykh 'Izz al-Dîn al-Qassam and the *kûfîya*. Chapter 2 discusses ways in which the dominant Israeli historical narrative is physically established and confirmed at national-historical sites like Masada and Yad Vashem, which function simultaneously as assertions of the Zionist-Jewish narrative and as erasures of the Palestinian Arab past. I examine the specific ways in which such Israeli official sites variously marginalize, vilify, and obliterate the Arab history of Palestine.

Next I turn from versions of official history to popular memories of the revolt. The subaltern memories of revolt are treated not as a unified and coherent outlook on the past but as a jumbled composite, as aspects of the people's "common sense" (Gramsci) of the past. I examine, in turn, what I term the subalterns' nationalist, populist, and collaborationist memories of the revolt. For the sake of analysis and compiling an inventory I treat each type separately, but in practice these forms of memory are often interconnected. Chapter 3 deals with popular memories that concurred with the official nationalist line. I show how old peasants who agreed with mainstream interpretations nonetheless often used nationalist terms to give the revolt's memory a subaltern inflection. I examine how a national-popular vision of the revolt has been created by erasures and condensations, as well as through rearticulations of dominant historical narratives. Chapter 4 focuses on memories that stressed the insurrection's popular character and emphasized peasants' autonomous actions in organizing it, in opposition to official views that marginalized the revolt's lower-class character. These popular histories had remained alive but were hidden from public view, as recollections that official nationalist discourses had not substantially recoded or hegemonized.

Chapter 5 concentrates on what I call "collaborationist" memories, those accounts that appeared to accord with the colonialist or Israeli interpretations of the past. I examine "collaborationist" narratives that explicitly contradicted the orthodox Palestinian nationalist version of the past and look closely at the recollections of two men who served as rebel commanders and defected to fight alongside the British. I argue that much accommodationist discourse should be treated as a kind of unauthorized critique of official nationalist narratives and not merely as naive or treasonous endorsement of Israeli or colonialist ideology.

Chapter 6 investigates how the social memory of the 1936–39 revolt was revived and recoded in the wake of the intifada that burst forth in December 1987. At the onset of the intifada, the revolt served as an inspirational model, but more recently the perceived excesses of the intifada's campaign against traitors has called forth a revised memory of the revolt as having failed to control internal bloodletting. I also examine a point of comparison between the revolt and the intifada that has not been publicly discussed: the mobilization of women and the campaigns against female activists that occurred during both insurgencies. An investigation of these points of interconnection between uprising and *thawra* urges a revision of the images of both these national-popular struggles. The Epilogue, finally, returns briefly to the image of the *kûfîya*, that symbol of Palestinian struggle in both the 1936–39 revolt and the intifada. We track its recent international travels and its current fate under the occupation.

1 / Popular Memory and the Palestinian National Past

It was an incident from the height of the *grand peur,* the Great Terrorism Scare that afflicted the United States from 1983 to 1986 (see Said 1988: 46), and it occurred just three days before a bomb went off at a West Berlin disco, killing a U.S. serviceman, wounding thirty-five others, and providing the pretext for the U.S. air raids on Libya. On April 2, 1986, a bomb exploded on a TWA jet approaching Athens, killing four U.S. citizens. A "shadowy" group—the "Ezzedine Qassam Unit" of the "Arab Revolutionary Cells"—claimed responsibility for the outrage and asserted that it was acting in retaliation for the U.S. Navy's earlier clash with Libya in the Gulf of Sidra.

The name "Ezzedine Qassam," unknown in the country whose citizens were the targets of violence, quickly faded into insignificance during the ensuing media barrage about the terrorist peril. The only fact that mattered was that U.S. citizens had been murdered. The *Washington Post* (April 4, 1986) identified "Ezzedine Qassam" simply as "a Palestinian who fought and was killed by the British during their occupation of Palestine in the 1930s," while the "newspaper of record" explained that Qassam was "killed in 1948 in Jerusalem in Arab Israeli fighting" (*New York Times,* April 3, 1986).

I encountered little such confused ignorance about Qassâm's memory in Palestinian communities in Israel and the Occupied Territories. For them, the name 'Izz al-Dîn al-Qassâm was saturated with historical significance, signifying a hero of the liberation struggle and a model of patriotic sacrifice. Most Palestinians know that he was born in what is now Syria, not Palestine, and that he took refuge in Palestine in the early 1920s after he was sentenced

1

to death by French colonial authorities for his leadership of the resistance to French occupation. Qassâm was a popular Islamic preacher at Masjid al-Istiqlâl (Independence Mosque) in Haifa, the country's most important port and its chief industrial center, and he used to attract large audiences of workers and lumpen proletariat as well as peasants from nearby villages. He spoke out fiercely against British rule and Zionist colonization, advocating spiritual renewal and political militancy as the appropriate weapons for defeating these dangers. One villager we met reported seeing Qassâm preaching jihad at the mosque and grasping a gun or a sword in his hand. One of his disciples recounted a sermon in which the shaykh urged bootblacks to exchange their shoebrushes for revolvers and to shoot the English rather than polish their shoes. "Obey God and the Prophet," Qassâm proclaimed, "but not the British high commissioner."

In the mid-1920s, Qassâm concluded that armed revolt was the only road to national liberation, and he began secretly organizing and training cells of guerrilla fighters, whom he recruited from among the urban workers and lumpen proletariat and the peasantry of villages in the vicinity of Haifa. In November 1935, Qassâm and his men took to the hills of northern Palestine with the aim of raising the countryside in revolt. But Qassâm's guerrillas were discovered after only a few days, and on November 20, 1935, some fifty years prior to the TWA operation, the shaykh and three of his followers fell in battle with the British mandate police forces in Ya'bad Forest. The martyrdom of Qassâm and his men electrified the Palestinian populace.[1] In a matter of months, owing in large part to the shaykh's example, Palestinians launched the general strike that evolved into the 1936–39 revolt, the last great popular insurgency witnessed in Palestine until the intifada (uprising) erupted in December 1987. The opening words of the intifada underground leadership's second communiqué (January 13, 1988) underscored the continuing significance of Qassâm and the 1936–39 rebellion for Palestinian's social memory of struggle: "O masses of our great people. O people of martyrs, grandsons of al-Qassam . . . O people of the uprising, which has been spreading from the roots of our homeland since 1936" (Lockman and Beinin 1989: 329).

My field research concerned Palestinian memories of the revolt Qassâm helped trigger. I was interested principally in how elderly villagers who participated in the *thawra* remembered this significant event in their past and in the relation of their disparate memories to official nationalist histories, or dominant memory. I chose to study this insurrection because of its symbolic importance as the first massive Palestinian mobilization on a national scale. Yet, despite its centrality as an image of resistance, published accounts, whether sympathetic or antipathetic, whether Israeli, Western, or Palestinian, had largely marginalized this national, anticolonial insurgency and, in particular, ignored its popular character. My aim was to find out what "popular memories" of revolt remained alive in this context and how they had been refigured, over time and in the context of the tumultuous and difficult struggle for national identity.

Palestinian memory, I soon learned, could be understood simply on its own terms. The "truth" of Palestinians' memories of revolt was not to be found solely in "the field" in which it was articulated. As Fredric Jameson notes, one notable characteristic of the modern imperialist era is that "the truth of experience no longer coincides with the place in which it takes place" (1988: 349). Palestinian memories were produced under those conditions peculiar to the third world, where "the problems and solutions of . . . culture are not only those that take place within a sacred national interior—the creative national mapmaking of the colonial powers made that clear. Instead, they take place in what is more like an international railway station than a national inner sanctum" (Layoun 1988: 57). But Palestinians, who have not yet won formal national independence, must produce their history and memory in a space that is more like a bomb shelter under continuous shelling than a railway station. Palestinians who live under Israeli rule are attempting to construct an "authentic" identity for themselves in a relation of subordination and antagonism to Israeli repressive and ideological apparatuses. Those agencies of domination, which weigh so heavily upon Palestinian productions of history, are underwritten by the Western powers, especially by the United States, which proffered Israel $53 billion in aid between 1949 and 1991, including $3.7 billion in 1991 alone.[2] In a very real sense, then, how Palestinians remember their past has a great deal to do with how they are "remembered" or imaged in the West. To begin to comprehend Palestinian memory therefore requires conceiving it in relation to the history of Jewish colonization in Palestine/Israel and to the history of broader Western support for that project.

It appears that the "Ezzedine Qassam Unit" that bombed the TWA flight was trying to point out precisely the historical parallels between the Palestinian national struggle against Britain's imperial support for Zionist colonization during Qassâm's day and the current battle against Israel and its imperial ally. But while the Qassâm group's deadly assault disrupted mundane life in the United States only momentarily, it simultaneously reconfirmed common perceptions of the Palestinians as savage terrorists. The ill-conceived message was fated to misfire, in part, because of the absence of ideological space for Palestinians in the West. The sheer force of the dominant Zionist narrative, Edward Said has observed, simply has not permitted the emergence of a "socially acceptable narrative to absorb, sustain and circulate" any counter-facts about Palestinians (1984: 34). That Palestinians were victims of the Zionist venture and paid a high price for its successes, for instance, was a fact that could not be placed meaningfully within, or against, the official narra-tives. The story of Western civilization advancing in the East through its proxy Israel has consistently pushed Palestinians to the margins. Western views have been remarkably continuous with those expressed in an editorial in the Zionist *Palestine Post* on July 3, 1936, which asserted that the aim of the Palestinian Arab movement was to "foment a struggle against European civilization in the Mediterranean and to keep this country not merely as a half desert but to continue it, as it had been for many centuries, 'a desert of history.'" Forced to lurk in the West's shadows, the "wild" Palestinian Other has occasionally managed to blast his or her way onto center stage with explosive charges and machine-gun bursts. Such disruptions of the Western narrative only lasted for a flicker of the television screen and ultimately proved counterproductive, for they were apprehended as irrational interrup-tions of an unfolding story of Western progress rather than as statements within a plausible counternarrative. Instead of reminding "us" of the crucial part the West plays in suppressing Palestinian rights, such violence served as retrospective justification for everything "we" in the West do (Said 1984: 37). The killing of U.S. citizens in the name of a Palestinian hero sparked mini-mal interest here in the Palestinian past, which only remained murky, impen-etrable, irrational, and violent.

Given the relative absence of any space for Palestinians to assert their nar-rative, U.S. support for Israeli suppression of Palestinians' civil and national rights has continued virtually unchallenged. This massive aid has underwrit-ten the censorship of Palestinian culture and the ongoing seizure of Palestin-ian land, which has in turn impinged upon the very possibilities for the main-tenance of Palestinian memory itself. Yet even horrific acts like the TWA bombing in Qassâm's name could be seen as ghostly reminders of a historical repression that remains largely unrecognized (see de Certeau 1986: 4). Such interruptions might be profitably taken as occasions to examine the sup-pressed and ignored interrelations between our own national history and that of others. They could be read equally as reminders that "our" history has been a story of the suppression of other histories and as tokens of the fact that our cultural identity can *appear* to be produced within a sacred inner shrine only because there are unmarked tombs, out of sight, in other places.[3] Palestinian attempts at historical self-representation must be understood, therefore, in relation to their narrative absence in the West. One of the aims of this work is to disinter some of those unseen documents of barbarism that underwrite our own claims to civilization. Such texts are part of that international frame within which the articulation of Palestinian popular memory must be viewed. The context for such an understanding of the memories of colonization and revolt, Michael Taussig suggests, cannot be limited to a "secure epistemic nest in which our knowledge-eggs are to be safely hatched." It involves instead the recognition of a kind of "connectedness incongruously spanning times and juxtaposing spaces" that are "far apart and . . . different from each other" (1992: 44). Contemporary Palestinian memories of the 1936–39 revolt must be seen as situated, therefore, within a complex, fractured, multiply situated global discursive field.

Rival Memory Modes

Memory is a battlefield.   *Alistair Thomson*

A discussion of colonialism is relevant to our discussion here not just because it highlights the interconnections between the "field" and the international frame, but because, despite all the claims that we have entered a "post-colonial" era,[4] colonialism still characterizes the relation between the state of Israel and the roughly 2.7 million Palestinians living under its rule (1.9 million under military occupation, 800,000 as citizens). Zionism, an exclusivist and settler variant of colonialism whose aim was the establishment of a strictly Jewish state, diverged from classical colonialism in that it aimed fundamentally to exclude the natives rather than to "civilize" them or exploit their labor power.[5] Unlike "classical" colonialism, such as in India, where the English tried to turn middle- and upper-class Indians into (lesser) Englishmen with brown skin (see Sharpe 1993), Zionist colonists in Palestine were never interested in making the indigenous Arab population over into imitation Jews. From 1882 to 1900, during the First Aliyah, the Zionist aims were to employ the "pure settlement" style of colonization, based on European control of land and labor and the removal of the native population. What evolved instead was an agricultural plantation type of colonization, like that pursued by the French in Algeria and Tunisia, which required the employment of some (displaced) local Arab labor. When this model faltered, the Zionist Labor movement won hegemony over the settlement effort and installed a true "pure settlement"–style colonization, in which only Jewish labor was to be employed. But throughout these developments, the Zionist movement tended to deny, ignore, or dismiss the natives' presence. Moreover, when the Jews in Palestine gained their national independence in 1948, the Zionist movement expelled the indigenous inhabitants in as great a number as possible and rubbed out the traces of their past existence. Not only was the Palestinian link to a past based in a territory violently severed when Israel was founded, but it has been "periodically and ritually resevered in [Israel's] sustained war upon [Palestinian] national peoplehood" (Said 1986: 149). Palestinians living under Israeli rule meanwhile were governed by a colonial-style system that Gramsci termed "domination" (*dominio*), in which the mixture of coercion and persuasion was markedly weighted in favor of repression, and which he contrasted to hegemony (*egemonia*), by which he meant the exercise of political control in which persuasion was the predominant feature.

Against Israel's exclusivist and expansionist brand of colonial nationalism, Palestinians have attempted to construct a historical identity and to "authorize" their own past by elaborating a "defensive" nationalism (Rodinson 1973). The effort to sustain the sentiment that all the Palestinian people share a national past is a significant part of their battle for their own independent state. When Zionists argue that Palestinians, unlike Israelis, have no special national identity because they are simply "Arabs" who can easily assimilate anywhere in the Arab world, they ignore the fact that although all nations typically claim to be distinct essences with timeless pasts, *all* are recent constructions (Anderson 1983: 16). And they miss the irony that it is chiefly in relation to Israeli actions that Palestinians acquired their notion of a distinctive identity, that Palestinian self-representation, formulated to a large degree in opposition to Israel, is inversely specular.[6]

Palestinian popular memory therefore is a contested terrain worked over by two markedly different historical apparatuses, each with rival strategies of memory control: the *dominio* mode of the colonizing machine versus the "incorporative" mode of the nationalist movement with its own aspirations for *egemonia* (hegemony). The Israeli state (with vast Western support) attempts to dominate Palestinian social memory by erasing its most visible remains and suppressing attempts to sustain collective, nationalist remembrance. The Palestine Liberation Organization (PLO), official representative of the Palestinian nation, attempts to forge a "national-popular" past by recalling memories of a unified national struggle, but since the Palestinian leadership does not control the apparatuses of state power, it is particularly dependent upon the support and goodwill of the Palestinian masses. This makes for a certain fluidity, given that the Palestinian subaltern classes cannot simply be treated as passive participants in the national movement. Having been invited to join the national struggle, the "masses" could potentially democratize it from within. This dynamic relationship, between the leadership and the people, creates a certain margin for the articulation of popular memories. On the other hand, the exigencies of a struggle that demands national unity tend to circumscribe this potentially oppositional space.[7]

Colonizing Memory

Historicizing a Territory

After Shaykh 'Izz al-Dîn al-Qassâm's remains were laid to rest, an imposing marble tombstone was constructed over his gravesite at the village of Balad al-Shaykh, located on the outskirts of Haifa. The mausoleum quickly became a popular site of pilgrimage for Palestinians, who regarded Qassâm as a kind of national saint. "A new form of worship was created,—the worship of martyrs, who had murdered Jews and Englishmen," a hostile observer remarked at the time. "Legends and stories were woven about them in order to impress the primitive people to whom the printed word is holy. . . . Visits were made to the martyr's [Qassâm's] grave and his picture was hung in all the Arab public buildings. His picture was displayed at all parades and demonstrations."[8]

On April 24, 1948, Balad al-Shaykh's five thousand Arab residents fled in the wake of an attack by the Haganah, following Haifa's earlier "emptying" (April 22) of Arab residents (Morris 1987: 93–94).[9] The community was renamed Tel Chanan and settled by Jews (it is now part of Nesher township). The graveyard at Balad al-Shaykh was allowed to go to ruin, and Qassâm's tomb has been repeatedly vandalized (Furani 1984).

To this day, meanwhile, no marker commemorates Qassâm's death at the site of the famous battle near the West Bank village of Ya'bad, west of Jinîn. When I visited Ya'bad in the winter of 1984, some university students pointed out the spot in the "Ya'bad forests" (*ihrâj Ya'bad*) where, according to local legend, Qassâm fell. The site is still remembered by many residents, although the terrain has been considerably denuded since the thirties. Several area inhabitants were of the opinion that some sort of historical marker should be erected at the spot where their national hero had fallen, but were convinced that if this were done, the military authorities would simply knock the memorial down and arrest those who put it up.[10] Youths from Nazlat Shaykh Zayd, the hamlet closest to the battle site, told me that a few years earlier, some Israeli Jews came around asking local residents, "Can you tell us where Qassâm was killed?" "Over there, on top of that ridge," they replied. Within a matter of months, bulldozers appeared where the men of Nazlat Shaykh Zayd had pointed, gouging great holes in the earth for the construction of a new Jewish settlement. But the men had lied. Like everyone else in the area, they knew that Qassâm had been martyred in the valley below the hamlet, not on the opposite hilltop, where the colony of Shoqayd soon appeared.

This story, perhaps apocryphal, highlights Palestinian awareness that their very memory sites are being erased and hemmed in as part of Israel's ongoing, expansionist processes of nation-building. For among the major tasks of the modern state is the establishment and fixing of the special relation between the people's history and its land. The construction of a unified national identity, writes Poulantzas, requires "the historicity of a territory and the territorialization of a history" (1980: 114). National existence requires the confirmation of a solid link between a delimited space and an undivided culture and history. When it comes to anchoring a colonial settler-state in contested territory, this process requires the violent suppression of the past of the indigenous population. "The modern nation-state," observes Poulantzas, "involves the eradication of the traditions, histories, and memories of dominated nations involved in its process." However, a "nation without a state of its own," he continues, "is in the course of losing its tradition and history" (1980: 113).

The modern Zionist movement originally imagined that Eretz Israel (the land of Israel) was uninscribed and empty: "a land without a people," as the saying goes.[11] So as they gradually settled the land, all disruptions of that fantasy, all previous Arab inscriptions, had to be effaced. In order to implant an exclusive national identity in that space, Zionists had gradually to eliminate the sites that memorialized the Palestinians' past and embodied their relation to this territory. Every parcel of land had to be plowed with Jewish history, for as Benedict Anderson observes, "In the modern conception, state sovereignty is fully, flatly, and evenly operative over each square centimetre of a legally demarcated territory" (1983: 26). The territory, imagined as uninscribed, had to be "worlded" as well as textualized as Jewish (see Spivak 1985: 133; 1990: 1). Qassâm's ruined or absent memorials are illustrations of how the Israeli state has established a Jewish national identity on the land while obstructing or extirpating Palestinian memory.

"Zionism came fully into its own," Edward Said once observed, "by actively destroying as many Arab traces as it could" (1980: 103). At the end of the 1947–48 war, Israel held a little over 80 percent of Palestine's original surface area, about one and one-half times what the 1947 U.N. Partition Plan allotted to the Jewish state. In the course of the war there occurred the most radical act of Zionist "worlding," as Jewish military forces dispersed some 770,000 Palestinians from the newly created Israeli territory in 1948.[12] About 70 percent of the Palestinian people were transformed into refugees. The new state then proceeded to obliterate most of the historical vestiges of those vanished people, wiping some 418 Palestinian Arab villages off the face of the earth.[13] Those Arab traces subsequently acquired Jewish identities as they were variously ploughed under by Israeli farmers, resettled and given new Hebrew names, or planted over with Jewish National Fund (JNF) forests (Jiryis 1976: 79).[14] The conquest of land went forward as well: by 1966, the state had seized about half the land belonging to the remaining Palestinian-Israeli villages; by the mid-1970s, it had confiscated two-thirds (McDowall 1989: 127). Once seized, the state ensured that the formerly Arab land could never be returned by effectively "deterritorializing" it. The Israel Land Administration (jointly administered by the JNF and the Ministry of Agriculture) and the Land Development Authority (run by the JNF) are responsible for developing, leasing, and administering 92 percent of all the land of Israel. The territory under their purview is held "in perpetuity" for the Jewish people—whether Israeli citizens or not—and can only be used for the benefit of Jews, not on behalf of non-Jewish citizens (McDowall 1989: 126–27).

The process of land confiscation entered a new stage after the 1967 occupation of the West Bank and the Gaza Strip.[15] In 1947, before partition, Jews made up 45 percent of the population of Palestine but possessed only 7 percent of the land. By 1983 the relationship of Jews to the territory had been radically reversed: Jews accounted for about 60 percent of the population within the boundaries of historic Palestine and held 85 percent of the land. Palestinian Arabs meanwhile constituted 40 percent of the population[16] and held less than 15 percent of the territory (Benvenisti 1984: 19; Benjelloun-Ollivier 1983: 87). Land expropriations and the establishment and expansion of Jewish settlements in the Occupied Territories have continued virtually unchecked (even after the September 1993 accord).[17] As Palestinians lost lands on both sides of the Green Line (the 1948 armistice), they were impeded from, or lacked funds for, maintaining or restoring many Arab historical sites that remained in existence. Meanwhile, Israeli historical apparatuses sponsor an array of activities like hiking, archaeological digs, tourism, environmental activism, and the planting of trees on Arbor Day (Tu Bishvat), all integral parts of the ongoing Zionist program of "worlding" the land, investing it with the victor's identity, normalizing the conquest, and obliterating others' links to that territory.

Westerners are invited to participate in this process, especially as tourists. When we vacation in Israel/Palestine—"one of the chief goals of European and North American international tourism"—the historical and touristic apparatuses ensure that we encounter a country with which we feel an empathy, even an identification, both in the present and the past. We "find" a vibrant, modern Western nation built in our image even as we encounter the monuments of a common Judeo-Christian past (Bowman 1992). This convergence is felt in especially powerful ways by the Christian pilgrims who visit the Holy Land "to walk in the footsteps of Christ" and who "are more interested in the ephemeral accretions of 2,000 years of history in order to 'see' original traces" than in present conditions (Bowman 1985: 7). Tourists have little opportunity to hear about or see much evidence of any alternative, living history. In 1984, there were only 38 Palestinian Arab guides with licenses allowing them to guide in Israel and the Occupied Territories, with another 33 who had licenses permitting them to work only in the West Bank. Few of those licensed found much work, in any case. Most Western tourists, therefore, are guided to sites by Israeli Jews (3,356 licensed in 1984), who warn them to be wary of Palestinian shopkeepers and who insulate them from the contemporary Arab reality (Bowman 1985: 15; Bowman 1992). By these means and others, Israeli touristic institutions magically occult the traces of the long Arab-Islamic historical interlude that separates the biblical era from contemporary Israel. Arab remains are made to appear merely as the decayed debris of an irrelevant interruption of the sacred narrative of the Jews' "return" to "their" land. And present-day Arabs, like the objects of study of classical ethnography, seem to inhabit some distant "allochronic" space, to emanate—unlike Westerners and Israelis—from some premodern era (Fabian 1983).[18]

Cultural Repression

The jailer who guards a body that has no words—and written words can travel—may sleep in peace.   *Assia Djebar*

Even to write about Shaykh 'Izz al-Dîn al-Qassâm can be dangerous for Palestinians. In 1983 the military authorities brought West Bank writer, physics lecturer, and political activist Sâmî Kîlânî to trial for publishing a volume of poetry dedicated to Qassâm. The charge sheet stated that to invoke Qassâm's name in verse constituted an act of "incitement," a punishable offense (*al-*

Fajr, November 11, 1983). When a military court failed to convict Kîlânî of poetic incitement, officials punished him with sentences of town arrest and administrative detention (which can be imposed without a trial) that lasted over three years. On three separate occasions, soldiers broke into the Kîlânî family household in Ya'bad during the early morning hours to take Sâmî away; each time they also confiscated his entire library (including, on the last occasion in 1985, a cookbook). Three times, after being released from jail, the writer had to rebuild his book collection from scratch.

Qassâm is one of the many images of insurgency engraved in Palestinian psyches, with the potential to inspire struggle against colonial domination. In their effort to tame the will to fight, the occupiers continually attempt to erase such pictorial inscriptions from native memory by hindering the circulation of national symbols and severely constraining Palestinian efforts to build the institutional framework of civil society. Since, as Benedict Anderson observes, nations accumulate memory through the printed word (1983: 77), it is not surprising that the Israeli state seeks to deny Palestinians access to recollection by blocking the production and circulation of books on Palestinian history and culture. The Israeli censor has banned thousands of books from the Occupied Territories—mainly titles dealing with Palestinian subjects but also including Shakespeare's *The Tempest,* Ezer Weizman's *The Battle for Peace,* and works by Aleksandr Solzhenitsyn, Jack London, and Yigal Allon (McMickle 1989; Benziman 1989). The censor's primary concern, according to Meron Benvenisti, is "to eradicate expression that could foster Palestinian nationalist feelings, or that suggests that Palestinians are a nation with a national heritage" (1983: 1, 3, 130–31).

The Israeli state also ensures that Palestinian children learn little about their people's history through the approved educational curriculum (Graham-Brown 1984: 37–81). According to Christine Dabbagh, public relations officer for the United Nations Relief and Works Agency (UNRWA), which operates 146 schools in refugee camps in Gaza, Israeli authorities routinely confiscate up to one-half of the Arabic textbooks UNRWA tries to import into Gaza. "You're talking about math texts for the second grade that are deemed to be 'inciting,'" Dabbagh asserts (Wood 1988: 22). Palestinian institutions—universities, research groups, newspapers—that attempt to preserve, produce, and accumulate a Palestinian countermemory have faced constant harassment and closure, and the heads of such organizations have been frequently arrested and even deported.

Even private memory is not exempt. Many veterans of the 1936–39 revolt I met had kept personal papers, diaries, photographs, communiqués, and other memorabilia from the insurrection, but almost all those personal archives were subsequently lost—either seized during Israeli military searches or destroyed by former rebels themselves out of fear of being incriminated if security forces discovered their cache.

Colonial Historiography

The "war" in Palestine is the work of a handful of partisans, guerrillas, and racketeers, under the orders of a small group of malevolent and absentee dictators who have not scrupled to bring ruin on their own country and people, in the hope of themselves forging to the top and remaining there.   *Palestine Post,* January 11, 1939

The rebels fight fairly and chivalrously, and rule with kindness. The British kill the innocent, when no other enemy is near, and loot and rob the poor and destitute.   *Elliot Forster Diary,* August 1938

On November 21, 1935, the British mandate government in Palestine issued an official communiqué announcing that its police forces had killed four members of a band of "outlaws," including their leader Qassâm, and had captured four others at Ya'bad Forest. Public statements from the Zionist movement similarly labeled Qassâm and his disciples "gangsters" and "terrorists." In private, Zionist leaders sang a different tune. Two weeks after Qassâm's death, David Ben-Gurion told his Mapai comrades, "This is the first time that the Arabs have had a sort of Tel-Hai. . . . Now, for the first time, the Arabs have seen someone offer his life for the cause. This will give the Arabs the moral strength which they lack." Ben-Gurion considered Qassâm "the Arab Trumpeldoor"[19]—someone who, unlike the Mufti Hâjj Amîn al-Husaynî or the Nashâshîbîs, was ready to sacrifice (Teveth 1985: 150–51).

Official public Zionist treatment of Qassâm has remained consistently and relentlessly antagonistic. Israeli historian Shai Lachman's study of Qassâm exemplifies the academic version of the party line. The shaykh, Lachman asserts, was motivated by a "religious fanaticism" that manifested itself in xenophobia and militant anti-Jewishness (1982: 62). In 1937, he writes, Qassâm's followers, who played a leading role in the armed revolt, unleashed a "terror" campaign against Jews and Arab "moderates"—all those disposed to making peace with the Jews, suspected of deficient nationalism, and having commercial dealings with Jews and Christians (1982: 79–80). When the exiled leadership in Damascus lost control over the rebel movement in the summer of 1938, "absolute anarchy" and an "unprecedented campaign of terror and violence" descended upon the Arab community (1982: 82). Lachman furnishes sensationalist details of this reign of terror, explaining, for instance, that suspected traitors were assassinated and left to rot in the streets for days as warnings to other collaborators. The Qassâmites, he maintains, played a leading role in these events and were personally responsible for the murder of dozens of Arabs in 1938–39 and for brutalizing and extorting from numerous others. As "one of the most anarchical and destructive forces ever to arise in the Palestinian community," the Qassâmites' terrorist excesses contributed heavily to the revolt's internal collapse (1982: 87). Shaykh Qassâm's movement, Lachman concludes, was "the first Arab terrorist movement in Palestine" (1982: 86). Given the West's ongoing panics about terrorism, such a designation is a potent means of disqualifying the Palestinian past.

The 1936–39 revolt has come in for special disparagement in Zionist discourse.[20] The official narrative of Israeli history allows space only for one authentic national liberation movement in Israel(-Palestine): the one that led to the foundation of Israel in 1948. Dominant accounts therefore occlude the anti-British and anticolonial character of the 1936–39 Palestinian revolt by naming it as a series of "riots" directed specifically against Jews, or by simply calling it HaMeora'ot, the "events," "happenings," or "disturbances" of 1936–39, rather than designating it as a national rebellion. During the course of the revolt, there was internal debate within the Zionist movement over whether the rebellion should be considered *meora'ot* (events) or a national insurgency. In public, however, Zionist leaders systematically denied the *thawra* any national character (Black 1986: 17). Those leaders who, like Ben-Gurion, disagreed with the prevailing view that the revolt was simply a disturbance fomented by criminals or outside agitators did not voice such sentiments publicly, lest they discourage rank-and-file Zionists or lend the Palestinian Arabs any credibility abroad, particularly in England (Haim 1983: 36). The Labor-Zionist paper *Davar le-Yeladim,* for example, informed its readers on October 22, 1936, that the Palestinian strike was strictly an elite affair. The strike's leadership, the paper proclaimed, was composed of wealthy effendis, shaykhs, large landowners, lawyers, and religious leaders, but it contained not "one representative of the working masses." It was these upper-class chiefs, *Davar* claimed, who were wholly responsible for organizing the gangs of robbers, murderers, and bandits who carried out armed actions (Black 1986: 54–55).[21] During the second phase of the revolt (after September 1937), Zionists usually attributed the revolt's persistence to outside forces that, with the backing of foreign money, had imposed themselves on the Palestinian Arabs by force (Haim 1983: 126–127).[22] But even for the minority of Zionist leaders like Ben-Gurion who privately considered the revolt a manifestation of Palestinian nationalism, the effect of the rebellion was to stiffen their resolve regarding the necessity of partition and the compulsory "transfer" of Arabs from the Jewish state (Teveth 1985: 166, 181).

The public image of the revolt presented by the Zionist movement in the 1930s, in which only the Jewish movement is worthy of being designated as national, has proved remarkably resilient. As the official historical narrative has been elaborated and embellished, inconvenient facts have been suppressed. For instance, the assistance that Jewish forces rendered to the British army's counterinsurgency campaign during 1937–39 has been consigned to the margins, and Britain's essential role in facilitating Zionist colonization prior to 1947–48 has been denied (see Rodinson 1973).[23] Official accounts therefore ascribe the revolt's failure not to the British military's superior firepower and brutal methods but to the movement's self-disintegration. The rebellion is therefore said to have degenerated into a reign of terror against the "moderate" internal opposition, an orgy of rebel plunder of wealthy Palestinians, and internecine rivalry among revolt commanders. This deterioration was inevitable, the argument runs, given the backward nature of a society characterized by the demagogic and manipulative rule of despotic feudal landowners and a venal and fanatical religious caste over an ignorant mass of peasants. Israeli historian Arnon-Ohanna's judgment, that rebel bands simply reflected the uncivilized conditions of the peasant society from which they emerged, is typical: "The absence of cooperation and mutual responsibility, the deep-seated divisiveness of a society based on patriarchal lines and hamulas, the ancient inter-village and inter-hamula wrangles over stretches of land and water sources, over blood feuds, family honor and marital problems—these were simply transferred to the [guerrilla] bands movement" (1981: 24).[24] Even accounts by Zionist leftists have sometimes described the insurgents of 1936–39 as mere bandits, gangsters, or mercenaries (Bauer 1966: 56) and claimed that, since the Palestinian revolt received arms and financial support from Germany and Italy, it was essentially "an arm of the international fascist movement" (Bauer 1966: 24).[25]

Elpeleg asserts that the Palestinian rebels of 1936–39 frequently employed "horrifying means" of violence and that they were unable to distinguish between criminal and political actions. By contrast, Elpeleg describes *havlaga*, the policy of self-restraint that the Labor Zionist mainstream practiced during the revolt, as "one of the extraordinary manifestations of the Jewish spirit to be seen in Palestine" (1978: 45). Bauer meanwhile states that *havlaga* "gave the *Yishuv* a feeling of moral superiority over its enemies" (1966: 22).[26] By asserting the essential polarity between the Jews' extraordinary moral behavior and abhorrence of violence and the Arabs' bloodthirstiness and abysmal absence of ethics (see Shapira 1992: 237), Zionist writers can call into question the legitimacy of the Palestinian movement of 1936–39 and undermine the credibility of the current Palestinian fight for an independent state.

The official story continues giving off sympathetic reverberations today. Take, for instance, Marc Charney's *New York Times* article of February 28, 1988, a purported analysis of the historical background of the intifada. Charney implies that the Palestinians' sole military targets during the six–month general strike of 1936 and the armed revolt of 1936–39 were the Jews, and he nowhere mentions Palestinian opposition to British rule. Charney asserts simply that the uprising "included bitter Arab attacks on Jews in Hebron, Haifa, Jaffa and Tel Aviv,"[27] and that Britain's role during the 1930s and 1940s was limited to obstructing Jewish immigration. Like official Zionist accounts, the *Times* "remembers" the revolt as anti-Jewish rather than anti-colonial and neatly occludes British imperialism's crucial support for the Zionist enterprise.[28]

The conclusion of official Israeli histories is that the internal disintegration of the 1936–39 insurrection signifies a lack of true national identity, a failure that in turn disqualifies today's Palestinian claims to nationhood. The reduction to ruin of the physical traces of the Palestinian past and the censorship of living Palestinian memory are consistent with such a logic.

Tracks of Repression

The effects of Israeli repression of memory were immediately apparent from the gaps, silences, and omissions in the accounts of the Palestinians I interviewed.[29] Surviving rebel fighters who remained in Palestine were often reticent regarding the revolt, even though nearly fifty years had elapsed since its conclusion. The successive experiences of Jordan's repressive rule and Israel's military occupation had etched fear and suspicion deep into the consciousness of many veterans still alive and dwelling in the Occupied Territories. Former fighters residing in Israel, who lived under military occupation until 1966 and still generally regarded the government as repressive, were equally leery of discussing the revolt with outsiders. Although a Palestinian colleague (usually Sonia Nimr) always accompanied me to interviews, a few *mujáhidín* refused to talk about the rebellion at all.[30] This reticence was due in part to their mistrust of a citizen of a country whose government's backing for Israeli policy was long-standing and unstinting, but the atmosphere generated by military occupation is poisonous enough to make people of the West Bank

and Gaza suspicious even of local researchers. Sharîf Kanâ'ana, director of
Birzeit University's Research and Documentation Center, reported in the
mid-eighties that researchers from the center conducting interviews with
refugees about their former villages were encountering difficulties similar to
my own: "People are not frank. They show fear and do not want to speak.
They also refused to speak on their tribal [sic] differences" (al-Ghazali 1986).

Such fears were not without foundation. Several former *mujâhidîn* living in
Israel told us that intelligence forces detained them for questioning about
their roles in the 1936–39 revolt immediately after the 1947–48 war, and
many West Bank revolt veterans were similarly interrogated after the
occupation of June 1967. Abû Saysân, a *qâ'id fasîl,* or "band commander," at
Qabâtîya (Jinîn district) during the insurgency, asserted that he was reluctant
to talk about his rebel past because he dreaded the return of his old enemies,
the English, to Palestine. "After all," he noted, "it's called Great Britain. And
as they say, the sun never sets on the British Empire." Some of my middle-
class Palestinian friends chuckled with me in disbelief after I told them about
Abû Saysân's far-fetched fears. But later I decided that his apprehensions
about the English were a displacement of his concerns about the Israelis. Ten
months after the interview, Abû Saysân's son—who was under town arrest
when we visited Qabâtîya—was charged with membership in a "terrorist"
organization and deported to Jordan without trial, one of the twenty-seven
Palestinians expelled from the Occupied Territories in the wake of the "iron
fist" of the summer and fall of 1985.

Nonetheless most revolt veterans ultimately did agree to speak about
their experiences, especially once they felt comfortable with my Palestinian
colleague. But even so, their recollections were punctuated by significant
silences about certain topics. One such subject was rebel attacks on Jewish
colonies. Former rebels who recounted the clashes in which they had participated usually remembered only engagements with the British military, and
some claimed that rebels made no attacks on Jewish colonies. But reliable
published accounts as well as official rebel communiqués make it clear that
Jewish settlements were an important if secondary object of rebel attacks,
while the British armed forces were their primary target.[31] Pitched battles
usually involved British forces, while Jewish colonies were mainly harassed,
raided, and shot up at night. Yet old *mujâhidîn* were so reluctant to discuss
assaults on Jewish targets that one might have imagined that such forays had
hardly occurred at all.

Some men explained that they wouldn't discuss this subject because they
still feared retribution from Jewish colonists or their descendants. 'Alî Bay-

tam, from the village of Abû Snân (near Acre), one of few fighters willing to describe such attacks, always took care to speak of them in the third rather than the first person. Veterans' reticence on this subject also appeared to be a reaction to official Israeli ideology, which claims that the Palestinian national movement was and is inherently anti-Semitic. These allegations have so successfully tainted Palestinian nationalism with Nazi associations that Palestinians handled the subject of hostile action against Jews very cautiously. Wishing to undercut the Israeli claims they assumed I had heard, the *thuwwâr* seemed to emphasize by their omission that the rebellion was directed strictly against British colonialism, not the Jewish people. In revising the past in such a manner, they contributed to the Palestinian nationalist movement's portrait of itself as unblemished by anti-Semitism. This remembrance of the revolt as purely anticolonial and untarnished by anti-Jewish feeling might also be interpreted as a sign of Palestinian desires to live peacefully alongside Israel, in their own state. Such silences and gaps, therefore, were usually not just unfortunate lapses in memory, but effects of repression. They could also be viewed more positively, as elements in a counternarrative to the standard Israeli accounts of the revolt.

Israeli repression also pushed a few old veterans to adopt defeatist versions of the past. Such men had been understandably overwhelmed by Israel's long string of military successes and apparent cultural and technological superiority. In their judgment, the Palestinian national movement was incapable of mounting an effective riposte. For all its efforts, it had only reaped an endless harvest of defeats and disappointments. "It was a mistake to rebel against the British in 1936–39," one former band commander told me, "because we were too weak to win. We should have compromised instead." He also implied that Palestinians were *still* too puny to defeat Israel and that they therefore should stop struggling, cut their losses, and make any compromises necessary to extricate themselves from their horrible predicament. Such defeatist sentiments were effects of Israel's coercive power, of nearly twenty years of military rule over Palestinians in the Occupied Territories or of almost forty years of life in the Jewish state for Palestinian-Israelis. Yet by voicing these opinions, former rebels still did not signify that Israel had won their active consent, especially since the same persons often simultaneously expressed bitter criticisms of Israeli government actions. Such negative assessments of the Palestinian past indicated not an endorsement of Israeli policies, but a passive acceptance of the powerful Zionist reality.

In any case, accommodationist views represented a minority opinion. Most veterans responded to Israeli propaganda by asserting counternarratives. Occasionally we would tell someone who was reluctant to speak, "Israeli and English books say that the rebels were merely bandits and terrorists who used the revolt as a pretext for robbery. What do you think?" Often the man would explode angrily that these claims were dead wrong, that the rebels were mainly honorable and heroic nationalists (*wataniyín*), and would (sometimes) go on to discuss the *thawra* in detail. The fact that, despite fifty years of defeats and disappointments, Palestinians *did* adhere strongly to a nationalist interpretation of the revolt testified to the PLO's success in molding consensus in the face of adversity. Furthermore, it exemplifies how Israeli attacks on all manifestations of Palestinian identity often incite instead of simply suppress a militantly nationalist memory.

Forging a National Memory

If the story of the rise of the nationalist resistance to imperialism is to be disclosed coherently, it is the role of the indigenous subaltern that must be strategically excluded.   *Gayatri Spivak*

On January 5, 1936, two separate public meetings were held in Haifa to mark Shaykh 'Izz al-Dîn al-Qassâm's *arba'ín,* the ceremony Muslims normally hold forty days after someone's death. One gathering, organized by the Young Men's Congress (*mu'tamar al-shabâb*) and supported by the political parties representing the interests of the traditional Palestinian leadership, was attended by five hundred persons who listened to the "moderate speeches" of political notables. The other meeting, arranged by the Young Men's Muslim Association of Haifa, of which Qassâm had been president, and supported by the radical nationalist Istiqlâl Party, was attended by a thousand persons of the "lower classes" who heard middle-class radicals' speeches that were "strong in their tone."[32] These evocations of Qassâm's memory in "moderate" versus "strong" tones, reflecting a wider division within the national movement that was often manifested during the revolt, are an example of the kind of gap in representation that the Palestinian national movement works hard to cover over.

Israel's chief official antagonist in the battle over memory is the Palestinian national leadership, the PLO. Rather than effacing the Palestinian people's recollections, the widely supported PLO seeks to incorporate them within a larger unified narrative. It attempts to articulate subaltern memories with its hegemonic principles in order to create an agreed-upon definition of what the "real" past was like (see Mouffe 1981: 173); it works to consolidate a vision of that history for the purpose of political mobilization, as well as to assert Palestinian existence and lay claim to a distinct history connected to a particular territory. In order to confront Israel's overwhelming strength effectively, the middle-class Palestinian leadership must necessarily depend upon and motivate the masses (Nairn 1981: 100). It must incorporate their concerns within its discourse and appeal to them in a language they comprehend.

Its attempts to construct a hegemonic position are hampered, however, by the fact that it is based outside of historic Palestine. Since 1969 the PLO gradually managed to gain the support of the overwhelming majority of Palestinians inside Israel and the Occupied Territories. It did not win this backing automatically or immediately: only in 1973, after six years of occupation, did the masses in the West Bank begin to detach themselves from "traditional" elites tied to the Jordanian monarchy and align with the PLO. The development of Palestinian national consciousness in the West Bank, manifestations of which were suppressed during Jordanian rule, has deepened during the Israeli occupation (Gresh 1985: 14, 63–64; Taraki 1990). Meanwhile Palestinian-Israelis increasingly identify themselves as Palestinian Arabs (as opposed to simply "Arabs" or "Israeli Arabs") (McDowall 1989: 153–54).

Support for the PLO was loosely organized and expressed in the mid-eighties through a variety of "national" institutions—universities, newspapers, journals, and research institutes—and popular organizations—trade unions, women's groups, student and professional organizations—that emerged as a result of the national movement's sustained effort to build a Palestinian civil society in the face of the occupation (see Hiltermann 1991b).[33] In recent years specialized bodies devoted to the preservation, collection, and dissemination of memories of the past have come to play a crucial role in a wider Palestinian struggle to articulate and sustain a national and cultural identity (Khalili 1980; Ashrawi 1978). Although constrained by military rule, these shadow historical apparatuses and their cultural practices have also contributed to the "outside" leadership's efforts to deepen its emergent hegemonic relation with Palestinians "inside" (those residing in historic Palestine).

The nationalist account of the past is at once continuist and progressivist. It presents today's leaders as the natural heirs of the earlier heads of the national movement. At the same time, standardized history depicts a progressive, teleological development since the 1930s. Whereas the *thawra* was an important moment of insurgency and unity, the national movement today is said to be even more mature and experienced. Today's leadership, then, represents the fulfillment of the heroic national struggles of the past.

The "Great Revolt" was the first Palestinian insurgency in which the peasant masses were significantly drawn into the national movement. Official

Palestinian accounts acknowledge their critical role,[34] partly because the PLO has had to invoke popular mobilizations of the past in order to motivate the populace in the present. But dominant histories simultaneously evoke images of popular struggle and tame subaltern traditions. The *fallâhîn's* practices are subsumed within a coherent narrative that deemphasizes their rupturing force. Standard histories incorporate peasants both by exalting their heroism and sacrifice and reducing them to bit players and ancillaries. The rebellion is depicted as a common undertaking, in which the urban elite, the protagonist of the narrative, coordinated its own actions against the British with those of its rural supporters. While more critical accounts from the left claim that "the masses" were responsible for pushing a reluctant elite leadership to take more radical positions, even these versions depict the peasantry as militant but politically mute, lacking in conscious agency (see 'Allûsh 1978: 143, 147, 156). According to al-Azharî, although the rebels of 1936–39 had the strongest of feelings, they lacked the appropriate "intellectual framework" necessary to defeat the enemy (1989: 11). Khilla (1974), meanwhile, underscores the revolt's popular character, asserts that the *fallâhîn* were the prime movers in the insurrection and made the greatest sacrifices, and stresses the rebellion's relative independence from the national leadership. Nonetheless, Khilla's narrative devotes considerably more space to the "official" elite sphere and its diplomatic negotiations than to the activities of the subaltern classes. Moreover, local peasant leaders generally remain anonymous in the official accounts, while the names of elite leaders like Hajj Amîn al-Husaynî, who are the authors of memoirs and the subjects of biographies, tend to function as metonyms for the whole movement.[35] The overall tendency is to downplay differences between elite and subaltern, to minimize popular initiatives, and to stress unity under the Higher Arab Committee (HAC), the official body that led the national movement during the revolt.

Conventional Palestinian accounts variously attribute the revolt's shortcomings to internal discord, to the failure of the people to follow the experienced leadership, or to the peasants' inherent deficiencies. Since the valiant and resolute *fallâhîn* were susceptible to manipulation and limited by their clannishness, localism, and inadequate political consciousness, they could not successfully go it alone. A leadership from the ranks of the educated classes was required to compensate for these failings: only it could organize, coordinate, and control the subaltern classes. Although some accounts do criticize the urban notable leadership for its disunity, its mistakes, and its timidity in prosecuting the revolt (see Kayyali 1978: 231), they nonetheless take it for granted that the peasantry was inherently incapable of furnishing effective leadership of the insurrection. In the end the rebellion splintered, it is said, either because the official leadership, mainly in jail or in exile, was absent or because the urban chiefs' internal disputes rendered them ineffective. Other observers, like al-Hût, blame the internal problems of the revolt on the fact that local commanders made decisions without consulting the revolt leadership in Damascus (al-Hût 1981: 401–2). Once peasants took control, the revolt was doomed to failure because of the *fallâhîn*'s congenital shortcomings. "In general," says Palestinian historian Issa Khalaf in a not untypical view, "the [Palestinian] peasant tends to be more inward-looking, localistic, and relatively isolated, perhaps mentally more than physically in his village world" (Khalaf 1991: 204). Nationalist discourse, therefore, positions peasants and urban middle classes within the dualistic structure of tradition/ modernity. Peasants occupy the pole of tradition, are found to be "inadequate," and must be raised out of their ignorance, parochialism, and false consciousness by the modern (whether liberal or leftist) educated middle classes (see Chatterjee 1986). These standard interpretations are also therefore characterized by a presentist orientation, for they imply that the masses today should continue to look to an educated, politically advanced leadership for guidance and orders. The implicit message of official accounts is that the people today must remain united under the current (middle-class) leadership. Alternatively, the people need to look to a different kind of leadership—but still a modern, educated one that will educate the subaltern classes out of their backward ideological state.

At the same time, official interpreters tend to handle the revolt gingerly, depicting it in reverential tones yet keeping it at arm's length, never examining its details too closely. It is symptomatic of such treatment that no in-depth Palestinian study of the revolt, particularly one dealing with the insurrection's popular base, has been undertaken.[36] Instead, nationalist discourse constantly evokes the rebellion as an inspirational symbol but rarely submits it to careful historical investigation. Even treatments of rebel commanders tend to be hagiographic and fail to discuss *mujâhidîn* mistakes or internal differences (see 'Awda 1984, 1988; Muhsin 1986). Thus, troubling subjects like class fissures, acts of treachery, or peasant initiatives that were independent of elite control appear to be exceptions. The events of the revolt's second stage (especially 1938–39), a period marked by sharp class antagonism as well as assassinations and executions of traitors and spies, remain particularly well hidden. Authoritative discourse smooths over the past's jagged edges and evens out its irruptions, serving up a national conformism.

The feeling that Palestinian history and society are threatened with radical extinction has encouraged preservationist work. Institutions like the Society for the Preservation of the Family at al-Bîra, the Birzeit University's Center for Research and Documentation, the Research Center for Arab Heritage of al-Tayyiba, and the Arab Studies Society in Jerusalem sponsor an array of projects designed to rescue the past: collecting testimony from refugees in order to document the histories of destroyed villages,[37] gathering and publishing folklore and folktales,[38] sponsoring folkloric dance and music troupes, and encouraging traditional crafts, particularly women's needlework. This salvage work tends to throw up idealized images of the past, signifiers of a national essence that work through "mythicizing vagueness" (Wright 1985).

One of the central signifiers of the national past to emerge from these preservationist efforts is the *fallâh,* or peasant. Nationalist discourse has transformed the *fallâh* from social actor into symbolic representative of the cultural and historical continuity of the Palestinian people. The traditional lifestyle of the *fallâh* is seen to encapsulate the shared values deemed worthy of preservation, and it provides a picture of traditional life "as it was" prior to the disaster of 1948. Owing to his crucial role in the 1936–39 revolt, the *fallâh* epitomizes the anticolonial struggle. The peasant additionally signifies a prolonged attachment and intense love for the land of Palestine in the face of land expropriations and population transfers. The *sumûd* (steadfastness) of the *fallâh* is the model for confronting these dangers and maintaining a permanence of place (see Shehadeh 1982). The olive trees that *fallâhîn* tend and the wild thyme (*za'tar*) village women gather have been elevated, through constant invocation in poetry and song, to almost sacred symbols of the relation of the people to the Palestinian soil. Through its imputed oneness with the peasant, the entire populace shares these bonds with the land of Palestine.[39]

Another reason for the symbolic centrality of the *fallâh* and the rural way of life is that the effect of Israeli repression has been to place them in jeopardy. Objects of significance frequently take on the aura of heritage when their basic terms of existence are put in question (Wright 1985: 95). The West Bank has witnessed massive land expropriation, as well as a decline in the economic significance of agriculture. Although by 1984 roughly 70 percent of the West Bank population still lived in rural areas, the percentage of the total workforce employed in agriculture had declined from 47.5 to 28.4 since 1970 (Graham-Brown 1983: 179; Benvenisti 1986b: 8). By the mid-eighties, approximately one-third of the West Bank workforce was commuting to Israel daily for waged work, and roughly three-quarters of that workforce came from rural areas (Tamari 1981: 39). Real Palestinian villages were becoming simulacra of peasant communities.

Such transformations of rural communities made a romanticized peasant centrally significant in national culture. Yet the *fallâh's* representative power was acquired through an erasure of internal differences and a forgetting of social antagonisms. As the agriculturalist was fashioned into a signifier of *national* resistance, he or she ceased to evoke conflicts with landlords, money-lenders, and state officials. When official nationalist discourse made the peasant into a symbol, it effaced his or her regional specificity. It also generalized the peasant as a hardy, independent small farmer—never an oppressed share-cropper or a landless laborer. As the repository of popular wisdom, the devotee of custom, and the keeper of a continuous tradition, the *fallâh* came to stand—in official discourse—for a solidifying past rather than a specifically subaltern history, a *symbol* conveying unity and permanence rather than an *image* that implies rupture and discontinuity (in Benjamin's sense) (see Buck-Morss 1989).

The national movement has forged an ideology of timeless rural tradition to confront the drastic ruptures and fragmentation of Palestinian society caused by colonialism. Urban Palestinians could participate in an imaginary identification with this romantic and idealized rural past-present through evocations of the peasant. Artists sketched scenes of the picturesque village and of pastoral simplicity, folklore collectors discovered an unbroken tradition of national resistance and authenticity, and left-wing folkloric troupes staged tableaux of a pristine time before the colonial onslaught when villagers lived in a kind of "primitive communism." Such constructions were not merely the mythicizing fabrications of an alienated middle class, for I also encountered comparable romanticizations of rural life among Palestinian villagers. Their views resembled the memories of Palestinian refugees "outside" in Lebanon interviewed by Sayigh, who described their existence in former Palestinian villages as "living in paradise" (Sayigh 1979: 10). Mainstream nationalism attempts to remold such nostalgia into a conformist vision of the past.

Enabling Memory

Forgetting represents a force, a form of robust health.
Friedrich Nietzsche

For understandable reasons, interviewees were often less willing to ventilate the revolt's shortcomings with me than with my Palestinian colleagues or with their family or friends. One issue they hesitated discussing was that of Arab sales of land to the Zionist movement, an issue causing great alarm within national circles in the 1930s. Zionist land purchases from non-Palestinian sources predominated until 1928, but thereafter acquisitions from Palestinians (big landowners and *fallâhîn*) constituted the larger portion, and by the mid-1930s, transactions with Palestinians were accounting for 89 percent of the total land purchases by Jews (Porath 1977: 83–84; Stein 1984: 178–87). The Arabic press, the national movement, and Hajj Amîn al-Husaynî's Supreme Muslim Council mobilized against such sales between 1930 and 1935 (Porath 1977: 90–98). During the revolt, moreover, rebels treated those involved in land sales to the Jews as traitors, and many were punished, fined, or executed.

When villagers I met spoke about the issue of land sales, however, they mainly told of famous cases of absentee Lebanese and Syrian landowners like the Sursuqs and Tayâns who sold large estates to the Zionists.[40] Rarely did someone suggest that any Palestinians—whether big landowner, small farmer, or particularly someone from their own village—were involved in land transactions. A significant slipup in this collective representation occurred when Sonia and I were interviewing the son and cousin of a former fighter at al-Tayyiba, a village near Tûlkarm, in the Israeli Triangle. Two men in their twenties came in to call on our hosts and sat in on the rest of the interview. At one point they interjected to indict a notable family from Tûlkarm, the al-Hajj Ibrâhîms, for selling land to Jews in the 1930s, and even went so far as to call the men of that family traitors (*khuwwân*). One of the older men, Abû Mahmûd, retorted that the only Tûlkarm family who sold to the Jews were the Samâras. I left the sitting room at one point to use the bathroom. Sonia informed me that while I was out of earshot, the elders upbraided the youths for exposing the seamy side of the Palestinian national movement to a foreigner.[41] It was not just the desire to maintain a pristine national image that motivated people's guarded approach to this subject, although this representation did accord with official accounts. The issue remained contentious within the community: covert land sales by Palestinians are still avenues (although less significant than outright expropriation, and much less important than they were during the thirties) by which Arab land falls into Israeli Jewish hands—a case of "deferred action," where "recent material gets strengthened by the latent energy of the repressed" (Freud 1967: 121).

Villagers also balked at relating stories about rebels' involvement in activities like assassination, robbery, or clan feuds. Another taboo area concerned the existence as well as rebel treatment of *khuwwân* (traitors) and *'umalâ'* (spies). As with most peasant insurgencies, the rebels of 1936–39 frequently meted out harsh punishment to those known to be traitors to the cause and spies for the enemy. Since the instances of internal division and bloodshed that occurred during the revolt often got entangled with preexisting clan or family differences within or between village communities, these events frequently remained important, troublesome, and alive issues for some elderly men. Perhaps more significant in this regard was the desire not to tarnish the luster of this central national symbol and forerunner of today's liberation movement. The fact that conventional Israeli historiography and propaganda has presented actions like robbery and murder as characteristic of the whole rebellion further strengthened the old men's reluctance to air dirty national linen in public and tempered any inclination to engage in public self-criticism. To cast a pall over the memory of the revolt might also enshroud the image of the PLO. Through narrative lacunae, elderly *mujâhidîn* often tried to project an unsullied Palestinian national past and present.

Another gap in memory concerned the economic situation in Palestine during the 1930s. Published accounts tell of a rural economy in crisis, of *fallâhîn* under tremendous pressure due to growing landlessness, high indebtedness, rising taxes, and the cycles of global economic boom and recession. Written sources stress that while British policies and Zionist colonization were crucial causes of the worsening condition of Palestinian rural communities, many Palestinian landlords, moneylenders, and merchants were full partners in and beneficiaries of the economic processes that were reducing many peasants to misery.[42] Armed with such "facts" about economic conditions during the thirties, I hoped to elicit peasant memories of exploitation at the hands of the Palestinian upper classes. But when I asked, "How were conditions back then?" old people frequently answered, "Life was good, we were very happy." Such remarks did not seem to indicate nostalgia for a lost past so much as critical judgments against a burdensome present. Life in the thirties, my interlocutors appeared to imply, was quite fine *by comparison* with current conditions. When tape recorders were turned off and formal interviews about the *thawra* were concluded or suspended for lunch, the old rebels in the territories complained continuously about their current problems: dispersal of families, relentless land expropriations, absence of civil rights, fears that the nightmares of military rule might go on forever. Even inside Israel, where Palestinians enjoyed relatively better conditions, old men typically bemoaned continuing land seizures, Israeli-Jewish racism against Arabs, and the Palestinian-Israelis' unequal access to civil and economic rights. The bleak present functioned as a kind of screen that filtered out dark memories of the thirties and highlighted that decade's golden tones. The selective vision afforded by present conditions blocked out many harsh features of daily life under British colonial rule. To many old people, the 1930s seemed an idyllic time compared with life since the earth-shattering catastrophes of 1948, 1967, and so on.[43] Such revisions of the past were also consistent with efforts to reduce the memory of class antagonism.

When pressed further, some old men shifted from the spontaneous, stereotypical, and ready-made levels of recollection to a more reflective layer of memory (see Passerini 1983: 195) and averred that the 1930s were marked by their share of economic problems. But instead of complaining about exploitation by Palestinian merchants or capitalists, many recounted a particular ideologeme—that in the thirties the British mandate government deliberately imported cheap agricultural products into Palestine (through the Steele Company, one interviewee claimed) as part of a conspiracy to wreck Arab agriculture and facilitate Zionist conquest of the land.[44] The dominant interpretation, in its popular inflection, accounted for past economic troubles by stressing external causes and obscuring internal class difference.

Other veterans who made critical judgments about the revolt often explained away its shortcomings by displacement. Even villagers who acknowledged that robberies, assassinations, or land sales occurred during the revolt were frequently vague on the details. Others claimed that such things happened only in other places, never in *their* village or *their* district. While acknowledging the partial validity of claims regarding unprincipled rebel practices, they shifted responsibility away from their own locale. One old peasant from the Ramallah area, by contrast, charged that although rebels active in his district were guilty of robbery and extortion, the *thuwwâr* did not behave in this fashion in the Jinîn area. For him, the practices of insurrectionists around Jinîn exemplified the revolt's true character. Remembrance through displacement and condensation therefore preserved the rebel movement's good name, but within regionally circumscribed limits.

Other revolt veterans faulted the enemy for all the unsavory acts that are usually ascribed to the *mujâhidîn*. Palestinians, they claimed, could not be blamed for internal divisions. Domestic turmoil was the result of conspiracies hatched by the British or Zionist intelligence services, who paid mercenaries to commit robberies and murders in the name of the revolt in order to stir up disputes between rival commanders, to exacerbate clan or family differences, and to break the back of the revolt.[45] The not-too-hidden lesson that was drawn for contemporary practice was that while no significant internal differences exist(ed) within the community, the Palestinian people nonetheless needed to remain ever vigilant in maintaining unity, because in the past the enemy exploited the slightest hint of weakness or vacillation and would continue to do so. There was considerable agreement at the popular level, therefore, on the need to maintain a unified, nationalist memory of the past.

Subaltern Traditions

Given that Israeli repressive practices heightened Palestinian tendencies to put forward a seamless nationalist memory, what space was left for the articulation of "popular" memories of revolt? I found that subaltern historical consciousness had neither been eliminated by Israeli censorship nor wholly shaped by mainstream nationalism. Interviewees did not simply echo the dominant versions or remain silent for fear of persecution. Popular traditions led a submerged existence in the everyday realm of private conversation rather than being expounded in the public arena. But there was no such thing as a "pure" popular memory: rather the memories of the subaltern classes were tangled up in the thick and intricate web of what Gramsci calls "common sense." Unlike the relatively coherent and systematic discourses that issue from official sources, common sense, according to Gramsci, is "ambiguous, contradictory . . . , multiform" and "strangely composite" (1971: 324, 423; 1985: 189). Common sense is the historical result of an "infinity of traces," bearing the deposits of "Stone Age elements and principles of a more advanced science, prejudices from all past phases of history at the local level and intuitions of a future philosophy which will be that of a human race united the world over" (Gramsci 1971: 324). Moreover, common sense is not a comprehensive knowledge shared in precisely the same way throughout Palestinian communities, but is characterized by distinctive local and regional differences.

Ironically, Israeli policies were partly responsible for the persistence of distinct subaltern traditions. The authorities' harassment of those institutions that sustained support for the PLO thereby limited the national leadership's ability to channel common sense. Israeli repression hampered the PLO's capacity to harness subaltern opinion to hegemonic principles and to produce or disseminate highly elaborated interpretations of Palestinian history. Mainstream nationalism, while enthusiastically embraced, was therefore able to imprint specific histories on people's minds only to a limited degree. Because official agencies had effectively circulated the mere outlines of a general historical narrative, many local versions of the past remained relatively untouched as long as they did not directly contradict the official story.

This partial opening permitted the limited circulation of local versions of history. Among these parochial versions were "popular-democratic" interpretations of the revolt that emphasized local initiatives and that emanated from submerged peasant traditions of independence from state control and were forged out of the experience of past struggles. These traditions could be put to use to contradict or reinscribe official historical discourses (Hall et al. 1977: 50). They resembled the kind of "negative" class consciousness or "subversivism" that Gramsci described in rural Italy—the countryside's dislike of the town, the peasants' hatred of state officials (1971: 272–73). But no red thread tied subaltern memory into a coherent pattern of class consciousness. Elderly villagers did not remember the revolt in the "pure" language of class but rather through a complex web of popular-democratic, nationalist, religious, clan, and localist discourses. Different groups and individuals combined strands of these discourses in various arrangements and articulations. Official Palestinian nationalist discourse tried to fit certain elements into its own system of meaning, to turn them into equivalents in a signifying chain, and to marginalize the dissonant strands. Therefore popular-democratic memory traces rarely appeared full-blown or articulated within a counter-discourse, but instead they were interwoven with other, discontinuous expressions of subordinate memory. "Subversivist" recollection was often expressed indirectly, in the interstices of a nationalist opinion, in conjunction with "religious," "regionalist," and sometimes even "collaborationist" discourse. And often that subversivism was articulated through images rather than through narratives. "History breaks down," Benjamin suggests, "into images, not into stories" (1983–84: 25).

Because of the power of the standard narrative, interviewees frequently couched popular-democratic statements in nationalist language, articulating divergent rather than openly oppositional versions of a national past. "Subversivist" accounts of the revolt were generally not linked to a fully counter-hegemonic discourse, but instead were inflections, negotiations, and maneuvers within the dominant Palestinian code. For instance, former rebels often disputed the official version's emphasis on the leading role and the "advanced" political consciousness of the urban middle class. Some villagers made the "subversivist" assertion that the revolt was the work of the urban and rural poor and not the rich. It was the *fallâhîn* and not the city people, they argued, who really "made" (*'amalû*) the revolt. "The revolt would have succeeded," claimed the old fighter Muhammad Kîlânî of Ya'bad, "if wealthy Palestinians had only sacrificed for it one-tenth as much as poor people did." The impoverished classes who fought, gave their lives, and contributed generously to the rebels, Kîlânî asserted, were the true nationalists. The rich, who made only small contributions and never joined in the fighting, played an insignificant role. Some veterans even claimed that the *fallâhîn* were more nationalistic and revolutionary than the effendi leadership. Glosses such as these, however, were also frequently ambiguous, as is characteristic of common sense. Men who expressed pride when recalling the rebels' independent actions nonetheless compared their level of military organization unfavorably with the PLO's fighting capacity of 1985. "We were dedicated," they would assert, "but the overall situation was one of *fawda* [chaos]." Some elders, in contrast, claimed that during the thirties the movement was more nationalistic and militant than it was in the mid-eighties, thereby deploying the past to criticize the chiefs of the present.

Some surviving *mujâhidîn* employed the language of regionalism in a "subversivist" fashion. They often presented popular initiatives as strictly local phenomena, actions initiated by the men of a village (or group of villages) without any orders or direction from the central leadership. For example, they told of peasants deciding on their own to form armed bands, of rebels supplying themselves with weapons and food, of local commanders planning when and where to hit the British forces, and so on. Interviewees often recounted such localized rebel actions with great pride. Their localist language unsettled official versions, which either claimed that the hand of the leadership guided effective action or that peasants were only capable of "spontaneous" activity. Veterans also frequently maintained that local practices and knowledges were essential for the prosecution of the revolt. One such rural practice was the *faza'*, or alert, a traditional village means of mobilizing in cases of outside aggression. This form of alarm, refunctioned for the purposes of the guerrilla struggle, was crucial to the rebels' abilities to get men into battle at a moment's notice. Interviewees also underscored the significance of their knowledge of local geography—the hiding places, the trails, the smuggling routes—that were necessary for the prosecution of the insurrection. Such essential skills, they emphasized, could only have been in peasant hands.

Some interviewees articulated democratic-popular positions through religious discourse. Most older men, for example, remembered Shaykh 'Izz al-Dîn al-Qassâm first and foremost as a good Muslim, a man of religion (*rajul al-dîn*). They also underscored that the practices of Qassâm, who recruited followers exclusively among the peasantry and the urban poor, who resided in the popular quarter of Haifa, and who sold his own belongings in order to purchase a rifle, simply involved acting in a proper "religious" fashion. Interviewees also stressed that Qassâm's association with the lower classes, his militancy, and his sacrifices for the nation set him apart from the other national and religious figures of the era. Such accounts provide further illustration of the disparate character of commonsense memory, its tendency to be articulated through a "multiplex" combination of religious, nationalist, regional, and populist elements.

Many old rebels gave the national past a subaltern inflection by recalling it via a kind of peasant condensation. They remembered the revolt through images of exemplary local rebel commanders or leaders like Qassâm who organized among the subaltern, rather than by recalling the names of official urban leaders. When asked about the revolt, they spontaneously cited the local heroes and martyrs with relatively unblemished reputations like Qassâm, 'Abd al-Rahîm al-Hâjj Muhammad, or Abû Khâlid as metonyms for a national movement that was popular, honorable, religious, and lofty in its aims and actions (see Swedenburg 1987: 18–20). In the eyes of elderly villagers, the *fallâhîn* were less signifiers of the entire people than a distinct part of the people with their own local traditions of revolt. They recalled peasants as much in terms of their difference from the privileged classes as they did in terms of cross-class commonalities. Villagers who voiced heterogeneous opinions about the revolt, through popular-democratic or subversivist inflections of mainstream nationalism, localism, or Islam, in fact articulated a more inclusive and heterogeneous "national-popular" tradition (Gramsci 1971: 130–33, 421) than did standard Palestinian historiography, which frequently tried to turn such polyphony into a conformism.

Sartorial Patriotism

Among the most important of all signifiers associated with the Palestinian peasantry is the *kûfîya,* the Palestinian headdress. The story of its adoption as a *national* signifier is illustrative of the processes whereby national unity is forged through the forgetting of difference. It also demonstrates the built-in tension between this signifier's function as a *symbol*—which offers a naturalized, unifying, and transcendent representation of the nation—and as an *image*—which stresses transitoriness, impermanence, and fragmentation; signifies the dangers posed to Palestinian existence, as well as to the constructed nature of the national past; and points to the contingent character of national identity. Prior to the outbreak of the rebellion in 1936, the cotton and usually all-white *kûfîya* (also known locally as the *hatta*) was one element in a complex and dynamic code of dress that differentiated people by rank, region, sect, age, gender, and—perhaps most significant—by whether they were from town or country. For, as Gramsci has observed, "dress is a fundamental element of distinction" (1971: 272). The *hatta,* usually all white, was worn almost exclusively by the men of the countryside, both peasants and Bedouin. Placed over a skullcap and held in place by a headcord known as the *'iqâl,* it staved off the winter cold and shielded against the summer sun, while simply by covering the head it also affirmed the religious modesty and respectfulness of the wearer. The turban, by contrast, distinguished the elders of rural communities from younger men (Seger 1981: 34).

In the terms of the sartorial system of this hierarchical society, the *kûfîya* also marked its wearer as a man of low status. This head covering distinguished the *fallâh* from the effendi, the educated middle- or upper-class man of the town, who demonstrated his social preeminence by donning the maroon-colored felt *tarbûsh* or fez (familiar in the United States for its association with parading Shriners). The reforming Ottoman government first introduced the fez in the 1830s as a replacement for the turban, whose various colors differentiated subjects according to their sectarian allegiance. The fez, by contrast, marked its wearer simply as an Ottoman subject without making any distinctions regarding his faith (Hodgson 1974: 229; Winkelhane 1988: 136).[46] Although it was initially resisted, the *tarbûsh* gradually took hold among males in Ottoman urban centers, and throughout the nineteenth century it remained *the* distinctive outward marker of (male) "Oriental" identity even as other clothing items underwent westernization (Winkelhane 1988: 138). In the course of this sartorial evolution, Ottoman subjects never adopted the Western hat, which was regarded as the emblem par excellence of the colonialists.

With the early stirrings of Arab nationalism in the Mashriq, the *tarbûsh* began to be contested. In the early twentieth century Arab nationalists in Damascus initiated a campaign to distinguish themselves from the fez-garbed "Ottoman" Turks by donning the "Arab" headscarf (*kûfîya*). Some men went bareheaded in order to remain aloof from this Turkish-Arab apparel conflict (Winkelhane 1988: 136). Photographic evidence suggests that the *kûfîya* was an important part of the uniform of the fighters in the Arab Revolt led by Prince Faisal (Khalidi 1984: 46). I do not know how involved urban Palestinians were in the early-twentieth-century struggle over Turkish versus Arab headwear, but photos show that by the twenties and thirties many educated young urbanites in Palestine had adopted the bareheaded pose, probably as a sign of "modernity." Snapshots of middle-class radicals of the Istiqlâl Party from the early thirties feature a mix of uncovered heads and *tarâbîsh* (Khalidi: 1984: 106–7). Palestinian Boy Scouts, also part of the nationalist movement, garbed themselves in unique hybrid outfits that included both Arab *kûfîya* and Western-style shorts (Khalidi 1984: 104). The *tarbûsh,* meanwhile, was never donned in the countryside, except by some village boys who attended school and by certain men who worked in urban centers (Seger 1981: 62). Up to the 1930s, despite some minor shifts, the *kûfîya* generally still signified social inferiority (and rural backwardness), while the *tarbûsh* signaled superiority (and urbane sophistication).

The status hierarchy based on rural–urban and class difference was momentarily yet dramatically overturned during the 1936 revolt. While the official political leaders of the struggle for independence came from the urban upper and middle classes, the armed rebel bands that began to operate in the highlands after the general strike broke out were composed almost exclusively of peasants. These guerrilla fighters took on the *kûfîya* as their insignia. Wrapped close around their heads, *kûfîyât* provided anonymity to fighters roaming the countryside, disguised their identities from spies, and helped them elude capture by the British. (Fighters also used teknonyms— names taken from their children, like Abû 'Abdallah, "the father of 'Abdallah"—as noms de guerre to mask their true identities. One old *thâ'ir* told us it was considered "illegal" to ask another fighter his "real" name.) Rebel leaders who embraced the *hatta* were also probably consciously invoking the memory of King Faisal's Arab nationalist followers in 1918 Damascus (Kayyali 1978: 212).[47] From the military point of view, however, there was one problem with the *kûfîya:* increasingly, whenever fighters slipped into towns along with other villagers, their conspicuous headdress made them targets for arrest by the British army.

On August 26, 1938, when the revolt was reaching its apogee and beginning to take control of urban areas, the rebel leadership commanded all Palestinian Arab townsmen to discard the *tarbûsh* and don the *kûfîya*. Rebel headquarters in Damascus announced that this was to "demonstrate the complete solidarity of the residents of the country with the struggle [*jihâd*], and as a sign that everyone in the country is a rebel [*thâ'ir*]" (quoted in Khilla 1974: 458). British officials were amazed that the new fashion spread across the country with "lightning rapidity" (*Palestine Post,* September 2, 1938).[48] While the order was issued in part to help *thuwwâr* blend into the urban environment, it was equally a move in the wider social struggle within the national movement. One rebel commander, harking back to the Arab Revolt and Damascus battles over headgear, asserted that whereas the fez was associated with the Ottoman Turks, the *kûfîya* was the headgear of the Arab nation.[49] The Palestinian director of the American Friends School at Ramallah, Khalil Totah, explained:

The Igal [that is, *kûfîya*] of the Arab today is surely a liberty cap but conceived in an original and native fashion. By making Supreme Court judges, big Government officials, important merchants and the entire professional class and in fact every body, wear an igal the rebels have made a grand sweep in the direction of democracy. The fellahin do not conceal their delight at seeing their "uppers," the effendis, come down a peg and look like them in the matter of head dress. They feel proud of having raised themselves in the social scale.[50]

Rebels accordingly resorted to force to make some reluctant effendis put on this new, lower-status garb.[51] An article in the *Times* (London) entitled "Sartorial Patriotism" reported on September 8 that "a regular campaign of tarbush-smashing has spread in the towns. It first appeared in Jaffa, and now is being made felt in Jerusalem. The *shabab* or young bloods have been quick to take it up, and young boys have followed suit." The *tarbûsh* soon became associated with the Palestinian Opposition, led by the Nashâshîbîs, and came to be regarded as an insignia of treason to the national cause (Nashashibi 1990: 103).[52] The significance of the struggle can also be gauged from an interview with Opposition leader Fakhrî Nashâshîbî at Jerusalem that appeared in the *Egyptian Gazette.* Conducted in December, shortly after Fakhrî had issued a statement attacking the Mufti, the article's headline reads, "The Tarboush Stands for Liberty."

> —"I see that you are still wearing a tarboush?" [the *Gazette*'s reporter asks.]
> —"Yes," laughed Fakhry Bey, "I think that I am the only man in Palestine today to have the courage of my head-covering."
> —"Don't you consider the keffiyeh the national headdress then?"
> —"There is no national significance in it at all. It was imposed by the rebels merely to evade capture by forcing all Arabs to look alike."[53]

Nashâshîbî's claims notwithstanding, the order to don the *kûfîya* was not just the imposition of a *national* symbol, but was also a symptom of the social antagonism against the wealthy urban notable class to which Nashâshîbî belonged. The promotion of the *kûfîya* represented a symbolic inversion, a reversal of the "natural" semiotic hierarchy of clothing, and a violation of the symbols of power (see Guha 1983: 61–63; Connerton 1989: 10–11).

The new national dress code should also be situated within the context of other rebel actions in the late summer and early fall of 1938. Commanders of the armed peasantry instructed urban residents to stop using the electric power produced by the Anglo-Jewish Palestine Electric Company. (Villages did not yet enjoy the luxury of electricity.) The *thuwwâr* extracted hefty "contributions" to the national movement from wealthy Palestinians, particularly the big orange growers and merchants of Jaffa. The rebel command declared a moratorium on all debts, taking effect on September 1, 1938, and warned both debt collectors and land agents not to visit the villages. (Usurious loans were one of the chief means by which large landowners exploited peasants and kept them dependent.) The command also canceled all rents on urban apartments, which had reached scandalously high levels. They warned Arab contractors and their workmen not to construct police posts and roads, and attempted to disrupt the orange harvests on plantations owned by big Palestinian landowners.[54] At the same time, the rebels were setting up an alternative state apparatus in the countryside that included law courts (complete with white-wigged judges and court stenographers), printed law codes, and taxation systems. This shadow infrastructure threatened not just the British administration but the Arab elite's hold over the countryside, as well. The *kûfîya* order therefore appeared in concert with rebel actions in support of popular interests, a "revenge of the countryside" that drove hundreds of wealthy Palestinians to seek refuge in Syria, Lebanon, and Egypt.

Colonial officials who noted the speed with which the fashion spread saw this more as the result of a conspiracy than as a manifestation of national spirit. The Zionist press similarly asserted that the townsmen's adoption of the *kûfîya* was an act of "cowardly submission" to the "terror" of the armed "gangs" and ridiculed the townsmen's "superficial" nationalism (Black 1986: 388).[55] For instance, the *Palestine Post* (September 1, 1938) wrote sarcastically: "When the history of these stirring times is written, and the devastation suffered by the Holy Land assessed, the chronicler will add a postscript: in the third year of the disturbances the Arab townsfolk acknowledged the hegemony of the wild banditry by substituting for the tarboosh or panama, the kefia and agal. That was their contribution to the national cause."

The subsequent reassumption of the *tarbûsh* by the effendis of the town was equally the result of struggle, of pressures from the British and the Nashâshîbî-led Opposition. The British commander in the north, General Bernard Montgomery—who made a name for himself fighting Palestinians before going on to do battle with Rommel—wanted to issue an order against wearing the *kûfîya* and *'iqâl*, not in order to prosecute men who refused to obey but to have an excuse to put them in a "cage" for a day or two "to cool off." Haifa's assistant district commissioner Thomas Scrivenor disagreed with Monty's plan and argued that enforcing such a measure would lead to riots.[56] So the *kûfîya* was simply eliminated from the cities without any official proclamation. In the town of Jinîn, the British police pressured the men to reassume the *tarbûsh* in the course of reestablishing "order" (Morton 1957:

98–100). In Nablus, Sulaymân Tawqân, mayor and prominent Opposition figure, commanded his subjects to replace the *kûfîya* with the fez after he returned from exile, under British protection, in January 1939.[57]

Even at the time the rebel order to put on the *kûfîya* was issued, Palestinian official accounts claimed that all urban Palestinians embraced it enthusiastically as a national symbol and ignored the fact that pressure had to be applied to certain elitist or conservative townsmen. Standard nationalist versions have repeated this story ever since (see al-Hût 1981: 381–82). Palestinian histories tend to explain the order to put on the *hatta* as a matter of military exigency rather than as a transgression of social hierarchy (al-Muzayyin 1981: 197; al-'Askarî n.d.: 90; Zu'aytir 1980: 440).[58] Although part of the motivation for asserting Palestinian unanimity about the *kûfîya* is no doubt in response to hostile Zionist and British propaganda regarding the campaign, the nationalist version of the tale is also part of the effort to "forget" past internal splits, in the interest of preserving a fiction of national unity.

In the mid-sixties the Palestinian *fidâ'îyîn* reanimated the *kûfîya* as an emblem of national struggle and as an image of unity. (The *kûfîya* they "revived," however, was not the all-white headscarf of the *thawra* but a checkered black-and-white one. The origins of the black-and-white checkered *kûfîya* as the distinctive Palestinian headscarf apparently date to the early 1950s. Glubb Pasha, the English commander of Jordan's armed forces, distinguished his Palestinian soldiers from his Jordanian ones by outfitting West Bank Palestinians in black-and-white *kûfîyât* and East Bank Jordanians in red-and-white ones.)[59] The *hatta* of the new Palestinian guerrilla both evoked and produced a memory of a moment when all Palestinians—rural and urban, Christian and Muslim, rich and poor—combined without distinction in collective action. The fact that an earlier generation of fighters *imposed* this item of apparel as a sign of the conjunctural hegemony of the rural over the urban and of the inversion of the social hierarchy was largely forgotten in the course of its revival by the guerrillas—despite the fact that the emergence of the *fidâ'îyîn* was itself a ruptural moment.

Indeed, people I met usually related this well-known story to me along conventional lines. Over and over, Palestinians young and old told of how townsmen donned the peasant *kûfîya* during the revolt. And generally, they too recounted this act as an allegory of national unity. The *hatta* was still being used in various ways in the mid-eighties, whereas the *tarbûsh* had all but disappeared. Palestinian elders of village origin still wore the distinctive *kûfîya* on their heads, held in place by the *'iqâl*. On one level, therefore, the *hatta* remained the mark of a peasant—but generally speaking, of an elderly one. Younger and middle-aged village men by contrast often went around bareheaded. Additionally, some young Palestinian men and women—in town and village—wore the *kûfîya* as well, but draped around their necks as a scarf rather than covering their heads, as a badge of national identity and of activism. The *kûfîya*'s revival among young people indexed the development of a more popular-democratic nationalism that incorporated women to a greater degree than in the past. Yet this adoption of the sartorial mark of the peasant and his "traditional" mode of life involved the simultaneous writing of the popular classes into national history and the partial erasure—in the name of national unity—of the memory of the subaltern struggles that prompted that initial rewriting.

Memories of Revolt

The *kûfîya* was not established for all eternity as the symbol of national unanimity. It could also be reinvoked as an image, a signifier of contingency and disruption. Sâmî Kîlânî once told me a story he heard in prison from a septuagenarian *fallâh* named Abû Muhammad, a fighter in the 1936–39 rebellion who was subsequently detained numerous times for his ongoing political activity. In the early 1980s he was serving time for offering military advice to young would-be guerrillas. Abû Muhammad spent hours recounting stories of the *thawra* to his prison comrades, men thirty or forty years his junior. One day, he recalled gleefully that many educated city dwellers, when ordered to don the peasant *kûfîya* in 1938, did not know the proper way to wear it. The effendis simply could not keep the symbol of national struggle from slipping off their heads. Geoffrey Morton, a British police officer in Palestine during the insurgency, offers a similar image: "Most of the merchants and shopkeepers found their new headgear decidedly awkward to manage, and many a curse was hastily stifled as its hanging tasselled ends knocked over a glass of tea or tangled inadvertently in a dish of olive oil" (1957: 53). I heard another such account in Austin from Makram Copty, a Palestinian friend from Nazareth. His grandmother used to tell him about the peddlers who hawked *kûfîyât* in the streets of Nazareth during the fall of 1938, chanting:

> Hatta, hatta bi 'ashr 'urûsh
> In'al abû illî lâbis tarbûsh
> [*Hatta, hatta* for ten *qurûsh* (piastres)
> Damn those who wear the *tarbûsh*][60]

Such anecdotes continued to be recirculated, reinvoked, and rewritten in unofficial channels. Counterimages were relayed through subaltern circuits, by means of tales told at home, smuggled books, privately recorded cassettes of nationalist songs, and banned poems. They were one means by which members of the popular classes, as well as progressive militants, worked to assert a Palestinian national identity in the face of tremendous cultural repression, and simultaneously tried to widen the space for equality and democracy inside the unified national sphere—in order to prevent nationalism from being merely a kind of slogan, chanted in unison, authored by the middle classes.

2 / Scenes of Erasure

If you shoot the past with a bullet, the future will mow you down with
artillery.   *Vietnamese proverb*

. . . the dead who rise to buffet you when you are indifferent to the twists
and turns of the present but are made to realize you are still vulnerable to
the caprices of the past.   *Anton Shammas*

Whitewash

"You've *got* to visit Acre Prison [*sijn 'Akkâ*]," Hishâm urged us as we sipped
sage tea together in February 1985, sitting in his cramped apartment on
Jabotinsky Road. Outside, in the public playground across the street, Jewish
children, protected by a guard cradling an Uzi, were enjoying the sparkling
sun and the salty breezes sweetly wafting off the Mediterranean. Hishâm, a
publisher, was one of the thirteen thousand Palestinian-Israelis living in this
"mixed" town of forty thousand in northern Israel, called 'Akko in Hebrew,
'Akkâ in Arabic. "You can still see the prisoners' scribblings on the walls
there," he continued. "You'll find Abû Hâkim's name among them. Take a
photograph of the graffiti he wrote, then take it along to show Abû Hâkim
when you go to Gaza. He'll start crying, and then he'll tell you great stories
about the years he spent in prison during the mandate. If I owned a camera
I would have photographed his signature myself."

Hishâm's words only whetted our eagerness to visit the prison. Sonia and
I were staying in Acre for several days, conducting interviews with former

38

rebel fighters in nearby villages and relishing the temperate littoral climate and our brief respite from military occupation. Other friends had already told us about the prisoners' writing on the cell block walls of Acre Prison. Several men we had interviewed recounted stories of prison life. During the 1936–39 rebellion, hundreds of Palestinians were incarcerated there, in what was then Palestine's Central Prison, and most of the 112 Arabs executed for security offenses connected with the revolt were hung in the gallows of Acre. Not only were we keen to get an *aide-memoire* for our interview with Abû Hâkim in Gaza, but we were interested in how the stories we had heard jibed with the representations of the Israeli historical apparatuses.

As we approach the Citadel (*al-qala'*) of Acre, which houses the old prison and is an important tourist attraction, we notice that, like most historic edifices in Israel/Palestine, the Citadel is constructed over the rubble of innumerable ancient monuments. Their indistinct layers bleed into one another to form the structure's foundations, testimony to the ancient and complex history of this seaport town. The Phoenicians named it 'Akko, and the ancient Israelites, who never captured the town, employed the same appellation. The Arabs who conquered the city in A.D. 636 renamed it 'Akkâ. The Crusaders seized the town in 1104 and christened it Saint Jean d'Acre. The Citadel building standing today was built atop the old Crusader fortress by the famous Ottoman governor of Bosnian origin, Ahmad al-Jazzâr Pasha, who is best remembered for holding out against Napoleon's siege of the city in 1799 and thwarting Bonaparte's ambitions of conquering Syria. When the British took control of Acre in 1919, they turned Jazzâr's Citadel into the Central Prison of Palestine. After the city fell into Israeli hands in 1948, the state turned the Citadel into a mental institution, and only transformed it into a tourist attraction in 1980.

Sonia and I enter the fortress and make a beeline for the prisoners' block. We search for Arab inscriptions, but find none. The walls of the old prison look freshly whitewashed, part of the ongoing renovation for the tourist trade. All traces of prisoners' writing are wiped out.

The execution chamber is equally devoid of vestiges that might evoke the memory of Arabs. Several old men we met recited stories of the "national heroes" Muhammad Jumjum, Fu'âd Hijâzî, and 'Ata al-Zayr, who bravely faced execution for their part in the bloody events of 1929. Other former rebels recalled Shaykh Farhân al-Sa'dî, an associate of 'Izz al-Dîn al-Qassâm. Shaykh Farhân, an important rebel commander in the Jinîn area, was the first *thâ'ir* (rebel) tried and executed under Defence Regulations prescribing the death penalty for anyone caught possessing arms and ammunition. His trial, in military court, lasted three hours. Shaykh Farhân was hung in the execution chamber on November 27, 1937, while he was fasting for Ramadan and despite lawyers' pleas for mercy on the basis of his advanced age (he was reportedly in his eighties).[1] We had heard names of others, too, now remembered only by a few elderly villagers, whom the British executed during the revolt for mere possession of a revolver or cartridge clip.[2] But it is just the eight Jews put to death during the British mandate who are now memorialized here (only one of whom was executed during the 1936–39 revolt.) A perpetual light burns in memory of these martyrs, whose massively enlarged photos line the chamber walls.

We leave the gallows and proceed to a section of the Citadel known as the Museum of Heroism, dedicated to the memory of Jewish underground fighters detained at the prison. Here, amid the memorabilia of Jewish prisoners, we find some Arab traces:

1. A dramatic mural portrays a scowling Arab wrapped in a *kûfîya*. A cluster of fists, some clenching knives, are raised over the Arab's head, ready to rain down blows on unseen victims. In style and content, the mural bears an uncanny resemblance to the PLO posters celebrating the guerrilla struggle that graced the walls of Beirut and Amman during the late sixties and early seventies. The English caption reads, "Attack of the Arab prisoners . . . on the Jewish prisoners."[3]

2. An enlarged reproduction of a *New York Times* article describes the celebrated jailbreak of May 4, 1947 (recounted in Leon Uris's *Exodus* and dramatized in the film that was shot on location in the prison), when a joint Irgun–Stern Gang team dynamited its way into Acre Prison to rescue 41 comrades. In passing, the article mentions that 131 Arab prisoners escaped in the course of the same incident.

3. A placard bearing the title "1936–39" states: "In 1936, Arab riots broke out all over the country, subsiding in 1939. *The Irgun Zevai Leumi* . . . retaliated with a series of reprisals, hundreds of its members were detained and imprisoned. One of them, Shlomo Ben-Yosef, was condemned to death and was executed here on the 17th April, 1938."

The public historical memory staged at Acre Citadel represents an episode in the drama of the Jewish national independence struggle. Exhibits enshrine the memory of the Jewish underground fighters and endow their escapades with meaning by framing them within the narrative of the Israeli nation. The key actors in this drama are the British colonialists—the former masters of the prison—and the Jewish prisoners. The outcome of their contest, the fulfillment of the narrative, is the creation of the state of Israel.

This story gains its coherence through various erasures, marginalizations, recodings, and disfigurations of Palestinian Arab history. The remnants of the Arab prisoners are effaced from the prison walls and the gallows. The 131 Arab detainees who escaped are rendered incidental to the tale of the 1947 prison rescue. The protagonists of the escape—"one of the most dramatic and crucial turning points of the pre-State era," according to the Ministry of Tourism brochure (*Akko* 1983: 9)—are the Stern Gang and the Irgun. And the 1936–39 rebellion of Palestinian Arabs is reinscribed as "riots" against the Jews, an act of naming that denies the revolt's anticolonial and nationalist character, designations reserved for the Zionist movement. By such a reckoning it was only the Jews who fought the British, and for whom Eretz Israel constituted "the homeland, the irreplaceable core of national existence" (*Facts about Israel* 1961: 11).

To make the Zionist struggle of 1947–48 into simply an anticolonial narrative also requires recoding and revising the history of the Zionist movement. For if the Palestinian struggle for national independence is to appear as anti-Jewish "riots" while the Zionist movement is to seem anticolonial, prior Zionist collaboration with the British must be excised. Such a narrative cannot contain Britain's role as imperial sponsor of the Zionist movement and as mother country for Jewish colonists. In 1922, after Great Britain assumed its mandate, the Jewish community in Palestine (83,790 persons) accounted for 11 percent of the population, whereas by 1943 it had grown, chiefly through immigration, to 539,000 or 31.5 percent of the total (Rodinson 1973: 56). Immigration on this massive a scale was possible only because British arms imposed it upon the Arab Palestinians. It was only in the last years of the mandate that tensions led to open conflict between the settlers and their imperial sponsors. Such inconvenient facts are neatly elided in the narrative presented at Acre Prison.

This public memory also purchases its coherence by papering over the substantial divisions inside the Zionist movement. Historical sites, Bommes and Wright (1982: 264) argue, represent the nation most effectively when they purge all internal contradiction in the name of a unified culture. Acre Citadel presents a fable of a unified Jewish struggle for independence and a "forgetting" that the "heroes" memorialized within—mainly members of the Stern Gang and the Irgun—committed many violent acts against Arabs that the mainstream Zionist movement, which advocated a policy of *havlaga*, harshly condemned.[4] One deadly spree was launched in April 1938, soon after the British authorities executed Shlomo Ben-Yosef, who was convicted of shooting at an Arab bus in retaliation for a previous murder of five Jews and who is named in the "1936–39" placard at the Acre Citadel. The Irgun (of which Menachem Begin took command in 1942) aimed its "reprisals" not at the British officials who ordered Ben-Yosef's hanging but at Palestinian Arabs. These involved stringing up one Arab in Haifa and employing young Sephardi Jews who could mingle anonymously with Arab crowds to set off a succession of bombs in the bazaars of the "mixed" towns of Jerusalem, Tel Aviv, and Haifa. By the end of June 1938, seven to ten Arabs had been been killed; in July 1938, seventy-seven more Arabs were murdered in these "retaliations" (Bell 1977: 42; Black 1986: 374–75), on whose details the Museum of Heroism narrative is silent.[5]

The remains of the Arab prisoners expelled from the prison cells reappear in inhuman form in the museum mural. This depiction remembers fierce Arab prisoners wielding knives, forever menacing innocent Jews who only resort to violence in self-defense or as "reprisals." The Israeli historical narrative is presented as the constant repetition of Arab aggression and terrorism against the blameless Jew. Yet the story establishing Jewish innocence is a frightening one. The mural Arab's savage demeanor is the troubling reminder of a repression, the infiltrating mark of the "wild" Other inscribed within the national narrative (see de Certeau 1986: 4). Maybe such fantastic fears *about* the Palestinian give a hint of what was done *to* them (see Taussig 1987), and perhaps the image of the Arab as a dehumanized beast is a terrifying token of the high price Palestinians paid for Israel's national independence. Although the museum Other must be named an "Arab," not a Palestinian, his head is swathed in a *kûfîya,* signifier of the Palestinian terrorist par excellence. The *kûfîya* here testifies to a past that constant rubbing out can never completely eliminate.

Similar efforts have been initiated outside the Citadel's walls to remove the Palestinian from the city of Acre. In early 1948, the city's population (all Arab since the 1936–39 rebellion, when the small Jewish population left) totaled 15,500. By November, after it fell to the Haganah in May, the Arab population had shriveled to 3,100 (Torstrick 1993: 71, 74). Shortly thereafter a policy of Judaization of 'Akko/'Akkâ was initiated; Jews were settled there (many in abandoned Arab properties), and the town was expanded to the east over the ruins of the Arab village of al-Manshîya (Torstrick 1993: 69, 77–82). Meanwhile the old Arab section of town was left to run down— causing severe overcrowding and the collapse of housing—and Palestinian-Israelis were denied the licenses necessary to improve or expand their dwelling spaces. As congestion and decay became severe in the Old City, the government launched an effort in the seventies to turn it into a "living museum city" (Lustick 1980: 132). Emptied of most of its Arab inhabitants, the historic Old City would be "safe" and appealing to tourists. Arab residents were encouraged to move out of Acre to government-sponsored housing near the village of Makr, eight kilometers east of the city.

Despite its persistent efforts, the state did not succeeded in eliminating the Arab population. Since 1970, the Labor-dominated municipality has consistently raised alarms about the impending Arab "threat" to the demographic "balance," even though this has remained at a fairly stable ratio of three Jews to every Arab between 1955 and 1989 (Torstrick 1993: 111, 260–61). In December 1988, the Likud candidate for mayor (who was also the deputy mayor in the Labor-dominated municipal council) announced that he would run on a platform calling for the "transfer" of Arab residents to nearby localities in order to "maintain a purely Jewish town" (Abdel Fattah 1988; Torstrick 1993: 262–91). "Transfer," of course, was the euphemism used in 1948 for the massive expulsion of Palestinians from the new state of Israel. The Likud candidate thundered that Arabs were guilty of disturbing Saturday prayer services by holding parties and picnics in the open square and by keeping their shops open, and that Arab youths were flirting with Jewish girls in the town's main street. The more "moderate" Labor Party mayor, who was reelected with the support of Arab voters, favored "coexistence" based on the maintenance of a Jewish majority (Torstrick 1993: 282).

Guidebooks meanwhile warn tourists off those remaining Arabs. Foreign visitors to old 'Akkâ are cautioned that "many local [Arab] men . . . consider picking up foreign women a full-time sport, and what begins as a pleasant conversation may turn into a dangerous encounter. . . . It's best not to prowl the alleys of the old city after dark" (Harvard Student Agency 1984: 153).[6]

Yad Vashem and 'Ayn Kârim

Forgetfulness leads to exile, while remembrance is the secret of redemption.
Baal Shem Tov
(inscription at Yad Vashem)

Earlier that same winter I paid a visit to Yad Vashem at Jerusalem, Israel's holocaust monument and injunction against forgetting. Besides a permanent exhibit, the site houses a research center dedicated to archiving, authenticating, elaborating, and disseminating the memory of the holocaust. By the mid-seventies, the institute, which traces and registers the name of each Jewish victim of the Nazis, had collected thirty million written documents and twenty-five thousand oral testimonies relating to the persecution, extermination, and resistance of European Jews during the fascist era (Thompson 1977: 37).

As anyone who has visited Yad Vashem knows, the exhibits effectively convey a message through eloquent understatement. One can only be deeply moved by these depictions of the enormity of the Nazis' crimes and the unspeakable suffering they caused. But despite its pretensions, Yad Vashem does not merely communicate a *universal* message about oppression. Diplomats visiting Israel are always shepherded through Yad Vashem prior to getting down to official discussions (Bowman 1992), and the lesson they are given is not a "universal" one. For Yad Vashem is equally a *national* historical site, part of a system of signs that together constitute an Israeli narrative (see Bommes and Wright 1982). As an element in the nation-making signifying chain, Yad Vashem too bears marks of repression and elision.

A slide show inside the exhibit hall recreates "The Jewish World That Was," evoking the bygone world of Jewish life in Europe without a trace of nostalgia, with no regret for the passing of this era. The exhibit's implication is that life in the Diaspora was *always* impossible because anti-Semitism is simply ineradicable. Anti-Semitism is presented not as a historical phenomenon but as a permanent feature of diasporic Jewish existence among the Gentiles. Yad Vashem, according to Tom Segev, "leaves [Nazi anti-Semitism] without explanation, as though it were a phenomenon with an obvious explanation, almost natural" (quoted in Rosen 1991: 10).[7] Israel's creation, according to this logic, was necessary to provide refuge from the future holocausts and pogroms that are inevitable as long as Jews continue to live in exile. Rather than urging visitors to oppose *all* oppression *in general,* therefore, Yad Vashem enjoins them not to forget one particular, *exceptional* act of repression, an atrocity more timeless than historical because it "is presented as one link in a long chain of anti-Semitic persecution" (Tom Segev, quoted by Rosen 1991: 10). The "memory" one should take away from Yad Vashem is that anti-Semitic violence might erupt again at any moment, in any place, and therefore only the existence of an ever vigilant Israel guarantees Jewry's continued survival. Moreover, such a depiction of *the* Holocaust seems to set the Jewish people "outside of history and the moral judgment of the world." Thus Menachem Begin could proclaim during the 1982 invasion of Lebanon, "No one, anywhere in the world, will preach moral lessons to our people about the concept of humanity" (Rosen 1991: 10).

Since Israel is the telos of this narrative, the Yad Vashem exhibits present the difficulties faced by Jews who wished to emigrate from Europe in the

1930s as due solely to England's restrictions on Jewish immigration to Palestine, and they neglect the closing-off of Jewish immigration to Great Britain and the United States. For if Israel must be the goal of all Jews fleeing persecution, other possible countries of refuge must be forgotten. The exhibit asserts as well that *all* postwar Jewish survivors of the Nazi massacres refused to return to their former homes in Europe and tried instead to get to Eretz Israel. The state of Israel, Yad Vashem informs us, was the *only* possible answer to the holocaust and endemic anti-Semitism. All other possible places and varieties of Jewish life are excluded (see Segev 1986: 114).

Like the Acre Citadel, Yad Vashem contains Arab traces, in the form of enlarged photographic reproductions that depict the Grand Mufti, Hâjj Amîn al-Husaynî—leader of the Palestinian national movement from the late 1920s until the late 1950s—in exile in Germany during World War II. Hâjj Amîn is shown being greeted by Heinrich Himmler and inspecting Muslim volunteers in the Wehrmacht. Beside the photos hangs a copy of a letter from the Mufti to Ribbentrop, urging the German government to prevent Balkan Jews from emigrating to Palestine.[8] Yad Vashem recalls the Palestinian leader *simply* as a collaborator with Hitler; through his image the entire Palestinian people is metonymically implicated in the crimes of Nazism. The effect of such propagandistic associations, according to Israeli commentator Boaz Evron, has been to make most Israelis feel that "there is no difference between an illiterate Palestinian refugee and an SS trooper" (1981: 25). Palestinian nationalism is thereby reduced to a garden variety of the anti-Semitism that produced the holocaust and still shadows Jewish existence. Little wonder that a *New York Times* reporter could claim in 1988 that the Yad Vashem mural shows Hâjj Amîn "calling on Arabs to slaughter Jews in the Nazi cause" (Clines 1988)—an outrageous misreading that accurately renders the display's unsubtle message: the Palestinian national leader was a savage war criminal.

Other photographs at Yad Vashem show the Nazis, in the course of their retreat from Eastern Europe, attempting to erase the traces of their unconscionable crimes from the face of the earth. Yad Vashem proclaims itself an act of defiance, a countermemory to Nazi efforts to cover up the signs of their transgressions. How grimly ironic therefore that, according to Ibrahim Matar (1983), the very memorial that challenges the oppressor's attempts to hide his sins would sit on lands once owned by the Palestinian village of 'Ayn Kârim, reputed birthplace of John the Baptist. Some 3,200 Christian and Muslim Palestinians resided in this farming community in 1948. Many fled in the aftermath of the joint Irgun–Stern Gang massacre of between 245 and

254 Palestinians at nearby Dayr Yâsîn in April 1948; the remainder departed in July after shelling by Jewish forces (Morris 1987: 212; Khalidi 1992: 269–73). Today this former Palestinian village is a fashionable suburb of West Jerusalem known as Ein Karem, its "exotic" chalk and limestone buildings and its panoramic views much coveted by Israeli yuppies. An estimated 30,000 former residents of 'Ayn Kârim and their descendants presently live as refugees in Jordan (Abdel Fattah 1985).

Yad Vashem, monument to the memory of human suffering, a warning against the dangers of ignoring persecution, is itself a material act of repression, an active forgetting. Yet it too is haunted by the continuing return of the oppressed: In 1987, the Histradut's Solel Boneh construction company hired Palestinian workers to build a stone monument at Yad Vashem commemorating the vanished Jewish communities of Europe (Friedman 1987).

From These Poor Remains . . . Speak the Men

Masada shall not fall again. *Yitzhak Lamdan*[9]

The fortress of Masada perches dramatically atop a four-hundred-meter high butte, amid the rugged beauty of the "Wilderness of Judea." From Masada's heights, the entire Dead Sea is visible. Here, in A.D. 73, according to the celebrated account of Josephus, a group of 960 Jewish Zealots revolting against Rome committed mass suicide rather than submit to imperial rule. Archaeologist Yigael Yadin intensively excavated Masada's remains in 1962–63, in what was "perhaps second only to the clearance of the tomb of Tutankhamun—the most publicized excavation in the twentieth century" (Silberman 1989: 89). Hundreds of volunteers from Israel and twenty-eight other countries assisted him, testimony to the tremendous local and international enthusiasm for Israeli archaeology. Ever since, Masada has been a pivotal national historical site and a much frequented tourist attraction. The career of Yadin himself, Masada's chief publicist, is illustrative of the ideological centrality of the discipline and discourse of archaeology for Israel. Yadin interrupted his archaeology studies to serve as commanding officer for operations of the Haganah in the war of 1947–48,[10] as commanding officer for operations of the Israeli Defense Forces (IDF) from June 1948 to 1949, and as IDF chief of staff from 1949 to 1952. Between 1963 and 1977, Yadin was professor of archaeology at Hebrew University. Entering political life in 1977 as a founder of the Democratic Movement for Change, he served as deputy prime minister in the Begin government between 1977 and 1981.

Archaeology was not always so closely identified with the ideology and practice of Jewish settlement in Eretz Israel. Theodor Herzl, founder of the modern Zionist movement, had little use for the science of ancient cultures and was indifferent to Palestine itself as the site for the proposed Jewish state, advocating Argentina, Cyprus, the Sinai, and Uganda at various times as other possible targets of Jewish colonization (Eisenzweig 1981: 263). For a time, archaeology even seemed unnecessary *after* Palestine was chosen as the site for Jewish settlement, for early Zionists, like ethnocentric Western colonialists, regarded the colonial world as a natural landscape (Eisenzweig 1981: 267). Prior to actual settlement, Zionism produced an idea of a natural Palestine, a nonhistoric space in which no Other was present. After imaginatively removing the Other from the land of Palestine, this discourse filled in the dreamed-for space where the question of Jewish emancipation would be resolved with the Jewish self, who was conceived of as a "natural" inhabitant.[11] And for a long time after their discourse had cleared out the Other by naturalizing the landscape, Zionists would "purely and simply, not *see* the Arab Palestinians." They *could* perceive "natives" who, like trees and stones, formed part of the virginal, natural space—but not an Other. These "natives" did not constitute any particular social group (namely "Arabs"), for "the vision of natural space, of landscape, is a correlative of the absence of otherness" (Eisenzweig 1981: 281–83). These natives were simply an element in the pristine space of nature, a space which the colonizers had every right to make over as they saw fit.[12]

Later a further twist developed in the colonizers' thinking. In the search for a new kind of Jewish identity that was both appropriate to the land of the Bible and in opposition to the despised image of the corrupted Diaspora Jew, the "Zhid," Zionists made a qualified identification with Arab "primitivism." The Arab, particularly the Bedouin nomad, began to be regarded as a kind of "noble savage." His bold independence, adaptation to the stern environment, and rootedness in biblical territory would henceforth be imitated by pioneering Jewish youth (Glover 1986: 28–29; Shohat 1989: 100; Shapira 1992: 61, 71). Thus the early socialist-Zionist settlement guards, Ha-Shomer (1909–20), accoutred themselves in ersatz imitations of Bedouin garb (complete with *kûfîyât*), developed a special warrior argot that was a mixture of Yiddish and Arabic, and derived their idea of heroism from the Bedouin. Nevertheless Ha-Shomer was known for its aggressiveness in dealing with real Arab villagers and Bedouins (Shapira 1992: 72; Shafir 1989: 140–42; Teveth 1972: 7).[13] Later, between the teens and the thirties, some Zionist writers advanced the Romantic notion that some Arab inhabitants of Palestine, particularly the *fallâhîn* and the Bedouin, were the descendants of Jews who had converted to Christianity, and later to Islam, after the destruction of the temple. Thus these Zionists regarded Palestinian *fallâhín* and Bedouin as the Jews' long-lost cousins, and hoped that these "cousins," the embodiments of Jewish origins in the land, would welcome their return (Shohat 1989: 100–101; Teveth 1985: 31).[14]

But whether they were seen as Biblical remnants, "noble savages," "cousins," or parts of the natural backdrop, the Arab natives seemed to inhabit a "primitive" time and an "allochronic" space. As noble savages or cousins, they were viewed as "monuments" of ancient times, who could speak and be "read" for insights into the past. As de Certeau observed regarding the native or aboriginal in early-modern Western discourse, "the *living* (Savage) permits the *dead* (ancient) to 'speak,' but the Savages are not heard except as voices of the dead, echoes of mute antiquity" (1980: 42, 61). Such Zionist denials of Arab coevalness (see Fabian 1983: 31) furnished the warrant for turning the land into a modern, progressive space.

Given these conceptions about the land and its inhabitants, therefore, the early colonists of the First and Second Aliyah (1882–1914) had little need or use for archaeology or for reestablishing "roots." Future-oriented and utopian in their vision, they scarcely noticed the first large-scale Palestine excavations conducted by European and American archaeologists (Elon 1981: 283–84), who chose—and continue to choose—sites primarily on the basis of their biblical connections (Glock 1985: 465).

The Jewish settlers began to perceive the Arab as a real Other only after violent Arab opposition to Zionist colonization erupted, especially in the wake of the Young Turk Revolution of 1908 (Shafir 1989: 202–8; Mandel 1976). Only then did the project of remapping the land and disintering its remains become of paramount concern. As they struggled to wrest the land of Filastîn (Palestine) from its Arab inhabitants, the Zionists began to rename its every detail according to the criteria of a preexisting biblical map of Eretz Israel (the land of Israel). This colonial remapping frequently prefigured the actual conquest, as in other non-European parts of the globe. European geographical sciences, in fact, developed in the service of the colonizing projects of the late nineteenth century (Said 1978: 215–16). But unlike most other colonialisms, Zionism, as it evolved in the early twentieth century, did not claim the land as "empty" territory, it *re*-claimed the land as the object of a return, on the basis of a prior, originary mapping.

The ground for the Zionist operation had been prepared by biblical scholars and imperial cartographers. The effort was inaugurated by Edward Robinson, a U.S. biblical scholar who belonged to a tendency in nineteenth-century Bible studies that felt that the most effective means of countering secular scientific skepticism was to employ "scientific" procedures to authenticate the Bible. (The biblical atlas I studied as a boy resulted from such efforts.) Robinson concluded that the surest way to identify biblical place names in Palestine was to read the Bible conjointly with existing Arab nomenclature, and during a three-month stay in Palestine during 1839 used this method to identify over a hundred biblical sites (Benvenisti 1986a: 195; Broshi 1987: 18–19).[15] Others followed up on Robinson's work, notably Claude Conder, who extensively surveyed Palestine in the 1870s under the sponsorship of the London-based Palestine Exploration Fund, which was founded in 1865 with the explicit purpose of verifying the Bible (Conder 1878; Broshi 1987: 20). Increasingly, there was a convergence of interests between Western scholars seeking to reclaim Palestine for biblical purposes and imperialists desiring to control it in order to protect British communication with India. Another well-known Holy Land geographer, George Adam Smith, noted proudly that his cartographic efforts assisted the British army's conquest of Palestine from the Turks during the 1914–18 war. "I have been much encouraged," he pens, "by the generous tributes from Field Marshal Viscount Allenby and many of his officers in Palestine to the real usefulness of my volume in framing the strategy and tactics of their campaign" ([1894] 1966: 23). It was the surveys carried out by Western biblical geographers, in fact, that established the political borders of the new territorial entity, the Palestine mandate, that was created by the League of Nations after the war (Silberman 1990: 31).

This Christian-colonial mapping paved the way for the Zionist movement's own renaming-remapping project. Meron Benvenisti, whose cartographer father played a prominent part in this undertaking, points out the endeavor's inherent ironies. It was the Arab conquerors of Filastîn, having slightly modified preexisting place-names according to the logic of their own related Semitic tongue, who were largely responsible for "preserving" the ancient Jewish sites that Western scholars would later "discover." Scholars like Robinson and Benvenisti's father had to master Arabic in order to identify the "original" Jewish locales. But once those sites were located, the Arabic names were eradicated and the fact that Arabs made the retrieval possible in the first place was quickly forgotten.[16] Western archaeologists had already established that this elision was not to be regretted, since Arab civilization and the ancient Semitic cultures they identified with the Arabs were so inferior. The Bishop of Salisbury, for instance, remarked in 1903: "Nothing, I think, that has been discovered makes us feel any regret at the suppression of

Canaanite civilisation [the euphemism for native Arab Palestinians] by Israel-ite civilisation. . . . [The excavations show how] the Bible has not misrepre-sented at all the abomination of the Canaanite culture which was superseded by the Israelite culture" (cited by Said 1980: 79).[17] In a similar vein, George Adam Smith in 1894 wrote of the Arab "swarms" who had invaded Palestine ever since biblical times. Smith likewise equated the modern Bedouin Arabs with the ancient Amalekites, the original enemies of the Old Testament Jews (1966: 192, 265).[18]

In the process of the Zionists' massive denomination enterprise, in what Derrida calls "the battle of proper names" (Derrida 1978: 107), even sites with no ancient Hebrew names or associations, only Arabic ones, were Hebraized. This project, known in Zionist idiom as "the redeeming of names" (Kimmerling 1983: 208), represented for Benvenisti an attempt "to eradicate the history of Arab Palestine" (1986a: 196).[19] Yet it marked an unavowed recognition of the existence of the Other whose traces had to be radically excised.

The growing Arab opposition to Jewish settlement during the Third Aliyah, which motivated redemption by nomenclature, simultaneously gen-erated an enthusiasm for authenticating the ancient Jewish presence through the recovery of material remains. This changing attitude toward the past on the part of socialist and revolutionary Zionist settlers was dramatized in 1928, when a sixth-century synagogue was discovered at the colony of Beit Alpha in the Esdraelon plain. Beit Alpha's left-wing secularist settlers, who regarded the synagogue as a find of "national importance," brought in Yigael Yadin's father, archaeologist E. L. Sukenik, to excavate the site. Secular kib-butzniks from throughout the area volunteered enthusiastically to work on the Beit Alpha dig (Elon 1981: 284–85).[20] These newfound roots no doubt provided a source of inspiration for the settlers of Beit Alpha, whose exposed position in the eastern Esdraelon made them objects of attack by Arab insurgents both in 1929 and in 1936–39. Such violence convinced Zionists to abandon the idea that indigenous Arab "relative-remnants" were the living proof of Jewish rootedness in the soil of Eretz Israel. Better, per-haps, to turn to names, ruins and bones, and animate them instead.

This same generation of socialistic Eastern European Jews of the Third Aliyah was also responsible for making Masada a national symbol. They selected Masada as a rallying point because it was susceptible to a nationalist as opposed to a religious interpretation. Labor Zionists admired the Jewish Zealots at Masada for having defied the Jewish religious and political estab-lishment to do heroic battle with the Romans. They also considered the

Zealot a fighting Jewish image, in contradistinction to the quietist, assimila-
tionist, and pious model of the diasporic Jew (Bruner and Gorfain 1984: 66).
As a result of Labor Zionists' efforts, the mass suicide at Masada came to
replace the destruction of the Temple at Jerusalem as the key moment of
Jewish history for the Zionist movement and for the nascent state of Israel
(Benvenisti 1986a: 35; see also Shapira 1992: 310–19). Yigael Yadin's assertion
that the "belief in history" is of more significance than religious belief for
young Israelis is an example of how secular Zionism has attempted to dis-
place or recode the Jewish religion with a nationalism rooted in history.
Through archaeology, Yadin writes, Israeli youth "discover 'religious' values"
and "find their religion." Archaeology teaches young Israelis "that their forefathers were in this country 3,000 years ago. This is a value. By this they fight
and by this they live" (quoted in Elon 1981: 281). Here Yadin mobilizes the
language of religion ("beliefs" and "values") to sanctify the national cause. As
Benedict Anderson has argued, nationalist discourse generally extends and
modernizes, but does not replace, "religious imaginings." Instead nationalism
incorporates religion's concern about death, continuity, and desires for origins
(1983: 18–19). Archaeology has played a crucial role in the process of nation-
alizing and modernizing religion in Israel.

The function of Israeli archaeology, as Yadin makes clear, is to find and
reveal ancient Hebrew origins in the land and thereby establish connections
between modern Israelis and their ancestors. The chief function of Israeli
archaeological research, which concentrates almost exclusively on Jewish
objects and sites, is to reassure Israelis of their roots in the land (Elon 1981:
280). Excavations like Masada and Beit Alpha are spectacularized in order to
comfort the psyche of a nation locked in combat with an Other with claims
to a rival originary network of signs linked to territory. Israelis have asserted
their rights to possess the land by establishing that their ancestors lived there,
by excavating and monumentalizing their remains. So by the early 1950s,
archaeology had become something of a popular amateur pastime for Israelis, a "tangible means of communion between the people and the land." Perhaps the most renowned (and somewhat infamous) amateur archaeologist in
Israel was Moshe Dayan, who as chief of staff was able to mobilize military
resources in the pursuit of his hobby and amass a huge collection of antiqui-
ties (Silberman 1989: 125).

Perhaps the exigencies of the Arab-Israeli struggle—in which both Dayan
and Yadin played major roles—account for the abrupt shifts in register that
punctuate the latter's internationally best-selling account of the Masada
excavation, *Masada: Herod's Fortress and the Zealots' Last Stand*. Throughout

most of the volume, Yadin writes in the appropriate tone of the objective, sober scholar. But when it comes to describing the unearthing of ancestors, his prose suddenly takes on the ecstatic timbres of the passionate nationalist (re)discovering his "religion" in archaeology. At the moment when the excavation team uncovered three Zealot skeletons, Yadin writes, even "the veterans and most cynical of us stood frozen, gazing in awe at what had been uncovered, for as we gazed we *relived* the final and most tragic moments of the drama of Masada." The extreme desert aridity had preserved the scalp on the skeleton of a woman, whose "dark hair, beautifully plaited, looked as if it had just been freshly coiffured. Next to it the plaster was stained with what looked like blood" (1966: 54; emphasis added). Similarly, when the team found charred children's' sandals and broken cosmetic vessels in a Zealot room, the excavators "could sense the very atmosphere of their last tragic hour" (1966: 16). "From these poor remains," Yadin proclaims in the National Parks Authority brochure distributed at the site, "from these ashes, speak the men who made their last stand at Masada" (Yadin n.d.).

Yadin drenches these (accidentally) preserved residues with emotion, simultaneously evoking the holocaust (Paine 1991: 22) and inviting the reader to imagine, with the excavators, that Masada's defenders had only just perished. He thereby empties out nineteen hundred years of history, merging past and present so that excavators and readers alike "relive" that horrible moment of suicide. Modern Israel is thereby textually identified with A.D. 70 Masada. Yadin makes the heroic yet tragic experience of the Zealots equivalent to that of contemporary Jewry and allows for direct communication between the Zealots and "us," encouraging the implied Western readers to participate vicariously in that identification of Zionist and Zealot.

But the casual visitor to Masada might miss the humble remains of the Zealot hovels amid the splendid columns and mosaics of the Herodian palaces and the wild beauty of the desert, were it not for the massive ideological labor undertaken by the Israeli historical apparatuses to ensure that visitors recognize the modern state of Israel in the ruins. Tourist literature, souvenirs, guides, and state ideology all lend their collective efforts to producing that mythical equivalence. The Israeli Defense Forces conduct elaborate swearing-in ceremonies for Jewish recruits at Masada,[21] "the anvil on which the younger generation forges its awareness of history" (Yadin n.d.). Hundreds of young North American Jews and their families celebrate Bar and Bat Mitzvahs on Masada each year. Masada's excavators tried to reinforce the synonymy between Israel and Masada by dubbing the simple dwellings of the Zealots *ma'abarot*—the term for the "hut camps" erected for immigrants to Israel in the early 1950s (Livneh and Meshel n.d.). (This romanticization of the immigrant experience managed to overlook the fact that the *ma'abarot* mainly housed Mizrahi ("Eastern" Jewish)—not Ashkenazi (European Jewish)—immigrants, and that their decrepitude signified the Ashkenazi elite's systematic discrimination against Mizrahim [Shohat 1988: 18; Segev 1986: 136–38].) Yadin also strongly suggests an equivalence between the simple lifestyle of the Zealots and that of the ideologically committed kibbutznik pioneers—who were considered "the personification of highest Zionist purposes" (Elon 1981: 314–15)—when he calls attention to the "vast contrasts" between the "grand" and "luxurious" palaces of Herod and the Zealots' primitive remains. The magnificence of the palaces meant nothing, Yadin claims, to the Zealots, who "faced the brutal challenge of life or death, the stark problem of existence" (1966: 16–17). Yadin here suggests that Israel, too—like Masada, a fortress surrounded by a threatening and hostile desert—faces a life-or-death struggle. Yet there is one significant difference: modern Israel represents a significant improvement over the Zealot community, because "Masada shall not fall again."

Yadin's attempt to create a textual "reliving" of the Zealot past and a reexperiencing of their emotions represents a forgetting of the invented nature of the Masada tradition. Meron Benvenisti argues that the Zionist movement was fundamentally misguided in adopting Masada as the national symbol. Its story, he claims, is a "myth" unknown in the Jewish sources; its sole chronicler, Flavius Josephus, a Jewish official who defected to the Romans, is probably unreliable. Jewish texts are silent about Masada, Benvenisti maintains, "apparently because the mass suicide committed by its defenders is entirely alien to the spiritual characteristics that sustained the Jewish people in their land and . . . in the Diaspora" (1986a: 35).[22] Other archaeologists have also raised questions about Yadin's interpretation of the remains at Masada, claiming there is no compelling material evidence that any suicide took place. Shaye Cohen, moreover, argues that Josephus probably invented the collective suicide and employed a classical literary motif according to which the Zealots admit their mistake in rebelling against Rome. But such scholarly doubts have neither punctured the popularity nor diminished the ideological power of Masada (Silberman 1989: 95–101).

Although Benvenisti points out correctly that the elevation of the myth of Masada to the position of national symbol cancels two thousand years of Diaspora history (1986a: 35–36), he neglects how Masada equally erases the intervening thirteen hundred years of Arab settlement *in Palestine* (not to mention a Mizrahi Jewish presence in Palestine; see Alcalay 1993). By evacuating the gap between past and present, official representations of Masada render meaningless all events in Palestine between the exit of the Jews and their "return" in the late nineteenth century. Robert Paine terms this Israeli nationalist and religious conception of time "totemic" as opposed to "historical," and explains that "the past that counts dates back 2000–3000 years and that the intervening years are for the most part considered transitional, liminal, of little interest on their own without the biblical and the Zionist period to flank them" (cited by Dominguez 1989: 55). If the Masada site does not materially efface any Arab remains, it nonetheless performs an ideological erasure. For all such national sites portray Israel as a "return" to a "previous state of affairs" (Said 1980: 87) and render nugatory the existence of an Arab community in Palestine in the interim between the departure and the return.

Ella Shohat observes that Zionist ideology conceives of "historical 'strata' within a political geology. The deep stratum, in the literal and figurative sense, is associated with the Israeli-Jews, while the surface level is associated with the Arabs, as a recent 'superficial' historical element without millennial 'roots'" (1989: 64). Such "superficial" or "surface" Islamic archaeological remains are therefore usually either ignored or, according to Israeli archaeologist of Islam Miriam Rosen-Ayalon, sometimes "shoveled aside or bulldozed over" in pursuit of Jewish or more ancient remains (Hamilton 1987). Recent observers like Magen Broshi claim that Israeli archaeology has undergone a significant transformation over the last two decades and that Amos Elon's 1971 assertion—that Israeli archaeologists ignore Hellenistic, Roman, Byzantine, and Muslim sites—no longer holds true. According to Broshi, Israeli archaeology now studies all periods (1987: 27) and "bias" is being eliminated.[23] Neil Silberman claims less optimistically that "the uncritical archaeological acceptance of modern concepts of ethnicity—with regard to the ancient Israelites, Eblaites, and Arabs, among others—and the assumptions about the inevitability of ethnic conflict have yet to be challenged" (1990: 34).[24]

But if academic archaeology is undergoing some liberalization,[25] state policy has evolved very little. Ever since the Israeli National Parks Authority (NPA) assumed control of the archaeological sites in the Occupied Territories in 1967, it has neglected or left undeveloped existing Arab sites. For instance, the locale of Hisham's Palace at Jericho, built by Umayyad caliphs in the eighth century, is bereft of signs explaining its history, and the palace rarely appears in publications of the Israeli Ministry of Tourism (Aboudi 1985). Yet because of the continuing biblical orientation of "Holy Land" archaeology, ancient (pre-Arab) Jericho remains the most excavated site in Palestine/Israel after Jerusalem (Broshi 1987: 25–26).

And archaeology continues to be put to political purposes. In March 1988, Prime Minister Yitzhak Shamir took the inauguration of a tourist site at a fortress built by Herod the Great as the occasion for a speech aimed at intifada activists. "Those who say we the Israelis are invaders [in] this country . . . "he proclaimed, "[to those] killers [and] terrorists we say . . . from the heights of this mountain and from the perspective of thousands of years of history that compared to us they are like grasshoppers." And just like those insects who periodically blow in from the desert to infest settled lands, Shamir went on, the terrorists will have their heads "smashed against the boulders and walls of these fortresses" (*New York Times,* April 1, 1988; Kifner 1988a). On another occasion Shamir declared that the intifada was merely a continuation of the war that has continued ever since the time of the Hasmoneans (166 B.C.) (Cockburn 1989: 151). Two years later, in a televised speech, Shamir called Palestinians "brutal, wild, alien invaders of the land of Israel that belongs to the people of Israel, and only to them." And, he asserted, "There will be no Palestinian state here. Never" (*Seattle Times,* February 6, 1990: 2). Translation: Masada shall not fall again.[26]

Making the Desert Bloom

Few things are as evocatively symbolic of the Zionist dream and rationale
as a Jewish National Fund Forest.   *Amos Elon*

Closely connected to the Israeli passion for archaeology is the love of the *moledat* or homeland. Activities such as hiking in the land, learning the intimate details of the terrain, and using the Bible to identify sites are typical manifestations of this form of secularized worship (Benvenisti 1986a: 20). Whenever I went hiking in the craggy "Judean" wilderness together with Mâzin, one of those rare Palestinians whose enthusiasm for rambling matched that of Israeli Jews, we invariably ran into hiking parties, one of whose members sported an Uzi or M-16, engaged in *moledat* worship. Often they were groups of schoolchildren or soldiers on outings that constituted part of their formal training in *yedi'at ha'aretz* (knowledge of the land), an important subject in school and army curricula. An extensive network of institutions promotes the love of the *moledat* and *yedi'at ha'aretz:* research institutes, field schools, the Society for the Preservation of Nature in Israel (SPNI), youth movements, the Jewish National Fund, and paramilitary units (Benvenisti 1986a: 19–20). Like the enthusiasm for archaeology, this passion for Eretz

Israel represents a nationalist displacement and modernization of the Jewish religion. Indeed, "new conscripts in Israel are given a bible as a present in the preface of which the chief army rabbi tells them that this book is Israel's title deed, or registration document, for the land of Israel" (Broshi 1991: 4).

Benvenisti argues that the practices of *moledat* worship, such as sighting and identifying flora and fauna and traversing the mountains and deserts, constitute "symbolic acts of possession" (1986: 23). In Israel, the accumulation of such knowledges, like the practice of archaeology, is a massively popular and amateur activity not reserved for academicians and government functionaries. This enterprise originated in the prestate period (see Shapira 1992: 270–71) and, appropriately, was the subject of *Oded the Wanderer* (1933), the first feature-length film produced in the Yishuv (Jewish community in Palestine) (Shohat 1989: 29). Organized *moledat* activities like hiking animate citizens' sentiments that the land belongs to all Israeli Jews and are openly acknowledged as having "security" connotations. Azarya Allon has stated, "There are important sections of the country which are not inhabited by Jews and they are in danger. Hiking is thus a tool for displaying Jewish presence in those areas" (Israeli Broadcast Service, September 1, 1974, quoted by Kimmerling 1983: 208). The acts of finding and identifying natural features that are integral to such "nature walks" also encourage Israeli Jews to feel that they *care* about the land. The personal emotional attachment to Eretz Israel engendered by *moledat* worship offers further proof of national and individual proprietorship (Benvenisti 1986a: 23).

This ideology was partly responsible for the tragic events of April 6, 1988, at the West Bank village of Baytâ. The armed Israeli settlers who were leading a group of teenagers on a hike and who shot to death two Palestinian youths and (accidentally) a teenaged Jewish girl were on a provocative march through hostile and disputed territory, not an innocent stroll through the countryside. As one teenaged settler injured in the stone-throwing remarked afterward, "We had to show them that we are the owners of this country" (Vitullo 1988a: 12). (The incident motivated the army to demolish fifteen Baytâ houses, damage fifteen others accidentally, and deport six residents for throwing stones [Cantarow 1989: 85].)

Caring for the land is also expressed through ecological activism. Green activity in Israel is often motivated by an unstated judgment that those who live on the land but neglect it have no rights to it (Benvenisti 1986a: 23). Israeli popular and scholarly writing alike abounds with examples of Arab carelessness regarding the land.[27] The diminution of forests is blamed on the voracious appetites of goats raised by Arab nomads and on Arab villagers who cut down trees to manufacture charcoal, while topsoil erosion is ascribed to Arab negligence of the agricultural terraces constructed by the ancient Jews (Benvenisti 1986: 24). These judgments are consistent with the long-standing Zionist project of the "redemption of the land" that accompanied the "redeeming of names." The purpose of the Zionist venture was and continues to be the rescue of the land from both its non-Jewish occupants and its desolation—the latter also usually attributed to the Arabs (Kimmer-ling 1983: 201).

"Ecological" arguments provide the authorities with pretexts to proscribe "traditional" Palestinian economic practices said to harm the environment. In the early eighties, for instance, the authorities in the West Bank banned charcoal production in Palestinian communities near the Ya'bad Forest Reserve. The military administration informed Arab residents that their charcoal manufacture was causing air pollution and jeopardizing the health of Jews living in nearby settlements. Villagers regarded such justifications as racist and complained to me about the ban's negative impact on their economic livelihood. The authorities were also motivated, they said, by a concern to protect the forest reserves from further "Arab depredations."

Local residents' explanations for the denuding of the once vast Ya'bad Forest (where Shaykh al-Qassâm fell in battle) directly contradicted these official claims. Mu'în, an al-Najâh University student from the village of 'Araqa, explained to me that much of the forest had been cut down during World War II to feed the British army and its railroads' tremendous appetite for fuel. More trees, Mu'în said, were felled in the aftermath of the 1948 war. The influx of refugees, who at first lived in the open fields, exacerbated the drastic local economic disruptions caused by partition. Destitute villagers and refugees alike cut down large quantities of trees and produced and sold charcoal simply to survive. No doubt Mu'în's version is not the whole picture,[28] but it does suggest that the razing of forests is better explained by the Arabs' structurally subordinate, historically specific position than by their supposed "backwardness." Israeli environmental discourse is consistent in this regard with that of Western development agencies like the World Bank, which tend to blame the planet's environmental problems on the third world poor instead of on the overdeveloped world, which consumes the bulk of global resources (Ress 1991: 18). Thus Israel's own ecological record is rarely interrogated. One rarely hears about its lack of a comprehensive policy to regulate pesticide poisoning and storage, its use of 75 to 80 percent of water resources for high-production agriculture (Young 1992: 190, 192), or the consumption by Jewish settlers in the West Bank of four times more water per capita than

Palestinian residents. Official Zionist accounts obviate the need for historical or structural explanation by essentializing Palestinian Arab culture as eternally destructive of the land.

Ecological struggle is likewise waged against Palestinian citizens of Israel, especially the Bedouin of the Negev (al-Naqab). The agents of the struggle are the "armed nature lovers" of the Green Patrol, a paramilitary police unit set up in 1976 as a branch of the Nature Conservancy Agency and run in coordination with the Israel Lands Administration and the Ministry of Agriculture (Margalit 1978: 143; Maddrell 1990: 10). Under the cover of environmental concern, the Green Patrol has implemented government policies designed to drive Bedouin out of herding and agricultural pursuits, to concentrate and "sedentarize" the Bedouin—who are already restricted to a small zone in the Negev and who have lost much of their lands in previous state expropriations—in government-sponsored townships, and to create pools of cheap labor (Falah 1989; Maddrell 1990: 8–10). The patrol's efforts were abetted by media propaganda that presented the Bedouin as ecological bandits, welfare chiselers, and encroachers upon Jewish territory (Maddrell 1990: 11). The aims of the Green Patrol constituted a curious environmental-colonialist amalgam.[29] Its head, Alon Galili, asserted that the patrol's work was motivated by the fact that "stretches of land which the Israeli nation bought with blood and money are slipping through our fingers as a result of the Beduin reconquest of the land" (quoted in Abdel Fattah 1984b: 9). Avraham Yoffee, head of the Nature Conservancy Agency, meanwhile claimed that the Green Patrol's official aim was to protect state lands—"nature reserves" originally created from properties confiscated from Bedouin—and to guard farm crops "against the damage from grazing herds of sheep and goats" (quoted in Abdel Fattah 1984b: 9). The Green Patrol enforces such measures as the Black Goat Ordinance, which authorizes the state to confiscate goats pastured on lands that do not belong to their herders, and the Plant Protection (Damage by Goats) Law of 1950 (Margalit 1978: 144; Goering 1979: 16–17; Maddrell 1990: 13). In the course of their work, the gun-toting Greens have ripped down hundreds of tents, razed numerous permanent houses, and evicted their residents from the "state lands" they were occupying. They have ploughed over crops and uprooted fruit and olive trees (Maddrell 1990: 10). The patrol also seized thousands of sheep and goats for any apparent infraction, and subsequently either slaughtered them, sold them on the open market, or returned them to their owners in return for the payment of heavy fines. The confiscations were in accordance with a government plan, first proposed by Agriculture Minister Ariel Sharon in the late 1970s, to reduce the Bedouin herds by one-half

(Abdel Fattah 1984b: 9; Maddrell 1990: 13). Armed nature lovers were still chasing Bedouin off their lands in the early 1990s (Torney 1991).

A further example of Green-Zionist policies' negative impact on Arabs is the military administration's ban on gathering wild thyme or *za'tar* in the West Bank. Rural women in the Jinîn district have been collecting *za'tar* for generations, for domestic consumption as well as for sale in the cities. Sâmî Kîlânî's aunt and grandmother, whom I met on my first visit to Ya'bad, complained vigorously about the recent edict, which deprived them of a valued food source as well as a small income and which imposed a heavy fine on violators. Many Palestinians will tell you that the most savory *za'tar* comes from the Jinîn region. *Za'tar*—dried in the sun; blended with salt, sesame seeds, and sumac; and consumed principally with unleavened Arabic bread dipped in olive oil—is among the most delectable mainstays of the local diet. Parents remind their children in the morning, as they ready themselves for school, that eating *za'tar* for breakfast will make them smarter. Over the last three decades the herb has also become an almost sacred symbol in Palestinian literature, a signifier of the peasant's attachment to the land in the face of Israeli expropriations. In 1976, Tal al-Za'tar (The mountain of thyme), a Palestinian refugee camp on the outskirts of Beirut, was overrun after a nine-month siege by right-wing Lebanese forces (assisted openly by Syria and covertly by Israel). The camp was reduced to rubble, and hundreds of its inhabitants massacred. As Tal al-Za'tar became another powerful symbol of heroic resistance and suffering, another affective dimension was added to the herb's polysemy.

According to my friend Abû 'Alî, a Birzeit University professor, gathering wild *za'tar* was banned because a single Israeli settler in the West Bank had started to grow thyme as a commercial crop. The law was passed, word had it, to limit Arab competition with the settler's herbal enterprise. Given past experience, Palestinians were more inclined to credit this explanation than any ecological justification propounded by state agencies. Benvenisti asserts that "there is a genuine concern" in Israeli circles for *za'tar's* "ecological survival," but adds that the real purpose of the ban is to send this message to Palestinians: Because you despoil the land and have no feelings for it, you have no rights to it. Since Israelis do care for it, they are its rightful owners (1986a: 24). Because Israelis alone appear to be concerned about ecology, their rights to the land are confirmed; Palestinians' apparent indifference to the upkeep of the natural environment meanwhile disqualifies their claims to a homeland. It is normal for colonialism to masquerade as a mission of benevolence. What seems distinctive about Zionist colonialism is that, most often, altruism is expressed toward the land rather than toward the indigenous population living on it.

Perhaps Israel's vision of itself as the land's (proper) guardian is expressed most clearly in the publicity surrounding afforestation. Tu Bishvat (Arbor Day) is a major national holiday, the occasion for school children's outings to plant trees throughout the country. A *Jerusalem Post* editorial on the occasion of Tu Bishvat in 1985 (February 6) spelled out the observance's ideological meanings. Over one hundred years ago, the *Post* editors wrote, Mark Twain and Herman Melville toured Jerusalem and were appalled by the barrenness of the hills of Judea.[30] But not long after Twain and Melville's visits, the "Jewish renaissance" began, and "soil reclamation and afforestation became the order of the day." The formerly treeless hills of Judea "now begin to recall Biblical glory," while the hills of Galilee and the Negev desert are finally "clothed."[31] The planting of trees in Israel, the *Post* went on to proclaim, is a universal moral value, beyond reproof. Not even Israel's critics, the liberal daily (which turned right-wing in the early 1990s) asserted, can "question the value" of the reforestation of "denuded mountain slopes" and "sandy desert wastes."

Western tourist-pilgrims are encouraged to participate in this moral mission by donating money for tree planting. My family, in the course of our visit to Israel in winter 1962, made its own contribution and received a certificate in return. Although after three weeks in the West Bank we were somewhat disenchanted with the Zionist enterprise, my father nonetheless felt that planting trees in Israel was a neutral humanitarian project we could support without moral qualms. Israel's reforestation venture, like its archaeological digs, enjoys popular support on a truly *international* scale. Planting trees confirms the undeniable ethical value of Israel's (and by extension, the West's) project in the East. Afforestation is also linked, materially and symbolically, to the holocaust, for thousands of trees have been planted in memory of lost communities and individual victims (Elon 1983: 200). The Israeli forest is a central symbol of Israelis' love of the land and a signifier of their rights to it insofar as the forest materially embodies their renewal of Eretz Israel. The forest's emotional charge is redoubled by its additional function of memorializing the victims of Nazi persecution. It is therefore a veritable holy sanctuary.

What this official narrative excludes is how the Israeli state deliberately *used* reforestation to conceal the ruins of some of the 418 Arab villages that were "disappeared" after the creation of the state. Afforestation was usually employed where Arab villages sat on rocky or hilly terrain; "abandoned" villages situated on cultivable land were plowed under and the land used for farming.[32] "By the mid-1960's," writes Sabri Jiryis, "the Israeli government was carrying out the last of its projects for 'cleaning up the natural landscape of Israel' by removing the remaining traces of ruined Arab villages" (1976: 80; see also Morris 1987: 155–56; 169). Since 1967, the authorities have employed afforestation as a pretext for seizing Arab lands in the Occupied Territories. Meron Benvenisti cites a government document stating that the aim of creating parks and nature reserves is to prevent "unsuitable [Arab] development" in the Occupied Territories. "Afforestation is a method of land seizure," write Jewish National Fund planners, "that can be implemented in areas that otherwise are difficult to seize" (quoted in Benvenisti 1986a: 27–28).

The most egregious instance of such environmental hypocrisy, according to Benvenisti, is the "Peace Forest" at Canada Park, planted on the lands of three West Bank villages in the Latrûn district. Fierce battles (al-Qastal, Katamon, and Bâb al-Wâd) were fought in this region during the 1947–48 war, over control of the strategic Latrûn Heights that dominate the steep, winding road linking Jerusalem and Tel Aviv. Unable to wrest control of the heights from either Palestinian irregulars or Glubb Pasha's Arab Legion, the Zionists were forced to cut a "Burma Road" through the mountain wilderness in order to connect Jerusalem to the coastal areas.[33] After capturing the highlands of Latrûn in June 1967, the IDF (whose chief of staff was Yitzhak Rabin) immediately razed three villages strategically situated there ('Imwâs, Yâlû, and Bayt Nûbâ) and expelled their fourteen thousand inhabitants.[34] At 'Imwâs, fourteen residents who were either too old or ill to leave died when soldiers dynamited their homes over their heads (Abû Ghûsh n.d.). Still others expired on the road out. Money raised abroad, particularly from Jewish philanthropists of Montreal and Toronto, financed the JNF's development and planting of the seventy-five-hundred-acre "peace forest" (Dirlik 1991). The ruins of two of the "disappeared" villages ('Imwâs and Yâlû) are located within the boundaries of the park; those of Bayt Nûbâ are situated outside, but most of its former lands are within.

By the time I visited there I was sufficiently familiar with patterns of Palestinian village settlement to discern that Canada Park's terraces and the fig and olive trees signified previous Arab habitation. The park's markers, which speak only of a distant archaeological past, are designed precisely to prevent the average tourist from noticing such traces of pre-1967 agricultural activity. The only intact Arab structure at Canada Park was a *mâqâm* (saint's tomb) in memory of a general who served the thirteenth-century Mamluk

Sultan Baybars. A placard notes the *mâqâm*'s antiquarian interest and its age but not the religious significance it played in the lives of Palestinians who resided nearby until 1967. The *mâqâm*'s aged and rundown appearance creates the impression that any Arab presence is long since past. At the entrance to a section of the park that serves as a picnic area is a sign reading "olive grove." The trees' size indicate that they were planted well before the park's establishment, but the tourists and the Israeli visitors enjoying their cookouts beneath the olives' gentle shade would not suspect that they were signs of prior, and recent, Arab habitation. As another manifestation of the grand national project of "reforestation," the park's message precludes the possibility that people who cared enough about the land to plant orchards could have lived here prior to June 1967. Canada Park presents itself as though established on empty, abandoned, antiquarian space.

For Benvenisti, the demolition of 'Imwâs, Yâlû, and Bayt Nûbâ and the organized cover-up of that action, aided by money raised abroad in the name of peace, constitute striking evidence that the 1967 occupation ushered in a new age of corruption (1986a: 200). But Sabri Jiryis's important study, *The Arabs in Israel,* suggests that such corruption—in which the signs of the Other are erased with Western philanthropic support and the result is sacralized by reference to moral missions and the Holocaust—constituted Israel's foundations. Canada Park's placards are merely a continuation of normal Zionist afforestation policy.

I became aware that forests can camouflage the remains of Arab villages while traveling around Israel with Palestinian friends. When Palestinians sight cactus plants (*sabr*) on the Israeli landscape, they know immediately that an Arab village formerly stood on that spot. Arab farmers planted the cacti to fence off their property; the plant also produces a fruit, the cactus pear, a source of cool, honeyed refreshment during the hot summers. Palestinians claim that the Israeli authorities, despite unceasing efforts, cannot eradicate *sabr.* Even when burned to the ground, the plant always springs back to life. Cactus has thus become a folk metaphor for the indelible Arab character of the land. Since *sabr* means "patience," it equally connotes persistent Arab steadfastness on Palestinian territory. The other story about the cactus—its association with the native-born Israeli or Sabra who, like the cactus pear, is said to be "prickly on the outside, but sweet on the inside"—is the one known in the West. Ironically, this contested prickly-sweet signifier of Arab and Jewish aboriginality was imported to the region from Mexico via Spain (Lavie 1992: 1986).

One day in March 1985 I accompanied Sonia Nimr's family on a picnic outing at the Sea of Galilee. Driving from Nazareth to Tiberias, we spotted a clutch of cacti, an unruly patch of desert growth amid the bucolic order of a planted pine forest. Sonia's father, an electrical engineer in his late fifties, exclaimed, "I remember, there used to be a village here, it was called . . . Lûbyâ." Later I consulted a map and discovered that the Jewish settlement across the road from the forest was a kibbutz, founded on village lands in 1949, named Lavi—presumably a Hebraization of Lûbyâ.[35] The ruins of the village are buried under two JNF forests, one planted in the name of the republic of South Africa (Khalidi 1992: 527). Former rebels in the Galilee recalled Lûbyâ as a major smuggling depot where they used to purchase rifles and ammunition for use in the revolt.

Other *mujâhidîn* from the Acre district recounted other afforestation projects that covered over their natal villages. Shaykh Rabbâh al-'Awad reminisced about his ancestral home al-Ghâbisîya, which he was forced to leave for al-Mazra'a village in 1950.[36] Today the lands of al-Ghâbisîya are the site of a Jewish National Fund forest and Netiv Ha-Shayyara, settled by Iraqi Jews (Khalidi 1992: 15). 'Alî Baytam quit his village of Kuwaykât (population 1,000) in 1948, after it fell to Zionist forces on July 10, and took up residence in nearby Abû Snân as an "internal refugee." The village was demolished, pine and eucalyptus were planted on its lands, and a kibbutz called Ha-Bonim, later renamed Beit Ha-Emek, was founded there in January 1949 and settled by immigrants from England, Hungary, and the Netherlands (Khalidi 1992: 22).

Green Patrol Strikes Again

On January 11, 1986, the Green Patrol uprooted two thousand olive trees at Qattana, a Palestinian village northwest of Jerusalem. The trees were planted on land claimed by Israel, but villagers reportedly possessed titles showing that the land was theirs, as well as proof that the unearthed trees were between twenty and fifty years old. Two weeks later, in commemoration of Tu Bishvat 1986 (on January 25), a group of one hundred Palestinians, Israelis, and expatriates planted five hundred olive seedlings on the land where the olive trees were unearthed. At first Israeli soldiers, police, and Green Patrol members harassed the volunteers, then left them alone. The next day, Green Patrol workers pulled up all the newly planted seedlings. Sixteen of the deracinated olive trees were subsequently located on the newly named Martin Luther King, Jr., Street in West Jerusalem. A protest was organized; finally the peasants of Qattana agreed to "donate" their olive trees in honor of the African American civil rights leader (Hentoff: 1986a, 1986b.)

In June 1988, the *New York Times* reported that an ad hoc group of Israeli citizens planned to visit Baytâ in order to replant 150 olive trees the army uprooted in retaliation for the shooting of a young Israeli Jewish girl (Brinkley 1988). (Typically, the *Times*'s report failed to mention that the girl was shot by an armed Jewish settler guard.)

'Ayn Hawd Dada

A few "abandoned" Arab villages in Israel, seven in all, managed to escape being reduced to rubble, planted with forests, or ploughed under (Khalidi 1992: xix). 'Ayn Kârim, whose exotic structures were incorporated as a suburb of West Jerusalem, was one. Another village eluding dismantlement was 'Ayn Hawd, whose rustic stone houses on the pine-forested slopes of Mount Carmel were renovated in 1954 and turned into a picturesque artists' colony known as Ein Hod. The "artists' village" (or Kfar Omanim, as it is sometimes referred to in Hebrew) was founded by the Romanian Marcel Janco, who is best known for his participation in the 1916 Dadaist Cabaret Voltaire, along with Hugo Ball, Emmy Hennings, Hans Arp, Tristan Tzara, and Richard Huelsenbeck. Janco's paintings are exhibited at the Janco Dada Museum in Ein Hod. In March 1984, the month before his death, Janco was involved in a recreation of Cabaret Voltaire; performances were given at Ein Hod and Jerusalem. At the time, he expressed his hope that "through Dada we can use the museum for cultural ties with the Arabs. . . . Artists can communicate better than politicians" (Pomerantz 1984: 7).

Although Dada's memory is enshrined at Ein Hod, one finds no signposts indicating that the restaurant-bar called the Bonanza was once a mosque or that the charming, timeworn buildings that house more than two hundred art galleries, studios, and craft workshops were formerly the homes of Árab tillers (al-Ghazali 1986; Kanâ'ana and al-Ka'abî 1987). But, in a kind of colonial montage in which Dada paradoxically figures, only three kilometers from the artists' colony a family of eleven from the expelled population of the old village managed set up a "new" settlement called 'Ayn Hawd. From 1949 to 1952 this group repeatedly petitioned the government for permission to return, but were turned down since they were not in their homes on the day the state of Israel came into being and thus lost all rights to their properties (Eber and O'Sullivan 1992: 272). By the late eighties the exiled community had built houses, a school, and a mosque and had achieved a population of about 150 souls. (The bulk of the refugees from 'Ayn Hawd settled in refugee camps in Jinîn and in Irbid, Jordan [Kana'âna and al-Ka'abî 1987: 58].) The "new" settlement is still struggling for official recognition, since all the land of the old village was taken over by the JNF, and residents of the new hamlet are technically squatters. The second 'Ayn Hawd, along with thirty-nine other Palestinian-Israeli communities, is considered illegal, omitted from maps, is denied all municipal services (including water, electricity, and roads), and is earmarked for eventual destruction (McKay 1989, Lavie 1992). I do not know whether Marcel Janco ever used his Dada museum to establish "cultural ties" with the Arabs of the new, illegal 'Ayn Hawd.

The Arab section of the Galilee town of Safad has also been turned into a "quaint" artists' colony, and one of its mosques functions as the General Exhibition Hall for local artists. The elite section of Old Jaffa, for its part, was reconstructed as a series of "art galleries, discos, expensive restaurants, [and] fancy shops" overlooking the Mediterranean. "No tourist or Israeli my age," Palestinian human rights lawyer Raja Shehadeh observed in 1982, "could ever guess that thirty-five years ago this was the vibrant, flourishing Arab [commercial] centre of Palestine" (1982: 21).

Club Med-ieval Atmosphere

Likewise no tourist or young Israeli would imagine that Achziv, a popular tourist and recreation spot on the shores of the Mediterranean, just six kilometers south of Lebanon, was formerly an Arab village called al-Zîb.

I consulted the Harvard Student Agency guidebook before visiting Achziv with Sonia in March 1985. My book promised that one of Achziv's chief attractions is a National Park with "beautiful lawns, a sheltered beach (complete with showers and changing rooms), and eighth-century remains of a Phoenician port town" (Harvard Student Agency 1984: 163–64). In September 1983, twenty-thousand people had attended a music concert on the grounds of Achziv national park; the concert was organized by the Israeli leftist group Yesh Gvul. The event raised eighty-three thousand dollars for the families of Yesh Gvul members jailed for refusing to serve in Lebanon (*al-Fajr,* October 14, 1983: 4).

It is a stormy day, and the Mediterranean seems angry. We pause at the entrance to Achziv National Park to read the placard, which rehearses the significant moments of Achziv's history: its name is mentioned in the Bible; the Israelites conquered it from the Phoenicians; a Jewish community flourished there up to the Talmudic period (third to seventh centuries A.D.); it contains a Crusader castle.[37] Then, we are told, decay set in. "In later centuries," the official chronology continues, Achziv "declined into a coastal village. Today the medieval atmosphere still clings to its quaint houses and narrow alleyways." Archaeological excavations have been carried out, the placard concludes, and the National Parks Authority has restored the site, developed the beach, and planted a national park.

Inside, few "quaint houses" are still standing. Grass covers most of the park's grounds. A sign in front of a cemented-up structure, clearly a mosque, reads "holy site." Adjacent to it are the remains of the Crusader castle. The beach, devoid of sunbathers on this blustery day, is strewn with huge, round, white grinding stones, apparently of Phoenician origin. Next to a simple restaurant that appears to have been a large Arab house are some half-ruined Arab buildings and piles of rubble.

My guidebook labels these "ruins" Phoenician (circa 1250 B.C.). The notice at Achziv's entrance calls the village "medieval" without naming its inhabitants. The deity worshipped at the "holy site" is likewise anonymous. Such oversights are not the innocent results of ignorance, but symptomatic of an official historical discourse that must disavow the relative contemporaneity of the Arab presence here. The material evidence of crumbling houses and mounds of debris helps produce a "medieval effect." The representation of the village as medieval seems merely to convey an "atmosphere" that already "clings" to the houses and alleyways. The official representations deny the very act of representing, disavow the fact that they *make* the houses of Achziv say "medieval" in much the same way as Yadin makes Zealot bones utter "Israel." The referent seems to speak for itself, and it functions as a sign that is not supposed to look like a sign (Barthes 1970: 149; 1977: 116). The placards describing Achziv's past as well the material juxtaposition of Phoenician and Crusader ruins serve to establish the "antique" character of the holy site and quaint houses. By failing to distinguish between the jumbled remains of "medieval" structures (dating perhaps from the twentieth century A.D.) and Phoenician remains (thirteenth century B.C.), the touristic discourses manage to produce a site and an era that is undifferentiatedly antediluvian. Arabs and Islam, names that might hint at contemporaneity, have no place in this public staging of a historical narrative.

A Club Méditerranée, closed for the off-season, abuts the southern boundary of the National Park. Peering over the fence, we spot some cactus plants and a couple of decayed Arab buildings that serve as changing rooms for sun worshippers and note that the remains of Arab al-Zîb lend a picturesque touch to the Club Med as well. I recall the Paris graffiti from May 1968: Club Med—A Cheap Holiday in Other People's Misery (Marcus 1989: 21).

Across the Nahariya-Rosh Ha-Nikra/Ras al-Naqura road is kibbutz Gesher Ha-Ziv, founded in January 1949 (at first named Beyt Ha-'Arava) on the lands of al-Zîb and settled by American, British, and South African Jews (Morris 1987: 187; Khalidi 1992: 37).

Adjoining the National Park on the north is a bohemian mecca known as "Achzivland." Its bearded, long-haired, middle-aged proprietor, Eli Avivi, ambles out to greet us. Avivi runs a youth hostel at "Achzivland" that doubles as a museum, on grounds leased from the government. Few guests are at the hostel now, but Eli invites us to return in summer, assuring us that it's full of young people who stay up half the night, playing guitars, drinking wine. (He does not seem to suspect that Sonia is a Palestinian from the West Bank and thus by law is not allowed to stay overnight inside Israel.) It's much cheaper, Eli adds, than Club Med.

The lintel over the entrance to the building reads "Eli's Museum." According to my guidebook it is an Arab mansion cluttered with artifacts "mostly from the Phoenician period" (Harvard Student Agencies 1984: 164). It turns out to be crammed with everyday implements of Arab village and manor life: farm tools, household utensils, tombstones, a Singer sewing machine, games, pottery, and so on. Ancient Phoenician, Roman, and Cru-sader artifacts are interspersed indiscriminately with the Arab relics; no item is labeled, no effort made to distinguish between historical eras. Wall paint-ings by amateur curators reinforce the impression that all the remains come from a homogeneous premodern era. A scene of a Phoenician ship sailing next to a Venetian boat is painted on the wall of a room where tombstones carved in Arabic script lie hard by Roman jug vessels. Passing through the kitchen of the museum-cum-hostel, we notice the remains of breakfast: gra-nola, a pot of honey, slices of home-baked, whole-grained bread. A pot of hearty vegetarian lentil soup bubbles on the stove. The next room holds a wardrobe crammed with what we recognize as Arab dresses suitable for the Palestinian aristocracy. A long robe of emerald-green velvet trimmed with gold embroidery catches my eye. A painting is drawn on the wall beside the cabinet, its style reminiscent of the ancient tomb drawings at Luxor: a woman garbed in the flowing, diaphanous dress of Pharaonic Egypt.

This juxtaposition assimilates the garments of the twentieth-century Arab noblewomen to the patrician attire of ancient Egypt. The years 1500 B.C. in Pharaonic Egypt and A.D. 1947 in Arab Palestine appear as moments in a single, undifferentiated ancient epoch. By producing an indistinguishably premodern essence, these representations magically remove Arab artifacts (never named as such) from modern times and place them in the time-space of the ancient. The haphazardness of display is the result neither of amateur-ishness nor of a deliberate strategy of montage that aims to rescue historical objects by "blasting" them out of the continuum of developmental histories (Buck-Morss 1989: 218–19). Nor is it a case of postmodernist pastiche, of "random cannibalization" of the various styles of the past (Jameson 1984: 65). Rather it is the effect of a "pseudo-archaizing" discourse (Koptiuch 1989) that achieves its coherence by simultaneously denying the Arab in Palestine *co*-presence and *recent* presence.

Like other Palestinian visitors to "Achzivland," Sonia is able to read this narrative against the grain. She urges me to imagine how the lives of those who once wore the embroidered dresses turned out. Perhaps, she ventures, they're still living in exile, in war-scorched Beirut. The mansion's former owner-occupant, Sonia tells me, was named Muhammad 'Ataya, a landowner who was a friend of her grandfather.[38]

But to the vast majority of tourists, the various exhibits and sites at Achziv collude to tell a story with no Arab presence on this site prior to 1948. As part of the discourse of official and unofficial agencies of Israeli public meaning, the displays and markers cannot identify the previous inhabitants by name, explain why they departed, or inform us where they might have gone. Placards and guidebooks either scrupulously avoid reference to Arabs and Muslims or banish the latter to ancient times. The salient point in the Achziv narrative is that Jews, who once had a flourishing community in this place (although there appear to be no identifiable archaeological traces of that presence), have returned to reclaim it. Muhammad 'Ataya's mansion becomes "Eli's Museum," the spacious grounds of the seaside mansion are renamed "Achzivland," and the village of al-Zîb—a name that preserved the traces of the Hebrew/Canaanite designation—returns to its "origin," Achziv. Al-Zîb's history is scripted as the "decline" of an unnamed, pitiful "coastal village." The mosque becomes a picturesque "holy site" once dear to adherents of some vague Eastern religion. The former fishing village serves up an archaic ambiance for Western tourists enjoying the relaxed pleasures of the eastern Mediterranean.

According to Israeli historian Benny Morris, the Haganah had a "long account" with al-Zîb. "The villagers under mortar barrage and fearful of Jewish retribution for their past anti-Yishuv activities, fled during the battle" of May 14, 1948 (1987: 124). Refugees from al-Zîb told Palestinian historian Nafez Nazzal that the attacking Haganah soldiers wore red-and-white *kûfîyât* and therefore tricked the village's defenders into thinking that their Arab brothers (from the Liberation Army) had come to rescue them. Al-Zîb's small force was overwhelmed, and the village was rapidly emptied of its nineteen hundred souls. Only the dead, wounded, and a handful of elderly people re-mained behind (Nazzal 1978: 56).

Haganah commander Moshe Carmel ordered most of the villages he captured in western Galilee razed, because he "wanted to punish the vil-lagers, especially of Az Zib . . . for past acts against the Yishuv, and to make sure the villagers could and would never return" (Morris 1987: 125). Yosef Weitz, chairman of the "Transfer Committee"—the semiofficial body charged with preventing Arab refugees from returning, advising the govern-ment on further expulsions, and organizing and overseeing the destruction of Arab villages (Morris 1987: 135–36)—visited al-Zîb in December 1948. Weitz's official position in 1947–48 was director of the JNF Lands Depart-ment; since the 1930s, he had been responsible for land acquisitions from the Arabs. Weitz observed that the village of al-Zîb had been "completely lev-elled" and he wondered "if it was good that it was destroyed and would it not have been a greater revenge had we now settled Jews in the village houses" (quoted in Morris 1987: 168). (The "revenge" concerned Weitz's son Yehiam, a Palmach officer killed by al-Zîb villagers in the course of a Palmach raid on the al-Zîb bridge [Morris 1987: 336].) Mapam critics referred to the work of Yosef Weitz's Transfer Committees as "landscape improvement" (Morris 1990: 14).

The bulk of the refugees from al-Zîb (but not the landlords) later settled at the 'Ayn al-Hilwa refugee camp near Sidon, Lebanon. They named their quarter of the camp, located near the railroad tracks, al-Zîb.[39]

No Room in the Narrative

As we left Achziv National Park, Sonia and I bumped into a middle-aged U.S. couple who had just visited Gesher Ha-Ziv kibbutz. We exchanged the pleasantries characteristic of chance encounters of U.S. tourists: "What state are you from? Did you enjoy your stay in Israel?" Then to my discomfort, Sonia launched into some agitprop. "You should go inside the park and look at the buildings," she told the couple. "What they've done to us Palestinians is awful, they've destroyed our village. My grandfather used to live here," she added, bending the facts a bit to establish her point. "They destroyed his house and expelled the rest of our family to Lebanon."

As Sonia spoke, I watched the couple's eyes carefully for any hint that her poignant tale might have some effect. There was not a spark of recognition: it was as if she had not uttered a word. The "facts" failed to sink in, the story carried no weight, because "facts only signify, only have human meaning, within explanatory frames" (Popular Memory Group 1982: 225). When she finished, the couple simply resumed the exchange of amiable, banal pleasantries. For they had already absorbed the message tourists to Israel routinely ingest, a story that confirmed, on the ground, what they already knew before coming. Perhaps they had already visited Acre Citadel, Yad Vashem, Masada, Canada Park, and the other historical sites that stage the Israeli national past, and learned all too well a story that could not contain any counterfacts. Palestinians and their tale could find no room in the narrative they knew—except, perhaps, as "terrorists."[40]

Countermapping

Many times, in Israel and abroad, I have seen maps from 1948, where hundreds of villages and towns which have disappeared are noted on maps distributed by Palestinian institutions in the diaspora. And these maps are more dangerous than any bomb.
                                                              Uri Avneri

The Palestinian refuses to satisfy the Zionist dream and dematerialise.
                                                              Haim Bresheeth

The ghostly presence of Palestinians still haunts the sites of the state's narrative. In 1972 a young Israeli columnist, Y. Geffen, wrote about a dream in which an old Arab came to his house: "He removes my grandfather's picture [a prominent figure in the Second Aliyah], and underneath it reveals a picture of his grandfather. . . . For a long time I have been feeling that this house is not mine. And lately I have had another feeling, which is very characteristic of the average Israeli adolescent: I feel that someone lived in this house before we came."[41] Refugees from Marcel Janco's "artist's village" of Ein Hod told Birzeit University researchers a similar story. The Jews who settled there, they said, had a difficult time staying in the Arab houses, for every night they would be awakened from their sleep by the clatter of rocks at their doors. They would get up and look, but no one would be at the door. This went on for a long time. Finally the new inhabitants questioned a former Arab resident who had settled in the nearby village of Dâliya after his expulsion:

> They asked, what's this place, who were its residents? How did they used to live here, what used to be here? He told them, this place was a poor village of good people (*awâdim darâwîsh*), they lived together in peace. The Jews told him, every night we see big stones thrown on our doors, we get up and no one is there. He told them, maybe your town is haunted by ghosts. Maybe they are venerable saints (*awlîyâ'*) who don't want you living here (Kanâ'ana and al-Ka'abî 1987: 33).

Despite the constraints imposed by a colonizing movement that has expelled their compatriots, drastically limited their access to land, and severely constrained their efforts to build national institutions, Palestinians living under Israeli rule assert their own history and presence in the land of Palestine: against Zionist mapping, a shadow cartography.

Like Jews in the Diaspora dreaming of next year in Jerusalem, Palestinian refugees yearn for their own "return" to the land of Palestine. After the June 1967 war, it became possible for 1948 refugees who lived in the newly occupied territories (and who constituted 44 percent of the West Bank population, 70 percent of the Gaza Strip) to return for a look at the sites of their former homes. Other refugees who had managed to acquire U.S. or other non-Arab citizenships also took advantage of the opportunity. Although Westerners commonly go back for nostalgic looks at homes we lived in twenty or thirty years ago, since we usually left them willingly we do not often ring the doorbell and assert our right to enter. But Palestinians appear to knock at the door routinely.

Many stories circulate about such return visits; they also turn up in fiction (such as Ghassan Kanafani's *Return to Haifa*) and documentary films. My friend George, a U.S. citizen, made such a visit to the house in West Jerusalem where his Palestinian father, now a California psychiatrist, was raised. His father never had the heart to make the trip back himself. After locating the house with the aid of old photographs and directions from relatives, George one day knocked on the door. An elderly Jewish couple answered. George asked to see the house, saying it belonged to his grandfather. They let him in, but told him, rather defensively, that they were given the house by the government, which told them it had been unoccupied for the few years prior to 1948. George, who possessed photos proving that his family had lived there until 1948, kept politely quiet.

In *The Third Way*, Ramallah lawyer Raja Shehadeh chronicles his own "return" to Jaffa in the late 1970s. "I had intended a grand tour," he writes, "beginning with my parents' home [in Jaffa] which they fled in 1948, of the landmarks in my favourite childhood stories." But his aim was frustrated by the "cute reconstructions" of Old Jaffa which erased any trace of its formerly vibrant Arab character and left him feeling deeply humiliated (1982: 21). He returned to the West Bank, relieved to get back to what he now felt was his true home. Shehadeh turns the realization that the transformation of Jaffa is a sign of Israel's permanence into a criticism of his own nostalgia for what will never return. He locates his real home, and the site of struggle, in the West Bank, under military occupation.

Others undertake the "return" to perpetuate the memory of the old map of Filastîn in the minds of their children. One day in 1985 my friend Samîr's mother whisked him off from work because it was time, she had decided, to refresh his memory of the old Arab sites in West Jerusalem associated with his family history. Samîr and his mother spent the afternoon visiting various locations that increasingly only the older generation can still identify as former Palestinian locales. It was characteristic of Umm Samîr that she made the tour without pathos or an outpouring of emotion, without bewailing the passing of "the good old days." She simply did what had to be done.

More eventful was the experience of the refugee family from the Gaza Strip depicted in the 1985 documentary, *Gaza Ghetto: Portrait of a Palestinian Family*.[42] They went for a look at their former village inside Israel, now the site of a Jewish settlement. The grandfather and great-grandfather point out Muhammad Ayyub's orchard and Uncle Khalil's sycamore to the children. A Jewish resident emerges and orders them to leave, claiming it is forbidden to be there without a permit. The mother objects. "We work in Jaffa and Tel Aviv and that's not forbidden." "Here it's forbidden," the Jew replies. While chasing the refugee family off, he asserts forcibly that the site is *his* home.

Institutional support for the reclamation effort has been provided by Birzeit University Research Center, which is bringing out a series of booklets on Palestinian villages and towns destroyed after 1948. Thirteen volumes had appeared by 1992 (see Kanâ'ana and al-Ka'abî 1987), and six more were scheduled for 1993. Many other studies of individual communities, often amateur efforts, have been produced by refugees (see Doumani 1992: 17). Recently the Institute for Palestine Studies brought out a massive study of all the 418 destroyed Palestinian villages inside Israel, called *All That Remains* (Khalidi 1992).

Acre Prison, where we started this tour, is also not forgotten, even though it is now a museum for the victors. The prison is associated in particular with the names of three Palestinians hung there, Muhammad Jumjum, Fu'âd Hijâzî, and 'Ata al-Zayr. The mnemonic device that keeps the names alive is a well-known song, "Sijn 'Akkâ," whose first verse goes:

Wa min sijn 'Akkâ tala't janâzî
Muhammad Jumjum wa Fu'âd Hijâzî
Wa jâzî 'alayhum ya sha'abî jâzî
Mandûb al-sâmî wa rub'ahu 'amûma

[A funeral procession went out from Acre prison
For Muhammad Jumjum and Fu'ad Hijâzî
He punished them, O people
The High Commissioner and his people punished them]

The tune is widely available on (probably illegal) cassettes recorded by various West Bank music groups.[43] The versions I heard are stirring dirges that emphasize the three martyrs' exemplary bravery and deep love of Palestine. But curiously, many Palestinians I met, young and old, were quite vague on the historical specifics of the martyrs' deaths. Several people thought that al-Zayr, Jumjum, and Hijâzî were involved in the 1936–39 revolt. An informant told Susan Clark, in the course of her research on the song, that Jumjum and company were executed for their role in riots in 1921 or 1922 (Clark 1992: 22). No one could tell me who had authored the song, whose lyrics are equally hazy on historical detail.

The song is an example of how the anticolonial struggle can often produce mythical and unselfcritical nationalist images and narratives, countermapping with its own elisions. I eventually discovered that the song's author was Nûh Ibrâhîm, a popular poet and a fighter in the 1936–39 revolt ('Awda 1988: 87–88). In fact, the three national martyrs (al-Zayr, Jumjum, and Hijâzî) were convicted of murder for their part in the 1929 massacres of 133 Orthodox Jews at Hebron and Safad, who had little connection to the Zionist enterprise. The lyrics, however, make no mention of the Jews, naming only the British as the enemy (Clark 1992: 21). The general vagueness about the men's demise and the tendency to assimilate them to other events indicated a general nervousness concerning anti-Semitism. The only critical statement I heard was from Imîl Habîbî, who in 1984–85 was the editor of the Israeli Communist daily *al-Ittihâd*. Habîbî argued that the three men should not be venerated as national heroes since they had participated in massacres of Jews.

Intifada: The Fire Next Time

During the torrid summer of 1988, six months after the start of the intifada, Israeli forests again became a hot issue that was covered extensively by the U.S. media. Fires broke out in woodlands throughout the country, allegedly the work of Palestinian arsonists.[44] Palestinian-Israeli novelist Anton Shammas observed that these blazes endowed Israeli novelist A. B. Yehoshua's celebrated short story "Facing the Forest" with new meanings. The story, known by virtually all Israelis, concerns an Israeli university student who takes a job as a watchman in a Jewish National Fund forest, where he is assisted by a mute Arab caretaker. At the end of the story, the Arab torches the woods, which burn to the ground and expose the ruins of a destroyed Arab village (Yehoshuah 1970; Marzorati 1988: 101). "The name Emmwas ['Imwâs] this summer," Shammas wrote, "began more and more to be heard." Israeli Jews "wondered if one day [Canada] park, and similar forests, would be set on fire" (Shammas 1988: 47). What if intifada fires exposed the ruins of 'Imwâs, Yâlû, and Bayt Nûbâ for all to see?[45]

But the U.S. and Israeli media largely ignored the 1991 Annual Report of the Palestine Human Rights Information Center, which estimated that between the beginning of the intifada in December 1987 and October 1991, Israel's occupation forces uprooted some 120,000 trees (including about 84,000 olive trees) in the Occupied Territories, mainly in acts of collective punishment. Many of the mature trees were subsequently replanted in Jewish settlements (Abu Aker 1990; Goldring 1991).[46] Settler vigilantes were also responsible for ripping out additional trees, damaging olive groves by spraying pesticides, burning down forests, and destroying crops in Palestinian areas (see *al-Fajr,* July 24, 1988, 14; Young 1992: 191).

Redemption by nomenclature continued, too. In September 1990, government-run television stations and radio networks banned the use of Arabic names for Palestinian towns and villages in the Occupied Territories and ordered the application of biblical names instead. According to Shlomo Kor, deputy authority of the Israel Broadcasting Service, the decision reflected the fact that the Jews had returned to "the land of Israel and not to Palestine" (*New York Times,* September 4, 1990). This marked another stage in the nomenclature of the occupation. In the first stage, the Jordanian term West Bank was maintained so as to identify the newly occupied areas with Jordan. The designation "administered territories" was then adopted, one that negated the land's Palestinian identity and kept its legal status ambiguous. The term "territories" was employed to deny the region its Palestinian, Jordanian, or indeed any identity. After the 1973 war and the upsurge of Jewish settlement, the annexationist nomenclature "liberated territories" and "Judea and Samaria" came into currency (Athamneh 1990). And in October 1990, the military authorities in Nablus informed printers in the city that it was "forbidden to print any text containing the word 'Palestine,' regardless of whether the text [was] political, social, educational or otherwise." Exemptions would require the military's approval (*al-Fajr,* October 1, 1990, 13).

The intifada also witnessed the arrival of the new Moledat Party, which won two seats to the Knesset in the November 1988 elections on a single-issue platform advocating forced "transfer" of Palestinians from the Occupied Territories and on the campaign slogan, "Keep Israel clean of Arabs." Moledat's leader Rehavam Ze'evi, nicknamed "Gandhi" because he was thin and ascetic as a young man, served as then prime minister Yitzhak Rabin's chief adviser on terrorism in the early seventies. Gandhi, who routinely refers to Palestinian Arabs as the "Ishmaelites," joined the Likud governing coalition in February 1991 (see Brown 1989). Polls taken in 1988 indicated that between 41 and 49 percent of Israeli Jews supported the "transfer" of Palestinians from the Occupied Territories as the preferred solution to the Israel-Palestine problem (Cockburn 1988; Katz 1988; Hentoff 1988).

Let us leave the final words to the suave Benjamin Netanyahu, currently the leader of Likud. Netanyahu is well known in the United States as Israel's former ambassador to the United Nations, a self-styled expert on terrorism, and a much-favored guest on the McNeil-Lehrer News Hour. Speaking to students at Bar-Ilan University at a time when he was deputy foreign minister, Netanyahu declared that "Israel should have taken advantage of the suppression of the [Tiananmen] demonstrations in China [in summer 1989], while the world's attention was focused on these events, and should have carried out mass deportations of Arabs from the territories. Unfortunately, this plan I proposed did not gain support, yet I still suggest to put it into action" (reported in *Yediot Aharanot,* November 24, 1989; quoted by Cockburn 1990: 43).

3 / Popular Nationalism

"I have done that," says my memory. "I cannot have done that," says my pride, and remains inexorable. Eventually—memory yields.

Friedrich Nietzsche

Strange Composites

Although they are ghostly presences at Israeli historical sites, the 2.2 million Palestinians who live under Israeli rule refuse to vanish. One of the ways they actively assert their presence, I have suggested, is by remembering a national past. In this chapter I begin to take an inventory of the "common sense" (Gramsci 1985: 189; 1971: 326 n. 5, 324) of elderly Palestinians concerning the 1936–39 revolt. Following Ranajit Guha's (1989) suggestions, I divide common sense into those elements that people use to make the compromises necessary to live under a system of domination and those elements by which they attempt to oppose or resist that ruling order. In political terms, therefore, I understand common sense as a contradictory web of submission and resistance. The presence and relative weight of each element within common sense varies according to the particular historical circumstances of dominance and subordination.

In the first instance, Palestinian commonsense memories must be viewed in relation to Israeli dominant discourses and practices, which attempt to erase, discredit, and marginalize the Palestinian past. Following Guha, we can say that Israeli dominance over Palestinians takes a specific form such that coercion outweighs persuasion. The Israeli state is "hegemonic" in relation

76

to its Jewish citizens but not in relation to its Arab subjects. It makes no effort to universalize itself as representative of a "general interest" that includes Palestinians, nor does it attempt to fulfill an ethical and educative function in relation to them (see Hall 1979: 338; Gramsci 1971: 258). In essence, then, the Israeli state is a colonizing force vis-à-vis its Arab subjects. Its efforts to elaborate ideologies designed to gain their active consent are minimal; its discourses and practices are instead designed variously to fragment, render invisible, and eradicate the Arab presence. It is not surprising, therefore, that Palestinian subordination is broadly characterized by *resistance* to Israeli institutions and discourses rather than by collaboration with them (see Guha 1989: 229–32).

In general, commonsense memory that opposes the Zionist narrative is framed within the broadly hegemonic discourse of Palestinian nationalism. In this chapter I examine those popular accounts of *al-thawra* that conform rather closely to the conventional nationalist versions, memories that simultaneously "resist" official Israeli discourses and "consent" to official Palestinian histories. Contemporary struggles against military occupation and colonization have helped foster a substantial zone of agreement between popular and official nationalist views of the past.

It should be stressed, however, that subaltern interviewees did not simply mimic the given historical narratives. Instead, in accordance with their "original thought" (Gramsci 1971: 419–20), they endowed conventional nationalism with particular inflections and emphases that sometimes verged on the oppositional. If popular accounts often followed mainstream nationalism's desire to present a homogeneous picture of the past, their interests and investments were often rather different from those of official nationalism. The terrain of the common sense of the past manifested a considerable state of play and was a zone where one found reappropriations and reaccentuations of official discourse and "strange composites" (Gramsci 1985: 189) of the dominant and the subaltern.

Vague Images and Condensed Motives

When we queried interviewees about why they decided to take up arms in revolt, former *thuwwâr* usually appealed to a very generalized notion of the nation or homeland (*watan*—literally, "home"). Abû Fâris, a band commander from Majd al-Krûm ('Akkâ district), explained why villagers wanted to join his guerrilla band in this way: "All the people were revolutionary. They said, 'Nation, nation, nation [*watan*]!' All the people wanted to go with the nation. Without comprehending. Did *I* understand? Did *I* understand what a revolt was? I understood the nation and that the Jews wanted it. The English wanted to take it and give it to the Jews. *That's* the revolt." Although Abû Fâris meant to be critical of his men's hazy motives for joining the struggle, the explanation was not atypical. Most other combatants I met gave similarly vague reasons for signing up. "I joined the revolt," said Abû Rajâ of Sha'b, "because there was oppression, killing and insult." Other *mujâhidîn*'s explanations resembled Abû Fâris's: we took up the gun, they declared, simply because the colonialists were allowing Jews to pour into Palestine and were helping them to take away our homeland.

When asked to be more specific about why it had been necessary to resort to armed violence, many recounted the famous incident of the *barâmîl* (barrels). In October 1935, they recalled, Arab dockers at Jaffa port were unloading a shipment of cement from a ship. One barrel accidentally broke open, spilling out guns and ammunition. Further investigation revealed a substantial cache of smuggled weaponry secreted inside the cement barrels. British authorities determined that the cement was consigned to a Jewish merchant, but did not discover the arms' ultimate destination and made no arrests. Arabs, assuming that the weapons were being smuggled in for use by the Jewish underground, were alarmed at the threat and incensed at the British failure to take any action.[1] This event was remembered as one of the main factors triggering Shaykh 'Izz al-Dîn al-Qassâm's decision to take to the hills in November. Nearly fifty years later, the *barâmîl* anecdote was recounted as proof positive that the British were secretly helping arm the Zionists. Old *thuwwâr* told the tale to demonstrate that it was absolutely critical for Palestinians to take up arms at that moment to defend against the Zionist threat.

Local Idioms

Interviewees fleshed out their hazy notions about the endangered nation by employing local discourses. They made nationalism comprehensible, concrete, and usable through local idioms, in particular through the use of certain key cultural concepts like honor (*al-'ard*), land (*al-ard*), woman (*al-mar'a*), the family, the village, and the *hamûla*. Old peasants saw their livelihood as clearly rooted in the land they had tilled. A man's position as a respected member of the community was viewed as closely tied to his possession of land, and hence the oft-repeated saying, "He who is without land is without honor." The women in a man's family were also regarded as integrally bound up with his *'ard*. In this patriarchal society, women's designated role was to provide domestic labor and produce children, particularly male heirs to perpetuate family honor and wealth. Women also served as the means by which men maintained and expanded social relations (for example, through arranged marriages with relatives or other clans). Women and land were virtually equivalent constituents of a male peasant's honor, and both were the main bones of contention in local disputes.[2] It was understood that an assault on a man's honor—a slight to his family, the molestation of a female family member, an attempt to encroach upon his property—would call forth revenge or retribution.[3] In addition to this domestic-based sense of honor centered around the adult male and his family, old *mujâhidîn* expressed a strong sense of community-based solidarity (see Sayigh 1979: 19–25). Although Palestinian village life was in fact frequently riddled with inter- and intraclan and family disputes, public ideology nonetheless stated that it was crucial for rural communities to unite to repel the threat of any outside invader.

As nationalist discourse articulated with and hegemonized Palestinian rural culture, nationalist sentiment at the village level was often expressed in terms of these local conceptions of individual and family honor and through notions of rural community solidarity. As one man stated, "We had to fight in order to defend our nation [*watan*] and our honor [*'ard*]." Old *thuwwâr* tended to regard *'ard* and *watan* as intertwined, to understand the nation in terms of a man's honor. They likewise comprehended the honor of the nation as extending to include the women under a man's care. "The nation is like the mother [*al-watan ka-al-'umm*]," opined Abû Sa'îd from Kâbûl. "Men protect their women, and that's why they revolted." The notion that a man without land was without honor was invested with a nationalist articulation as well. An individual's loss of land to Zionist colonization came to be regarded as an affront to the *national* honor. When incorporated into this wider symbology, these constituents of the (male) individual's identity—family, honor, land, women—resonated with the aura of the nation. Nationalist thought remade local commonsense conception and expanded its geographical horizons. The idealized village was also constructed as the model of national solidarity. Speaking of his own village, Abû Shâhir asserted that "Dannâba is like one *hamûla*. If one man was wounded, we all were." According to Abû Shâhir, although Dannâba was divided into several *hamâ'il,* "We're like one family until today." The local conception of the nation was that it functioned as a single homogeneous unit, just like the *hamûla,* the family, and the village. Local and national cultural elements therefore cohered as a fairly unified ideological discourse, such that each element fulfilled a role of condensation with respect to the others and each one operated as a symbol of all the others (Hall 1980: 335; Laclau 1977: 93). Nationalism articulated with and complemented local conceptions of identity at the village and family level. If nationalism was the discourse of an expansive "imagined community," it was given specific shape by and actualized through local discourse. "I joined the revolt," asserted the self-proclaimed nationalist Abû Rajâ, "as a son of Sha'b and the son of a big family."

Popular Primordialism

Many interviewees were anxious to have me understand that their national identity possessed a primordial genealogical continuity. In large part, their assertions represented a kind of rejoinder to constant Zionist allegations that Palestinians are relatively "recent" immigrants to Israel/Palestine. Several old men claimed that there was a long genealogical chain of Arab residence in Palestine that spanned the centuries. Many old Palestinians traced their people's collective ancestry back to the "Arab Canaanites." By such means they meant to affirm that their originary title to the land of Palestine predated and took precedence over rival Israeli Jewish claims. Such assertions resembled those made by Palestinian nationalistic folklorists like Tewfik Canaan in the 1920s and 1930s (Canaan 1927), as well as arguments found in more recent official nationalist discourse. Abdallah Frangi, for instance, claims that the Arab Palestinians are the descendants of the autochthonous Canaanite inhabitants of Palestine and that the Israelis are the offspring of ancient Hebrews who invaded Palestine *later.* The Zionist movement, Frangi therefore concludes, is simply another instance of the perennial interventionist projects of the ancient Hebrews (Frangi 1983: 1–16). Similarly, Akram Zu'aytir has asserted that Palestine was historically "Arab" long before the Islamic conquests. The Jews were not the original inhabitants of Palestine, according to Zu'aytir, but "foreigners" who owned only a part of Palestine and never comprised a majority of its population. The Jewish kingdom, he asserts, lasted only a short time and left no lasting influence on the country's civilization (Zu'aytir 1955: 35, 58–59). People I met told stories that elaborated or expanded upon these "official" narratives. Some alleged that because the prophet Abraham (revered by Muslims) was an *Arab,* the Jews were therefore the descendants of the Arabs. The Arabs, who were Abraham's original offspring, therefore possessed prior rights to the land of Palestine. One shopkeeper in Jerusalem was a veritable fountain of Arab-nationalist-inflected stories derived from the biblical tradition. He explained, for instance, that when Moses came to Palestine from Egypt, the Jews were reluctant to believe in him but the indigenous Arab Bedouin population of Palestine immediately accepted him as a prophet. The Arabs, by this account, were therefore more genuine followers of the Mosaic creed than the Jews and hence were the true and deserving heirs to the sacred land. Such claims represented a kind of shadow discourse to that of the Zionists, a discourse articulated in virtually the same terms as its rival's. Yet at the same time, many people also routinely referred to the Jews as "our paternal cousins," *awlâd 'ammnâ,* and recognized a common descent from Abraham (the Jews as offspring of Isaac, the Arabs as offspring of Ishmael). This view coded the struggle as a kind of feud occurring within the same Semitic family. Such "genealogical" discourse, typical of the nation's impulse to represent itself as having an eternal past, had the unfortunate side effect of reproducing Orientalist and Zionist assertions that the "Arab-Jewish" struggle is ancient and virtually natural, and thereby obviated any need to understand the conflict in its current context.

These primordialist claims regarding the Palestinians' primeval and prior roots in the land operated at the level of the collective. When it came to an individual's own *family,* however, Arab-Islamic discourse took precedence over archaeological justifications. I ran across no Palestinian villager (or urbanite) who claimed personal descent from the Canaanites. Villagers typically traced their family or their *hamûla's* origins back to a more recent past in the Arabian peninsula. Many avowed descent from some nomadic tribe that had migrated from Arabia to Palestine either during or shortly after the Arab-Islamic conquests. By such a claim they inserted their family's history into the narrative of Arab and Islamic civilization and connected themselves to a genealogy that possessed greater local and contemporary prestige than did ancient or pre-Islamic descent. Several men specifically connected their forefathers' date of entry into Palestine to their participation in the army of Salâh al-Dîn al-Ayyûbî (Saladin), a historical figure whose significance has been retrospectively enlarged by nationalist discourse such that he is now regarded not merely as a hero of "Islamic" civilization but as a "national" luminary as well.[4] (Modern nationalist discourse tends to downplay Salâh al-Dîn's Kurdish origins.) Palestinians of all political stripes viewed Salâh al-Dîn's wars against the Crusaders as a forerunner of the current combats against foreign intruders. Many considered Salâh al-Dîn's victory over the Crusaders at Hittîn (A.D. 1187) as a historical precedent that offered hope for their own eventual triumph—even if, like the Crusader wars, the current struggle with Israel was destined to last more than two centuries. Family histories affiliated to earlier "patriotic" struggles against European aggression tied interviewees to a continuous narrative of national resistance. Villagers claiming descent from Arabs who entered Palestine during the Arab-Islamic conquest equally viewed these origins as establishing their historical precedence over the Jews, whom they basically regarded as Europeans who only began arriving in Palestine in the late nineteenth century.

Elite Views

Unity was another crucial motif shared by both official and popular versions of the past. I begin my investigation of this theme by examining the views of some elderly men from urban "notable" Palestinian families. In their accounts of *al-thawra,* national unity meant that the leaders and the people shared common interests and that there was no significant class divide. However, both because the peasantry's role in the revolt was so patently central and because hegemonic nationalist ideology over the years had taken a populist turn emphasizing the people's historical role, the recollections of old members of the notable class were rather defensive when it came to the insurrection of 1936–39. Even though written histories took note of educated city folks' participation in the revolt, urban notable interviewees had a hard time representing the insurrection as predominantly the result of their own activity.

The difficulties involved in asserting the elite's national honor when it came to the issue of the revolt were exemplified in the account of Abû Ja'far, a retired banker from an upper-class Jinîn family. Abû Ja'far maintained that someone "could be considered a participant in the armed revolt through money and efforts. One didn't have to be *in* it." By his account, a man needn't necessarily have joined the rebel bands in the mountains to be reckoned an activist in the uprising. Abû Ja'far also displayed a defensive posture when discussing his relations with rebel commander in chief Fawzî al-Dîn al-Qâwûqjî. A Syrian by birth, Qâwûqjî had been an officer in the Ottoman army, played a prominent part in the Syrian (mainly Druze) revolt of 1925, and subsequently became an instructor in the Iraqi military school. In August 1936 Qâwûqjî entered Palestine along with two hundred pan-Arab volunteers, declared himself commander in chief of the revolt, and united most of the disparate rebel units in the Triangle (the Nablus-Tûlkarm-Jinîn area) under his command. When the strike ended in October 1936, he withdrew from Palestine. Despite his short tenure as commander (about two months), Qâwûqjî was remembered locally for having significantly raised the Palestinian rebels' level of military organization and effectiveness.[5] I queried Abû Ja'far further when he mentioned his association with Qâwûqjî:

—You were with Qâwûqjî in 1936?
—I was with him.

—In the mountains?

—In the mountains and in the streets.

—Were you involved in any battles?

—Not really, not exactly. I was with him always, every day. . . . *Always* with him. . . . Qâwûqjî was very brave. His nerves were very strong, very very strong.

The imprecision of Abû Ja'far's memories of cooperation with Fawzî Qâwûqjî contrasted sharply with the vivid accounts I had heard ten months earlier from Muhammad Kîlânî of Ya'bad, who had fought alongside Qâwûqjî in the highlands. Unlike Abû Ja'far, Kîlânî was able to supply details about specific battles, the names of local rebel commanders who served with Qâwûqjî, and so on. It was also symptomatic of Abû Ja'far's class position that although he identified himself with Qâwûqjî, a professional military man of urban background who enjoyed a pan-Arab reputation, he did not praise or claim intimate connections to any other rebel commanders operating in the Jinîn area, leaders who were virtually all of peasant background and who held the reins of local authority for far longer than did Qâwûqjî. Instead Abû Ja'far was critical of other rebel *quwwâd* simply on the basis of their being *fallâhîn*. His assertions that city people could be revolt activists just by contributing money and that he was an intimate of Qâwûqjî were meant to establish a respectable place for himself—and by extension, the educated elite—in the story of popular insurgency.

Two men I interviewed from the Husaynî clan made similarly recuperative claims regarding their family's prominence in the revolt. It should of course be acknowledged that the Husaynîs were unusual among elite Palestinian families for their high level of direct participation in the rebel movement (Porath 1977: 261, 395).[6] The only rebel commander to emerge from elite ranks, moreover, was the Mufti's cousin, 'Abd al-Qâdir al-Husaynî, who directed military operations in the Jerusalem region. (Leading contemporary West Bank nationalist leader and chief adviser to the Palestinians' 1992–93 negotiating team, Faysal Husaynî, is 'Abd al-Qâdir's son. Faysal is often referred to as *ibn al-shahîd,* or "son of the martyr"; his father died in the battle of Qastal in 1948.) One of the Husaynîs I met described 'Abd al-Qâdir as a man of the people:

> 'Abd al-Qâdir was from a big, rich family, the son of Mûsâ Kâzim al-Husaynî, the mayor of Jerusalem and the leader of the national movement [Mûsâ Kâzim headed the Arab Executive until 1934]. But at the same time, 'Abd al-Qâdir was a tough man. He could go to the mountains and live just like the others.

> Sometimes he would even give his shoes to one of the "soldiers" [rebels] and go
> around without shoes. So they felt that he was tougher than them.[7]

This description displays 'Abd al-Qâdir al-Husaynî as possessing both aristocratic and popular qualities. His noblesse oblige was what motivated him
to donate his shoes to his men—an action demonstrating that 'Abd al-Qâdir
al-Husaynî was not merely as hardy as the ordinary *fallâh,* but hardier. He is
portrayed here as superior, therefore, by virtue of his origins (from a big
nationalist family), by virtue of his transcendence of lofty backgrounds and
descent to the level of the *menu peuple,* and by virtue of his ability to outdo
the common man in sheer robustness. The 'Abd al-Qâdir anecdote resonates
with Abû Ja'far's in that it attempts to demonstrate that notables were equally as militant as *fallâhîn.* Although it, too, concerns a single notable family,
the tale of 'Abd al-Qâdir nonetheless also salvages some local credibility for
the entire elite. The account accomplishes this in a paradoxically elitist fashion, simultaneously abolishing distinctions between the people and the
notable leaders while confirming the latter's inherent superiority. The story is
typical of mainstream Palestinian nationalism in that it presents national
unity and comradeship within a hierarchical framework while it denies the
significance of class differences. At the same time, the anecdote does mark
something of a concession, in that it avers that the standard of militancy and
toughness during the insurrection was set by villagers.

Not Husaynîya but Wataniya

Unity was a key trope, but differently inflected, in popular memories of the
insurrection, as well. In part, peasant interviewees' emphasis on unity stemmed
from reactions to official Zionist historiography, which presented the revolt
as simply a time of fratricidal conflict. Former rebels often reversed the
standard Israeli story by foregrounding rebel unity and either relegating
internal schisms to a shadowy or distant place or attributing divisions to the
machinations of outside forces. Villagers in particular skirted discussion of
internal tensions within the national movement that had been played out at
the local level, preferring instead to present their local communities as mod-
els of confraternity. Alternatively, they handled intramural divisions through
displacements, by explaining that internal strife occurred in locales other
than their own, by asserting that dissension afflicted the elite but not the
people, or by claiming that internal conflict was provoked by the Zionists and
the British.

Rural people gave national unity a somewhat different articulation than did official histories or elite families' narratives. Villagers rarely praised the effendis' actions during the revolt, and in fact often blamed them for factionalism. Those interviewees who acknowledged that internal schisms were a problem for the movement generally attributed these to rivalries between the Husaynîs and Nashâshîbîs that originated in Jerusalem municipal politics. Several men minimized the impact of this national rivalry upon their own rural communities, claiming it was irrelevant to peasant interests and merely concerned issues pertinent to the city of Jerusalem. Reliable published and archival accounts, however, assert that although the Husaynî-Nashâshîbî rivalry did chiefly concern the capital city's religious and political affairs, the contest had effects in rural areas, for these two prominent families had organized rival networks of notable and peasant allies that spread throughout much of the country. In the early 1930s the elite confederacies were transformed into political parties, chief among them the Husaynîs' Palestine Arab Party and the Nashâshîbîs' National Defence Party. During the revolt, however, the Husaynîs came to be widely identified with the national struggle. The term *majlisî* was generally used to imply a true nationalist, and many interviewees used the terms *majlisî* and *watanî* (nationalist) interchangeably The designation *majlisî* (literally, "councilist") referred to the Supreme Muslim Council, the *majlis,* the national Islamic body that was created by the British and headed by Grand Mufti Hâjj Amîn al-Husaynî. When the Mufti assumed presidency of the Higher Arab Committee (HAC), the official national body established in April 1936 to guide the general strike, the expression *majlisî* came to connote affiliation with the Mufti-headed HAC, and hence the national movement. The Mufti, the Husaynîs, the Supreme Muslim Council (*majlis*), and the HAC were thus often used as equivalent metonyms for the national movement. When the Nashâshîbî-headed alliance split from the Higher Arab Committee in July 1937, it became known as the Opposition, or *mu'ârida.* Those affiliated with the Nashâshîbîs or their National Defence Party, the *mu'âridîn* or oppositionists, eventually came to be regarded not as the "loyal" opposition but as virtual traitors.

These two leading and rival notable factions of the movement patched up their differences during the first year of the revolt, when both were represented in the HAC. But later relations reached a breaking point, in large part because of the greater willingness on the part of the Nashâshîbîs and their allies to make concessions to the British, including acceptance of partition, and the Nashâshîbîs and their allies withdrew from the HAC. The split within the elite spread to rural areas, particularly in areas where both factions had allies, and each side tried to mobilize its rural clients against supporters of the opposing party. But because Hâjj Amîn was the titular head of the national movement, the Husaynî faction was widely identified with "the nation." In many locales, in fact, such political differences were transcended or mitigated, especially at the rebellion's high points. But as the insurrection dragged on and British pressures increased, the Nashâshîbîs and their confederates began to organize more vigorous opposition. In fall 1938, with British encouragement, the Nashâshîbîs, local opposition forces, and some outright mercenaries began establishing counterrevolutionary battalions that were given the name "peace bands" (*fasâ'il al-salâm*). These contras began to harass and attack rebel forces in the Jerusalem, Hebron, and Jinîn areas.

One way in which some interviewees "handled" such cracks in the national movement was simply not to mention them at all. In other cases, former *quwwâd fasâ'il* (band commanders) admitted that Husaynî-Nashâshîbî factionalism existed but claimed that they personally had overcome it at the local level. 'Abd al-Fattâh al-Mizra'âwî, a band commander in the Ramallah district (who, according to one account, served under regional commander 'Abd al-Qâdir Husaynî [Muhsin 1986: 179]), described his policies as follows: "I wasn't a *majlisî* or *mu'ârid,* but a nationalist [*watanî*]. I went to the villages and I said, 'Now there's no more Husaynî or Nashâshîbî, now there's *watan* [nation] and *bandûqîya* [rifle].' " From the standpoint of orthodox nationalist discourse, according to which a *majlisî* was a *real* nationalist and a *mu'ârid* was a turncoat, al-Mizra'âwî's statement might be considered rather heretical. Al-Mizra'âwî twisted conventional wisdom by implying that *majlisî* meant being bound to narrow Husaynî interests. Likewise, al-Mizra'âwî claimed he was able to incorporate villagers with Nashâshîbî ties into his domain because *mu'ârida* affiliation was irrelevant to his local-level definition of Palestinian nationalism. He presented his policy of uniting all villagers as more inclusive than that pursued by the urban leaders. Thus al-Mizra'âwî turned *mu'ârida* from a term denoting national disloyalty into a designation that had no meaning except in the domain of the elite and its petty squabbles. As al-Mizra'âwî saw it, *majlisî* and *mu'ârida* had no bearing on the interests of villagers; the nation and the gun were the true basis for the politics of the rebellion.

Al-Mizra'âwî did acknowledge that his nationalist conception of unity had regional limits. He contrasted the district under his control with the area immediately to the north. The commander Muhammad 'Umar al-Nûbânî, a lieutenant of 'Ârif 'Abd al-Râziq, held sway in this region, which was plagued by rebel aggressions based on Husaynî partisanship and by rebel misdeeds against villagers. Al-Mizra'âwî's metonymic model of national unity, by his own admission, was strictly local.[8]

A similar model of nationalist practice was presented by Abû Shâhir, who had served as the personal assistant of his cousin 'Abd al-Rahîm al-Hâjj Muhammad, the famous regional rebel commander responsible for the Tûlkarm-Nablus area. Abû Shâhir reported that one day (probably in 1938) an emissary from the Damascus rebel headquarters, Dr. Dâ'ûd al-Husaynî, turned up at 'Abd al-Rahîm's camp with a list of traitors for the commander to execute.[9] 'Abd al-Rahîm refused to comply with the leadership's behest, telling Husaynî, "I don't work for *Husaynîya* ["Husaynî-ism"] but for *watanîya* [nationalism]."[10] Abû Shâhir claimed that in commander 'Abd al-Rahîm's view, the revolt was being fought in pursuit of higher goals, not for the narrow factional interests (like eliminating political enemies) sought by the Husaynîs. Abû Shâhir represented 'Abd al-Rahîm as a more genuine nationalist than the political chiefs in Damascus because his notion of unity was more all-encompassing. For him, patriotism was incommensurate with political assassination, especially when such murder served partisan purposes. Abû Shâhir therefore remembered any excesses in the campaign of killing accused traitors (*khuwwân*), British agents (*'umalâ'*) or land dealers (*samâsira*) as being due to Husaynî intrigues. By contrast, he presented local rebel commanders as scrupulous practitioners of an expansive national solidarity. Abû Shâhir attempted to rescue the memory of the rebellion by holding up a paradigmatic *local* version of nationalism (although at the same time, he darkened the reputation of the Husaynîs and of Damascus headquarters). Abû Shâhir's picture is backed up by a British intelligence report of October 1938, which states that 'Abd al-Rahîm had become so disaffected with the Damascus command that he had ceased sending money there. The commander was said to have replied to a recent demand for funds with the words, "The shoe of the most insignificant mujahid is nobler than all the members of the Society [the Damascus-based leadership], who have indulged in pleasure while their brethren suffer in the mountains."[11] Abû Shâhir's local view of unity operated as a critique of dominant nationalist versions, which deny corruption on the part of the leadership and assert that any factionalism was due to rival commanders' manipulation of the "simple" peasants.

Faysal 'Abd al-Râziq recounted a similar populist-nationalist story concerning his father 'Ârif 'Abd al-Râziq, the regional commander responsible for the Banî Sa'b area south of Tûlkarm and, according to written accounts, a rival of 'Abd al-Rahîm al-Hâjj Muhammad. 'Abd al-Râziq, like most rebel commanders, routinely performed judicial functions during the revolt.

According to Faysal, on one occasion his father 'Ârif pardoned a man from a village near Nablus, who was brought before him on the charge of being a traitor. 'Ârif told him: "The accusations against you are lies. I don't care what your political opinion is, you're not against the revolt and that's the main thing. You're free to have your own political opinion. If you want to side with the Tawqâns or the 'Anâbtâwîs [local notable families allied with the Nashâshîbîs], that's something other than the revolt, that's just family disputes." Through this and other similar anecdotes, Faysal represented his father as someone who worked hard to overcome the Husaynî-Nashâshîbî disputes at the village level. This depiction was contradicted by several other interviewees' accounts, as well as by archival sources, which usually portrayed 'Ârif 'Abd al-Râziq as the Mufti's man. 'Abd al-Rahîm al-Hâjj Muhammad meanwhile was usually said by most sources to have maintained a degree of independence from the Damascus leadership. It was probably because of prevailing national-popular views of the revolt, which stressed the importance of local unity and looked with disfavor on anyone aligned to particularistic interests—especially outsiders—that 'Abd al-Râziq's son Faysal had also found it necessary to portray his father as nonpartisan.

Galilee villagers' notion of what constituted national consensus differed somewhat from the views presented by villagers in the Jinîn-Nablus-Tûlkarm region (the "Triangle of Terror"). The Triangle, part of the Palestinian central highland where a rural aristocracy (the *shuyûkh al-nawâhî*) developed during the Ottoman period, was relatively independent of central state authority.[12] During the mid-nineteenth century, in the course of the Ottoman "reform" period (which actually meant increased state control and the implantation of capitalist relations of production), the Porte reduced the power of the village-based aristocrats of the central highlands. Many such families (like the 'Abd al-Hâdîs of 'Arrâba) gradually relocated in the cities and merged with the existing urban notable class. In the mandate period, these aristocratic families nonetheless still retained networks of clients in the countryside. These links often combined political and economic relations (alliances and landlord-tenant links). Such confederations, which frequently shifted and realigned, were usually connected in various ways with either the Husaynîs or the Nashâshîbîs.

The Galilee by contrast had not witnessed the emergence of powerful aristocratic families with extensive rural clienteles, chiefly because this region was more closely controlled by the nearby Ottoman centers of power, at Acre, Sidon, and Damascus. Villagers of the north therefore were somewhat removed from the Husaynî-Nashâshîbî feuds, since large-scale notable-dominated confederacies were not so important there. *Thuwwâr* from the Galilee affirmed that the dissenters they encountered during the revolt did not go out under the Nashâshîbî banner. Elderly men from northern Palestine, moreover, usually did not recall the Mufti as a partisan figure who was mired in clan-based machinations but as the leader of the nation. "The Mufti was a good man," many Galilee interviewees repeated, "and there was no *majlisî* or *mu'ârida* here." Northern villagers could consider Hâjj Amîn a unifying national symbol because the Husaynîs played almost no part in their politics and alliances in the north, whereas in the hills of Nablus, Jerusalem, and Hebron, notable landowning families and their rural clients were frequently split along Husaynî-Nashâshîbî lines. In contrast to villages in the Galilee, therefore, West Bank *thuwwâr* were often more vocal in their criticism of the Mufti's partisanship. In the north, where Hâjj Amîn al-Husaynî was generally removed from parochial disputes, his name carried more symbolic and unifying power, yet he was less intimately known. In the central highland Hâjj Amîn had enjoyed greater influence and authority, but his image and power were more contested. In the Galilee, the Mufti figured more straightforwardly as a signifier of common national interests.

My Religion Is Palestinian

Many old *mujâhidîn* stressed that, during the revolt, Palestinians managed to transcend any religious divisions that might have beset the nation earlier, when it was not as "advanced." Over and over I was assured that no significant differences divided Christians from Muslims or Sunnis from Druze (members of a heterodox branch of Shi'ite Islam), because everyone was Palestinian and everyone was united within the nation. In many popular accounts, Palestinianness was said to be more important to the subject's sense of identity than religion. When queried about Arab Christians' role in the revolt, Abû Shâhir responded, "There's no *dîn* [religion; that is, there are no differences based on religion]. My *dîn* is *Filastînî* [Palestinian]." For Abû Shâhir, sectarian distinctions were simply outweighed by the fact of being Palestinian. His claim that Palestine was his "religion" was somewhat scandalous from a conventional Islamic standpoint, but it accorded well with the tenets of modern secular nationalism. Some villagers from the West Bank recalled a chant from the time of the rebellion that seemed to encapsulate this ecumenical spirit. "Sayf al-Dîn, al-Hâjj Amîn! [Sword of religion, Hâjj Amîn]" went the national slogan that the rebellion's supporters chanted throughout the country. But in the villages of the Galilee, where, unlike the case in the rural central highlands, there was a sizable Christian minority and

where some former rebels we interviewed were Christian, old people recalled shouting a modified version: "Sayf al-Din, al-Hâjj Amîn, muslimîn wa
masîhîyîn!" [Sword of religion, Hâjj Amîn, for Muslims and Christians]."
The Galileans' chant therefore presented the (Muslim) Mufti as the defender
of *both* religions, as the head of a nation that equally encompassed Muslims
and Christians.

This popular emphasis on national unity that rose above sectarian difference was partly the effect of a retrospective reinscription of memory. In the
mid-eighties, sectarian differences between Muslims and Christians were
seen as holding considerably less significance than they had in the past, mixed
marriages were becoming accepted at least among the middle classes, and the
contemporary discourse of Palestinian nationalism was more secular than it
had been in the 1930s. The current rhetoric (and practice) of sectarian unity
therefore tended to obscure any recollection of instances of sectarian conflict that flared up in the past. I heard nothing from interviewees, for instance,
about the kind of Muslim-Christian tensions discussed by Yehoshuah Porath
(1977: 269–71). According to Porath, sectarian tears in the social fabric were
manifested particularly during the second phase of the revolt, and especially
in summer and fall 1938 when the peasant *thuwwâr* imposed their hegemony
on the cities and in some instances forced Christians to observe Friday as the
day of rest and made Christian women veil.

But Muslim-Christian discord during the revolt appears to have been considerably less significant than conflicts that developed between rebels and the
Druze, a community of about ten thousand persons that was spread throughout the northern villages. When we questioned interviewees in the Galilee
about Druze involvement in the *thawra,* they replied that they had participated and usually named a few Druze fighters. But interviewees appeared
reluctant to discuss any past antagonisms involving Druze and did not usually remark on the apparent contradiction between Druze involvement in the
armed revolt and the Druze's current position, for the friction between the
Druze and the rest of the Palestinian community was very much on the surface of everyday life in the mid-eighties. Relations were agitated because, as a
group, the Druze enjoyed much closer ties to the Israeli state than other
Palestinian citizens of Israel. The Druze are the only Arab citizens of Israel
required to serve in the Israeli Defense Forces and are defined by the state as
a separate "ethnic" group that is not "Arab" (Hajjar 1992). While greater
opposition to the official Druze collaborationist position has gained ground
among the younger members of the community, the relationship of the sect's
members to other Palestinians remains problematic. This issue was especially

fraught for West Bankers, who almost daily encountered, and were on occasion beaten or shot by, Druze soldiers serving in the army of occupation. Particularly hated were the Druze members of the notorious border guards (*hâris al-hudûd*), who enjoyed a special reputation for brutality. Palestinians usually preferred not to broach this topic with an outsider, and those who did often took extra pains to tell me that not *all* Druze were collaborators.

One day in February 1985, Sonia and I drove to Shafâ' 'Amr (an Arab town located inside Israel, west of Nazareth) to drop in on an important Druze leader named Sâlih Khnayfus. We knew virtually nothing about him beforehand except that someone had told Sonia—she couldn't recall whom—that Khnayfus had fought in the revolt, and so his name was written down on our list. As we sat waiting for Shaykh Sâlih in his spacious *diwân*, sipping the fresh-squeezed lemonade one of his granddaughters had served us, we scanned with interest the Druze flag, the portrait of celebrated Syrian Druze leader Sultân al-Atrash, and the other mementos of the Syria Druze struggle that hung on the walls. Sâlih Khnayfus entered, looking like the epitome of the Druze chieftain, with his imposing demeanor; his dignified, straight-backed posture; his meticulously arranged, bleached-white *kûfîya* and neatly pressed gray *qumbâz;* and his prodigious, fastidiously trimmed white mustache. The trappings of Druze militancy arrayed behind him added to the shaykh's aura. We began to query him, but the great shaykh politely but firmly refused to utter a single word about the 1936 revolt. Instead he deftly steered the discussion to topics like the plans of the Shafâ' 'Amr municipality to turn the imposing eighteenth-century structure in the center of town, a citadel built by the son of Zâhir al-'Umar, into a museum.

After a half hour of polite but superficial conversation, we retreated, and headed down the hill to the home of Sâlih's son, Faraj Khnayfus. Faraj tried to put his father's silence into context for us. Toward the end of the 1936–39 revolt, Faraj said, one of the rebel commanders (either Abû Durra or Abû Ibrâhîm al-Kabîr, he wasn't sure which) had killed twenty Druze shaykhs from Shafâ' 'Amr. Five of the victims, among them Sâlih's own father, were from the Khnayfus family. Sâlih, who until then had fought on the side of the rebels, began to work on behalf of the British. The topic of the revolt still remained a sore point with his father. According to Faraj, the killings at Shafâ' 'Amr and similar rebel actions elsewhere turned many Druze against the national movement in the late 1930s, and they were an important factor in the Druze decision to break ranks with the rest of the Palestinian community in 1948 and to make a separate peace with the new Israeli state. Although we were keen to learn more about such conflicts and divisions, the

only person we ever met who was willing to discuss them was Faraj. In order
to sustain the image of a unified nation, most villagers preferred to consign
this past sectarian conflict to the memory hole—and all the more vigorously,
perhaps, because this rift still contributed to national disunity.

Faraj did not, perhaps could not, fill in all the details of this incident, but
additional information is found in Palestinian-Israeli anthropologist Majid
Al-Haj's ethnography of Shafâ' 'Amr (1987).[13] According to Al-Haj, because
of their minority status, the Druze of Shafâ' 'Amr had suffered a history of
abuses at the hands of the numerically superior Sunni Muslim villagers. During the mandate period they occasionally appealed to the British authorities
for protection against Sunni mistreatment, but such moves only exacerbated
Sunni antipathy.[14] Al-Haj does not indicate whether or not Druze from
Shafâ' 'Amr participated in the revolt, but he does report that on August 13,
1939, *mujâhidîn* attacked the Druze community at Shafâ' 'Amr and killed
three men, purportedly because the Druze had withdrawn their support
from the revolt. The assault prompted Druze to abandon the "mixed" residential quarters of Shafâ' 'Amr for all-Druze districts (Al-Haj 1987: 55–56).
Al-Haj does not inform us whether the attack pushed Druze into collaborating with the British. (In any case, the revolt was almost over by this date.) I
have been unable to determine if additional rebel attacks on Shafâ' 'Amr
Druze took place or if Faraj's claim that twenty Druze were killed was simply inflated.

Khnayfus's and Al-Haj's accounts, however, are limited by their local focus
and their inattention to the larger historical picture. (Perhaps this circum-
scription was motivated, too, by a desire to preserve the national reputation.)
Neither mentions, for example, the Zionist leaders' vigorous efforts to convince their contacts in the Druze leadership—in Palestine, Lebanon, and
Syria—to keep the community neutral during the revolt and not to attack
the Yishuv (Black 1986: 336–53; Porath 1977: 271–73). The Druze shaykhs
eventually promised their Zionist interlocutors that the community would
stay out of the rebellion, but they were not able to prevent the participation
of some Druze in the fighting. Nonetheless, Druze leaders' friendly relations
with the Jews and the refusal of a few predominantly Druze villages to
support the struggle angered some revolt commanders. Shaykh Hasan Abû
Rukn of 'Isfîya, for instance, was murdered by rebels in 1938 for cooperating
with the Jews. On November 27, 1938, Qassâmite commander Abû Durra
attacked the Druze villages of 'Isfîya and Dâliyat al-Karmil, located in
Mount Carmel, near Haifa. In the course of the assault Abû Durra reportedly desecrated Druze holy books, killed three persons, roughed up women and

children, and kidnapped village headmen.[15] By early 1939 Druze patterns of collaboration with the British and Zionists—which had increased in reaction to such rebel attacks—prompted all the Arab cigarette factories to boycott tobacco produced by Druze farmers (Black 1986: 352).[16]

Faraj Khnayfus's assertion that rebel aggressions during 1936–39 had a major impact on Druze decisions to defect from the Palestinian community in 1948 takes on additional meaning when we realize that Sâlih Khnayfus himself figured in the Zionist conquest of the north. In March 1948 Fawzi Qâwûqjî, commander of the Arab Liberation Army, put a Syrian Druze battalion commanded by Shakîb Wahhâb in charge of conducting the war in the Haifa district. Wahhâb set up his headquarters in Shafâ' 'Amr. In April, the battalion was defeated at the battle of Ramat Yohanon (known by the Arabs as the battle of Hawsha and al-Kasâyir) by a Haganah force led by Moshe Dayan. The Druze batallion, which was supported by Arab irregulars (including Druze) from throughout the north, suffered as many as two hundred casualties during the fight. Following the engagement, Sâlih Khnayfus, who had previously urged Shakîb Wahhâb to stay out of the fighting, arranged negotiations between the commander and Moshe Dayan.[17] Through Khnayfus's mediation, Dayan was able to persuade Wahhâb to withdraw his forces from the war. Shakîb Wahhâb's pullout was part of a broader Druze shift in allegiance from the Arab to the Jewish side in April 1948, a move in which Sâlih Khnayfus and Shaykh Labîb Abû Rukn of 'Isfîya played leading roles. The battalion's departure cleared the way for the Haganah to capture Acre with relative ease, and it set the stage for the Zionist conquest of all western Galilee—territory that the 1947 U.N. partition plan had allocated to the proposed Palestinian Arab state. Sâlih Khnayfus was subsequently decorated for his role in the founding of Israel, and he subsequently served as a member of the Knesset (Teveth 1972: 133–34; al-Qâsim 1976: 24–27).

But the medal Sâlih Khnayfus received from the Jewish state was not among the memorabilia we observed in his *diwân*. And while Sâlih's son Faraj was forthcoming about how the *thuwwâr* drove his father to collude with the British in 1939, he told us nothing about the shaykh's collaboration in 1948. (Perhaps because this was common knowledge among Palestinian-Israelis and he felt it was unnecessary to discuss it.) Faraj's living-room walls, unlike his father's *diwân*, were hung with posters of the Palestinian resistance movement, not sectarian mementos. Faraj had recently been released after three years in jail for refusing to serve in the Israeli army and was a leader of the left-nationalist Palestinian-Israeli organization, Ibnâ' al-Balad (The sons of the village). The variegated careers of the three Khnayfus generations—

grandfather killed by *thuwwâr;* father a *mujâhid,* then a collaborator with the British, and a hero of the Jewish state; grandson a Palestinian militant—display some of the seams that Palestinian nationalist discourse strains so hard, at the official and popular levels, to suture together in the interests of projecting unity.

Bandits or Heroes

Old *mujâhidîn* were also motivated by a sense of popular nationalism to deny enemy claims that rebels were thieves and criminals. During the insurrection, British officialdom and press routinely branded the *mujâhidîn* as "outlaws," "bandits," "gangsters," and "highwaymen" in order to discredit the movement's nationalist aims. The language of British counterinsurgency enjoyed an afterlife in the pronouncements of the Israeli historical apparatuses, which often made a case for generalized rebel criminality on the basis of a few cases of prominent commanders with criminal records (for example, 'Abd al-Rahîm al-Hâjj Muhammad, 'Ârif 'Abd al-Râziq, and Fakhrî 'Abd al-Hâdî).[18] Sonia tried to turn such defamations on their heads when talking to closed-mouthed interviewees. She would say, pointing at me, "Do you accept that people in America continue to read in their books that the rebels were all common criminals?" Not everyone, of course, was prodded into speaking by such a tactic, but sometimes the interlocutor would explode in anger, call such statements lies, and affirm that the rebels were truly honorable nationalists. "They were just defending their own land," exclaimed Umm 'Imâd (from Umm al-Fahm), in defense of rebels said to be robbers or terrorists. Other interviewees made a connection between the British practice of naming Palestinian nationalists criminals (*mujrimîn*) and the Israeli designation of them as terrorists (*irhâbîyîn*). But such was the force of such accusations that, although they were rejected by elderly Palestinians, they had helped turn "crime" into a touchy, even proscribed subject.

Former rebels therefore generally claimed to be innocent of any personal involvement in "criminal" behavior (except those involving "honor") at any time before, during, or after the revolt. Faysal 'Abd al-Râziq of al-Tayyiba, whose father 'Ârif 'Abd al-Râziq was often referred to by historians as a simple thief, was especially vociferous on this subject. Faysal claimed that it was because 'Abd al-Râziq had secretly organized the Black Hand band in the early 1920s to launch attacks on Tûlkarm-area Jewish colonies that the Zionists and the British intelligence services brought trumped-up charges of robbery against him. To support this claim, Faysal stressed that prominent nationalist lawyers like 'Awnî 'Abd al-Hâdî defended 'Ârif because they regarded his case as a national, not a criminal, issue. According to Faysal, the British and Zionists induced witnesses to lie and so 'Abd al-Râziq was convicted and spent three years in prison (1923–26).[19]

Some interviewees acknowledged that rebels did occasionally engage in petty thievery, but they usually added that these constituted a tiny and unrepresentative minority amid a multitude of scrupulous *mujâhidîn*. Some men allowed, in the course of discussions, that they had been in jail prior to 1936. But they never recounted this fact with pride. Usually the case involved killing or injuring someone in a brawl (*tawsha*) that they explained as an affair of *damm* ("blood," or homicide) or as the result of a feud between or within families. Interviewees presented such events moreover as something that *used to* occur but was no longer a problem in the villages, because the Palestinian community was now more modern, developed, and united on a national basis rather than being divided by clans. (Disputes of this sort, in fact, continued to occur in Palestinian communities, but they too were explained away as examples of "backward" and therefore exceptional behavior.) The unfavorable and defensive attitudes toward "criminality" (even affairs of *damm*) in Palestinian villages marked a general shift within rural culture, which was an effect of modernizing discourses and changing attitudes toward property and outsiders (see Sayigh 1979: 23).

By contrast, during the mandate such "crimes" were often regarded not with shame but with pride. Local robbers who stole from outsiders and not from locals and who never bothered women or the poor were the particular objects of both fear and admiration in rural society. Views like that expressed by the Qassâmite *mujâhid* 'Arabî Badawî, while exceptional by the mid-eighties, once typified rural opinion: "When I was a boy I decided that when I got older I would be like Abû Kabârî. He was commander of a band here [in this area]. They called them outlaws [*ashqiyâ'*]. They used to rob and plunder, but really they were heroes [*abtâl*]."[20] Badawî's statement echoed the Palestine Communist Party's propaganda concerning another and better-known bandit, Abû Jilda. In 1934, the party issued communiqués hailing the activities of Abû Jilda in the central highlands and claiming that his "partisan detachments" were pulling the country toward disorder and armed revolt (Budeiri 1979: 77). The bandit's actions and reputation were known in the Yishuv, as well. An article in the English-language Zionist daily, the *Palestine Post* (July 16, 1936), described Abû Jilda as an Arab "national hero" who was responsible for leading an insurrection in the villages of Wâdî Hawârith (whose lands had been sold by the Tayâns to the Zionists).[21] Former Palestine policeman Edward Horne states that Abû Jilda had a reputation as a vicious killer who terrorized villagers, but nonetheless he was admired by the Arabs for his ability to elude capture for so long and was regarded as a "token of resistance" (1982: 180). Contemporary folklore collections also mention songs composed in praise of Abû Jilda (al-Salhût and Shahada 1982: 25). By the mid-eighties, however, the only people we met who recalled this famous bandit in a positive light were older members of the Israeli Communist Party who did not hail from the rural areas where Abû Jilda had operated. Most elderly rural people expressed decidedly contrary views about such law-breakers of the past. Villagers who remembered Abû Jilda generally emphasized that he was simply a *qutta' turuq* (highwayman) and a murderer, and they denied that he was in any way a hero or a protorevolutionary.

Ranajit Guha has shown how peasant struggles in colonial India often transformed criminals into insurgents by providing a new context for activities that were already widely seen as a legitimate form of social protest (1983: 89–95). A similar transition occurred during the rebellion in Palestine, in the course of which village criminals and toughs (known as *zu'rân* or *qabadâyât*) were transformed into *thuwwâr.* But as a national memory of the revolt was constructed and sanctified, this close connection between the rural outlaw and the nationalist rebel was erased, and now "criminal" behaviors previously regarded in a positive or ambivalent light are branded as simply backward and antisocial.[22] Another factor in this shift was the hostile propaganda emphasizing that the Palestinians' "national heroes" were simply bandits and thieves like Abû Jilda and 'Ârif 'Abd al-Râziq. That the *thuwwâr* had emerged out of a rural culture that fostered social banditry was largely forgotten, both by official nationalist mythmakers and by the people themselves. Although the forging of the rebellion as a *national* movement had involved a transcription of preexisting forms of peasant radicalism, contemporary nationalist discourse portrayed this remaking of rural traditions of revolt as the invention of an entirely new form of modernist politics. In the course of the official displacement of the revolt's bases in peasant life, popular views on crime were also substantially recoded.

Rebels and Jews

Another form of popular-nationalist argument was that the revolt was aimed primarily *not* at the Jews but at the British mandate government and Zionist colonization. This subject was introduced in chapter 1 with regard to rebel attacks on Jewish settlements. Such a recasting of the character of the revolt involved the suppression of memories of Arab-Jewish hostilities and the emphasis on examples of good relations with the Jews. Abû Shâhir, the assistant to commander 'Abd al-Rahîm al-Hâjj Muhammad, recalled one such incident. A Jew from Natanya, he claimed, once spent a month in the mountains with 'Abd al-Rahîm's band, in the course of which he learned that the rebels were nationalists and not terrorists. Abû Shâhir deployed this anecdote as a counterclaim to Zionist allegations that the *mujâhidîn* were all anti-Semitic brutes and the PLO's guerrillas were just the same. The Jew from Natanya's reported seal of approval lent added credibility to Palestinian claims about the nature of their national movement. In addition, by showing how rebels welcomed a Jewish visitor into their midst, Abû Shâhir's tale was designed to demonstrate that Palestinians desired in the thirties (and still wished for in the eighties) amicable coexistence with the Jews. Similar assertions were often made by Palestinians I met, many of whom also took pains to claim that Islamic civilization *always* treated both Jews and Christians quite well.[23]

On the other hand, most persons I met did not raise the thorny issue of the Palestinian national movement's relationship to the Nazis. There is some evidence of popular Palestinian sympathy for the fascist movements. A British intelligence report, for instance, states that the Prophet's birthday in May 1937 was celebrated as a national event, complete with the hoisting of Arab, Italian, and Nazi flags and the display of photographs of Hitler and Mussolini.[24] Zionist propaganda has routinely stressed such examples of Arab profascist tendencies, which may have been marginal phenomena. This subject was rarely addressed by interviewees. The few men who did bring up the claim that the Mufti collaborated with the Nazis in the slaughter of Jews vigorously rejected the charge. They did acknowledge that, during the Second World War, the Mufti and his lieutenants (including Abû Ibrâhîm al-Kabîr, Hasan Salâma, and Wâsif Kamâl) took refuge in Berlin and supported certain Nazi policies. But, they argued, the Mufti's chief motivations for working with the Germans were that he and the Führer shared a common adversary, British imperialism, and that Hitler had promised to aid the Palestinians in gaining national independence. They underscored that Hâjj Amîn did not accept asylum in Germany out of any sympathy with Nazi persecution of European Jews, that he had been hunted by the British and had no place else to take refuge. While some of these men regarded the Mufti's relations with the Nazis as misguided, they defended his motives, which they claimed were genuinely nationalist, not anti-Semitic. A few took to the offensive and compared Zionist actions against Palestinians, like mass expulsions and military rule, to the Nazi oppression of Jews. "The *Israelis* are the Nazis," some veterans of the *thawra* insisted, "not us." These persons thereby attempted to deploy the memory of the horrible Nazi crimes against the

Jews by drawing parallels between the Israeli state's actions and Hitler's.[25] Faysal 'Abd al-Râziq (the son of rebel commander 'Ârif 'Abd al-Râziq, who took refuge in Axis-controlled Bulgaria during the war) went further, recalling the 1940 proposal of Stern Gang leader Avraham Stern (whose loyal lieutenant and successor was Yitzhak Shamir) to cooperate with the Nazis. (The Stern Gang not only expressed its sympathy for Hitler's goal for a *judenrein* Europe but also affirmed that it considered itself "closely related to the totalitarian movements of Europe in its ideology and structure" [Hitchens 1989].)[26] Such claims constituted attempts to create an unblemished nationalist memory of the revolt's relations with the Jews by emphasizing examples of rapport and by radically denying any Palestinian hostility to the Jews per se, Nazi affiliations, or fascist sympathies. The claims were also efforts to naysay the supposedly inherent and "natural" antipathy between Arabs and Jews.

Land Sales

The question of land sales was another domain of agreement between popular accounts and standard Palestinian histories (as discussed in chapter 1). This general silence about Palestinians who sold land to the Zionist movement bolstered a unified national-popular memory. Accounts of this issue focused chiefly on absentee Lebanese and Syrian landowners who turned over their large estates in Palestine to the Zionists. Villagers recalled certain well-known transactions and the names of those families involved. It was the Lebanese Sursuqs' sale of twenty-two villages in Marj Ibn 'Âmr (Esdraelon) and the Syrian Tayâns' transfer of Wâdî Hawârith that were recalled most often and that were presented as virtually paradigmatic cases. Such mnemonic condensations, usually presented as encapsulating the story of land sales, allowed the involvement of Palestinian landowners and small farmers in such transactions to be ignored.

It is indeed true that, on the whole, purchases from non-Palestinians constituted the major means by which Zionists acquired "legal" title to land. According to Kenneth Stein, of all land transactions up to 1945 for which figures are available, sales by *fallâhîn* accounted for 9.4 percent of the total land area purchased, sales by Palestinian large landowners amounted to 24.6 percent of the total, and transactions involving non-Palestinian Arabs made up 52.6 percent (1984: 226–27). The picture looks somewhat different, however, if we follow the story chronologically. Zionist land purchases from *non*-Palestinian sources predominated only until 1928. Beginning in that year, sales by Palestinians (both large estate holders and *fallâhîn*) constituted a larger proportion (in terms of total area) than sales by non-Palestinians. By the mid-thirties, transactions with Palestinians accounted for 89 percent of total Jewish land purchases (Porath 1977: 83–84). In 1934, for instance, over 60,872 dunums of land was transferred by Arabs to Jews. Of 1,178 sales, 1,116 involved transfers of less than 100 dunums.[27] The growing number of real estate sales by Palestinians explains why this issue was of such major concern to the national movement in the thirties, so serious in fact that the Mufti launched vigorous public campaigns against the notorious Palestinian *samâsira,* or land agents, and branded them as heretics (see Yasin 1975: 147–48; Porath 1977: 90–98). But by the eighties Palestinian participation in the marketing of the national patrimony was generally absent from popular memory, at least as relayed to me.

Local recollection of the land sale question was therefore broadly in accord with much standard Palestinian historiography, particularly the propagandistic variety. Abdallah Frangi, for instance, asserts that land transfers were the work of "two or three influential families from other Arab countries." By contrast, "Palestinians farmers with small plots . . . definitively refused to sell their lands" (1983: 60). And even though this statement might be read as implying that some Palestinian farmers with *big* plots did sell, Frangi never identifies them. But he does specify the non-Palestinians.[28] This strategy of not naming Palestinian names is generally employed even by Palestinian writers critical of wealthy families' involvement in land dealings. But perhaps the reluctance is understandable, given the tremendous stigma attached to such transactions. I first learned about Kenneth Stein's study of the land question in mandate Palestine (1984) from a Palestinian university administrator, who provided me a photocopy of the appendix to Stein's book, which lists prominent Palestinian notables who sold land to the Zionists. The educator claimed that if this list of names were translated into Arabic and circulated in the Occupied Territories, the whole Palestinian community would go up in flames, since so many still prominent local families had members who had been involved in such dealings.

Through the operation of displacement, therefore, a social memory was enshrined of land transactions as a non-Palestinian activity. More curious, perhaps, is that the actions of the big Palestinian landowners, whose sales to Zionists were more significant in terms of total acreage than those of the *fallâhîn,* were particularly obscured from local view. The owners of small plots, whom Frangi's nationalist account purports to represent, did not in practice always present a united front even when talking to an outsider. Interviewees attached the greatest blame to Syrian or Lebanese landowners but also sometimes displaced culpability for treacherous real estate deals onto *other* villages (or, less frequently, families). Rarely did they attribute such actions to their own villages or families. It should be added that the *thuwwâr* were probably the least likely persons to have sold out to Zionist land agents and that there was a great deal of regional variation in land transactions, meaning that some villages were hardly involved in such sales.[29] The point, however, is that old villagers in all likelihood were trying to protect their local community's reputation as well as rescue the good name of the nation, even to the extent of keeping actions they considered perfidious hidden from public view.

Plots (*al-Mu'âmarât*)

Other events that might cast the national past in an unfavorable light were sometimes explained by reference to British and Zionist plots. For instance, I heard one particular explanation of how land fell into Jewish hands at least four or five times. In the twenties, this story ran, the British authorities imported grain into Palestine from abroad in order to make local prices for grains fall. The *fallâhîn,* who were consequently forced to market their produce at low prices in order to compete with the cheap imports, became impoverished and fell into debt. Eventually they had little option but to sell their property to the Jews. Raconteurs rarely discussed how Palestinian merchants and usurers helped along and profited from such pilferings and dispossessions of Palestinian peasants. As mentioned in chapter 1, I had expected villagers to be more critical of landlords' and moneylenders' greediness, but both dominant nationalist discourse and popular memory seemed to minimize resentment toward the elite. The contribution of the Palestinian upper classes—usurers, traders in agricultural goods, and landowners—to the *fallâhîn's* worsening condition in the early 1930s had virtually no place in popular accounts. Local versions instead transposed full responsibility for peasant landlessness to the conspiracies orchestrated by outside forces.

Although 'Abd al-Rahîm al-Hâjj Muhammad was not a small farmer, his career was often given out as a paradigm of the rural economic crisis. According to Abû Shâhir, 'Abd al-Rahîm was one of the biggest grain traders (*tujjâr hubûb*) in Palestine, but was bankrupted by British policies of importing cheaper grain from abroad in order to favor Jewish interests.[30] 'Abd al-Rahîm's business failure, according to Abû Shâhir, was one of the key factors prompting him to get involved in the revolt. Faysal, son of 'Ârif 'Abd al-Râziq, told a similar story about his grandfather, a landowner and a trader in agricultural produce:

The English struck at him and those like him. They imposed a tax on water-melon and sesame. He sent a boatload of watermelons to Egypt, but it lost money due to the taxes. He was in debt to Nablus merchants, usurers. And to Jewish usurers—Arab Jews, the old Jews—in Jaffa. To make up for the loss, he bought a shipload of oil. The Shell Oil Company lowered the price of oil in Jaffa. He unloaded it at Haifa, they lowered the price of oil in Haifa. He sold it at a loss. As a result he got sick and died.

Faysal's explanation for the economic crisis that afflicted his family (and that was a factor prompting his own father to take up arms) was characteristic of mainstream nationalism in that it put the onus of guilt on imperialist (out-side) forces and it generally exonerated the Palestinian upper classes. In these accounts it was the local elites and not the ordinary peasants who bore the brunt of England's anti-Arab policies. Such tales maintained the purity of the national reputation.

Revolt veterans also recounted conspiracies hatched by the English and Zionists against the insurgency itself. These plot theories provided alternative rationalizations for untoward occurrences like disputes between rival band leaders, rebel assassinations of suspected traitors, and robberies by *thuwwâr* of villagers, actions that official Israeli historiography attributed wholesale to the revolt. According to Faysal 'Abd al-Râziq, both the Zionist and the Eng-lish intelligence services employed native collaborators to publish bogus bul-letins in the name of rebel commanders. A fake leaflet might claim, for instance, that 'Ârif 'Abd al-Râziq had assaulted some personality or it might slander 'Abd al-Râziq in the name of another commander. Such forged com-muniqués, according to Faysal, both created artificial disputes and exacerbat-ed preexisting differences.[31]

After another interviewee mentioned that disputes between *hamâ'il* used to occur in his village, Sonia asked him, "Were the English involved in such fights?" He replied: "The English like wickedness [*fasâd*], foreigners like wickedness. Doesn't Israel like it when the people destroy each other? It was the same with the English." Abû Shâhir observed similarly: "The English did two things: divide and rule. If they saw a village that they could intervene in and make evil [*fasâd*], they did it. But if the whole village met them with one hand, they couldn't." Although these men acknowledged that villagers or rebels bore a certain responsibility for quarreling with each other, they regarded the British as the primary instigators of local disputes.

Interviewees also used British conspiracies as a means of explaining away well-remembered assassinations of prominent Arabs, killings that Western and Israeli accounts usually attribute to the rebel movement and that Palestinian histories rarely mention. One famous case was that of Hasan Sidqî Dajânî. A prominent activist in the Nashâshîbî-led National Defence Party with close ties to Transjordan's Prince 'Abdallah, Dajânî broke with the Opposition after his release from three months' political detention in 1936 (*Palestine Post,* July 9, 1936; October 14, 1936). According to an official government bulletin, Dajânî's death occurred in the following manner: On October 12, 1938, Dajânî was invited to meet rebel commander 'Ârif 'Abd al-Râziq in a village in the Ramallah area. On his return to Jerusalem, his car was stopped by armed men and he was led away. His body was discovered the next morning (*Palestine Post,* October 16, 1938). Fakhrî Nashâshîbî, a leader of the Opposition, merely stated directly what the official British communiqué implied when he publicly accused 'Ârif 'Abd al-Râziq, whom he considered the Mufti's agent, of luring Dajânî to visit him so that he could be killed. Meanwhile no Arabic newspaper in Palestine dared lay blame for, much less even mention, Hasan Sidqî Dajânî's death.[32]

Ever since the incident, the official British government version blaming 'Abd al-Râziq and his boss the Mufti for Dajânî's death has circulated by word of mouth, although it is rarely discussed in "official" Palestinian accounts.[33] This account, however, is also frequently contested. One elderly member of the Husaynî clan I met claimed that the English planned the assassination of Hasan Sidqî Dajânî and then pinned responsibility for the crime on the Husaynî faction. This man alleged that the actual assassin was a Yemeni Jew, a servant of 'Ârif 'Abd al-Râziq who was known as Abû Muslim. Another interviewee, a relative of commander 'Abd al-Rahîm al-Hâjj Muhammad— 'Ârif 'Abd al-Râziq's rival—likewise alleged that Abû Muslim was responsible for the crime. He asserted that only years later did people finally discover Abû Muslim's true identity: that he was Jewish. What both these men insinuated but left unstated, since it was meant to be so patently obvious, was that since Abû Muslim was really Jewish but had disguised his origins, the Zionists or the British or both must have sent him to do the job. Some other old men without any personal or family stake in this issue equally blamed the assassination on the British; still others attributed it to the Opposition. (The case is discussed further in chapter 5.)

I heard a similar range of tales concerning the assassination of notables Muhammad and Ahmad Irshayd, members of a large landowning family from the Jinîn region who were well-known supporters of the Nashâshîbî-led Opposition. Their killing was sometimes attributed to rebel commander 'Abd al-Rahîm al-Hâjj Muhammad, and even those who denied this acknowledged that the claim was widely disseminated within the Palestinian community. (This assassination is likewise scarcely discussed in nationalist histories.) But many people contested this story, including—surprisingly—one old woman from the Irshayd clan itself. She asserted that the killing of her two relatives was actually carried out not by 'Abd al-Rahîm but by the British. Other persons told me Muhammad and Ahmad Irshayd met their demise after they were unjustly accused of supporting partition, and in the course of a popular mobilization (*faza'*), not on the orders of 'Abd al-Rahîm. Another old man blamed the Jarrârs (a prominent family from the Jinîn area) instead of 'Abd al-Rahîm.

In this case, interviewees in general made a great effort to divert blame from the well-regarded commander 'Abd al-Rahîm. In the case of Hasan Sidqî Dajânî's death, by contrast, there was less aversion to blaming 'Abd al-Râziq, a commander about whom old *thuwwâr* were considerably more ambivalent.[34] The effort to exculpate 'Abd al-Rahîm sometimes even involved the downplaying of hostility between the commander and the Irshayds. Former fighters usually acknowledged that Muhammad and Ahmad Irshayd's kinsman Farîd Irshayd *had* blamed 'Abd al-Rahîm for the murders, had organized "peace bands" to fight the revolt in the Jinîn area, and was instrumental in helping the British army locate and kill 'Abd al-Rahîm at his hiding place at Sânûr in March 1939, an event that was a great calamity for the revolt (see Porath 1977: 253, 257). Some people even claimed that Farîd Irshayd dispatched 'Abd al-Rahîm with his own hands. But despite the considerable feelings of antipathy toward the Irshayds among rebel circles in the Nablus-Jinîn-Tûlkarm region, there was a general unwillingness to lend credence to official non-Palestinian explanations for the hostility between this notable family and 'Abd al-Rahîm al-Hâjj Muhammad. The aim of the stories I heard was to point the finger elsewhere.

National Condensations

A coherent and exemplary national memory was constructed not just through the active forgetting of disturbing events and actions, but also through the celebration of admirable ones. Popular memory therefore conjoined with official history as well by throwing up heroic figures, particularly stories and legends clustered around persons whose actions and characters seemed to sum up everything positive and admirable about the Palestinian nation and people. (The creation of such a mythical figure, of course, necessarily involved its own forgettings—for instance, 'Abd al-Rahîm's possible role in the Irshayd killings.)

One of the most significant national-popular figures considered to stand for the revolt was Shaykh 'Izz al-Dîn al-Qassâm. It was remarkable how many people I met, young and old, from various regions, and of differing political affiliations, who responded in precisely the same way when I explained that I was doing research on the 1936–39 revolt. "Oh," they would reply, "you mean al-Qassâm." Part of the reason for Qassâm's importance can surely be attributed to the fact that he was a martyr for the cause and thus achieved heroic status quite rapidly. Tales of virtue and heroism also clustered around revolt commanders 'Abd al-Rahîm al-Hâjj Muhammad and (to a lesser degree) 'Abd al-Qâdir al-Husaynî, both of whom were martyrs ('Abd al-Qâdir in 1948). As the number of those who died for Palestine continued to mount, the martyr, or *shahîd,* acquired a central position in popular Palestinian political ideology (see Wood 1991). But it was not merely Qassâm's sacrifice of his life that made him so exemplary a figure, it was how he lived and struggled as well.

Qassâm's elevated stature was based in part on the fact that he is considered to have detonated the revolt. He was remembered for preaching jihad at the Istiqlâl mosque in Haifa, for organizing and training cells of guerrillas, and for going out in the hills in November 1935 to raise an armed insurrection. His example was seen as leading directly to the general strike and armed rebellion of 1936–39. Old men recalled as well that many Qassâmites (like Abû Durra, Abû Ibrâhîm al-Kabîr, Abû Khalid, Shaykh Farhân al-Sa'dî, and Shaykh 'Attîya) were leading rebel commanders.

Although Qassâm's martyrdom preceded the rebellion's outbreak by five months, his name was nonetheless closely associated with it. So strong was this identification that many Palestinians I met spontaneously placed Qassâm as a *qâ'id* during the 1936–39 insurrection itself. The names of others who *did* serve as rebel commanders, like 'Abd al-Rahîm al-Hâjj Muhammad, 'Ârif 'Abd al-Râziq, Yûsuf Abû Durra, Abû Ibrâhîm al-Kabîr, or even 'Abd al-Qâdir Husaynî, were less well recalled by the general population than the name of Qassâm, especially by the younger generation. One day, in fact, I got into a heated argument with two recent graduates of Birzeit University, who maintained that after Qassâm's death the revolt was left without significant military leaders and therefore went quickly downhill. Qassâm's blazing glory as a fighter seemed to eclipse the military prowess of the real rebel leaders. My friends were unfamiliar with the names of *any* of the commanders who actually led the *thuwwâr,* who unlike Qassâm did battle *successfully* (on occasion) with the British, who fought for over three years, and who were still well remembered by less-educated village graybeards.[35] But similarly, Qassâm was one of the few names of military leaders familiar to veterans in all the regions where we conducted interviews. Unlike the *quwwâd* named above, Qassâm's reputation was not just regional but national. Qassâm's name was fused so powerfully with the memory of the *thawra*, in fact, that some interviewees' recollections had become telescoped. One former fighter we spoke to reordered the chronology of events so that it accorded with the logic of Qassâm's importance. In his revision, Qassâm was the first armed fighter to appear in the hills *after* the strike began (in May 1936, five months after Qassâm's death). Such a rearrangement of the historical sequence was in no way illogical, given Qassâm's centrality in social memory and given the significance of his lieutenants during the armed rebellion. In this regard, popular memory tallies to some degree with official memory: Elias Sanbar observes that Arab and Palestinian sources have concentrated almost exclusively on the character and personality of Qassâm himself and have paid little attention to the movement he created or to the Qassâmites who served as revolt commanders (1988: 53).

Qassâm was also remembered as unique among national figures, particularly the urban leadership, in that he argued publicly for the necessity of armed struggle as the only way to defeat British rule. In this he opposed the moderate strategy favored and practiced by the national leaders: organizing peaceful demonstrations, submitting petitions, and friendly negotiations with the authorities—a strategy followed at least until the outbreak of the strike of April 1936. It is for this reason that Qassâm's memory in particular was revived when Palestinian guerrilla fighters made their appearance in the late sixties and armed struggle again moved to the top of the national agenda. In fact, before they finally decided to adopt the name Fath, the Palestinian militants who relaunched the armed struggle seriously considered naming themselves *al-Qassâmíyín* (the Qassâmites), because they regarded their own movement as a rupture in the historical process, much like Qassâm's (Sanbar 1988: 66–67). As the resistance movement reconstellated the national symbols of the past, it reanimated the memory of Qassâm and made him into the precursor of the *fidâ'íyín*. According to celebrated and infamous airplane hijacker Leila Khaled, "The Popular Front for the Liberation of Palestine begins where Qassam left off: his generation started the revolution: my generation intends to finish it" (1973: 23). Qassâm's example as a military figure had achieved such prominence that many Palestinians I met, particularly young men, regarded him as the *originator* of Palestinian armed struggle, as the virtual progenitor of the concept and the practice. They therefore forgot completely those Palestinians who picked up the gun prior to 1935.[36]

Qassâm was also remembered for his piety, which was often closely tied to national feeling in popular accounts. He was likewise venerated as someone whose whole life was devoted to the cause of Palestine. Qassâm sold his belongings, people said, to purchase a rifle, and encouraged his followers to do likewise. Interviewees also praised him for recruiting among the working class and lumpen proletariat of Haifa and among the peasantry. Qassâm was widely revered for having chosen to reside in the poor quarters of Haifa, with "the people," rather than opting, like other national leaders, for middle- or upper-class districts. One interviewee even claimed that Qassâm was descended from a saint. In short, Qassâm's reputation among the popular classes was virtually untarnished. This was partly because of his martyr status, but is also attributable perhaps to the fact that, unlike the other commander heroes of the revolt, Qassâm never held administrative control over a local area and population. Qassâm's unblemished aura was also a product of some distortion, a tendency to forget certain aspects of his career. For instance, both Palestinian historiography and popular memory remained silent about Qassâm's activities during World War I, when he requested a military assignment and was posted as a chaplain to the Ottoman garrison.[37] Such activities did not befit the ideal of the Arab nationalist hero.

Qassâm was remembered therefore as the preeminent symbol of the 1936 revolt. He "represented" it as the story of militancy, sacrifice, heroism, and piety. By choosing Qassâm to symbolize the insurrection, Palestinians presented a memory of the revolt as a pure and honorable national struggle. The telling of stories about Qassâm's noble character and selflessness also permitted them to "forget" any negative, dishonorable, or disintegrative aspects of the revolt. Palestinians' tendency to depict the revolt through such honorable condensations was heightened by the pressures of the ongoing national conflict. Yet, as we shall see in the next chapter, Qassâm was both a symbol of national purity and a figure over which there was considerable argument. Because he could appeal to virtually all Palestinians, Qassâm also lent himself to populist interpretations of the revolt (see Sanbar 1988).

4 / Memory as Resistance

We had heard wonderful and intriguing things about the militant spirit of
'Alî Husayn Baytam, a *thâ'ir* originally from Kuwaykât who had lived as an
"internal refugee" at Abû Snân in the Galilee since 1948. But when we
finally did meet 'Alî he was reluctant to be interviewed, and it took us at least
half an hour of heated discussion to convince him of our trustworthiness.
After we were finally allowed to turn on our tape recorders, the first thing
'Alî did was pull a sheet of paper out of the pocket of his *qumbâz* and hand
it to Sonia. Explaining that he was illiterate, 'Alî asked her to read its contents
into the microphones. She read:

> Massacre (*madbaha*) at Kuwaykât, April 1938. In it fell the martyr (*shahîd*) 'Alî
> Baytam, the martyr Sâlih Sanûnû, the martyr Muhammad Muhammad al-
> Husayn, the martyr 'Alî al-Safadî, the martyr 'Alî Husayn 'At'ût, the martyr
> Muhammad Khalîl 'At'ût, the martyr Muhammad Sâlih Iskandar, the martyr
> Ahmad al-'Abaday, the martyr from Sabalân, name unknown.

These were the names of men from Kuwaykât, 'Alî explained, who were
killed by the British in April 1938. He had kept the list with him for about
forty years, hoping to meet someone who would record the names in a book.

Later in our discussion 'Alî provided further details about the incident.
A rebel commander from the region, Shaykh Ahmad al-Tûba, had come to
the rebel group at Kuwaykât, which was led by 'Alî's brother Fayyâd Baytam.

—Shaykh Ahmad al-Tûba brought a mine to my brother Fayyâd and
told him, you should put this in the Yarka road [which ran through

107

Kuwaykât and Kafr Yâsîf]. Fayyâd told Shaykh Ahmad, I'm a son of this area (*balad*). I can't go and put a mine here, because they'd take revenge on this village. So Shaykh Ahmad al-Tûba and 'Alî Hammûda from Tarshîha and a group with him, they placed the mine. When they planted the mine, an English army car came by and the mine blew up the car and nine soldiers died. They went to Kafr Yâsîf and started burning up the village. Then someone came and told the soldiers, "It wasn't us who planted the mine, it was the people of Kuwaykât." They left Kafr Yâsîf and came to the people of Kuwaykât and made the massacre there.

—How did they make the massacre?

—As soon as the army entered the village they started to fire on one side and the other. The people were overwhelmed. There were people hiding in houses and they were unable to sleep. They went out to the street and were shot.

—Young men? Women weren't among them?

—Women, no. Just men. There was a group hiding in the mosque, they took them out of the mosque to the threshing floor and they killed them. There was also a group they shot from a distance. My father was riding on horseback, leaving the village, and they got him and beat him and threw him down. 'Alî al-Baytam. That's what happened.

The incident 'Alî Husayn Baytam recounted was one of many atrocity stories we heard, an example of the bloodlettings that are largely invisible from published Western and Israeli accounts of the revolt, which portray Palestinians as the terroristic aggressors and Jews as the victims. The British archives do contain some traces of such outrages, mainly because Palestinians lodged so many complaints. But the official response of the British authorities was usually a denial or a misrepresentation of the event, and the occasional cursory investigation. The British government never admitted publicly that its armed forces engaged in actions like the Kuwaykât massacre and never assumed responsibility for such inhumanities.[1]

The sketchy archival evidence suggests that the men on 'Alî Baytam's list were killed in an incident that occurred between February 14 and 17, 1939. The accounts inform us that a British army truck ran over a land mine placed on a new road under construction near the village of Kafr Yâsîf, killing one Royal Ulster rifleman and wounding two others. (During the revolt the British constructed such roads for security purposes throughout rural areas of Palestine.) According to a private communication by Eric F. Bishop, minister of the Anglican Church at Jerusalem, after the mine detonated British soldiers went on a rampage, torching between sixty-eight and seventy-two houses at Kafr Yâsîf, most of them Muslim-owned but a few belonging to Christians and Druze.[2] The British high commissioner's report on the incident, the usual snow job that blames the victim, stated that "about 50 houses were burnt down owing to the ignition of a quantity of gunpowder or similar material in a house which was being demolished."[3] When we visited Kafr Yâsîf on another occasion, we met a young man in his thirties who recalled village elders telling him that in February 1938, after a mine exploded and wounded several soldiers, the army retaliated by burning down seventy-two houses.[4]

This young man said nothing, however, about the massacre that transpired after the houses at Kafr Yâsîf were torched—an example of the regional limits of popular memory. According to the Reverend Bishop's account, when residents of Kuwaykât sighted the flames at Kafr Yâsîf, three kilometers away, "the men came down to see what it was all about. The machine guns were turned on them; and nine men were killed. I know nothing about the wounded, even if there were any." The British high commissioner's laconic report states that after the land mine went off, two villages were searched, and in one of them "eight Arabs were killed." Someone at the Colonial Office penned in the margins of the high commissioner's report: "This sounds as though the troops went wild and 'savaged' the villages—a not unknown procedure, one hears." A marginal note was the extent of official acknowledgment of British "savagery."

It was this massacre, typical of peasant experiences during the revolt, that 'Alî insisted that we preserve for posterity before he would discuss anything else. While the dominant Palestinian accounts typically report a few such incidents, these are not their central focus. In 'Alî Baytam's view, however, such iniquities demonstrated that the people (*al-sha'b*) were the true heroes of the revolt, its main supports as well as its main victims. Other old revolt veterans also emphasized that *al-sha'b*, as opposed to the elite leadership, were the real protagonists of revolt. But it was 'Alî Baytam, an active supporter of the Communist-led Democratic Front for Peace and Equality, who probably expressed the most consistently populist analysis of the revolt among all the former rebels we encountered. His adherence to Islam, he maintained, did not contradict his Communist sympathies. "By God," he told us, "I've made the *hâjj* [to Mecca—a sign of his piety], but I support the *jabha* [the Front— that is, the Communists]." While recounting his memories of the revolt, 'Alî constantly underscored that the people (*al-sha'b*) or the masses (*al-jamâhîr*) played the primary role in the rebellion, and at the same time he denigrated the actions of the rich, whom he held responsible for the revolt's failure.

Yet if 'Alî's interpretation of the revolt was the most uniformly populist and class-conscious, the coherence of its analysis had limits. It too was a construction, the result of exclusions and particular emphases. The incongruencies in his account were characteristic of that strange amalgam of commonsense memory. After Sonia finished reading the list of names, 'Alî added that one other person from Kuwaykât, whom he pointedly did not dignify with the nationalist appellation "martyr" (*shahîd*), had also died during the revolt: Ahmad Sâlih Sanûnû, who was blown up by a land mine on another date. 'Alî explained that Ahmad Sanûnû's name was not recorded on the paper he kept in his pocket because Ahmad's brother was "no good" (*'âtil*). 'Alî declined to elaborate further. But Sanûnû's absence from the list exemplifies how local disputes or quarrels could create gaps and inconsistencies in the memories of even the most progressive old *thuwwâr*.

Such discrepancies were characteristic of the commonsense memory that was resistant to official Palestinian national discourse. Dissidence to official views, as suggested in the previous chapter, was usually couched in the idiom of nationalism, the accepted framework within which to conduct political discussion. The oppositional memory that I examine in this chapter takes two basic forms. The first type involves interviewees' use of nationalist categories to make negative judgments about the elite, including both the Husaynî-led Arab Higher Committee and the Nashâshîbî-led Opposition, as well as the urban and educated classes in general. Such expressions of dissidence fractured official discourse from within by turning it against itself (Frow 1985: 206). This form of resistant discourse also frequently involved the articulation of nationalism and local peasant, clan, or village idioms, which worked together to produce populist inflections. It emphasized popular contributions to the revolt, as well.

The second type of oppositional memory examined here concerns those remembered *popular practices* that official historical discourse neither criticizes nor celebrates, but simply ignores. Authoritative historical accounts have relegated a whole range of peasant activities during the revolt to the margins, no doubt because they are regarded as "prepolitical" and insignificant. In general, the popular contributions to the movement are not discussed, acknowledged, or interpreted in standard nationalist accounts (see Guha 1982: 3). Official Palestinian accounts of the revolt concentrate on elite activity and define "politics" as the activities that take place within the realm of the state apparatuses. These standard histories of the mandate period, by and large, present a story of British governmental actions—the issuing of White Papers, convening of diplomatic negotiations, and sending out of missions of inquiries—and the Palestinian elite's responses—attending meetings with the high commissioner, issuing statements of protest, organizing political parties, meetings, demonstrations, armed revolt, and so on. Such a conception relegates unofficial and subaltern activities to tertiary importance and places them outside the purview of "history." The effect of the conventional nationalist histories' emphasis on elite antagonism toward the British regime, moreover, has been to render insignificant the notables' daily acts of collaboration with colonial rule (see Guha 1982: 2; Abou-el-Haj 1982: 187). Even leftist or progressive Palestinian histories have tended to neglect popular participation and initiatives, which they have regarded as inherently deficient because these were not rooted in "true" political consciousness, namely, some form of "modern" ideology such as socialism or communism.

But precisely because so many of these popular practices have been simply overlooked rather than actively maligned by official nationalist discourse, interviewees did not necessarily regard them as "oppositional." (By contrast, memories of active hostility to the upper classes, such as the rebel conquest of the towns in the fall of 1938, the *kūfīya* campaign, and peasant assaults on elite power [see chapter 1], seem to have been official targets of active forgetting. We heard only faint echoes of such events.) The memories examined here are "residual" (Williams 1977: 122–23) narratives that were relatively untouched, unrevised, and unincorporated by national ideological apparatuses. Due to the relative weakness of Palestinian national institutions, such memories were often neither colonized nor silenced by hegemonic discourse. Standing "outside" or "adjacent" to national histories, they were often recounted unselfconsciously. Having remained relatively unaltered by dominant discourses, they represented potential rather than overt counterdiscourses to the official nationalist views.

Nationalism as Critique

Elite actions during the revolt came in for considerable reprobation by villagers. If official national histories occasionally criticized the elite or sections of the leading classes, popular critiques had a much sharper edge. Whereas the written accounts stressed the elite's guiding role in the national movement and its antagonism toward British rule, a number of villagers remembered an upper class that was prone to collaboration or accommodation with the British (and sometimes even the Zionists). Some revolt veterans indicted not just the upper classes in general, but the official leaders (including middle-class radicals) of the national movement, as well. Mainstream nationalist discourse emphasized national unity under the leadership and the participa-

tion of all classes, but popular accounts occasionally recalled a revolt characterized by distinct differences, in terms of sacrifice and participation, between the subaltern and the dominant classes. While villagers acknowledged
the necessity for national unity, some saw themselves as having been more
committed to it than the elite.

A number of old *mujâhidîn* employed nationalist criteria to level criticism
at the leadership. The elite leaders who made themselves out to be nationalists, according to Abû Marwân of Dayr al-Ghusûn, were merely "superficial-
ly" so. Their dedication to national goals, he claimed, was just outward appearance, merely their "face." In reality, Abû Marwân asserted, the "national"
leaders were secretly involved in conspiring with the British. He named Hâjj
Amîn al-Husaynî and 'Abd al-Rahmân al-Hâjj Ibrâhîm, the mayor of
Tûlkarm, as well as prominent Oppositionist Sulaymân Tawqân, the mayor
of Nablus—that is, leaders from both the Husaynî *and* Nashâshîbî camps—
as being in cahoots with the British. Other interviewees made similar allegations about the national leadership's active assistance to the British efforts
to turn Palestine over to the Jews. Abû Râ'id, revolt veteran from Jerusalem,
was even harsher. The members of the Higher Arab Committee, he maintained, led double lives: by day they made political speeches attacking the
British and the Zionists, while at night they slept with Jewish girls. In Abû
Râ'id's version, the elite chiefs were not merely collaborators, they were
morally debased.

Abû Râ'id's statement verged on placing the leadership outside the national camp altogether. And although "oppositional," claims like these were not
necessarily elements within a coherent narrative of progressive politics. Rather,
such opinions were often stitched together with contradictory views, were
constituents of an odd composite. Abû Marwân, for instance, favored what
was considered in the mid-eighties a "rightist" political solution to the Palestine question—the return of King Hussein's dominion over the West Bank.
His paradoxical position therefore was to censure the Palestinian elite of the
thirties as collaborators (a "radical" memory) while backing King Hussein in
the present (a "conservative" orientation). Abû Ra'id, by contrast, was reso-
lutely anti-Hashemite and was even reputed to have had a hand in the assassination of King Hussein's grandfather, King 'Abdallah. Yet his memories were
so full of incredible anecdotes about the intrigues and betrayals of the leaders as to verge on the slanderous. Some would even consider his radical
attacks on national leaders antinationalist.

Memories of elite faults of the past also sometimes colored views of the
present. A worker in a small shoe workshop located near my house in Nablus

vehemently denounced Ahmad al-Shak'a, a prominent Oppositionist from the Nablus elite, as a "traitor" (*khâ'in*) during the revolt. Ahmad al-Shak'a had organized "peace bands" (*fasâ'il al-salâm*) late in the rebellion (winter 1938–39), which both "defended" villagers when they were attacked for withholding support for the revolt and aggressively kidnapped the rebels' supporters (see Porath 1977: 254–55). This recollection of Ahmad al-Shak'a as a traitor also tarnished this worker's view of Ahmad's son Bassâm al-Shak'a, the former mayor of Nablus who was still widely regarded in the mid-eighties as a major figure in the progressive wing of the national movement. Bassâm was revered by many because he had lost both his legs to a Jewish terror bombing and had been dismissed as mayor of Nablus for his forthright pro-PLO positions. Western sympathizers with the Palestinian cause who paid their respects to al-Shak'a in 1984–85 were invariably treated to a staged spectacle in mid-interview: a young girl entering the room to hand the esteemed former mayor a red rose. Despite Bassâm al-Shak'a's patriotic reputation, the shoe-maker saw Bassâm chiefly as the son of a treacherous father. Just up the road from the cobbler's workshop on Jabal Garzîm, one could find al-Shak'a's plush villa nested among the estates of the Tawqâns, 'Anâbtâwîs, Kamâls, and the rest of the Nablus upper crust, all affording spectacular views of the city. No doubt that fact, too, gave the underpaid and poorly housed worker's views about the former mayor's politics their particular flavor.

Another type of criticism we heard concerned Husaynî partisanship during the revolt. Persons making such judgments turned the prevailing notion—that disunity is contrary to the pursuit of national goals—against the leadership itself. Several men claimed that the Husaynîs simply pursued family interests during the revolt rather than the common good of the nation (in somewhat stronger terms than the suggestions of this sort we encountered in the previous chapter). In official accounts, the charge of self-interested, particularistic, or clannish behavior was frequently leveled at "backward" peasants. But subalterns occasionally expressed the view that the Husaynîs (and sometimes other notable families who played parts in the insurrection) exploited the revolt for their own political ends. The leadership was to blame, they said, for at least *some* of the *fasâd*—the bloodshed or "wickedness"—that beset the movement, and for using the cover of the national struggle to eliminate local political rivals. A few men claimed that the Husaynîs ordered the assassination of their political enemies under the pretext that they were traitors or spies—not because the latter had betrayed the revolt but because eliminating them increased Husaynî power. According to Faysal 'Abd al-Râziq, son of the well-known commander 'Ârif 'Abd al-Râziq, it was *the*

Mufti who ordered the killing of Hasan Sidqî Dajânî, not 'Ârif 'Abd al-Râziq, as was widely believed (see chapter 3). 'Abd al-Râziq, according to this version, was not the agent of the Mufti but his innocent victim, since he was forced to carry the blame for a murder he did not carry out. (And to preserve national unity, 'Abd al-Râziq never publicly blamed the Mufti.) According to Faysal, the Mufti was also responsible for authorizing the assassination of notables Muhammad and Ahmad Irshayd, for whose deaths the commander 'Abd al-Rahîm al-Hâjj Muhammad, 'Ârif's rival, was often held to be responsible. Both killings, according to Faysal, were connected with long-standing Husaynî family disputes with the Dajânîs and the Irshayds.

Old *mujâhidîn* likewise took the upper classes to task for their inadequate militancy. "The leadership should die before the people, not go into exile," one man complained, in reference to the fact that so many of the elite and the chiefs fled to Lebanon or Syria during the revolt, and did so again in 1948, both times leaving the mass of the population unprotected. Villagers also claimed that "the people" sacrificed in every way for the rebellion while the leaders did not. According to Abû Kamâl of Kafr Qûd (Jinîn district), "People paid to the revolt, and they were willing to pay. Willing! As for the *zu'amâ'* [chiefs], they never behaved properly [*mâshîya mazbût*]." (By *zu'amâ'*, Abû Kamâl was referring specifically to the shaykhs of big families in the Jinîn district like the 'Abd al-Hâdîs.) The rich, many elderly *fallâhîn* claimed, simply did not suffer on behalf of the nation like the people (*al-sha'b*) did. No one ever recalled a member of the elite perishing in a massacre like the one at Kuwaykât. According to many old peasants, the leaders, who asked that the entire populace participate in the insurrection, did not shoulder their proper share of national responsibilities.

Negative Class Consciousness

Dissident opinion also took the form of "negative" class consciousness, which Gramsci called "subversivism" (see Guha 1983: 18–76; Gramsci 1971: 272–73), some instances of which we have already encountered above. This kind of class consciousness was "negative" insofar as it was the class being criticized (the elite) that defined the notion of class, rather than the subalterns directly articulating their own class interests. Negative consciousness involved the reversal of dominant views, not the articulation of a positive lower-class program. It represented a form of consciousness, moreover, that was circumscribed by regionalism and that often overlapped or combined in rather inconsistent ways with religious, kinship-based, or nationalist discourse.

The most common type of negative class consciousness I encountered was one that identified "the rich" (*al-aghniyâ'*) as lacking in nationalism because they failed to contribute financially to the revolt to the same degree as the poor and the *fallâhîn*. Some interlocutors, like Muhammad Kîlânî, went so far as to call the rich Palestinians as a whole "traitors" (*khuwwân*) and to blame their treasonous actions (organizing "peace bands," cooperation with the British) for breaking the revolt. 'Alî Baytam blamed both the defeat of 1936–39 and the disaster of 1948 primarily on the diffidence of the rich and the educated Palestinian classes. For many other persons, however, "rich" was a category that applied specifically to members of the Nashâshîbî-led Opposition and not to elites aligned with the Husaynîs and the official leaders of the revolt. In these cases a "class" discourse was filtered through support for the Husaynî-led wing of the national movement. Although the Husaynîs and the other national leaders affiliated with them came chiefly from the notable and middle classes, they were nonetheless regarded in such instances as representing "the people."

A few former rebels asserted that it was specifically the national *movement's* leaders who were guilty of corruption. Abû Fâris from Kafr Yâsîf (Acre district) claimed that the middle-class leaders of the revolt based in Damascus—the "Central Committee of the Jihad," which included 'Izzat Darwaza, Jamâl al-Husaynî, and Akram Zu'aytir—"ate," that is, consumed for their own benefit, the donations they received from fundraising efforts on behalf of the rebellion instead of using the funds to purchase weapons and supplies for the fighters in the field. Certain persons in the leadership, he asserted without naming names, took advantage of the revolt to enrich themselves. Claims of this sort were not limited to men like Abû Fâris, whose testimony might be considered suspect since he was a rebel *qâ'id* who later went over to the British side (see chapter 5). Leftists like Muhammad Shraydî of Umm al-Fahm, a veteran of the 1936–39 insurgency who joined the Communist Party in the early 1940s and was still a party militant when we met him in 1985, made similar accusations. According to Shraydî, the national leaders based in Damascus sent little financial assistance to rebels in the field, drew large salaries for themselves, lived in plush homes, and drove automobiles (a luxury item in the thirties). (Shraydî did not name names, either.) When the revolt ended in the summer of 1939, the French authorities incarcerated the exiled Palestinian leaders, as well as average fighters who, like Shraydî, had managed to escape to Syria. He was one of about four hundred men, including elites and peasants, who were held in a Damascus prison. The leaders were able to pay for special treatment in prison, like decent food and clothing, whereas the common *mujâhidîn* enjoyed no such benefits because they possessed few resources. But the fighters were well aware of the sources of their superiors' funds. One day they got so exasperated with their chiefs' aristocratic airs and privileges that they beat them all up.

Critical anecdotes of that kind had no *inherently* or necessarily "progressive" quality, and they could equally be recounted by a Communist like Muhammad Shraydî or a "traitor" like Abû Fâris. And part of the reason why so *few* former rebels voiced such criticism was undoubtedly because their enemies had exploited internal disputes in the past. The British disseminated similar—although highly exaggerated—allegations of rebel corruption in 1939 as part of a disinformation campaign aimed at discrediting the revolt within the global Arab and Muslim community. Between September 20 and December 16, 1938, according to information obtained by the Colonial Office, the Palestine Defence Committee in Damascus had collected £3,346 in donations from Muslim or Arab communities in countries like India, Guatemala, Argentina, the United States, Honduras, Brazil, Singapore, Mexico, Martinique, Canada, Chile, South Africa, and El Salvador. British colonial officials worked diligently to ensure that the flow of monies, as well as the funds of sympathy, were choked off. The mandate government released a statement (patently forged although not entirely false) by "anonymous" dissident rebel commanders who complained about the leaders' corruption,[5] and it encouraged local newspapers to publish similar allegations by Opposition figures like Fakhrî Nashâshîbî. Articles claiming that the revolt leaders were embezzling moneys raised abroad were also planted in pliant newspapers in Damascus and Beirut. British diplomats throughout the world made certain that copies of these articles got into the hands of all the Syrian Arab societies abroad that had contributed to the Palestine Defence Fund. By May 1939, these British machinations had caused the flow of contributions from overseas to completely dry up.[6]

The "truth" of allegations of corruption therefore depended in part upon who was making them. Criticism of the leadership based on class criteria can and did provide grist for the enemy's propaganda mill. The memory of the British distributing black propaganda during the revolt in order to discredit the rebel command may have persuaded other interviewees to be wary of giving support to such claims fifty years later, even if they did believe in their veracity. So even critiques of upper-class treachery within a "progressive" discourse were not often voiced, since charges of corruption could still be quickly turned against the reputation of the national movement, past and present.

Condensations of the Popular

Oppositional memories of revolt also took the form of memorializing local or popular heroes. Even persons who looked back on the revolt with skepticism often remembered with favor local rebel figures whom official history tended to overlook or forget. Or, more commonly, they recalled a hero with a national reputation in a populist light. Perhaps the remembered national hero who was most often given a popular inflection was Shaykh 'Izz al-Dîn al-Qassâm. Qassâm is of interest precisely because his stature is such that mainstream nationalism asserts an exclusive claim to his image. I am classifying these particular views of Qassâm as resistant to dominant nationalism because they represent a subaltern insistence that Qassâm belonged to them and not to the elite. Several informants, for instance, stressed that Qassâm was a man of the poor, of the simple classes. Although he was a man of advanced religious learning—he had studied at al-Azhar—elderly villagers recalled that Qassâm chose to reside among the impoverished, the lumpen proletariat, the "scuffling petit bourgeoisie," and the working classes of Haifa.[7] Qassâm's follower 'Arabî Badawî, an itinerant laborer from the village of Qabalân, asserted that the shaykh was "one of our class" and that he used to donate all his money to the poor. Villagers stressed that Qassâm recruited his followers from the laborers of the shantytowns of Haifa and from the peasantry of surrounding regions.[8] Qassâm's men, Muhammad Kîlânî of Ya'bad insisted, "were not educated or philosophers." Many elderly peasants remembered seeing Qassâm in their villages during the twenties and thirties, doing his public rounds as a marriage registrar (*ma'dûn*) and secretly recruiting *mujâhidîn* at night. What they regarded as truly remarkable and unique about Qassâm was that he was a national leader and religious scholar who affiliated with villagers and urban workers on an egalitarian basis. They did not recall seeing other national or religious figures, who were all too conscious of status hierarchies, moving around the villages, rubbing shoulders with *fallâhîn*. Other villagers recalled attending Friday prayers at al-Istiqlâl Mosque in Haifa in order to hear Qassâm preach about the need for the common man to struggle against British rule. 'Arabî Badawî, a member of Qassâm's organization, asserted that the group was democratic. Its decisions were taken collectively, in the course of discussions, he said, and not made by Qassâm alone.[9] Villagers stressed that Qassâm and his followers, despite their poverty, purchased their weapons with their own money, often at great personal sacrifice. Informants additionally made much of he religious piety and forthright behavior of Qassâm and his followers, and recalled Qassâm's emphasis on jihad—involving *both* political combat and the moral struggle to improve and control one's character (*jihâd al-nafs*)—as the most important feature in Islam (see Schleiffer 1979: 69–71).

In these accounts Qassâm figures as a kind of metonym of the national leader who was a man of the people. In marked contrast to other leaders drawn from the urban elite, Qassâm was seen as a truly national-popular figure who fraternized, even merged, with the subaltern classes. Peasants remembered Qassâm as a member of their class, a man who was distinguished only by his character, not by his birth or wealth. Unlike the elite, he did not speak down to them in an official hierarchical language, but he employed a religious and democratic idiom that was on their level. He called the people to a national-popular struggle in which they would be equal participants and for which he would sacrifice as much as they. Popular stories that still circulated about Qassâm therefore were implicitly and sometimes overtly critical of the urban elite, emphasizing Qassâm's difference from the latter—his relentless combativeness, his common touch, and his selfless sacrifice for the sake of nation.

The rebel commander Yûsuf Abû Durra, a follower of Qassâm who assumed command of the Jinîn-Haifa region in spring 1938 after the death of the commander Shaykh 'Attîya 'Awad, represented a much more contested and contradictory condensation of the popular than Qassâm. Both hostile official accounts and many villagers presented Abû Durra as excessively, sometimes stupidly, brutal. In particular, some villagers condemned his predilection for executing *makhâtîr* and others accused of being traitors. In many local versions, Abû Durra served as the model of a brutish rebel *qâ'id* who, out of ignorance or cruelty, executed men who were falsely charged with betraying the revolt. An example of the type of excess for which Abû Durra in particular was recalled was recounted by the commander Rabbâh al-'Awad from al-Ghâbisîya (Galilee). An educated Palestinian man, according to Rabbâh, was executed as a traitor by fighters in his band (but not on his orders) simply because they had heard him conversing with a British policeman in English. Although al-'Awad meant to fault rebel brutishness, his anecdote suggests that there was a great cultural distance between the peasants and the imperial forces, a gap that made them regard the most rudimentary interaction with English culture as a form of collaboration.

Given such criticisms, it is possible to regard the views of those old *mujâhidîn* who *did* endorse harsh methods—like those practiced by *quwwâd* such as Abû Durra—as a form of oppositional memory. For instance, Fawzî Jaradât, a farmer from Yûsuf Abû Durra's village of Sîlat al-Hârithîya and a critic of many of Abû Durra's actions, told us that people used to say about Abû Durra what the Quraysh of Mecca had said in admonition of the prophet Muhammad—that it was the *ardalîn,* the despicable and the lowly, who followed him.[10] In the view of several grizzled veterans of the revolt, traitors had to be dealt with severely because they were the enemies of the people who threatened the national movement's survival. Village *makhâtîr,* who often represented the interests of local elites and were tied to land-owning families, were in many instances the most likely elements in a village to collaborate with the British. Salîm Mas'ad of Sîlat al-Hârithîya estimated that Abû Durra executed eighty-five *makhâtîr* in the course of the rebellion. This is no doubt a fantastic figure, and probably another man's estimate that Abû Durra dispatched twenty village headmen is closer to the truth. But despite the fact that he believed Abû Durra had executed so many village chiefs, Salîm Mas'ad still expressed support for his actions, explaining that *makhâtîr* used to pass information to the British. The police chief at Jinîn (Mr. Moffatt), Mas'ad elaborated, used to call village *makhâtîr* in for a chat each week, an action that put them under suspicion. (Mas'ad did not mention that village headmen in many parts of Palestine were involved in the detested activity of facilitating land sales to Jewish buyers, actions that frequently entailed bribery, coercion, and forged documents. Nor did he note that during the revolt the army made the *makhâtîr* responsible for keeping and updating a register of all male inhabitants between seventeen and fifty years old in certain "bad villages." Or that during the army's May–July 1938 campaign of village occupation in the "Triangle of Terror" [Nablus-Tûl-karm-Jinîn] and the Galilee, village headmen and elders were charged with seeing that all male members were present in the village during curfew hours and with reporting all absences. In "good" villages, consultations were held with *makhâtîr* and elders regarding local security, for example, issuing licenses for firearms.)[11] Mas'ad stated in addition that many executions of accused traitors were in fact the work of local Arab notables or *shakhsîyât* ("personal-ities"), who used to allege that a particular person with whom they had a personal grudge was a traitor, arrange to have him killed, and then ensure that blame for the slaughter was pinned on Abû Durra.

According to Ranajit Guha, the kind of severity Abû Durra employed to deal with reluctant villagers and traitors is typical of peasant rebellions. Coercion was often necessary to generate rebel authority, writes Guha, because of the "want of uniformity" of peasant consciousness. "Informers, they ought to be hanged. It is no sin to kill them": according to Guha, this is how peasant insurgents, from early-modern England to colonial India, have felt about informers, spies, and other active collaborators (1983: 215). So despite what critics of the 1936–39 partisans claim, the Palestinian *fallâhîn* were probably no more guilty of excessive bloodletting than insurgents in other peasant movements. Yet no doubt because of all the negative propaganda, it was rather unusual for old *thuwwâr* to endorse the roughness their movement employed in the past. Most tended retrospectively to remember critically or cautiously executions like those allegedly carried out by Abû Durra, perhaps because it was difficult to recall the atmosphere of this unusual and ruptural moment, when everyday acts of collaboration were no longer tolerated.

Western sources and even some Palestinian accounts also make the claim that rebels employed excessive force in their treatment of the urban elite. The *thuwwâr's* demands for payment of contributions from the upper classes, their imprisonment of those failing to pay, and their cutting down of orchards owned by suspected elite collaborators, are actions usually represented in these hostile sources as acts of simple thievery, revenge, and brutality.[12] Nationalist versions meanwhile have often simply overlooked this facet of the insurrection, which forced many hundreds of upper- and middle-class Palestinians to flee to Syria or Lebanon. After the elite was restored to a position of influence, those aspects of the revolt that had to do with class hatred were forgotten or recoded as criminality or backwardness. Yet there was still some subaltern contestation of such an analysis. Many written accounts and even some oral narratives we heard cited ʿÂrif ʿAbd al-Râziq as the prototype of a commander who extorted excessive sums from the elite. But Abû ʿAzma, the son of a *thâʾir* who served as ʿAbd al-Râziq's lieutenant in Jaffa, defended the heavy-handed methods ʿAbd al-Râziq and his father employed to raise funds. Their harsh means were fully justified, Abû ʿAzma said, because they were collecting money mainly from rich merchants and capitalists. Again, the fact that rebels treated the elite unkindly is not surprising, for an important part of the struggle—albeit disguised by its self-declared status as a nationalist movement—consisted of peasants' efforts to seize or violate the symbols of prestige employed by the elite (see Guha 1983: 75). The rebel order for city people to put on the *kûfîya,* of course, was one such a symbolic inversion. According to Abû ʿAzma, after the rebels issued this edict Abû Shaʿbân, one of ʿAbd al-Râziq's lieutenants, urged, "We should *kill* anyone wearing a *tarbûsh.*" But memories of such generalized class hatred were generally hidden or forgotten in the interest of presenting a unified and unsullied depiction of the revolt.

According to Abû Saysân, a commander from Qabâtîya, the *thuwwâr* did not "honor" or "respect" rich urban families living in the cities, the big land-owners and merchants like the Tawqâns or the Masrîs of Nablus. These notable clans, he insisted, were agents (*ʿumalâʾ*) of the English who never contributed any money to the revolt. The elite families named by Abû Saysân were prominent members of the Nashâshîbî Opposition. Sulaymân Tawqân, mayor of Nablus, supported the rebellion in 1936, but was widely considered a traitor after he came out in favor of partition in 1937. Al-Hâjj Tâhir al-Masrî was known as a close associate of Sulaymân Tawqân and as the ally of Ahmad al-Shak'a, the organizer of anti-*thuwwâr* "peace bands" in early 1939 (Porath 1977: 187, 229, 255). In January 1939, a British report states, the security situation in Nablus was sufficiently calm to permit Sulaymân Tawqân to return home from exile. "It is understood," the report continues, "that he intends to demonstrate his independence by requiring the townsmen to wear the tarbush in place of the peasants' kaffiye and 'agal."[13] Is it any wonder that rebels responded to this attempt to restore the elite's trappings of prestige by uprooting orange and olive groves belonging to Ahmad al-Shak'a and Tâhir al-Masrî in February 1939?[14]

The apparent class consciousness implied by Abû Saysân's statement that "the rich" were not "respected," however, had its own particular limits. For he then went on to add that the 'Abd al-Hâdîs, a notable landowning clan that was based in the nearby village of 'Arrâba but that had largely removed its interests to the city in the 1930s,[15] were "good landowners." It eventually emerged that Abû Saysân's family had belonged to a political alliance (*hilf*) whose ranks embraced the 'Abd al-Hâdîs. His expression of disdain for the urban rich was qualified by his admission of "traditional" loyalties to one particular rich family. This praise for the 'Abd al-Hâdîs was especially curious given the fact that Fakhrî 'Abd al-Hâdî, a prominent rebel commander during 1936, later became a notorious turncoat. Fakhrî was put on the payroll of the British consul in Damascus, became a "peace band" commander, carried out many attacks against the rebels in 1938–39 from his stronghold at 'Arrâba, and collaborated with Sulaymân Tawqân in these counterrevolutionary efforts (see Porath 1977: 252–54).

Popular Initiatives

A more common form of "oppositional memory" than the expression of class antagonism was the description of certain rebel practices that suggested the degree to which the revolt was a product of local initiatives and autonomous actions rooted in peasant customs. Fifty years later, the memories of these actions, unlike the attacks on elites, were not completely marginalized or denigrated by official discourse. Neither had such peasant practices been embraced as exemplars of historical oppositionality by progressive Palestinian political groups. Such traditions had not been substantially reshaped or recast. They had simply been ignored, left relatively untouched by both official and leftist nationalist discourse.

Organization of the Armed Revolt

The armed bands that appeared in the countryside in May 1936, the second month of the general strike, were remembered largely as the products of spontaneous village organization. There was a great deal of regional variation in this regard, however. According to Ibrâhîm Hanna, the rebellion began in al-Bi'na (near Acre) after a gang of unknown insurgents from elsewhere in the Galilee came to the village and demanded that it contribute money for weapons. While Ibrâhîm Hanna considered this rebel action coercive, he claimed it did not alienate the villagers. Guha's analysis suggests that such an action might in fact have increased the partisans' prestige among the more timid elements of the peasantry (1983: 197). Indeed Ibrâhîm Hanna claimed that the action spurred him to organize the collection of funds from community members in order to purchase weapons for local use. The men who received the rifles—five Muslims and four Christians—subsequently chose Ibrâhîm Hanna as their *qâ'id*. When he objected that it was inappropriate for a Christian to be commander in a village whose population was predominantly Muslim, they replied, "We don't want Islam or Christianity. You're in charge." So by this account, the villagers of al-Bi'na organized their own rebel band (*fasîl*) and chose their own commander (*qâ'id fasîl*). Ibrâhîm Hanna said that the next step he took was to inform the higher-up rebel leadership about the action the al-Bi'na villagers had undertaken, and that regional commander Abû Ibrâhîm al-Kabîr then put him in charge of the local region, an area including a number of nearby villages.

Revolt veterans from other areas also related that the men in their hamlets set up bands spontaneously, in response to the general atmosphere of insurgency, rather than at the suggestion or order of rebel commanders. (Both archival and secondary sources suggest that during the first few months of the rebellion there was no real centralized rebel command, although some regional commanders were organizing forces and actions in their own areas.) Such impromptu mobilization occurred in the city of Jerusalem, as well, according to two interviewees reportedly active there. Small groups of young urbanites, fed up with the timorous attitude of the elite leadership and galvanized by Qassâm's courageous example, formed secret "fighting cells" of four to five members. Only later did these groups affiliate with larger rebel organizations.[16] (By contrast, one would get the impression from Muhsin's hagiographic biography [1986] of 'Abd al-Qadir al-Husaynî that all military activity in the Jerusalem area was the exclusive result of 'Abd al-Qadir's efforts.) In the town of Tûlkarm and the nearby village of al-Tayyiba, according to Faysal 'Abd al-Râziq, it was the local Boy Scouts troop that set up autonomous fighting groups.[17] The early organization of the revolt, therefore, was frequently recalled as a highly variable process that involved considerable local initiative.

In other places, the insurrection got under way when rebel *quwwâd* appeared in villages to press men into service. Rabbâh al-'Awad, a commander in the western Galilee, asserted that after he was appointed a regional commander, he visited every village in the area under his command and informed residents that he wanted each family (this was not an area of *hamâ'il*) to furnish his band with two fighting men armed with rifles. At the village of Sha'b, according to Abû Rajâ, the regional rebel leadership came to the *lajna al-ikhtiyâríya* (council of elders) and ordered it to decide how many fighters to provide for the revolt, to assess the necessary contributions from village residents, and to purchase weapons. Abû Shâhir of Dannâba reported that during the winter of 1937, 'Abd al-Rahîm al-Hâjj Muhammad gathered the elders of all the villages in his area and demanded that each community supply him with one armed man. In this way he was able to recruit a rebel force of fifty fighters.

Such rebel acts of drafting men into service did not seem to have estranged village communities. The use of pressing, according to Guha, has been almost universally necessary during peasant insurrections in order to enforce the solidarity of a heterogeneous peasantry and to raise the standing of the insurgency in the eyes of less militant members (1983: 195–98). Former *mujâhidîn* who reported being drafted in such a fashion usually maintained that they were willing and eager to fight for the nation. Fighters were frequently enlisted, therefore, *through* the agency of the family, the *hamûla*, or the village. A *thâ'ir* who was fighting in the revolt was often considered the responsibility of the entire extended family. It was his family or clan that raised the money necessary to purchase a fighter's rifle, ammunition, and supplies and that determined which of its young men would fight and which ones would stay at home to till the soil. But other men reported that the decision to fight was a personal one and that they bought their weapons themselves. 'Alî Baytam, for one, told of how he defied the wishes of his father, who felt that since he had already furnished one son—the village commander Fayyâd—to the rebel movement, the family had made a sufficient sacrifice for the sake of the *watan*. 'Alî's father refused to supply the funds he needed in order to enlist, so 'Alî borrowed the money from a

usurer and turned it over to the rebel *qâ'id* Abû Khadr, who supplied him
with a rifle. Other men raised their pikes in rebellion as much to represent
their communities and kin as to defend the honor of the nation. Thus Abû
Rajâ explained that he signed on as a *thâ'ir* "as a son of Sha'b and a son of a
big family." Territoriality and the threat to the land therefore were not simply perceived in terms of the nation. Defense of territory was also manifested in terms of the intersection of two referents—membership in a common
habitat and membership in a lineage (Guha 1983: 279). If Palestinian nationalism had not connected with such local feelings and institutions, the revolt
would not have developed its popular base.

Abû Shadîd of 'Aqqâba (Jinîn district) argued that while local initiative
was crucial for *launching* the revolt, village-based insurgent organizations became much more effective once they were coordinated within the broader
rebel movement. According to him, peasants of 'Aqqâba and the neighboring communities organized groups to attack the British military in the spring
of 1936. But they did not establish permanent bands (*fasâ'il*) or coordinate
their military actions with other communities on a regional basis. The usual
mode of operation was simply for groups of men to come together on an ad
hoc basis and fire on passing British patrols. Only after Fawzî Qâwûqjî took
over command of the revolt in August 1936 did more formal military organization come to the villages. In the 'Aqqâba area, according to Abû Shadîd,
Qâwûqjî's lieutenant Abû Khâlid (a Qassâmite) set up a framework of band
commanders in each village, under the leadership of regional commanders.
In addition, a few men joined the permanent bands that were stationed in the
hills with the regional commanders, but the majority of fighters belonged to
bands based in the villages. These men stayed at home and farmed by day,
only going out to launch raids at night or when called into battle by the
regional *qâ'id*. By this account the beginning of the insurgency was characterized by considerable local initiative, but later the national movement provided it with a more organized structure. Since none of the men I interviewed were regional *quwwâd fasâ'il* of high rank, they did not have a very
precise idea of how the larger rebel framework was organized from on top.
Nonetheless, even though the middle- and upper-class national leadership
controlled the purse strings of the rebel movement, the rebel command
emerged from a popular base. Even the highest-ranking rebel chiefs—with
the exception of 'Abd al-Qâdir al-Husaynî—were men of the villages or the
shantytowns, and the Qassâmites were particularly important among them
(see Porath 1977: 260–64).

Military Engagements

Interviewees remembered the majority of military engagements as being the result of indigenous initiative. Typically, they said, a village *qâ'id* decided on his own or together with two or three other *quwwâd* from nearby hamlets to plan an attack on a British army patrol that would be moving along a main road. "The rebels got together, the English went by on the road, we'd start shooting. That's what the battles were like," was how Abû Fâris of the western Galilee characterized most *mujâhidîn* military encounters. Sâlih 'Ayyûsh, the *qâ'id fasîl* of Sakhnîn (western Galilee) asserted that he never received military orders or instructions from higher-ups.[18] He would plan a raid, then contact other local bands and ask them to join him in carrying it out. Ibrâhîm Hanna described the activities of his band at al-Bi'na similarly: "We didn't go to [the regional commanders] when we wanted to make operations. The operations came from our heads."

But several men, who described the rebels' behavior in such sorties as courageous, were equally critical of what they considered an absence of coordination between the various rebel groups. The military situation, according to Abû Hanna, another old veteran from al-Bi'na, was chaos (*fawda*). The revolt had no organization (*tanzîm*), Abû Fâris complained for his part. These sorts of negative judgments often stemmed from an unfavorable comparison the interviewee made between the rebels of 1936–39 and the guerrillas of the PLO. The latter, they asserted, possessed a much better infrastructure, more advanced weaponry, and superior coordination. But *"fawda"* was not the only judgment I heard. Many fighters reported participating in some military operations that involved a number of bands and were coordinated by regional commanders. Ibrâhîm Hanna, who stated that most of the action he saw involved only local fighters, also described one major battle at Safad, planned by the rebel command, in which he and his band were involved. So although the majority of engagements were remembered as being local, some battles also were recalled as being more carefully planned and regionally organized.

While some revolt veterans who were influenced by more recent discourses of modernization stressed the drawbacks inherent in the absence of overall coordination, others affirmed the positive advantages of a rebellion that was local and decentralized. 'Abd al-Fattâh al-Mizra'âwî, regional *qâ'id* at al-Mizra' al-Sharqîya (north of Ramallah), avowed that he was able to use his and his men's knowledge of the local environment to make his rebel force evaporate after doing battle with the British. He would keep a tiny group of four or five men with him permanently in the maquis and order the rest of his fighters back to their homes. So when the British army mounted a search-and-encirclement operation (known locally as a *tawq*) in the area of an encounter, hoping to capture the large rebel force that had earlier pinned them down for hours, they frequently discovered only peasants at work. British archives bear out al-Mizra'âwî's claim: the colonial troops, a report from 1939 states, "were continually finding themselves shot up on all sides only to discover on advancing . . . that the hostile area was apparently populated by unarmed peaceful shepherds and agriculturalists" who had already cached their weapons.[19] The "heavily booted British soldiers are no match in the hills for lightly clad natives who, at any moment, can drop their weapons pro tem and become peaceful ploughmen and goatherds until the military have passed by," observed another entry from 1936.[20] The stable force that stayed with al-Mizra'âwî was so small that it was able either to slip through the British lines undetected or else to hide out in caves whose locations were unknown to the military.[21] Rabbâh al-'Awad claimed to employ a similar style of organization, keeping no more than ten full-time fighters with him at all times, but possessing the capacity to mobilize two to three hundred men whenever he issued a battle order.

Another of Shaykh Rabbâh al-'Awad's anecdotes illustrates how rebels considered grassroots organization to be a military advantage. One day a leading regional commander from Balad al-Shaykh (outside Haifa) named Shaykh 'Attîya 'Awad reportedly came to him, with the intention of setting himself up as head of Rabbâh's band.[22] Rabbâh replied that this was impossible, because as a stranger to the area Shaykh 'Attîya would be unable to survive in the course of the struggle. We know more than you, he told the shaykh. If there was a *tawq* (a British encirclement operation), you wouldn't know how to escape. Our relatives know us here, so we can take refuge with them. When there is a battle, we know the terrain, we know the trees and the rocks, the trails and the caves. So Rabbâh refused to let Shaykh 'Attîya, an "outsider," take over command, because he understood that such local knowledges were essential to the rebels' ability to survive. It was this familiarity with the lay of the land that allowed the peasant insurgents to escape, time after time, through the nets of the army's search-and-encirclement campaigns—to the repeated consternation of the British High Command. "The hill country in Palestine is well suited to guerrilla warfare," reported Air Vice Marshall Peirse in 1936. "There is plenty of natural cover. The hills are steep and boulder-strewn and infantry have difficulty in covering the ground quickly. The enemy on the other hand is very mobile and knows the country perfectly."[23] A *qâ'id fasîl*'s mastery of the regional terrain and his men's personal ties to surrounding villages were also important sources of a band's local autonomy from the higher rebel command.

Rebel military engagements, in these recollections, were a matter of raids, of harrying the enemy and keeping him off balance, of maintaining effective control of the maquis, rather than of large pitched battles. In such tactics lay the strength of the guerrilla campaigns. The colonialists were forced to commit a large number of forces, but were unable to truly dominate the countryside until the summer of 1939. In certain respects, the decentralization of the Palestinian rebel forces resembled that of the Vietnamese guerrillas. As Herman Rapaport argues, the Vietnam War was characterized by an absence of battles and by constant guerrilla harassment. Vietnamese forces were "molecularized," forcing the United States to spread its forces thin. Those areas that the U.S. forces "coded" by day, the National Liberation Front (NLF) guerrillas "decoded" by night (1984: 137–39). Decentralization, following this argument, was key to whatever successes the Palestinian rebellion enjoyed.

Battles were also recalled as typically involving another significant local practice. Whenever rebels initiated a battle themselves or when a group of *mujâhidîn* was discovered and attacked by the army, the rebels were rapidly able to call auxiliary fighters from surrounding villages to arms. They did so by means of a long-standing rural practice known as the *faza'*, or alert. In peacetime, whenever a fight or dispute broke out in a village, a shout went up and everyone came running, stick, rocks, or rifle in hand. If the dispute involved rival families, *hamâ'il,* or sects, the people who came to assist fought on the side to which they belonged or were allied. But the *faza'* was also a means of alerting the village in case of a threat from the outside. Rosemary Sayigh (1979: 25) has called the *faza'* a rural tradition of "collective militancy."

The rebels of 1936–39 recalled building upon and extending this tradition of combat. The revolt transformed the *faza'* from an informal into a formal method for mobilizing men under arms. When a battle began, designated persons—known as *fazzi'yîn* (alerters) or *sâyihîn* (shouters)—would raise the call to arms throughout the area of conflict. "The voice would call," recounted village commander Sâlih 'Ayyûsh, "and they'd come." Shaykh Zabrî of 'Arrâba (Jinîn) reported what transpired on September 3, 1936, during the celebrated battle of al-Mantâr (near Tûlkarm), in which rebel combatants were under the command of Fawzî Qâwûqjî: "A caller came to the door of the mosque. They said, whoever has weapons, whoever has something, should *faza'.* They got out everyone. I didn't have a weapon then. By God, we used to *faza'* without weapons. The women would carry water and food and drink on their heads to those who were fighting. Some *faza'û* [mobilized] with sticks, some with rocks, some with rifles." In this description of the *faza'*, the first to go off were the auxiliary fighters from the villages, who dropped their work, collected their stashed rifles, and rushed off to join the fray. But Shaykh Zabrî adds that others mustered out as well, grabbing clubs, axes, or whatever else was at hand. According to 'Alî Baytam, everyone who possessed even the merest "fragment [*qita'*] of a weapon" would rally to the call. Sometimes the message summoning people to *faza'* was heard quite far from the battlefield. Muhammad Kîlânî reported with amusement that, during the battle of al-Mantâr, the signal to *faza'* reached all the way to the southern coastal port of Gaza, and cars packed with fighters, rifles protruding from the windows, arrived from Gaza hours after the battle had ended.[24]

The memories of *faza'*, however, were not untouched by more recent and "modern" nationalist discourses. Several former fighters expressed disdain for their combat experiences during the insurrection by saying that most battles were "just *faza'*"—that is, merely spontaneous, unorganized, and ineffective military actions. Such former *mujâhidîn* retrospectively viewed the *faza'* as a manifestation of the Palestinian rebels' backward consciousness and of primitive forms of military organization. Others, however, saw the *faza'* as the expression of popular combativeness. 'Alî Baytam of Kuwaykât, himself a full-time fighter, reiterated that *fazâ'îyîn* (those mobilized by the *faza'*) always outnumbered regular fighters at any particular battle. Other persons regarded the *faza'* as a form of action that involved more than just fighters. Once when we were discussing the organization of battles with a *thâ'ir*, his wife interrupted to insist that village *women* used to *faza'*, too. For her, the *faza'* meant women bringing food and water to fighters, an action that put "auxiliaries" like her in the range of hostile gunfire. She recounted her role in the struggle with pride, for to her the *faza'* illustrated that one could actively and courageously participate in the *thawra* without carrying a rifle. Other persons stated that the *faza'* was also an occasion when villagers rallied to confront British soldiers who had invaded their rural communities on the trail of fighters or weapons. This type of "alert" principally involved women, children, and older men, since any male of fighting age was automatically a suspect and would likely be hauled off by the British forces.

Another form of "popular" warfare mentioned by some old *mujâhidîn* was the ambuscade, a practice that was also used widely by bandits—although most interviewees did not acknowledge this genealogy of the ambush.[25] What this involved, usually, was blocking the road with branches and rocks so that when a British military patrol passed by, it would have to stop and remove the barricade. This provided the perfect opportunity for rebel bands to open fire at the exposed troops. According to Palestine Police veteran Edward Horne, insurgents usually chose a spot where it was impossible to turn the vehicle around. Even if the vehicle—in the revolt's early stages, usually an open Ford tender with a Lewis gun mounted in the rear—were able to turn around, the *thuwwâr* quickly put up another obstacle behind it. All the soldiers (or police) would be ordered out of the Ford except the Lewis gun operator, who covered the men's attempt to clear the barricade. Usually as soon as the first police officer left the vehicle, the area would be splattered with bullets and the man would have to take cover in a ditch. In July and August 1936, rebel forces were putting up about five such roadblocks per day (Horne 1982: 214–15, 218).

Old fighters we met also asserted that it was not *thuwwâr* alone who put up the barricades and that they were often assisted by ordinary villagers, as well. Prior to the rebel occupation of the "mixed" town of Tiberias on October 2, 1938 (an operation in which nineteen Jewish noncombatants were massacred), the main roads leading to Tiberias were barricaded to hinder the movements of any British forces coming to the aid of the army garrison in the town. Fourteen roadblocks were erected on the Nazareth-Tiberias road, twenty-two between al-Tâbigha and Tiberias, and it was estimated that this took many hours of work by hundreds of local villagers.[26] Villagers also sometimes participated in the sabotage of railways. We heard of one renowned case during the short time we spent in the Gaza Strip—an area where, according to the elders, the main activity of rebels and villagers during the revolt was harassing British communications. This event took place in September 1938, when rebel forces organized local villagers to tear up the railway tracks in order to prevent the arrival of a large body of troop reinforcements from Egypt.[27] The most concerted sabotage effort took place, according to a British report, on the railway between Yibna and Rafah on the night of September 24–25, 1938. Seventy-five kilometers of railway were affected, and a total of seven kilometers of track were torn up and destroyed. Interviewees we met in Gaza stated that the work of destruction involved hundreds of villagers, who toiled virtually the entire night. The British account tells us that: "a marked feature of the incident was the determined attempt on the part of the inhabitants of the district to hold up repairs. A boycott was organized to prevent the sale of food to [railroad] employees [mainly Arabs], and to prevent the hire of taxis, donkeys or any other transport to railway staff. The tools of the gangs were taken, and every effort was made to intimidate the men." After the destruction of the line, the Lydda train went out daily and worked its way southward doing repairs. But the work was beset by "labour troubles," due in part to the troops' treatment of the Arab staff, which included shooting into their houses and "the accidental machine gunning of employees' huts and wounding of an Engineering labourer" on September 29. The southern train working up from Rafah likewise encountered "considerable opposition from armed bands and from villagers. On the 28th, when the train was at Khan Yunis, the situation became so bad that the train escort and trolley crew had to bombard the village with rifle grenades."[28]

Popular Participation

We heard other accounts of wider village participation in and support for the revolt. Abû Rajâ of Sha'b reported that when rebels were trapped in a village under siege (*tawq*) by the English, a *thâ'ir* could take refuge in a peasant's house. The *fallâh* would give the fighter a change of clothes, so that when soldiers searched the village they would think the *mujâhid* was merely another local farmer. They would also hide rebels wanted by the British army by caching them in the nooks and crannies of their homes, dressing them in drag and throwing them together with the women of the family, or secreting them in wells and other village hiding places.[29] Abû Sâlih of Maysar (north of Tûlkarm) recalled an incident when 'Abd al-Rahîm al-Hâjj Muhammad was injured and stayed in his house during a British encirclement-and-search campaign. A similar incident occurred when 'Abd al-Rahîm

> was sick at Kufr Ra'ei, with him was his special guard, consisting of five men and these the military surrounded. From there Abu Kamal [as 'Abd al-Rahîm was known] was put in a well, and bushes covered the door of the well, also black manure was placed there. The five comrades all changed into civilian clothes like the villagers. Afterwards the military entered, searched the village, found no one and were unable to recognise anyone. They afterwards left the village and Abu Kamal with his guard joined his party.[30]

At one point during our interview with Abû Rajâ, the *qâ'id* at Sha'b, he went out of the room for a few minutes. During his absence Abû Rajâ's wife complained that some nights during the revolt found as many as forty to fifty armed men sleeping on the floor of her house, their guns cradled in their arms and their muddy boots on their feet. The armed guests used to wake her in the middle of the night to cook for them. She would make the rounds in the village, collecting contributions of food from each household. The stereotypical public memory of old villagers who had lived through the revolt, in fact, was that when fighters showed up in the community it was an occasion for a celebration resembling a wedding feast, with people singing songs and bringing food and drink. The rebellion was therefore remembered by some as having forged new forms of collective struggle. By contrast, modern nationalist discourses that stressed the importance of armed action by a political avant-garde and minimized the element of popular mobilization gave little credit to the initiative of members of the popular classes who may not have carried rifles or Klashnikovs but whose labor (especially female) supported the rebels and who endured house demolitions, arrests, beatings, searches that destroyed their stocks of provisions, and other collective punishment for the sake of rebellion.[31]

A related aspect of the collective memory underscored to what degree the *mujāhidīn* relied upon the village economy. Another reason military activity was localized and decentralized was that rebels were completely integrated into the economic life of rural villages and depended in particular upon their domestic labor. It is for this reason that the British soldiers so often assaulted that domestic base, by breaking into homes, ripping apart its insides, and pouring the supply of olive oil over the grains and pulses, thereby ruining the household's store of basic provisions for the year.[32] We heard this story, about the mixing of *zayt zaytūn wa ʿadas* (olive oil and lentils), on numerous occasions, from villagers who regarded this action as a veritable economic atrocity. Western observers also occasionally noted the importance of the local economy to the movement. For instance, when the authorities ordered Arabs to carry identity cards and traffic passes in November 1938, the response was a boycott. In late December the high commissioner noted that the boycott, which meant that Palestinians did not travel or carry on any commerce via the system of roads controlled by the army, was still continuing. It had not "produce[d] the hardships which were anticipated" because the peasants had "adapted themselves to the times. Commodities are brought to market now on the heads of the women, on asses or on camels. A change of this kind is not difficult for the Palestinian Arab; it merely means that the clock is put back twenty years."[33]

Kinship and Revolt

Rebels also frequently recalled the organization of the revolt as having been built upon preexisting local alliances. In some villages the rebel military structure reflected rather than transcended existing divisions in rural areas. But some veterans claimed that when rebel groups overlapped with already established local systems of alliance, this made for rebel cohesiveness and internal strength. According to 'Alî Baytam, all the full-time rebels of Kuwaykât came from the small *hamûla* to which he belonged, Dâr Baytam. Their *hamûla* used force to persuade the members of the other *hamâ'il* in the village, four large and two or three small ones, to take action on the side of the revolt. When asked why Dâr Baytam was especially militant, 'Alî replied simply, "It came from God: the Baytams had love for the nation."[34]

But others remembered that basing bands in particular families or *hamâ'il* could lead to internal disputes or antagonism. Yûsuf Abû Durra, who became regional commander of the Haifa-Jinîn district in March 1938, hailed from the Jaradât *hamûla* of the village of Sîlat al-Hârithîya. Fawzî Jaradât, one of Abû Durra's relatives, explained to us that during the thirties the Jaradât *hamûla* belonged to a wider confederation (*hilf*) that also included the notable Jarrâr and Tawqân families and the Saqr Bedouin of the Jordan valley. The other three *hamâ'il* of Sîlat al-Hârithîya were allied with another confederation led by the landowning 'Abd al-Hâdîs of 'Arrâba. Occasionally, according to Fawzî Jaradât, these preexisting divisions within the village were the bases for certain disputes that erupted during the revolt. Moreover, the fact that the chief rebel *qâ'id* in the region, Abû Durra, belonged to a *hamûla* traditionally opposed to the other main *hamâ'il* of Sîlat al-Hârithîya caused local resentment and friction. Nonetheless, although the British army was constantly throwing the men of Sîlat al-Hârithîya in jail in an attempt to pressurize the community, the villagers never provided the British any information leading to Abû Durra's capture. For a time, so many men of the village were behind bars, according to Fawzî, that Friday prayers could not be held in Sîlat al-Hârithîya.

The village of Maythalûn, also in the Jinîn district, contained only two *hamâ'il,* the Ruba'îya and the Nâ'irât. According to revolt veteran al-Hâjj Yûsuf, the Ruba'îya *hamûla* was aligned with the 'Abd al-Hâdîs—not because the Ruba'îya worked as sharecroppers for 'Abd al-Hâdî landlords but simply because they were part of its notable-led *hizb,* or party. The Nâ'irât *hamûla,* for its part, was tied to another regional notable family, the Jarrârs. According to al-Hâjj Yûsuf, Maythalûn rebels from the Nâ'irât *hamûla* usually fought alongside regional commander Fawzî Jarrâr (from nearby Jaba'). *Thuwwâr* from the Ruba'îya meanwhile declined to join up with the Jarrârs. To show their distinction, they signed on with Abû Khâlid, a Qassâmite *qâ'id* from Sîlat al-Zahr, and they also cooperated with Abû Saysân, the commander from nearby Qabâtîya, who was allied with the 'Abd al-Hâdîs. Yet villagers also claimed that such local divisions could be superseded. Abû Saysân, aligned with the

'Abd al-Hâdîs, asserted that he enjoyed decent relations with Yûsuf Abû Durra, whose *hamûla* belonged to a *hilf* opposed to the 'Abd al-Hâdîs.

On other occasions local divisions were simply exacerbated in the course of the revolt, and a village would splinter into armed factions aligned with different rebel leaders. No old rebel cared to relate such a case to us, however. According to British records, a serious split of this sort occurred in the village of al-Râma in the Galilee, where a thirty-year-old feud between the Hanna (Greek Orthodox) and the Nakhla (Greek Catholic) families was played out in the course of the *thawra*. Each village group tried to exploit rival rebel factions for its own purposes; each group occasionally denounced a member of the opposing family alliance as a spy in order to incite the rebel *qâ'id* with whom it was aligned to punish the other side. Although it was located only a quarter of a mile from a military base, the village of al-Râma was divided into two armed camps, each tied to a different regional rebel commander.[35]

Counterstate Apparatuses

Another local institution that the rebels built upon and recoded was the traditional legal system. As rebel organizations extended their control over all aspects of rural life, villagers quit going to British courts and turned to rebels for the adjudication of disputes. It appears that by September 1938, rebel commanders in most areas had forbidden Palestinian Arabs from resorting to mandate-government courts.[36] According to Ibrâhîm Hanna of al-Bi'na, whenever a disagreement or conflict broke out between people within the area under his command, he was the one responsible for arranging a *sulha,* or peaceful compromise, between the opposing parties. Under "normal" conditions this sort of mediation would have been the task of local village notables and not entrusted to the most marginal elements of the village. In the legal arena, the rebel *quwwâd* not only utilized existing structures but also replaced the rural elite as the local figures of authority. Since the commanders generally hailed from the lower and junior ranks of the village order—Ibrâhîm Hanna, for instance, was in his twenties and had worked as a camel driver before becoming a rebel leader—by taking over such functions they reversed local hierarchies of status, class, and age. No doubt this explains in part why some old members of the elite I spoke with did not have fond memories of the rebels.

Another function assumed by the *qâ'ids* was to sit in judgment of those charged with crimes like theft, assault, forgery, treason, spying, and land sales. The maximum penalty for acts of treason was summary execution. But with one exception—discussed in chapter 5—no commanders or ordinary fighters I met ever admitted to any involvement in the execution of accused traitors. The old *mujâhidîn* preferred to represent the rebel legal system as having acted in a compassionate manner, and they downplayed its toughness.

Some higher commanders reportedly developed more formal legal institutions. According to one old man's account, rebels even possessed a written code of laws and regulations. A few *quwwâd* also appointed legal specialists as *qudâh* or judges, and in 1938–39, the major commanders established a central "Court of the Revolt" (Porath 1977: 248). A refugee from 'Ayn Hawd— whose local rebel "judge" was Shaykh al-Hâjj Hasan al-Mansûr (a Turkman from al-Mansî)—observed, "The people didn't know there was a [British] government. There was the revolt, and it was the one that authorized, granted divorce, made appointments, judged, and discharged [*tajauwaz wa tatalluq wa tarassam wa tahakkam wa tanaffad*]" (Kanâ'ana and al-Ka'abî 1987: 52–53). British reports about rebels who set up these alternative institutions often have an offended and exasperated tone. Colonial authorities seem to have regarded the attempts of the subaltern classes to invest themselves with the trappings of authority as the pinnacle of impertinence. The officials considered such actions—just as the rebels appear to have intended—as systematic violations of the colonial symbols of power (see Guha 1983: 39). The archives record that one army search of villages conducted in late 1937 resulted in the capture of two presidents, five members, a clerk, and a messenger who were part of a rebel court.[37] A report from November 1938 states that the army "succeeded in capturing a Headquarters Group, complete with banner and documents; and a Court of Justice, with wig, warders, and witnesses" in the Acre-Safad area.[38] On another occasion, troops near Tûlkarm "surprised a rebel court in session, arresting the two judges, and seizing typewriters, telephones and a quantity of documents."[39]

Rebel commanders also reportedly developed a fairly refined and graded system of punishments, fines, and even incarceration. They might require that those convicted of crimes like robbery or spying be flogged, pay a fine, or be sentenced to two to three months in a rebel "jail," which was most often an empty well. Although the old *mujâhidîn* I met tended to emphasize the clemency and generosity of rebel legal decisions rather than discuss in detail the penalties imposed, even some British observers felt that the punishments imposed by rebel commanders could be quite effective. Elliot Forster, who was serving as a physician in Hebron during the revolt, reports that the father of one of his patients was caught fighting in the Hebron *sûq* with another man. Within fifteen minutes of the fracas, both men were arrested and arraigned before a rebel court on the charge of brawling. The father of Forster's patient received twenty-five sticks, his opponent fifty. Forster admits his admiration for rebel efficiency in dealing with such behavior.[40]

Forster's assessment of the legal authority of Hebron area commander 'Abd al-Halîm al-Jawlânî between August and November 1938 is also notable both for its details and its sympathy. The physician describes Jawlânî's rule as "just and equitable." The *qâ'id*'s rebel courts, according to Forster, heard courts-martial and land, feud, and financial cases, and "their justice and common-sense does not appear to me inferior, and their expedition is demonstrably many degrees superior to that of H.M.G." Forster reports the case of two Arab doctors from the Health Department who were hauled before the rebel court and reproved for taking too much money from poor patients, yet were treated courteously by al-Jawlânî. Others, including Arab police, government clerks, and "persons of doubtful loyalty" were abducted in the "most brazen manner" and tried by al-Jawlânî on charges of "oppressing the poor," refusing to give money to rebels, passing information to the government, and so on. In most instances, says Forster, these men were let off with a warning; one or two "purchased their lives . . . only by joining rebels." Such abductions and trials were not just random acts. "Their justice was generally acknowledged, even, in most cases, by the victims themselves."[41]

Elderly *thuwwâr* also reported that the revolt developed taxation systems as a means of encouraging (or requiring) villagers to support the rebel infrastructure instead of paying fees to the mandate government. (Rebel commanders even printed stamps that functioned as receipts for those who paid taxes, an example of which is preserved in the Central Zionist Archives.) And several veterans of the *thawra* reported proudly that they possessed strong networks of intelligence and support among the Arabs employed in the British bureaucracy, particularly among Arab police.[42] According to 'Alî Baytam, "Every *qâ'id* had a spy who'd come and give him information, that at such a time the army would pass by a particular spot. The *qâ'id* would close the road and hit the army when it came to them." Many former *thuwwâr* told tales of Arab police who stole weapons from the British and turned them over to the *mujâhidîn*. Even some members of the Opposition were said to have passed along information to the rebels, such as 'Umar Sâlih al-Barghûthî of Ramallah, who reportedly sent word to the rebel commanders whenever he learned that the British were about to mount an operation against them.

Finally, rebels were said to employ elaborate smuggling networks for procuring weapons and supplies. Many men we met in the Galilee knew the illegal border crossings into Lebanon quite well and had traveled these routes to Lebanon themselves to purchase their rifles. Those who didn't leave the country to procure their own rifles depended upon professional smugglers. According to Rabbâh al-'Awad, the usual procedure was for smugglers to go to the first house on the outskirts of a village, knock on the door, and inform those inside that they had weapons to sell. That household then informed other villagers, and interested parties would show up at the house to purchase rifles and ammunition. Another means of transporting weapons, according to one fighter, was for people to bring weapons along with them when they visited relatives in another village.

That It Keeps Going On Like This . . .

The popular memories of such grassroots practices and initiatives are indicative of the extent to which the revolt was to a large degree a movement of subaltern, local-level mobilization. That old men still clearly recalled such events and actions in the mid-eighties reflects the fact that such memories had not been hegemonized or erased by nationalist discourse. These memories and practices, however, remained *potentially* oppositional, for they were hardly incorporated within modernist left-wing or progressive discourse, which tended to consider the peasant as heroic but lacking in political consciousness. It should be stressed again that these "resistant" memories were chiefly articulated through the rearticulation or reaccentuation of nationalist discourses and through condensations of the popular. We have also seen that such memories were frequently tendentious constructions that involved silences regarding certain practices. Events and actions that were relatively "untouched" by dominant memory were recounted fairly freely. But other incidents that involved direct antagonism toward the wealthy landlords and merchants tended to be occluded, in part because of the pressures of nationalist discourse. Such silences were particularly noticeable when it came to the issue of rebel attacks on the wealthy classes who were considered collaborators with the enemy, an issue we will return to later.

Yet there were other pressures that *reinforced* a specifically subaltern memory of the revolt. That the popular classes have provided most of the militants and have shed the most blood in the course of the ongoing struggle serves to buttress the view that the people, not the elite, were and still are its true protagonists. 'Alî Baytam, whose account of the 1938 massacre at Kuwaykât opened this chapter, was one of the few members of his family who remained behind in Israel after 1948. Most of 'Alî's relatives fled Palestine in 1948 and eventually ended up in Shatîla refugee camp in Beirut. 'Alî managed, over the years, to maintain regular if intermittent contact with his clan and to stay abreast of their births, graduations, marriages, and deaths. Many of his relatives were among those slaughtered at Sâbra and Shatîla camps in 1982, in a massacre carried out by right-wing Lebanese Phalangists who operated under the noses and with the probable connivance of the Israeli command. 'Alî did not need to keep a list in his pocket to remember the names of his relatives slaughtered at Shatila. Among them he named "Kâmil Sâlih al-Baytam, *ibn ûmmî,* my father's brother's son. Fayyâd Hassan al-Baytam, whose father was my brother [the son of Fayyâd Baytam, Kuway-kât's commander in the 1936 revolt]. There were many people. *Ibn khâlî,* my mother's brother's son, named Walîd."

Sonia and I felt in awe of the fierce spirit burning so brightly in the diminutive man who repeated the names of the dead, as if that act could arrest the storm of progress and halt the historical progression that is "one single catastrophe which keeps piling wreckage upon wreckage and hurls it in front of his feet" (Benjamin 1969: 257). Remembering 'Alî reciting the martyr's names over the wreckage, I think: "That it 'keeps going on like this' is the catastrophe" (Benjamin, cited in Buck-Morss 1989: 375).

5 / (Un)popular Memories

Accommodation and Collaboration

This chapter focuses on that component of subaltern memories that, according to Ranajit Guha's terms, could be classified as "collaborationist" vis-à-vis official Israeli or Western discourses. In the strong sense, collaboration implies willing cooperation with the enemy. Just as "consent" describes the ideal type of subordination under hegemonic rule, "collaboration" names the ideal subaltern behavior for colonial systems where *dominio* prevails. But there are also more ambiguous kinds of relations between the colonized and colonizer that lie somewhere between outright opposition and enthusiastic collaboration. These could be described as *accommodation,* that is, adjusting or adapting, and *compliance,* that is, yielding or acquiescing in a subservient way. Given the urgency of the nationalist struggle, such forms of Palestinian commonsense memory might appear collaborationist, but James Scott's work suggests that we consider the possibility that such deference or subservience involves dissimulation and even covert resistance.[1] We will therefore examine whether what appears to be adapting or yielding to coercion in fact involves ambiguous, nuanced, or even oppositional forms of subordination, not outright subservience. We will also consider the possibility that "collaborationist" pronouncements are equally expressions of opposition to mainstream nationalist practices or notions, albeit articulated in an extreme or "inappropriate" manner. That is to say, we will examine whether *resistance* to orthodox nationalism may have been a significant conjunctural motivation for the subject's apparently "collaborationist" statements. (The enemy, of course, knew how to take advantage of such sentiment.)

The accommodationist, compliant, and collaborationist memories examined here take a variety of forms. I include a number of statements, anecdotes, or opinions that seem to break sharply with nationalist consensus. One such "accommodationist" type of view proposed a nonnationalist explanation for the revolt: that the *British* orchestrated it. Another type of "collaborationist" memory is the echo of various Zionist ideologemes in interviewees' statements. I also investigate memories that seemed compliant not in the sense that they repeated Zionist ideology but rather that they caved in to Zionist pressure. Harsh criticisms of the rebel movement that seemed to break with nationalist decorum are examined here, as well. Finally, I discuss narratives that appear more overtly "collaborative": personal accounts of men who were involved in actual collaboration with the enemy during the insurgency.

It should be noted that such accommodationist and collaborationist memories represented minority opinions among the former *thuwwâr* we interviewed. Furthermore, we discovered that in most cases, when we took an interviewee's accommodationist statements in combination with his other assertions, nationalist arguments in fact outweighed or undercut acquiescent ones. Thus statements of compliance or complicity with the enemy were rarely articulated within coherent narratives of submission but were usually accompanied by nationalist sentiments. Such accounts were composed of "bizarre juxtapositions," and therefore typical of common sense.

"The English Made the Revolt"

I had been in the West Bank for about six weeks when some friends took me to meet Abû Zayn at Dayr al-Ghusûn. I was eager with anticipation. Finally, I was about to meet someone who had actually fought in the revolt I had been reading about for the last few years. I was especially keen after I learned that my first encounter was to be not with a mere *thâ'ir* but with a local *qâ'id fasîl* (band commander).

But when I introduced myself to Abû Zayn and told him I wanted to pose him some questions about his role in the revolt, he responded: "The revolt was pointless. We were too weak to win. We should have compromised instead of fighting and grabbed what we could get. Now we're left with nothing. We're *worse* off for having fought the British. Just like Arafat in Beirut, who was too weak to beat the Israelis in 1982. Because he refused to compromise, we're now left with nothing. In any case, the *English* plotted the revolt." Abû Zayn's assessment of the entire Palestinian experience was so pessimistic that he was completely disinterested in discussing the revolt's details with me. Finally I asked, impatiently, "But weren't you proud, in 1936, to be a fighter?" "Yes, I was," he replied, "but I've learned better since then."

After about twenty minutes of this sort of conversation I gave up and left. My friends were rather embarrassed, but they tried to reassure me by saying that Abû Zayn was a sick old man (which turned out to be true) whose words I should disregard (which I did not). I would be able to get more reliable information about the revolt, they promised, from Abû Marwân, the acknowledged local expert.

I was surprised, for this was my first encounter with "accommodationist" statements from Palestinians, and it was hard for me to imagine how someone, and particularly a former rebel, could articulate such a position given the strength of Palestinian nationalism. As far as eliciting any usable historical "facts" about the revolt, my encounter with Abû Zayn was a dismal failure, but it forced me to begin to think about defeatist interpretations that, although decidedly the minority opinion, turned out not to be peculiar to Abû Zayn. It also introduced me to an astonishing mode of explanation of the revolt, for I was to encounter the claim that the English (al-Inglîz) were the ones who made or orchestrated ('amalû) the revolt many times and throughout the country: in the western Galilee, in the Tûlkarm district, and in the Gaza Strip. I was bewildered when I heard this pronouncement, especially from men who had participated in and organized the revolt. The claim was also confounding because the rebellion was a crucial icon of struggle in social memory, and I had come across no published accounts that ventured such an argument. Finally, the explanation was perplexing because it wrested all agency away from the insurgents and handed it over to the colonialists.

The mujâhidîn who asserted that the English were responsible always "proved" their case metaleptically, citing some outcome of the revolt to explain its cause. One old man claimed that the English, foreseeing war with Germany on the horizon, manipulated the Arabs into rebelling to gain the pretext for establishing massive military bases in Palestine. It was obvious that this was their purpose, otherwise why would they have dispatched important generals, like Montgomery, Dill, Wavell, and Haining, who played major roles in the Second World War, to a small and insignificant country like Palestine? After using these new outposts to quell the rebellion, the English then had them conveniently on hand to utilize during the 1939–45 war. Another version of this tale was recounted by four men from different localities. This stated that the English had goaded the Arabs to insurrection so that they could defeat them militarily and then be able to turn the country over to the Jews in 1948 without encountering significant opposition from the weak-

ened Arab community. Since the ultimate result of the uprising's failure was
the establishment of the state of Israel, they reasoned, this must have been
England's plan all along. Abû Ilyâs from Acre claimed that the British cooked
up the scheme of the revolt to spark hostilities between Arabs and Jews,
which would give them an excuse to partition the country. Even the leftist
'Alî Baytam, while not going so far as to claim that there was a plot, blamed
the English for stirring things up:

> The [mandate] government took the Arabs and threw them in Haifa. They told
> the Jews, look, he came and put mines against you. The Jews took him and
> killed him. They [the English] took a Jew and threw him to the Arabs, and said
> to the Arabs, look, this Jew came to you and threw bombs at you. So there
> would be a bigger dispute. And disputes started. They [the English] went from
> village to village, from city to city, until there was a revolt in the whole country.

Finally, Abû Marwân (the expert at Dayr al-Ghusûn) claimed that the English had conspired to start the Arab insurgency to give an excuse for the
Jews to build a harbor at Tel Aviv, and then take away all the commerce that
had passed through the Arab-controlled port at nearby Jaffa.[2]

It was no use arguing with the old *thuwwâr* about the validity of such
explanations. These men could not be convinced otherwise, although the
only real evidence they could cite as proof of their view was the end result.
Whenever Sonia or I disputed such a claim, the man typically responded:
"But look at what happened! We fought the English for over three years,
and not only did we *not* win our independence, but Israel was created with
their help. England *must* have wanted the rebellion so it could achieve what
it desired."

Another shock was that such assertions usually came at the conclusion of a
narration by a man who remembered the revolt *as if* Palestinians (particularly the peasantry) had organized and initiated it. After a long discussion in
which the interviewee represented the revolt as the work of the Arabs, he
would conclude, "But later we learned the English had really contrived the
whole thing." Although these men reportedly believed the plot scenario, they
did not rewrite the story of the *thawra* to make the English its prime movers.
Their metaleptic explanations of the cause of the revolt generally did not
move them to dismiss either their own actions or the uprising as a whole as
pointless exercises. As if to confirm Gramsci's claim that common sense is a
"strange composite," the plot theory generally appeared as a kind of jarring
postscript to a relatively coherent nationalist account.

The first "authentic" rebel I met, Abû Zayn, was located at the extreme end of the spectrum of plot theorists. Since Abû Zayn regarded the British as the protagonists of the revolt, he saw no point in rehearsing the minutiae of his involvement for my benefit. He could hardly look back with pride on his actions if he had simply been the unknowing pawn of a grand design. Yet although his views were excessive, they were not unrelated to those of other *mujâhidîn*. For clearly his subsequent historical revision, like those of other *thuwwâr,* was motivated by the experience of nearly fifty years of successive Palestinian disasters, defeats, and shattered hopes. The Palestinian resistance movement's recent expulsion from Beirut in 1982 was just the latest blow.

One plausible explanation for the prevalence of the "plot theory" of the revolt is that it served to explain away personal and collective failure by attributing responsibility to an outside agent. Through such a theory former *mujâhidîn* could reconstruct a story that accounted for their lack of success and helped them cope with defeat. The revolt's failure becomes comprehensible, almost inevitable, if one sees the British as its orchestrators. The theory also helped explain an apparent historical anomaly—the fact that other Arab countries of the Mashriq (Syria, Lebanon, Iraq, and Egypt) were able to win their national independence from the colonialists, while the Palestinians, who fought much longer and harder than any of their neighbors, not only failed to achieve independence but were driven from their land. Given the trajectory of Palestinian history, its many bizarre twists and turns, which often seemed to defy rational explanation and frequently appeared incompatible with any coherent narrative framework, the real surprise may be that old people did not invent even more fanciful explanations. In fact, were it not for the existence of the national movement, it is likely that many more people would have evaluated the revolt as Abû Zayn did. (Luckily for us, no other fighters used such grounds as a reason not to talk about the revolt.) Palestinian nationalist ideology provided a plausible narrative of a people-nation marching forward to victory that most people could believe in most of the time, a collective identity within which a person could situate the experiences of his or her past in a meaningful way. Yet it became difficult to sustain this "indispensable fantasy" (Eagleton 1980: 72–73) during periods of reversals and setbacks, when this narrative failed to account for why the movement kept encountering so many detours along its path and why this epic struggle so often swerved into tragedy.

After two former rebels, one in Ya'bad and the other in Gaza, told us that after the *thawra* was over, Palestinian landlords had informed them the whole thing had been a British plot, Sonia provisionally concluded that the plot theory was invented by upper-class collaborators who spread such rumors to cast aspersions on the revolt. I do not wish to dismiss this possibility out of hand, but I think it makes more sense to view the conspiracy (*mu'âmara*) explanation as symptomatic of a tendency in Palestinian political culture to think and explain events in terms of cabalistic machinations than to account for the conspiracy theory as just the result of another *mu'âmara*.[3]

While the tendency to reckon in terms of intrigue seemed particularly marked among the older generation, it was not confined to old-timers. The highly partisan Palestinian newspapers of East Jerusalem frequently fed such modes of thinking, with headlines and lead articles sometimes giving the impression that the Palestinians' enemies devoted all their waking hours to hatching intrigues against them. The various political tendencies all resorted, at times, to using *mu'âmarât* as weapons against their rivals, claiming that their foes were party to the schemes of an enemy. The "battles of the camps" that erupted in Lebanon during the summer of 1985, for instance, provided grist for such plot-mongering. At the time, Palestinian leftist groups (chiefly, the Popular Front for the Liberation of Palestine [PFLP]) were tactically allied with the Syrian regime and with those Palestinian organizations directly tied to the Syrians (Fath Uprising, Sâ'iqa, PFLP–General Command) in order to contest Yassir Arafat's policy of cozying up to Jordan's King Hussein. Meanwhile, the Syrian regime—already implicated in the massacre of Palestinians at Tal al-Za'tar in 1976 and in the expulsion of Fath forces from Tripoli in 1983—was encouraging the Shi'ite 'Amal militias to attack refugee camps in Lebanon, where Palestinian guerrilla organizations, Fath in particular, were making a comeback.

Only three years after the horrors of the Israeli invasion, and just as the Palestinian resistance movement was rising again, phoenixlike, out of the rubble of the camps, a new round of siege, slaughter, and starvation ensued, this time at the hands of Palestinians' erstwhile Lebanese and Syrian allies. These events caused great anguish among residents of the Occupied Territories, who saw their destiny as tightly knit to the fortunes of an independent PLO. At roughly the same time, U.S. diplomat Richard Murphy was shuttling in and out of Damascus, attempting to improve Washington's relations with Hâfiz al-Asad. The headlines of *al-Fajr*, a Jerusalem newspaper close to Fath, warned that the United States and the Syrians were cooking up a "Camp Murphy" in Damascus, implying that Asad, in much the same manner as Anwar al-Sadat in 1977 at Camp David, was on the brink of selling out the Palestinians to curry favor with Washington. Murphy's visits to Syria, *al-Fajr* suggested, were also connected to the camp wars. By linking all these events and actors, the paper also subtly suggested that Palestinian leftists who opposed Fath's rapprochement with Hussein and who were tactically linked to Syria were implicated in a grand conspiracy involving 'Amal, Syria, Israel, and the United States. *Al-Fajr* made these insinuations despite the fact that Palestinian leftists were fighting and dying inside the Lebanon camps *against* 'Amal and alongside Fath forces. Such thinking was summed up in a slogan I saw painted on a stone wall in Ramallah that was usually decorated with denunciations of the Israeli occupation, a graffito denouncing George Habash, the leader of the leftist PFLP: *Al-kalb Habash, khâ'in* (The dog Habash, traitor).[4]

My suggestion is that former rebels pushed the conspiracy logic that dominant nationalist discourse peddled one step further. If powerful outside forces are always plotting against the Palestinians, then those almighty powers might even have controlled or manipulated the Palestinian resistance in the past. Conspiracy theories, used variously by Palestinian leaders to incite the masses to act, to explain away defeats, and to beat up on rivals, took an unforeseen but understandable turn when popular memory ascribed the *thawra* to British orchestrations.

Although such plot discourse provided imaginary solutions to vexing dilemmas, it reflected a politically disabling conception of the past. Patrick Wright has termed this type of historical thinking "heliocentric," referring to the notion that historical forces break in from outside, that they cut in from above. The events that occur in "heliocentric" history are beyond an individual's control and not integrated into his or her system of personal, lived meanings. Heliocentric conspiracy theories provided a kind of astrological chart to explain the uncontrollable spasms and deviations of history whenever events failed to accord to nationalist logic.[5]

This heliocentric conception of past events was probably also connected to residual forms of subject interpellation still operative within Palestinian culture. A subject in precapitalist formations, unlike the bourgeois subject, is not "hailed" by ideology so as to imagine herself the author of her own actions. Rather than supposing herself to be self-determining, she sees determination as imposed upon her (Pêcheux and Fuch 1982: 17). This form of subjectivity is also linked to dominant forms of religious consciousness, in which the subject sees her destiny not as a function of her own will and action but as caused by forces beyond and independent of herself (Guha 1983: 268). Within the political discourse of conspiracy, it is not god or monarch that controls destiny, but those mighty yet vague and mysteriously shifting political forces. The tendency of official Palestinian political discourse to explain particular events by intrigue represented a kind of transcription of such religious or precapitalist discourses. This brand of mainstream discourse served as a framework of explanation that permitted nationalist leaders to escape self-criticism, to externalize problems, and to deflect popular dissent. Conspiracy thinking also enabled political manipulation of the masses, for it encouraged them to think that power lies not in their own hands but elsewhere. Such religious-style interpellations coexist in juxtaposition with bourgeois interpellations, which are equally necessary for political mobilization.

While such modes of explanation could provide an individual a modicum of psychological relief by accounting for the inexplicable, they could also, by their exaggeration of the all-controlling power of outside forces, encourage or reflect passivity and inaction, as in the case of Abû Zayn.[6] It should be emphasized, however, that even if a man's plot explanation was motivated by a defeatist sensibility, this did not necessarily mean his active endorsement of Israeli or British policy. The memories of one interviewee who identified very closely with the imperial West illustrate some of the complexities and limits of accommodationism under the conditions of Israeli rule. Colonel Sa'dî Jallâl of Tûlkarm had served as a police officer under both the British and the Jordanians.[7] Before he would speak with us he insisted on recording our names in a notebook, in case the Israeli military governor (*al-hâkim al-'askarî*) came to interrogate him about our conversation. His *diwân* was resplendent with medals and lined with photographs featuring the colonel in full military regalia, greeting visiting dignitaries (Egyptian, Iranian, and Pakistani ministers) to Jordan. Jallâl's sense of self was so bound up with the colonial powers, in fact, that, although he was by no means fluent in English, he spoke Arabic with an ersatz English accent. And he was full of scurrilous tales about the 1936–39 revolt. He asserted that all the *thuwwâr* (except 'Abd al-Rahîm al-Hâjj Muhammad) were ignorant, whoring, brutal men. Abû Durra, he claimed, used to decide whether or not to execute suspected traitors by counting his *misbaha* (prayer beads). Yet the colonel was equally a wellspring of implausible stories about English machinations against the Arabs. He maintained, for instance, that the British had planted two spies with Shaykh 'Izz al-Dîn al-Qassâm's gang, and that these operatives were responsible for murdering the shaykh while he was saying prayers in Ya'bad Forest on November 20, 1935. So this loyal servant of the British Empire paradoxically remembered his beloved masters as forever conspiring against the Palestinians.[8]

"Why Should We Kill a Jew?"

Another form of compliance involved the evasion of sensitive issues. I classify this avoidance as "accommodationist" because it represented a kind of caving in to the pressures of Zionist discourse. That old men, when asked to recall certain features of the days of the revolt, frequently answered by dissimulation, I assert, was a product of the repression attendant on Israeli rule. Some of the most noticeable regions of silence concerned rebel attacks on Jewish settlements, an issue raised in chapter 1.

One force that shaped men's reticence about discussing what "really happened" was the stated policy of the national movement during the revolt. The leadership's political line was that the rebellion was directed against the British mandate government rather than at Jewish inhabitants of Palestine. By defeating British imperialism, the national movement proclaimed, it would succeed in halting Zionist colonization. Several interviewees articulated such a position. Others advanced a related one, that the rebellion was directed not against the Jewish people but against Zionism, the political movement whose goal was the transformation of Palestine into a Jewish state. This position's origins are more recent, and reflect official PLO policies of distinguishing between Judaism as a religion and Zionism as a colonial movement. Interviewees who asserted that rebels made such a distinction were in all likelihood retroactively imposing the contemporary PLO position upon rebel policies.

Such interpretations, however, also represented something more than simple repetition of official propaganda. The preexisting image of a movement that was untainted by anti-Semitism was given fresh strength by current nationalist ideology, in a manner similar to what Freud terms "deferred action" (1967: 12). This reinforced memory served as a screen that blocked out the recollection of armed attacks on Jewish colonists. Thus a *thâ'ir*'s reticence on this subject indicated a concern to show that he personally was not anti-Jewish and that the revolt, by metonymic extension, was not anti-Semitic, either. For example, many interviewees underlined that they were never involved in military engagements in which Jews were killed or wounded. Abû Fâris, a commander at Majd al-Krûm, told us: "The armed men [*musallahîn*] with me, they brought a Jew to me. They caught a Jew. Why did they bring him? He's a Jew, so what? Why kill a Jew? Let him go. I told him, go! These Jews were working on the road [the British] were opening to Safad." In this instance, it is in fact plausible that Abû Fâris's men brought this Jew to their commander for punishment not simply because of his ethnic-

religion origins but also because he was employed in roadwork that represented a real threat to the rebel movement, since it would enable the British
army to better penetrate the Safad area. But Abû Fâris wanted to prove his
lack of anti-Jewish feeling. Both the taboo against anti-Semitism that was the
effect of Israeli power and the Palestinian movement's current anti-Zionist
(as opposed to anti-Jewish) policies prompted old men to tell stories that
presented themselves as untainted by anti-Semitism. These narratives of
selves who acted according to stated political ideals were meant to represent
the nation, as well.

A similarly motivated trope was the tale of the interviewee's personal
friendship with Jewish individuals, intended to demonstrate a lack of ani-
mosity toward Jews.[9] The son of regional band commander 'Ârif 'Abd al-
Râziq took special pains to construct an unblemished image of his father by
such means. According to Faysal 'Abd al-Râziq, his father began organizing
military actions in the early 1920s, when he established a secret organization
known as the Black Hand. The Black Hand's aim was to prevent Jewish
colonies from gaining a secure foothold on the land. It attempted to frighten
the settlers and keep them off their guard by destroying their crops and
orchards, but it did *not*—Faysal emphasized—slay colonists. Faysal made a
careful distinction between the struggle against colonization and the killing
of Jews. Similarly, when 'Abd al-Râziq launched rebel attacks on Jewish settlements during the rebellion, his aim was simply to halt the conquest of
land, not to drive the Jews as a whole out of Palestine. Faysal told us that in a
published interview with a foreign journalist, his father had stated that the
revolt's enemy was Zionism, not the Jews. In 1938, he said, 'Ârif made a
direct appeal to the Jews of Palestine in a communiqué calling for the establishment of a democratic Palestinian government that would include both
Jews and Arabs. The leaflet was distributed within Yishuv by Jewish Communists.[10] According to Faysal, 'Abd al-Râziq's plan showed him to be a
political visionary whose ideas prefigured the PLO's 1970 platform advocating a democratic secular state in all of Palestine.

Faysal also recounted several anecdotes attesting to his father's good personal relations with Jews. One of these concerned a Jewish doctor who used
to treat Arab villagers in the al-Tayyiba area. A few years prior to the revolt,
'Ârif had rescued her from the clutches of Arab thieves. When 'Ârif became
a rebel chief, she returned the favor by treating his battle wounds and concealing him from the British army in her house. 'Ârif also reportedly maintained personable relations with the Jewish farmers in the al-Tayyiba district.
During the revolt his fighters used to plant mines in the roads with the aim of

blowing up passing British military vehicles, but before they did so 'Ârif would inform Jewish agricultural workers in the area where the land mines had been placed so they could take a different route. (The Jewish workers never passed this information on to the British.) The last of the anecdotes dates from the 1939–45 war, during 'Ârif 'Abd al-Râziq's time in Sofia, where he fled after being involved in the abortive Rashîd 'Alî Kîlânî uprising in Iraq. While in Sofia 'Ârif aided a Jewish Communist active in the Bulgarian resistance, despite the fact that he was a guest of the pro-Axis Bulgarian government.

Other than the existence of 'Abd al-Râziq's leaflet distributed by the Palestine Communist Party, I have been unable to confirm the veracity of any of these stories about 'Ârif and views and practices regarding Jews. But their importance lies not in their truth status, but in the reasons for the telling. Faysal, who was working on a book about his father, relayed the stories he had collected from his father's friends and relatives in order to convey a memory of a revolt commander who was the antithesis of an anti-Semite. His stories responded directly to Israeli claims that the revolt was *essentially* anti-Semitic ("riots" or "pogroms against Jews"). The anecdote about the Bulgarian Jew was undoubtedly in part a reaction to Zionist assertions that since several key figures in the revolt (like Hâjj Amîn, 'Ârif 'Abd al-Râziq, and Hasan Salâma) took refuge with Axis regimes during the war, the Palestinian nationalist movement was not merely anti-Semitic but also pro-Nazi. Moreover, there is Bar Zohar and Haber's claim that 'Ârif 'Abd al-Râziq used to wear a Hitler mustache in imitation of his idol (1983: 26).[11] The tale of 'Ârif 'Abd al-Râziq's assistance to a Jewish fighter in the anti-Nazi resistance served as a kind of riposte to the picture of Hâjj Amîn and his letter to Ribbentrop that are displayed at Yad Vashem.

Such accounts therefore were much more than *mere* conciliatory gestures toward dominant discourse. On the one hand they made concessions by virtue of their sensitivity regarding anti-Semitism. On the other, they refused that charge. Accounts that avoided the topic of rebel attacks on Jewish settlements were equally effects of Israeli oppression and deflections of the claims of dominant Zionist discourse. Subaltern common sense accordingly slid in and out of conciliatory and oppositional modes. Interviewees' stories depicting a self (a metonym for the nation) that was (and still is) not anti-Semitic represented the cumulative historical result of fifty years of experience with settler-colonial violence. Palestinians tended to regard Israel as an unwelcome but accomplished fact, a reality that was unlikely to be unmade. Furthermore, Zionist discourse had the power to define "anti-Semitism" very expansively. Thus the former *mujâhid* was made to feel that even to acknowledge that Jewish colonies were rebel targets was taboo. (Just as in the eighties, any armed attack on the army of occupation was labeled "terrorism.") To mention 'Ârif 'Abd al-Râziq's Hitlerian mustache or other apparent instances of Palestinian sympathy for Nazis or fascists therefore became virtually unthinkable. Interviewees' descriptions of a revolt that was solely anti-British and their tales of friendship with Jews represented perhaps a grudging acceptance of hard fact. At the same time, these concessionist statements were to some degree oppositional in that they were connected to contemporary Palestinian nationalist discourse that distinguishes between Jews and Zionists and holds out a utopian vision of a secular state that does not discriminate among Jews, Muslims, and Christians. By remembering an uprising that was fought against the British *alone,* interviewees were not just dissimulating or caving in; they were also imagining a future in which relations with Israeli Jews would be peaceful and equitable. (What is ironic, of course, is that the net effect of the revolt was to harden even further divisions between the Arab and Jewish communities.)

"We're Happy Here with the Jews"

A few interviewees, and even some whose lands were confiscated by the Jewish state after 1948, were so accommodationist as to express support for certain aspects of official Israeli policy or propaganda. Three elderly Palestinian men, all Israeli citizens, praised the government for paying old-age pensions. No government in the Arab world, they asserted, looked after its people so well in their old age. One, Abû Rajâ, an internal refugee who had lived in Majd al-Krûm ever since his natal village of Sha'b was destroyed, told us, "We're happy here with the Jews. Yes, they took our lands. But we're living well. In Sha'b, even though I owned land, I didn't have a house like this." It was his pension from the government, he added, that had enabled him to build the new abode of which he was so proud.

Other old men repeated well-known Zionist ideologemes. "It was the Jews who built up this country, which was nothing before they arrived," said Abû al-'Abd of Haifa, some of whose properties were also seized after 1948. "They had the money to build it up. They made Haifa what it is today. We were nothing before they showed up." Fawzî Jaradât, a resident of Sîlat al-Hârithîya in the West Bank, ventured, "The ones who taught us farming were the Jews."[12] When the younger village men present began chuckling at this assertion, he exclaimed, "One has to tell the truth!" Sonia responded in exasperation, "Before the Jews came didn't we know how to farm?!" "By

God," Jaradât retorted, "we didn't know how to grow one tomato plant!" These statements, too, were surprising, especially given that Fawzî Jaradât lost most of his farmland when Sîlat al-Hârithîya's cultivable properties in the Marj Ibn 'Âmr (the Esdraelon Valley) fell under Israeli control in 1948.

I did not hear such assertions of direct support for Israeli claims or policies very often. Other Palestinians present when old men made such statements usually greeted them with protests or nervous laughter. Yet even these claims were not threads in a neatly stitched discourse of support for or compliance with Israeli rule, for each man who voiced such "pro-Israel" statements also made declarations critical of Israeli policies. Several men whose properties had been confiscated protested bitterly. Fawzî Jaradât grumbled that his *hamûla* didn't have "even one furrow" left to them. Their accommodationism in no way implied that they had ceased to harbor resentment about the expropriation of land, which was so tied up with men's personal sense of honor. Moreover, all these men remembered the 1936–39 revolt in a positive, if somewhat nuanced, light. Abû Rajâ of Sha'b recounted his role as village band commander proudheartedly. When asked to assess the uprising, he responded, "The revolt was good, but *zu'rân* [thugs] wrecked it." The others similarly gave favorable but mixed reviews.

Accommodationist rhetoric of this sort could be interpreted simply as successful effects of Israeli persuasion backed up by coercion. But if it represented a concession to power, the imprint of coercive force upon historical common sense, it did not constitute agreement with Israeli ideology. Accommodationist pronouncements were usually juxtaposed with oppositional ones: they were elements of a contradictory blend in which resistive parts usually outnumbered the collaborationist. The rarity of such statements attested to the Israeli ruling bloc's failure (at least within this population) to achieve even a spurious form of hegemony over those whom it had ruled for the last twenty to forty years.

Ignorant Rebels

Another form of accommodationism involved the slamming of rebel leaders and practices. Such harsh detractions broke with the desired national consensus by giving credence to official Zionist claims that the rebels were all brutal mercenaries and criminals (like Sa'dî Jallâl's calumnies, mentioned earlier). But although such attacks tallied with the enemies' criticisms, they usually tended to be the products of local political dynamics rather than compliance with Zionist ideology. Men made these statements, which bordered on treason from the standpoint of nationalist etiquette, *despite* the fact that they

constituted agreement with Zionist claims. In such instances, vigorous dis-
satisfaction with certain actions of the revolt overrode the censorship that
normally sustained nationalist decorum.

Most (although not all) of the severe faultfinding came from members of
big landowning families or their village allies. Usually such figures said they
had supported the revolt in its early days but had fallen out with it later.
Others, like Sa'dî Jallâl, had served in the mandate police force and similarly
disparaged the rebels. The criticisms made by such men usually resonated
with elite class hatred and disdain for the lowly. Such detractors reiterated,
variously, that the rebel commanders were all thieves (*quttâ' turuq*), thugs
(*zu'rân*), uneducated (*mish muthaqqafîn*), or ignorant (*jâhilîn*). They reserved
some of the harshest invective for Yûsuf Abû Durra, the Qassâmite who
became regional commander in the Jinîn-Haifa area in 1938. In the accounts
of elites and their clients from this region (as we have already seen), he functioned as a prototype of the brutish and uncouth rebel *qâ'id*. Several persons
accused Abû Durra of executing an inordinate number of *makhâtîr* on the
flimsiest of evidence that they were agents of the English. Abû Ja'far, who
belonged to a Jinîn landowning family and who had a relative who was killed
by Abû Durra (a fact he never mentioned during our conversation), labeled
the *qâ'id* "crazy, a fool." Wasif Abboushi's dismissal of Abû Durra as an "illiterate *fellah*" (1977: 42) is typical of what the elite of Jinîn thought of this
village upstart. They clearly resented the fact that a former railway porter and
lemonade vendor from a low-status clan had upset their political hegemony
in rural areas and even in Jinîn itself, although elites never stated this directly
when they criticized such commanders. In the course of the insurrection,
villagers began to take their orders from the parvenu commanders and to
go to them to level complaints, obtain legal judgments, and the like, administrative functions that were previously the monopoly of local notables. And
as we know, at the height of the rebellion (summer and fall 1938), rebel commanders forbade debt collectors from entering villages, abolished rents in
urban areas, and forced the urban effendis to replace their high-status *tarbûsh*
with the headdress of the lowly peasant, the *kûfîya*. Hundreds of members of
the elite fled the country, to avoid such humiliations and to escape paying
the excessive donations demanded by the rebel leaders. But members of the
elite rarely mentioned such class-based harassment. Instead, they railed about
the low social status of rebel *quwwâd*. Abû Ja'far asserted, "Our problem was
that our [military] leaders were ignorant. *Fallâhîn*. What was Abû Durra? A
worker!"

A Single Grain of Truth and a Very Small One

In part because their foes have paid intensive historiographical attention to the revolt's internal troubles, with the aim of depicting the Palestinians as inherently bloodthirsty and fanatical, official Palestinian histories on the whole have handled the whole question of the revolt's factional disputes gingerly and circumspectly. Given the Palestinians' lack of a state and their sparse national historical apparatuses, the construction of the national historical narrative is still very much in process, and in the Occupied Territories it has been under virtual siege. In this crisis-ridden and beleaguered atmosphere, it is little wonder that historical self-criticism has not been high on the Palestinian agenda. The revolt has scarcely been the subject of systematic or critical academic study by Palestinians, but rather has been depicted reverentially and held like an icon at a respectful distance.

A good example of the official view regarding infighting during the revolt is Yassir Arafat's explanation for why he decided not to use force against his leftist and rejectionist opposition in the early eighties. His reasons, he says, are based on lessons drawn from the 1936 rebellion. "During the revolt," Arafat states,

> our Palestinian leadership was divided and the rival groups fought each other. . . . Because of this internal fighting many of our leaders were assassinated. Now, when the history of those times came to be written, the British and the Israelis put their own cover on the story. They said what had happened was proof of the difference between the civilized Jews and the uncivilized Arabs. . . . As always there was a grain of truth in what the Israelis and their Western allies said—but it was only a single grain and a very small one. . . . The truth was that when our leaders turned to the gun to solve their internal problems, our enemies took advantage of the situation and launched a campaign of assassination to destroy our leadership. Many of the killings were done by British agents. . . . [After studying these matters] I made a vow that my generation would never repeat the mistakes of the past. (Hart 1984: 332–33)

While acknowledging that the Palestinian leadership committed errors and that it resorted to violence to enforce unity, Arafat concentrates our attention both on how the Palestinians' adversaries subsequently exaggerated the significance of those mistakes and on how the British army exploited the internal Palestinian struggle and was itself responsible for much of the killing.

Perhaps the sensitive nature of the subject of infighting during the revolt is one of the reasons why the PLO, which funded numerous projects in Lebanon during the seventies and early eighties, never supported a study of the *thawra* based on the testimony of refugees living in Lebanon. Maybe the resistance movement was hesitant to allow any details about the internal struggles of the thirties to be brought to light because bad feelings persisted in the diaspora community. The account of Bayan al-Hût (1981: 401–6), published by the Institute for Palestine Studies in Beirut, goes further than most standard nationalist accounts in its handling of this subject. Al-Hût at least concedes that the campaign of assassinations and executions alienated part of the population and was a serious problem for the revolt. But she goes on to attribute such killings primarily to *local* initiatives—to rebel commanders or to secret societies who acted without orders from the political leadership—and to Zionist and British intelligence operations. She reports that Jamâl al-Husaynî, a member of the Higher Arab Committee and a leading figure in the rebel headquarters at Damascus, admitted to her that the leadership was responsible for assassinating thirty or forty persons who were engaged in land sales to the Jews. These were dispatched, Husaynî insists, only after the national movement had exhausted all peaceful means of persuasion. Al-Hût criticizes Hâjj Amîn al-Husaynî for failing to take the necessary steps to halt the assassinations once they got out of hand but does not address the claim that Hâjj Amîn ordered such assassinations himself.[13] Al-Hût's version therefore skims lightly over the issue of internal struggles. To the extent that she does deal with it, she largely exonerates the leadership of responsibility for abuses and pins the blame on local leaders of peasant origin or enemy intrigues. Thus, in a move typical of official nationalist history, the lower classes are held responsible for excessive brutality and "errors" in the conduct of the revolt. A few Palestinian accounts are more critical of the assassination campaign, but these are unfortunately marred by a dogmatically Oppositionist (pro-Nashâshîbî) position. Thus they tend to portray the Opposition as having been completely innocent of resorting to violence, collaborating with the British, or supporting the Peel partition plan.[14] The factor of rebels' class hatred toward the wealthy, an important element of the anti-collaborator campaign, is virtually absent from Palestinian reports, whether official or dissident.

But despite the fact that the subject is virtually taboo, I did hear some stories about the activities of collaborators, traitors, spies, and those who sold land to Jews, as well as tales of rebel efforts to deal with such persons, including by execution or corporal punishment. If former rebels discussed these issues, they usually defended the execution of traitors or spies, whom they frequently identified as members or allies of the wealthy classes. But more often they dealt with the charge of excesses through the mechanisms of condensation and displacement. On the one hand, many emphasized cases of rebel commanders who caught spies and treated them fairly and leniently (condensation). Another way of turning aside criticism was by admitting that abuses took place but preserving the honorable memory of the revolt by asserting that these excesses were the work of other commanders in other places (displacement). And some like Abû Shâhir, as we have seen, blamed the Husaynîs for the assassinations. But no one I interviewed admitted to any personal involvement in the execution or assassination of traitors—with the single exception of Abû Fâris, whose case I discuss later. Finally, another common defense of the revolt was something like Arafat's: that many if not most killings were the work of Zionist or English intelligence. Such were the usual representations of the issue of collaboration and the struggle against it that went on during the revolt.

The continuing volatility of these issues was brought home to me after I interviewed the grandmother of Faysal, a friend of mine with progressive politics who came from a notable, landowning family. Faysal had previously taken me around to interview some elderly men of his clan, who had been hesitant to discuss their family's relations to certain revolt commanders. By contrast, Faysal's grandmother addressed the issue directly, telling us that the men of her family had cooperated with the British in capturing a local rebel commander who had killed one of their relatives. I later sent Faysal a copy of the notes I had taken of the discussion with his grandmother and asked him to check their accuracy. He wrote back saying that his father and uncles were very upset when he showed them the old woman's words, especially that the family had "cooperated" (my translation) with the British in capturing a rebel commander. They understood this to mean "collaborated," since the Arabic word ta'âwana can mean both cooperate and collaborate. Faysal asked me to amend my notes to show that although his family had "stopped coop- erating" with the rebel commander, they had not "collaborated" with the British. "Please try to deal with this carefully," he concluded, "and do not try to make a new confusion between the families. We still have to respect these old people's opinions and demands, because it seems that these things are still very sensitive subjects to them and to their honour."

I will not deal with the issue of Faysal's family, but with three stories of collaboration and informing that are exceptional because they were told by men who were actually involved in these activities. They are of interest because of the light they shed on the subjectivity and motivation for collabo- ration and on actual collaborators' memory of collaboration. These are excep- tional narratives in that their subject concerns the taboo issue of betrayal of the national movement; on the other hand, they also turn out to be rather ordinary in that their authors attempt to conform their personal stories to normalizing, nationalist dicta.

Thuggish *Thuwwâr*

I heard one straightforward tale of collusion with the British from Abû Tâhir, a former *mukhtâr* of Bidya, a West Bank village in the Qalqîlya district. Abû Tâhir explained frankly why his clan, the al–Zabans, owners of extensive properties in several villages in the area, did not fight alongside the rebels. The landed classes in this region, he asserted, were not involved in the armed rebellion, which they regarded as the business of low-class hoodlums. "We were big landowners, and the revolt was for the *zu'rân* [thugs]."

Abû Tâhir went on to illustrate how, as he put it, "the revolt wrecked the country" (*al-thawra kharbat al-blâd*) and opened up wounds in the social body that had yet to heal. A doctor from Bidya, Hasan al–Ghâwî, informed the local rebel band that Nâzim al–Zaban was a British agent. According to Abû Tâhir, the doctor's motivation for making this false charge was a strictly personal vendetta. The *thuwwâr* believed the doctor and executed Nâzim. So the al–Zabans set about to get their revenge, first by giving the British exact information about the rebel band's whereabouts. The army surrounded the *mujâhidîn* in their hideout, and in the ensuing shootout several rebels, including the man responsible for executing Nâzim, were killed. A few days later, men from the al–Zaban clan opened fire on a car driven by the doctor, leaving him unscathed but killing his father. Al–Ghâwî absconded to Iraq. In 1985 he still resided outside the country, in Jordan. Although nearly fifty years had elapsed since these incidents, bad feeling between families on opposing sides persisted in the village.

Other old men told me stories of men falsely accused of treason by their adversaries, who were motivated by personal or family reasons, and how those wrongly charged were executed on the order of rebel commanders. These were recounted as examples of how certain individuals and clans took advantage of the revolt's atmosphere of suspicion to settle personal accounts. Abû Tâhir's story differed from most other tales of mistaken death sentences in that—like official Israeli histories—it represented such killings as the *norm* during the *thawra*. Most other old men I met regarded rebels' erroneous judgments and excesses as exceptions and not the rule.

Abû Tâhir's narration was also singular for its matter-of-fact discussion of his family's assistance to the army's counterinsurgency effort. He stressed, however, that the al–Zabans passed along information to the English strictly for local, family reasons—merely to get revenge. In his account, this relaying of intelligence to the army was just a onetime affair; since the al-Zabans were not normally informers they could not be considered traitors (khuwwân), agents ('umalâ'), or collaborators (muta'âwanîn). In fact, the English were incidental to the plot of his story, serving simply as the tools of a landed aristocratic family settling a score with lower-status thugs. In Abû Tâhir's report, the al-Zabans manipulated the English to their advantage, and there is no suggestion that the English might have played on local divisions in order to shatter the national revolt from within. Local issues of class, status, and family conflicts rather than nationalist orthodoxy determined Abû Tâhir's assessment of the revolt. It was the revolt that "destroyed the country," not British oppression or aristocratic collaboration with the enemy. His clan's actions, in his view, were in no way to be regarded as antinationalist or treasonous. Agency in Abû Tâhir's account, in fact, is the obverse of agency in the conspiracy tales discussed earlier, in which the outside forces are all-powerful.

In this instance, the subject's parochial (class, family, personal) concerns were so powerful that they enabled defamations of the revolt exceeding the normal limits of nationalist etiquette. Abû Tahir's clan's act of collusion with the British forces was likewise justified in terms of local custom. There was no question in his mind, moreover, of such actions being viewed as antinationalist.

Then, as if to demonstrate what real collaboration meant, Abû Tâhir related a story from the more recent past. The authorities had dismissed Abû Tâhir as mukhtâr a few years prior to our conversation, after slogans denouncing the occupation materialized on some village walls, and they replaced him with someone more pliant and corrupt. The new mukhtâr, Abû Tâhir complained, was falsifying property deeds to facilitate fraudulent land sales to Israeli speculators. Indeed, some details of the scandal were emerging, and soon after our discussion the local press reported that the Bidya mukhtâr had been accused of forging land purchase documents for 330 dunums belonging to sixteen villagers (al-Fajr, February 15, 1985: 3). As Abû Tâhir spoke we were driving on the Qalqîlya-Nablus highway, right past the fruits of the chicanery of the current Bidya mukhtâr and others like him: the rapidly expanding Jewish settlements, full of red-tiled villas and modern flats.

Treacherous Narratives

But the most dramatic stories about collaboration came from two other men who had served as band commanders during the first stage of the revolt and had subsequently betrayed it to join the counterrevolutionary military units known as "peace bands" (fasâ'il al-salâm).[15] Sonia and I were surprised when these elders, who had been considered traitors (*khuwwân*) by other revolt veterans, agreed to discuss their actions. Unlike the al-Zabans, whose work as informers was covert and of limited duration, these men publicly took up arms in league with the enemy. Yet despite their treachery, our friend Abû Ilyâs, who brought us to meet these men and who himself was involved in the revolt as a teenager, remained on speaking terms with his erstwhile opponents. He alleged, however, that if the insurgents had been victorious both these men would surely have been executed, suggesting the situational as opposed to the essential character of collaboration.

In the course of our discussions, the two men presented narratives that tried to make nationalist sense of both their revolutionary and counter-revolutionary careers. They attempted to weave their contradictory actions into consistent patterns and strained to represent themselves as men with honorable and nationalist pasts. They proudly, even boastfully, recounted their careers as revolt commanders. Both men rendered the act of going over to the enemy as somehow not antithetical to Palestinian national aims. Betrayal was recast and was portrayed not as the essence of their beings but as an episode in complex and convoluted narratives that each did his utmost to harmonize with nationalist dicta.

"A Biscuit, Not Bread"

Shaykh Rabbâh al-'Awad was eighty-five years old when we interviewed him in 1985. An Israeli-Palestinian "internal refugee," he resided a few kilometers north of Acre in al-Mazra'a, where he had settled in 1950 after being expelled from his village of birth, al-Ghâbisîya (see chapter 2). During the thirties Rabbâh al-'Awad earned his livelihood from two citrus and sugarcane orchards (lucrative capital-intensive commercial crops), which he farmed with the help of the occasional hired hand, so unlike most other *mujâhidîn,* Shaykh Rabbâh was a fairly well-off farmer. But like so many, he had a "tough" reputation, having served time in prison, so he told us, for violence committed during interfamily conflicts in al-Ghâbisîya.

A framed photograph of the late mufti of Acre, Shaykh As'ad al-Shuqayrî, gazed down on us as we conversed in Shaykh Rabbâh's sitting room. The photo hung high up on the wall, close to the ceiling, occupying the spot usually reserved for pictures of one's father. Although he was not Rabbâh's relative, Shaykh As'ad loomed large and paternal in his life story. Al-'Awad was reportedly on good terms with the al-Shuqayrî family, and one of his orchards, located near Umm al-Faraj (about seventeen miles west of al-Ghâbisîya), was not far from the orange grove Shaykh As'ad's son, Dr. Anwar al-Shuqayrî, owned at al-Nahr.[16] One eventful day in 1937, Rabbâh told us, while he was working at his Umm al-Faraj orchard, Anwar al-Shuqayrî sent a man to fetch him:

—I went. Shuqayrî was sitting in his car. He said, "Get in beside me."

—I said, "Okay." We went to the gate of their orchard and got out. We went in about twenty or thirty meters. By God, I remember, his face was facing northeast, mine southwest.

—He said, "Did you hear what happened at al-Dâharîya [where a police post had been attacked and weapons stolen] in the hills of Hebron?"[17]

—I said, "How could I not know?"

—He said, "The umma [the revolt leadership][18] wants you to answer the call here in the north."

—I laughed.

—He said, "Why do you laugh?"

—I said, "I have many enemies here in the north. Besides, I have a [police] record. I'm afraid the government will catch me and lock me up."

—He said, "No."

—I said, "What do you mean, no?"

—He said, "It's not possible. The umma is backing you up."

—I said, "But this is a government [that is, the British mandate is very powerful]."

—He said, "The umma is charging you to rise up."

—I said, "Excuse me, let someone else go with the revolution publicly and I'll go out with him secretly."

—He said, "The umma wants you secretly and publicly. The umma took a sieve and sifted the men of Galilee. It didn't find anyone as good as you. Now it's up to you."

—I told him, "Suppose I died."

—He said, "Someone would go in your place."

—"Okay, let that person come out now."

—He said, "No, now it's your turn."

—"Doctor, doctor." I tried to bargain with him.

—He said, "Never."

—I said, "What if I don't want to go out?"

—He said, "The umma's not responsible for your life."

—I said, "This is the justice of the umma?"

—He said, "If the umma wants someone and if he wants to turn against them, the umma can dispense with him."

—I said, "Okay."

Most rebel veterans I met by contrast claimed they joined the armed revolt by choice, and several asserted they had organized local bands of fighters on their own initiative. Even the few former *mujâhidîn* who were conscripted by rebel *quwwâd* contended they were already convinced nationalists who were eager to fight. Shaykh Rabbâh's story was unique in its assertion that the decision to join up was made *for* him by a status superior. Other former *thuwwâr* we interviewed also took pains to explain what political factors motivated them to pick up the gun, whereas Shaykh Rabbâh merely cited the entreaties of a respected notable, which were backed up by threats of rebel violence, as the key factors that induced him to assume his position in the rebel command.[19] His explanation was typical of the subaltern mentality under noncapitalist systems, in which determination was seen as held by status superiors. Even when he inflated his own image ("the *umma* sifted the men of the Galilee"), his boast was based on the endorsement of higher-ups.

Rabbâh also recalled that Dr. Shuqayrî ordered him to finance his band of fighters by collecting money from villages. When Rabbâh objected, the doctor responded, "You're a *thâ'ir* [rebel] and you're obligated to take [money] from the villages. . . . You're taking *for* the *umma*. Go and take, on my guarantee." But the first time he demanded donations, at al-'Amqâ[20] and Kuwaykât, villagers objected, and shots were exchanged between the peasants and Rabbâh's rebels. Village elders applied to Dr. Shuqayrî, complaining that Rabbâh had threatened them and stolen their money. Shuqayrî brought Rabbâh before the villagers of al-'Amqâ and Kuwaykât and proclaimed:

—This is Rabbâh al-'Awad. He came here on the *umma*'s order, he's shooting on the British patrols in the roads, on the army outposts, on the Jews. *This* is Rabbâh al-'Awad, and *you're* sleeping in the laps of your wives. *He* put his blood in his palm and went out fighting, and *you* come to complain against him! If one of you contacts the police or the district commissioner, the *umma*'s not responsible for his life."

—They said, "Doctor, if only he'd told us that we would have given him more, but we didn't know."

—He said, "Now you know. Be aware."

—They said, "Finished, don't worry."

According to Rabbâh, villagers in the area reportedly regarded his demands for assistance as legitimate once the notable Shuqayrî had intervened. So, he recalled, "whenever we were hungry we could go to a man and he'd feed us. If we wanted money, we'd take it and buy whatever we wanted—clothes, bullets, rifles, parts, and so on." Once again Rabbâh presents agency as the attribute of the status superior, whose word is all-powerful. Any abuses in the collection of money for the revolt—about which criticisms had been raised—therefore were the responsibility of Shuqayrî, not Shaykh Rabbâh.

On June 6, 1939, during the revolt's waning months, Rabbâh's patron Dr. Shuqayrî was murdered. Many Palestinians in the Acre region assumed then that rebels were responsible, and many who remembered the incident still believed that in 1985. But the stories we heard from men other than Shaykh Rabbâh never really made clear *why* rebels made this hit or who exactly was responsible, and so the entire affair remained quite murky. A closer examination of the contradictory politics of the al-Shuqayrî family is not particularly illuminating. Anwar's father As'ad al-Shuqayrî, the mufti of Acre, did have a somewhat questionable reputation from a mainstream nationalist point of view. Shaykh As'ad was a vocal and early rival of Grand Mufti Hâjj Amîn al-Husaynî. He objected when the British appointed someone who was his junior in age as well as religious learning to the highest post in the Islamic hierarchy in 1921 (the position of grand mufti was a British innovation). There were also question marks about Shaykh As'ad's politics prior to the mandate. As a Committee of Union and Progress delegate to the Ottoman Parliament prior to the 1914–18 war, he had opposed the rise of Arab nationalism. During the war Shaykh As'ad served as mufti for the Ottoman Fourth Army, and was reportedly one of the first to report to Jamal Pasha about a revolt planned by Arab nationalists in Syria. Shuqayrî also apparently maintained ties with Zionists during the 1920s (See Porath 1974: 24, 212, 217, 226; al-Hût 1981: 181; Lesch 1973: 45, 111–12; Muslih 1988: 91). In the early thirties Shaykh As'ad was one of the leading figures in the Nashâshîbî-headed Opposition movement, the National Defence Party, the main rival of the Mufti's Palestine Arab Party. But Shaykh As'ad split with the Opposition in 1937 over the issue of partition, which was supported by many leading members of the Opposition from Nablus and Jerusalem (Porath 1977: 229). No doubt Shaykh As'ad opposed the Peel Commission plan—as did most Arabs in the north—because it included the virtually all-Arab Galilee and Acre districts within the boundaries of the proposed Jewish state and recommended that Arabs be "transferred" from it, if necessary. Several former rebels claimed that the shaykh and his sons had aided the armed rebellion; some reported they had witnessed Dr. Anwar Shuqayrî treating wounded *thuwwâr*.

A careful look at the political activities of Shaykh As'ad's best-known son, the lawyer Ahmad Shuqayrî, makes the issue of Anwar's murder appear even more obscure. Ahmad was known as a radical nationalist who was close to the Istiqlâl Party (founded in 1932), which, although composed of middle-class members, pursued a more militantly anti-British political line than did the Mufti-led official national movement. Ahmad was part of the team of lawyers that defended the Qassâmite fighters captured in the Ya'bad Forest in November 1935. According to his memoirs, during 1938 and 1939 Ahmad Shuqayrî lived in Beirut, where he had taken refuge to avoid arrest. In exile he acted as a publicist for the revolt and was on good terms, if not always in total agreement, with Hâjj Amîn, who was also based in Lebanon (al-Shuqayrî 1969). But Ahmad al-Shuqayrî is best remembered in the West for his torrid, demagogic rhetoric as a Palestinian spokesperson after the revolt. Shuqayrî repeated such bombast for years: first as the Mufti's spokesman in 1948, then as Saudi Arabia's delegate to the United Nations, and finally as first chair of the PLO, created by the Arab League in 1964. Shuqayrî's reported remarks on the eve of the 1967 war—"Those native-born Israelis who survive the war will be permitted to remain in the country. But I don't think many will survive"—are frequently cited as proof of the Arabs' genocidal intentions toward the state of Israel (Elon 1983: 4; Hirst 1977: 288).[21] Ahmad's close affiliation with Hâjj Amîn therefore raises questions about claims that the Mufti's men bore responsibility for the assassination of his brother.

As for details about Anwar Shuqayrî, his political beliefs, activities, and how he died, these are virtually absent from published Palestinian accounts of the period—an act of national self-censorship?[22]

Rabbâh's garbled account of Anwar al-Shuqayrî's death ran as follows:

—There was a woman who came to the doctor. He was going to Haifa. She said, "Take me with you, Doctor." She was hitchhiking on the 'Akkâ road. (Only God and I know about this.) Her husband, an officer in the police, got suspicious. So he started giving reports to the rebels, that Anwar Shuqayrî is coming to the police and giving us information. So they shot him.
—What group shot him? [we asked.]
—They hanged the one who shot him.
—What group killed him?
—They were . . . [he coughs].
—Abû Durra's group?
—No, Abû Durra wasn't here.
—Abû Ibrâhîm?
—Yes! [interjects Abû Ilyâs.]
—Abû Ibrâhîm's group wasn't around then [says Rabbâh].

—So which group?

—There was a group, there were people who worked in assassination. The police officer revealed to the messengers going to the rebel command in Damascus: The story is so and so. The doctor comes to us the police, this is not right. So they killed him.

—So the Mufti sent the message to kill him?

—No.

—So who?

—A group.

—[Abû Ilyâs interjects again,] The English were behind it!

—I can't speak [Rabbâh protests].

—You don't know?

—No. I want to speak, I want to speak. It's a biscuit, it's not really bread [that is, it's something different than it looks]. Either some of the oppositionists [mu'âridîn] got to the umma by way of the officer . . . [at this point Rabbâh was interrupted and the subject shifted].

After much hesitation, considerable prompting, and interpolations from Abû Ilyâs—who first opined that commander Abû Ibrâhîm al-Kabîr was responsible, then fingered the English—Shaykh Rabbâh finally settled on condemning unnamed members of the Opposition (mu'ârida) for the killing. By this reckoning, the mu'ârida exploited the situation and got the police officer to pass information to the rebel leaders, who ordered the hit. Rabbâh did not venture to explain why the Opposition wanted the doctor murdered. There is good reason to be skeptical of this version, since the Nashâshîbî Opposition was not noted for its strength in the north.[23] While Rabbâh's narration blames rebels—a shadowy group specializing in assassination—for actually perpetrating the murder, it casts the true villains as some anonymous Palestinians who opposed the national movement. But Rabbâh's reluctance to name any specific group and his statement, "It's a biscuit, it's not really bread," also may have been intended as a hint that there was a darker secret—perhaps that Jews were ultimately behind the murder. He appears to have wanted to suggest this explanation but to have been afraid to state it openly.[24]

The explanation Rabbâh gave in 1985 for Dr. Anwar's killing was clearly secondary revision, for in the passion of the moment the rebel qâ'id had felt no such hesitation in assigning culpability. When al-'Awad broke with the thuwwâr in 1939, he was certain that Shuqayrî's blood was on the hands of the Mufti's men. He dispatched a letter of condolence to the Shuqayrî family right after the doctor's murder. Shaykh As'ad's son 'Afû urged him to help his patrons avenge the death by going to work for the English.[25] Rabbâh agreed, and was quickly installed at al-Farda with a force of sixty-five former rebels under his command and a British army officer to "assist" him. He showed us a photo of some members of his contra band, which included a man in shorts whom he said was a Jew. The British army, Rabbâh claimed, paid him a salary of sixty pounds a month—no doubt an inflated figure. This well-paid job, by his account, simply entailed arranging pardons for rebels wanted for political offenses (such as firing on English soldiers) but now willing to lay down their arms. Rabbâh never referred to his group as a "peace band," and he avowed that he never fought in any clashes with the rebels. "No rebel ever bothered me," he concluded.

Rabbâh therefore remembered going over to the British not as an act of betrayal but as an innocuous action that did the revolt no harm. It was as if he had simply performed a "service" for war-weary *mujâhidîn*. At the same time, Shaykh Rabbâh had earlier on recounted his activities as a *thâ'ir* with great pride and claimed to have been the responsible commander at several major, locally known battles. He deployed other strategies, as well, that allowed him to protect his personal as well as the national honor. First, he appealed to local cultural mores: the necessity of exacting revenge and the importance of demonstrating loyalty to one's aristocratic and religious superiors and patrons. Second, Rabbâh claimed that he inflicted no damage on the *thuwwâr*—or the nation—while working for the English, and that the rebels had not been hostile to him, either. Third, by associating his actions with a family that maintained a nationalist reputation (mainly because of the activities of Ahmad al-Shuqayrî), he covered his own activities. Finally, he looked back positively on his career *in* the revolt, and he refrained from defaming (although he did sometimes criticize) the rebel commanders or the political leadership, even when it came to the matter of Anwar Shuqayrî's murder. By such means he managed not to sully the reputation of the national movement. His tale of "betrayal" navigated an unsteady course between local discourses (although the "feudal" one he advocated was by the eighties generally discredited) and nationalist discourses, and thereby managed, in a tangled manner, to preserve his own, as well as the nation's dignity, intact.

I have found no mention of the "peace bands" organized by Shaykh As'ad al-Shuqayrî or of Rabbâh al-'Awad's activities in published Palestinian accounts.[26] But other fighters we met were more forthcoming than were official histories, and their assessments of Rabbâh's career were more critical than his own. 'Alî Baytam of Kuwaykât was the most trenchant. According to 'Alî, Rabbâh did not quit his command but was "retired" by the rebel lead-

ership (al-umma) for stealing money from villagers. After Shaykh Rabbâh started working for the English, he and his men attacked the rebel *fasîl* of Kuwaykât to which 'Alî Baytam belonged; following the battle the British blew up
eight houses in Kuwaykât, including the Baytam family's. 'Alî was subsequently captured, subjected to torture (which included being tossed into a
cactus [*sabr*] patch), and finally persuaded to intervene to get his brother, band
commander Fayyâd al-Baytam, to surrender to Rabbâh. According to 'Alî,
Rabbâh's mercenary activities were directly responsible for the demise of the
rebel movement in the north. (Baytam also asserted that Shaykh As'ad al-
Shuqayrî had been a *khâ'in* [traitor] ever since the days of the Turkish rule,
and therefore his son Anwar al-Shuqayrî deserved to be killed.) Another former rebel, Abû Rajâ of Sha'b, reported that he was detained for two months
at an army camp in 1939, after British forces besieged a village he was visiting to attend a wedding and Rabbâh al-'Awad fingered him as a rebel commander. Somewhat surprisingly, Abû Rajâ declared that Rabbâh was a "good"
man. A third *mujâhid,* band commander Ibrâhîm Hanna of al-Bi'na, remembered al-'Awad as an "arrogant" character but insisted that the revolt had
already disintegrated by the time Rabbâh went over to the army. He confirmed that one of Rabbâh's functions was indeed to encourage rebels to collect testimonies of good behavior from village notables, after which the army
pardoned them. Ibrâhîm Hanna himself was recruited to the Palestine police
force after receiving such a dispensation.

"He Who Extended His Hand to the English"

The second tale of treachery came from Abû Fâris (a pseudonym), a Druze
in his seventies whom we interviewed at his home in Kafr Yâsîf, half an
hour's drive from Acre. Abû Fâris had been the band commander in his natal
village of Majd al-Krûm. "The first one to rise up in revolt in the Galilee,"
he boasted, "was me. The first house that the government demolished was
mine." (House demolition was adopted by the British as punishment for
"terrorist" suspects and is a practice Israel continues to employ today.) After
a stint as local commander (a lower rank than Shaykh Rabbâh's), Abû Fâris
grew dissatisfied with the rebel movement, he said, because it opposed the
1937 Peel Commission partition proposal. According to Abû Fâris, the rebels
were against the splitting of the country because "they wanted to throw the
Jews into the sea." Continuing this line of argument, Abû Fâris alleged that
the rebel movement intended to kill all Palestinians who supported partition,
and that this forced eighty-five thousand persons to take refuge abroad. (Critical accounts of the revolt also claim that the rebellion was out to get sup-

porters of partition, but their estimates of those who went into exile are usually much lower.) When the Mufti's men finally ordered *him* to assassinate a supporter of partition in 1938, Abû Fâris quit the rebel movement and took refuge in Lebanon.

One example of rebel misdeeds that Abû Fâris cited was the attempt to kill Father Ya'qûb of al-Rama. Rebel *quwwâd* told him they wanted to execute the priest because he was a traitor and informer, but the true reason, said Abû Fâris, was that Father Ya'qûb backed partition. He named the Qassâmite Abû Ibrâhîm al-Kabîr, a leading regional commander in the north and a member of the rebel headquarters in Damascus, as the chief orchestrator of the terror campaign against partition proponents. Abû Fâris also made light of the social origins of Abû Ibrâhîm and other *quwwâd*: "All those commanders in the revolt, what did their work in Haifa used to be? They all had carts, they used to buy empty sacks. . . . Abû Ibrâhîm didn't even have a cart, he carried the sacks on his shoulder. This man who was second to Hâjj Amîn— he went around carrying sacks on his shoulders, buying sacks!"[27] Abû Fâris contrasted his own social position to this low-class manual laborer's by stressing that all *his* friends were from the notable class. But like Shaykh Rabbâh, Abû Fâris hesitated to blame all executions on the Mufti's group, and sometimes accused anonymous "intriguers" or "plotters" who killed for money.

In 1939, after learning that the Mufti's men had ordered *his* execution, Abû Fâris arranged through his friends among exiled Palestinian notables in Lebanon to return to Palestine and work with the British army. Among those who assisted him in his efforts to join up with the British-sponsored counterrevolution was Muhammad 'Ataya, the landowner from al-Zîb whose mansion is now Eli Avivi's museum cum youth hostel (see chapter 2). Muhammad 'Ataya had sought refuge in Lebanon, Abû Fâris said, after the Mufti's men killed his brother. We asked whether Muhammad 'Ataya's ability to arrange such matters with the English didn't make him a collaborator. "He didn't go with the government, ever," was Abû Fâris's response. "He didn't have relations with anyone [that is, the British]. The *zu'âmâ* [notable leaders] didn't have relations with anyone, just acquaintances." In Abû Fâris's reckoning, Muhammad 'Ataya, like other notables, acted independently of the British and was innocent of any treachery. (This justification resembles Abû Tâhir's.)

Abû Fâris returned to Palestine to work with the British under the protection of the army, together with the group Rabbâh al-'Awad had organized. The returning mercenary's first stopping point was Shaykh As'ad al-Shuqayrî's house in Acre. According to Abû Fâris, the Shuqayrîs, like other notables, were independent souls, and this explained why trouble broke out between them and the rebel movement. Abû Fâris attributed Anwar Shuqayrî's murder to the Mufti's men, but did so in an ambiguous fashion: "Anwar Shuqayrî worked with the *thuwwâr*. . . . Wherever he found a wounded rebel he would treat him. Hâjj Amîn's group killed him . . . because they didn't want him with the revolt. The Shuqayrîs were independent. Hâjj Amîn's group—*or another group*—got paid and killed him" (emphasis added). Although he had returned to Palestine in the company of Rabbâh al-'Awad and under the Shu- qayrîs' patronage, Abû Fâris declined to join al-'Awad's group at al-Farda because he objected to the latter's methods. According to Abû Fâris, during his earlier tenure as rebel commander Rabbâh used to extract "donations" from villagers for his personal use. Abû Fâris claimed he had even tried to help villagers to defend themselves against Rabbâh's depradations. At al-Farda Shaykh Rabbâh ran a prison, Abû Fâris asserted, where he hauled in suspects and only released them on condition that they brought back either ten pounds or a rifle. Because most of the accused were not rebels and so were unable to procure weapons, they paid the ten pounds and helped line Rabbâh's pocket. Not wishing to participate in such activities, Abû Fâris joined a British army camp at al-Râma, where he served as follows: "They wanted me to take them to the *thuwwâr* so we'd surround and kill them. The English were an ignorant people. They didn't know where God put them. . . . The army says, we will go to a certain place. I would send information to the *thuwwâr*, please go somewhere else. Then we would go there, and no rebels would be there. That was our work. I stayed there until the 1939–45 war got bigger and the revolt ended."

Abû Fâris justified his defection from the rebels by pointing to the Pales- tinian leadership's incorrect position regarding partition (*taqsîm*). But both in 1937–39 and again in 1947–48, most Palestinians, especially in the Galilee, opposed all partition plans, and it was *taqsîm* that inflamed Arab opinion in the Galilee and galvanized support for armed insurrection (Porath 1977: 228).[28] It was only much later that the U.N.-sanctioned partition of 1948 (which unlike the Peel plan did not include the western Galilee) was widely accepted among Palestinian-Israelis, largely because of the influence of the Israeli Communist Party, the most influential "nationalist" force in the Pales- tinian-Israeli community. It is more likely that rebels harassed and even exe- cuted Arabs in the Galilee not for their position on *taqsîm*, but for suspected collaboration with the British or opposition to the national leadership. The rebel intimidation campaign against Opposition members and notables favor- ing partition appears to have been centered in the Nablus and Jerusalem areas and not the Galilee (Porath 1977: 229). Archival evidence also suggests that what Abû Fâris described as rebel hostility toward Father Ya'qûb, the Greek Orthodox priest of al-Râma, over the latter's support for partition should be interpreted somewhat differently. There was a long-running feud between two main families in al-Râma, the Greek Orthodox Hannas, to whom Father Ya'qûb belonged, and the Roman Catholic Nakhlas. The conflict was played out in the revolt, with both factions trying to use their ties with rival rebel leaders to gain an advantage over their opponents. According to Father Ya'qûb's own testimony (as recorded in the archives), certain rebels charged him with being a spy and having connections with Arabs who worked in the mandate administration or the police. He suspected that it was Jamîl Nakhla, leader of the Roman Catholic community, who denounced him to the rebels. Father Ya'qûb's statement says nothing about support for partition as a cause of rebel antipathy.[29] Abû Fâris's assertion that internal struggles and his own defection were based on differences over *taqsîm* appears to be a revision based on partition's retrospective respectability. Abû Fâris also implies that the supporters of partition, unlike the rebels, were not anti-Semitic. But the slogan about throwing the Jews into the sea was not in use by Arabs during the 1930s, and was probably never employed as widely as Israeli propagandists have claimed. Abû Fâris's explanation therefore diverts attention from the possibility that some of his notable friends might have been lukewarm in their support for the revolt or even opposed it, perhaps because of their class position.

In addition, Abû Fâris distinguished his own mercenary endeavors from Rabbâh al-'Awad's. Even when assisting the army's counterinsurgency operations, he claims to have acted as a double agent, passing messages to the *thuwwâr* so that they could escape capture.[30] In this sense Abû Fâris, like Rabbâh, was representing his defection as bringing no injury to the rebel movement. In fact he paradoxically rescues his reputation by placing himself squarely *within* the nationalist ranks, as a double agent.

But the most remarkable feature of Abû Fâris's narratives is his open admission of participation in the execution of traitors while a rebel leader. As he neatly summed up rebel policies toward *khuwwân,* "He who extended his hand to the English would die." Abû Fâris then proceeded to recount an incident involving a man called Ya'qûb. Ya'qûb's cousins, including Ramzî and Samîr 'Abbûd, who belonged to Abû Fâris's rebel band, refused to allow him to carry through with his marriage to his *bint 'amm* (father's brother's daughter), to whom he was engaged. Ya'qûb asked Abû Fâris to mediate with the recalcitrant cousins on his behalf. Abû Fâris told Ya'qûb he would help him

after he got back from a wedding at Kafr Yâsîf. While he was savoring the
nuptial festivities, the British army besieged the village. Abû Fâris managed
to escape, but was certain that Ya'qûb had informed on him. He ordered
Ya'qûb's cousin Samîr 'Abbûd to trick Ya'qûb into accompanying him to
Majd al-Krûm. Samîr did so, and brought Ya'qûb to him. Abû Fâris told us:

—I said to Ya'qûb, "What's happened with you and your uncle's family?"

—He said, "Nothing, I'm waiting for you."

—I said, "Let's go." We went there and then. Fawwâz [another member of
Abû Fâris's group] came after me. I told Fawwâz to take off Ya'qûb's *kûfîya*
[a sign of humiliation]. I told Fawwâz, "Tie him up." Ya'qûb walked in
front and Ramzî 'Abbûd followed. There was a rock. I said, "Sit [as though
on a pedestal] on this rock. *Now* you're a bridegroom." Ya'qûb sat down.

—I said, "Why did you send the army to Kafr Yâsîf?"

—He said, "So they'd capture you."

—I said, "How much money did you get for turning in me and Ramzî?"

—He said, "They gave me a hundred pounds."

—I said, "Okay, great, that's one."

—I said, "Why did you take dynamite from your other cousin and put it
in your cousin's house, and five minutes later the English came and got the
dynamite from his house?"

—He said, "My cousins oppose my marriage to my *bint 'amm*. I went to
that cousin and said, 'Give me the dynamite to put at the bridge, I want to
blow up the road.'"

—[Abû Fâris explains for us:] Ya'qûb's cousin believed him, he gave him
the dynamite. Ya'qûb pretended he was a *thâ'ir*. He placed the dynamite in
the house of his cousin, Ahmad al-Hasan. The army came and arrested
Ahmad.

—I said, "That makes two."

—I said, "Why did you send the army to the orchard, to your cousins'
women? You waited until your cousins were out harvesting tobacco and then
sent the army to your cousins' women, and the soldiers raped them. It happened with you or not?"

—He said, "It happened."

—"Why?"

—He said, "Because my cousins didn't agree to my marrying my *bint 'amm*."

—I took out my pistol, shot him and left. Ramzî 'Abbûd lifted his jacket
and emptied seven bullets into him. We left him there and withdrew.

As we drove back to Acre from Kafr Yâsîf, our friend Abû Ilyâs, who had introduced us to Abû Fâris, commented on the interview. He was surprised that Abû Fâris had been so candid, and said that even a few years earlier he would not have told the story, because of its implications for family politics in the village. (By 1985, almost all the principals were dead.) Before the revolt, Abû Ilyâs claimed, Abû Fâris served time for killing a man in Majd al-Krûm for the price of two guineas, and he had joined the revolt both to protect himself from revenge seekers and to cleanse his reputation. But after the revolt ended Abû Fâris moved to Kafr Yâsîf in order to escape retribution for both the earlier contract killing and the revolutionary execution of Ya'qûb. When we had asked Abû Fâris why he left Majd al-Krûm, he responded simply that he "didn't like the politics there."

By taking responsibility for executing a traitor and by asserting so forcefully that such men deserved to die, Abû Fâris stood out from other interviewees, who largely evaded this problematic issue. Rabbâh al-'Awad, for instance, stressed that suspected spies whom his men caught were never executed on his orders, only by commanders superior to him. "I'm innocent of his blood," Rabbâh said of a prisoner he turned over to Abû Ibrâhîm al-Kabîr, who was responsible for ordering the accused traitor's execution. I read Abû Fâris's exceptional admissions as a statement of his own absence of guilt regarding charges of betrayal. By establishing his credentials as a rebel commander who was extremely tough on spies and collaborators, Abû Fâris hoped to demonstrate his own unimpeachable nationalist credentials.

Irreducible Dregs?

Even the stories of Abû Fâris and Rabbâh al-'Awad, at first blush straightforward cases of treason to the national cause, serve to demonstrate that "collaboration" and its representation in popular memory are quite complex and contradictory phenomena. The question of betrayal, in these cases at least, seems not to be as unambiguous an affair as Ranajit Guha, writing about peasant insurgencies in colonial India, would have it. Collaborators, informers, and traitors, Guha asserts, "personify the irreducible dregs of a backward consciousness which even the force of an insurrection cannot fully flesh out. They stand for servility, fear of change, fatalism, and urge for self-preservation at any price which go with the petty proprietor's mentality everywhere" (Guha 1983: 198). But Shaykh Rabbâh and Abû Fâris represented their motivations for turning against the revolt as being rooted in local ideology and custom, in particular, feudal loyalty and the desire for revenge. Their testimonies contained no hints that they joined up with the British out of

admiration for colonial traditions or for the Zionist project of settling Palestine, or out of "fear of change" or "the urge for self-preservation." What is
more, they retrospectively depicted themselves as having manipulated, and
even outsmarted, the British.

But these stories offer us more than just a sense of the complexities of a
traitor's subjectivity. They also press upon us the retrospective force of hegemonic nationalist discourse. For in a sense, the accommodationist stances
examined here represent relatively minor tears in a commonsense fabric that
was broadly, if loosely and complexly, nationalist. Although both Abû Fâris
and Rabbâh al-'Awad interjected some criticisms of the national movement
into their stories, they equally tried to weave their own contradictory actions
into life patterns that would appear consistent with the national honor,
refiguring nationalism idiosyncratically in order to fit their own biographies
within its parameters. Personal mistakes or inconsistencies—especially in
Rabbâh's case—were presented as products of the machinations of mysterious, outside forces beyond their control. Finally, these narratives give us a sense
of the limited options for expressing any dissent from the national movement
at the height of the insurgency. It was extremely difficult to articulate any
criticism of the rebel movement at that moment without being considered a
traitor. Guha argues that at the apex of peasant insurrections, "the notion of
betrayal tends to acquire a certain degree of elasticity . . . when the usual
thresholds of tolerance are considerably lowered and all neutral markings
erased between sharply polarized positions" (1983: 199). Rabbâh al-'Awad and
Abû Fâris provide accounts of exceptional situations, of actions taken by partisans during times of all-out war. At such a juncture, the ambiguity that normally characterized everyday common sense and practice was simply no
longer acceptable: one had to choose between one of two sides. It also seems
that, at a distance of decades and in the context of more "normal" times, it
was difficult for protagonists to make sense of the exceptional moments in
which they were involved. In such cases, the retrospective "cleaning up" of
the interviewee's self-portrait is not just the normal use of a "life story" as "a
way of excusing [oneself] in public, an effective means of building an
enhanced self-image" (Peneff 1990: 39). Such recastings of memory may also
be due to the difficulty, under "ordinary" circumstances, of recalling or imagining the intense atmosphere of a time of crisis and revolutionary ferment.
When past events such as betrayal and assassination appear strange and murky
in retrospect, it is not surprising that one might attempt to explain them in
terms of mysterious intrigues and secret societies.

6 / Memory Recoded:

Intifada/Thawra

When the intifada erupted in December 1987, the memory of the 1936–39 revolt was quickly revived and reinscribed in Palestinian public discourse. Initially Palestinians in the Occupied Territories recalled the revolt as a symbol of mass struggle and rupture, as the starting point of a modern tradition of national resistance in which the intifada was the latest episode. Militants likewise identified the intifada's protagonists with earlier national heroes of the thawra like Shaykh 'Izz al-Dîn Qassâm and 'Abd al-Qâdir al-Husaynî. These names were frequently invoked in the leaflets issued by the intifada's underground leadership, the United National Leadership of the Uprising (UNLU), and on November 19, 1988, the UNLU called a general strike to mark the fifty-third anniversary of Qassâm's martyrdom (Lockman and Beinin 1989: 390). In the uprising's early days the image of the thawra that was particularly emphasized was that of the six-month general strike of 1936 and its popular unity. This memory of the revolt was presumably stressed because both commercial strikes and the discourse of national unity were so central for the intifada.

While symbolic links between revolt and uprising were asserted and circulated in popular and political circles, Palestinian intellectuals ventured some analytical comparisons between the two movements. In general, these writers drew up balance sheets whose conclusion was that the intifada was more "advanced" than the heroic revolt. Salim Tamari, a sociologist at Birzeit University, argued that unlike the general strike of 1936, which was enforced with a fair amount of coercion, the strikes of the intifada were carried out

171

voluntarily. Tamari stressed, too, that the leadership in 1936–39 represented classes (the urban aristocracy, the big landlords and merchants) that had no equivalent in today's Occupied Territories. "The current uprising," Tamari wrote, "was (and is) led by a strategic coalition of forces and social groupings that bear little resemblance to the elitist and semi-feudal character of the Higher Arab Committee of the 1930s" (1990c: 160–61). Bethlehem University historian Manuel Hassassian for his part observed that the 1936 revolt was more "effective" than the intifada because it was an armed struggle. Hassassian also argued that among the causes for the *thawra*'s ultimate failure were elite factionalism, the rural-urban split, and the rebel forces' predominantly peasant character. The intifada, by contrast, had thrown up a unified leadership representative of all elements of Palestinian society, including rural and urban (Hassassian 1988). Muhammad al-Azharî, an intellectual based outside the Occupied Territories, likewise underscored that the intifada, unlike the *thawra,* was characterized by mass participation and total unity (1989: 9–10). He claimed, too, that the 1936–39 revolt lacked a revolutionary ideology, was afflicted by tribalism, was largely spontaneous, and involved no widely established popular organizations (1989: 11–12, 19–20). The intifada, al-Azharî implied, suffered no such failings. Finally, he argued that the 1936 revolt was crippled in its later phases because its political leadership, located outside Palestine, possessed all the political expertise, whereas the local rebel commanders retained only military abilities (1989: 12). By contrast, the "inside" leadership of the intifada, al-Azharî suggested, was as politically sophisticated as the "outside" PLO chiefs in Tunis.

In sum, such analyses hailed the earlier revolt for its militancy but concluded that the uprising represented a significant advance because it was clearly characterized by greater national unity and political savvy. (These analyses also either ignored the *thawra*'s peasant character or saw this feature as a deficiency.) Such comparisons were voiced during the early, optimistic phase of the uprising, when national unity and popular mobilization were at their peak.[1] They seemed in part to express desires and convictions that the intifada, unlike the *thawra,* would ultimately succeed and usher in national independence. But these assessments, by presenting the history of the Palestinian national movement as a narrative of *progress,* tended to mute the ruptural and discontinuous charge of the revolt's imagery even as they recognized its importance as a symbol of resistance. Nevertheless, that insurrectionary vision of the *thawra* was kept alive by the evocation of figures like Qassâm.

The Israeli government also drew its own comparisons. Continuing long-standing Zionist policies dating back to the thirties, official sources generally labeled the Palestinian national uprising as "riots" and "disturbances." President Chaim Herzog's 1988 Independence Day speech declared that "many Palestinians know in their hearts that the violent uprising is a dead-end, useless struggle, that will produce no more results than the Arab rioting of the 1930's." Like other functionaries, Herzog publicly blamed the "rioting" on the outside agitation of the "extrem[ist]" PLO leadership (Kifner 1988b; Schenker 1988). But unlike the thirties, some cracks appeared in this official orthodoxy. Israeli chief of staff Don Shomron, for instance, declared in early 1989 that "there is no such thing as eradicating the intifada, because in its essence it expresses the struggle of nationalism," but his statement was immediately dismissed as "superfluous" by Prime Minister Shamir (*al-Fajr,* January 16, 1989).

Other observers raised additional comparisons between the revolt and the intifada, noting in particular the Zionist state's use of many of the same repressive policies (and laws) to deal with the uprising that the British mandate government initiated during the revolt: deportations, house demolition, and administrative detention of "terrorist" suspects.[2] But other significant, hidden connections might be raised, as well. Consider the following.

Bad Girls

Winding its way through the hills, a convoy of Jewish civilians and its army guard comes under attack from a volley of stones. Army troops storm the nearest village and take away three suspects. Women hurl a fusillade of rocks at a police detachment remaining behind to search for more offenders, and one policeman is badly injured. The constables open fire over the women's heads in order to effect their escape. A "stray bullet" mortally wounds a Palestinian girl of sixteen. According to a government official, the girl is said to be "bad," and her death is "thought by many to be a good riddance."[3]

The incident just described occurred at the Galilee village of Kafr Kanna—the biblical Cana, where Jesus is said to have turned water into wine—during the early days of the revolt (May 1936). It suggests obscured links between the *thawra* and the intifada. Brought to light, such connections urge a reconstellation of our views of both these struggles.

The most obvious point of comparison is stone-throwing, the renowned international signifier of the intifada. Innumerable popular songs and poems have been composed in praise of *awlâd al-ahjâr* (the children of the stones), hundreds of whom have been killed or injured in their unequal confrontations with Israeli soldiers. Stone-throwing is less commonly associated with the 1936 revolt, but the anecdote from Kafr Kanna suggests that this oppositional Palestinian practice predates the intifada. I'm reminded of how incredibly rocky the highlands of the Galilee and the West Bank seemed when I first visited there in 1962, and of the legend I heard: that soon after the creation God sent the angel Gabriel out to distribute rocks throughout the earth, but when he reached Palestine Gabriel tripped and spilled most of his load. I recall that a Palestinian boy demonstrated how to hurl rocks with a sling like the one David used to slay Goliath; boys used the same kind of sling for similar purposes in the intifada. One British police officer, thinking back on the hazards he faced from Palestinian youths during the insurrection of 1936–39, claimed that "Arabs for some reason can throw a stone more accurately than anyone else in the world. They rarely miss" (Horne 1982: 201).[4] The confrontation at Kafr Kanna underscores that the *thawra* was not just the work of *mujâhidîn* shouldering rifles.

But more important, this tale provides a rare picture of *women* as actors, protagonists, and martyrs in the earlier national liberation struggle. Kafr Kanna suggests that the kind of Palestinian women's mobilization that became visible for a time during the intifada was not entirely novel, and that it has a history that has been systematically neglected. Finally, the woman martyred at Kafr Kanna is described as a "bad girl" and "good riddance," an assessment shared by colonial officials and certain inhabitants of the village. Similar moral judgments against female activists emanated from the Palestinian community during the revolt as well as the intifada, with consequences negative not just for women but for the national struggle as a whole.

It was fall 1988 when I rediscovered the Kafr Kanna anecdote among my research notes. Throughout the first months of that year, I had witnessed almost nightly television images of Palestinian women in the Occupied Territories demonstrating, confronting soldiers, and even throwing stones. Some observers were claiming that such activities indicated that Palestinian women had come "to the fore as equal partners of men" (see Said 1989: 20), while others made more guarded but still optimistic appraisals. It was this new level of mobilization and visibility of Palestinian women that prompted me to return for a closer look at women's role in the 1936–39 revolt.

Although women had not been the focus of my field research on memories of the *thawra,* I had not meant to ignore them. Both Sonia and I were keen to collect samples of women's memories of the insurrection, but since our research priority was the armed revolt we concentrated chiefly on locating and interviewing *thuwwâr.* Moreover, we introduced ourselves to villagers as researchers interested in the revolt, so the local experts we were referred to virtually always turned out to be men—fighters, relatives of *mujâhidîn,* or others reputed to have "good information." Rural men as well as women considered *men* to be the primary authorities on the revolt and on local history and public affairs in general. Old women might be repositories of the folklore and songs of the *thawra,* but they could not be experts on its "history." To elicit women's views regarding the revolt would have required us to present ourselves as interested in some subject other than one coded as a "male" activity and domain of expertise—"life during the thirties," for instance. Such an approach would also have required different methods of research. The procedure we adopted for old fighters, formal interviews lasting a few hours, was not productive for eliciting recollections from elderly rural women. Initially we did interview a few elderly women, but we discontinued this avenue of research after it proved mostly unrewarding. One elderly woman, for instance, protested that we shouldn't bother interviewing her because the older men of the village were much better informed. Another old woman we tried to interview was repeatedly interrupted and "corrected" by her "better-educated" sons, daughters, and in-laws, and was constantly having to attend to her grandchildren. (By contrast, elderly males were rarely bothered by interjections from their offspring, and young children were always kept out of the room when we interviewed them.) We subsequently tried to compensate for our neglect of elderly women by querying male *thuwwâr* about women's actions during the revolt, but this too proved unsatisfactory, since we mainly heard stereotypical stories about women's auxiliary work during battles. Since I learned so little about women's activities while doing fieldwork, this account of women and the 1936–39 revolt relies chiefly on a reading of archival and secondary sources.

"Arab Ladies"

A look at the British archives and at secondary sources leaves one with the impression that the chief female actors during the insurrection were the members of the Arab Women's Committee (AWC). Established in the wake of the violence of 1929, the AWC's stated aims were to advance the cause of women's equality within the framework of the Palestinian national movement.[5] A photograph from the early thirties shows a delegation of AWC leaders posed outside the high commissioner's Jerusalem residence, sporting an array of head coverings. Christian members of the delegation are outfitted in Western-style hats, while Muslim AWC leaders are variously attired in black headscarves (*manâdîl* or *hujub*) that cover their hair, light veils, and heavy veils (Khalidi 1984: 101). As a whole, this "respectable" yet elegant apparel testifies to the women's class background: most AWC leaders hailed from "good," upper-class families and were related or married to prominent nationalist figures. Sayigh notes, however, that some of the AWC's most active organizers did not hail from notable families and that their high-class backgrounds did not prevent these women from undertaking some militant and innovative actions (1989: 155). When General Allenby visited Jerusalem in April 1932, for instance, the AWC organized a dramatic protest, in the course of which a Christian member addressed the crowd from the pulpit of the Mosque of 'Umar and a Muslim member spoke at the nearby Church of the Holy Sepulchre (Mogannam 1937: 94–100). AWC members also played prominent parts in the October 1933 nationalist upsurge, marching alongside men in urban demonstrations and addressing the crowds. Official British sources claimed that the October 13 clashes in Jerusalem were instigated by veiled women who encouraged protestors to stone the police (Taggar 1986: 254). Government reports likewise asserted that Jaffa's October 27 disturbances were incited by "Arab ladies" from Jerusalem who spoke at the rally.[6] The high commissioner's comments on the Jerusalem events indicate officialdom's concern about women's actions: "A new and disquieting feature of this demonstration was the prominent part taken by women of good family as well as others. . . . They did not hesitate to join in assaults on the Police and were conspicuous in urging their menfolk to further efforts."[7] At the same time, Labor Zionist leader Moshe Shertok privately observed that these women's militancy testified to a new depth of Arab nationalist sentiment (Black 1986: 25).

When the Higher Arab Committee (HAC) was established in April 1936 to take control of and guide the nationwide strike and insurrection, no woman was selected to serve on this body, which represented a coalition of male political groups. Instead the AWC and women in general were assigned auxiliary roles. But despite their subordinate position, elite women were quite vigorous. Colonial Office archives preserve a record of the AWC's frequent protests to the high commissioner—by letter and by deputation—regarding the British forces' repressive actions: house demolitions, canings and whippings of suspects, torture of prisoners, deportations, lootings of homes, administrative detentions, summary executions, and the like. It is largely thanks to this correspondence that a documentary record exists of British abuses, a subject to which insufficient attention has been paid. AWC branches also raised money and donated jewelry to support the resistance, administered funds collected for the relief of Palestinian victims of the hostilities, and aided families of prisoners.[8] The AWC likewise appears to have played a role in organizing several demonstrations of urban women.[9] AWC leaders from families that belonged to opposing political factions (*majlisî* and *mu'ârida*) managed for a long time to work together and to transcend the deep and eventually violent divisions that plagued the official national movement. When the women's movement did definitively split along Nashâshîbî-Husaynî lines in late 1938, the division took place over a year after the rift in the official movement.[10]

The AWC also made efforts to mobilize international solidarity. In particular it urged the Egyptian Feminist Union (EFU), headed by Huda Sha'râwî, to support Palestinian women and the Palestinian national struggle (Hatem 1989: 59). The EFU accordingly lodged protests with the British authorities and in October 1938 organized an Arab Women's Conference on Palestine that was attended by delegates from Palestine, Egypt, Iraq, Lebanon, and Iran. The meeting affirmed support for Palestinian national independence, pledged to contact international women's organizations on the Palestinians' behalf, criticized British abuses, and established women's committees on Palestine in each of the Arab states represented at the conference (Hatem 1989: 64–65).

Perhaps the most militant and active AWC branch was located in Haifa, Palestine's most industrialized city and home to the largest concentration of Arab workers. Several reports describe women (including AWC members), accompanied by children and "street Arabs," or *shabâb* (young men), forcing shopkeepers in the Haifa *sûq* to observe commercial strikes declared by the rebel movement. On occasion female strike enforcers were arrested and charged with "intimidating" merchants and smashing shop windows.[11] The leading AWC figure in Haifa was Sâdij Nassâr, wife of the editor-owner of the newspaper *al-Karmil,* Najîb Nassâr, and a professional journalist in her own right. Sâdij Nassâr's name crops up frequently in the British archival record, as organizer and participant in street demonstrations and as a strike monitor. Nassâr was also involved in the AWC's extensive welfare projects with families of prisoners and victims of the disturbances. In 1939 the mandate government placed her under administrative detention (without formal charges or trial) for nine months; she was the only Palestinian woman to be so interned during the revolt. The authorities reportedly had come to regard Nassâr's newspaper articles as "incendiary" (Sayigh 1987: 21) and the marches she organized as "more virulent and dangerous."[12]

Although the AWC set up women's societies in some villages (see Peteet 1991: 48), its political orientation, like that of the official national leadership, was essentially hierarchical and elitist. The AWC never articulated a specifically women's agenda or demanded new rights for women; instead it viewed itself as the female wing of the national movement. Like their husbands, fathers, and brothers, these elite women saw their class as the natural leader of the struggle and regarded the peasant and lower-class women who cooperated with them as their "assistants" in the movement. Accordingly, they made little sustained effort to involve rural or lower-class urban women directly in their organizations or to establish mass-based women's organizations (Peteet 1991: 56, 101).

We do know, however, of at least one urban women's group operating outside middle- and upper-class circles. That was Rafîqât al-Qassâm (Women Comrades of Qassâm), an underground women's organization established by 'Izz al-Dîn al-Qassâm.[13] Our sole source of information on Rafîqât al-Qassâm, which continued operating after the shaykh's death, is Ruqayya Khûrî, the daughter of a Muslim shaykh. Khûrî joined the organization as a Haifa schoolgirl and continued her activities after getting married at age eighteen. Although she received some weapons training, Khûrî never engaged in actual combat during the revolt; her chief tasks were to prepare and transport food to fighters in the hills, to act as a courier,[14] to smuggle weapons, and to collect money for the movement (Antonius 1983: 71; Sayigh 1987: 26–27).

Women in the Countryside

Ruqayya Khûrî described villagers' reactions to her nationalist work as follows: "As we were involved in the struggle no one ever criticized us, although we were in our teens and roamed around quite freely. Even when I went to a village I didn't know and was taken by a guide—a man whom I also didn't know—to the caves to deliver a message, even then no one thought anything of it; on the contrary, the peasant women would salute you if they saw you were in the movement" (Antonius 1983: 71). These peasant responses not only reflected the fact that leaving home in the service of the national cause had gained legitimacy during the revolt, they also indexed important differences between urban and rural women. In general, upper- and middle-class urban women were more restricted in their movements than their rural sisters and, if Muslims, were frequently required to veil. (Of course there was considerable regional and family variation; the coastal towns of Jaffa and Haifa were generally more "liberal" than Nablus or Jerusalem.) The veil, in fact, was still widely considered a signifier of urban women's elevated class status and respectability. And although the AWC's work did expand the "acceptable" scope of public activity for many women, its impact was not universal. Nationalist poet Fadwa Tuqan's account (1990) of her cloistered upbringing in an upper-class nationalist Nablus family during the thirties, for instance, reminds us that quite severe strictures could be imposed on elite women.

By contrast, rural women enjoyed more freedom of movement and generally did not veil.[15] Because economic exigencies usually made it necessary for peasant women to toil outside the home—in the fields, in crafts, as gatherers of herbs, as sellers of produce in urban markets, and so on—they were less constrained by confinement in domestic space.[16] (Rural women who migrated to lower-class districts in the cities generally preserved their greater relative freedom of movement, their lower status, and their greater work burdens.) Moreover, in times of crisis when husbands or sons were absent, some rural women supported their families by their own labor.

Rural women were also more routinely involved in the armed rebellion than were their urban sisters, in the main because the revolt's centers were in the countryside. But only a handful ever carried guns into battle.[17] Female resistance activities in rural areas generally meant "support" work that involved an extension of normal women's duties. Whenever we queried a former fighter about village women's part in the struggle, his typical response was that women used to provide food to rebel bands hiding out in villages and carry food and water to fighters in battle (see chapter 4). A few *thuwwâr* told of women who performed another customary function—singing or ululating in order to stiffen men's resolve as they went off to combat (see Peteet 1986: 21; al-Hût 1979: 450). Although these accounts are stereotypical, they do attest to the essential role women played as producers, preparers, conveyors, and procurers of food and supplies for the rebel economy. Other women took up the slack for absent men and performed "male" activities like plowing. Rosemary Sayigh (personal communication) tells of the widowed mother of one full-time *thâ'ir* who supported her son's partisan activities by manufacturing cheese to sell in Acre. "Without women's responsibility for the continuation of the economy," as Maria Mies reminds us, "no successful liberation war can be fought" (1986: 195).

The British army recognized the critical importance of the domestic economy to the revolt and consistently attempted to cripple it. The collective punishments they imposed on villagers frequently involved an invasion and assault on domestic space, which incited some women to lend the rebel movement more active support. And in the course of searches for weapons and suspects, as we saw in chapter 4, soldiers routinely turned houses topsy-turvy, mixed staple foodstuffs like oil, rice, and lentils together; and destroyed household provisions set aside for the year. This oft-repeated story of olive oil poured over lentils functioned as a kind of trope for the British army's extreme economic cruelty.[18]

Women were likewise crucial to the rebels' amazing ability to blend in with the rural population, to sustain the armed resistance, and to escape detection and capture repeatedly. Frequently this support for the armed struggle required that women manipulate their inferior status and bend the "strict" boundaries of the domestic sphere. For instance, after the government declared the possession of weapons or ammunition a crime punishable by death in late 1937, fighters began to entrust women with hiding and transporting guns and bullets in their clothing or baskets. The British seemed at first not to have suspected women, and even after they began to mistrust them the authorities often did not have sufficient policewomen on hand to conduct systematic body searches of females. One woman we interviewed, Umm Muhammad of Ya'bad, recounted how she once got spontaneously involved in weapon transport. One day in 1938 she was riding a bus from Tûlkarm to Jinîn, a trip she took frequently to sell her pottery work. When the bus came to an army checkpoint, she noticed that a man sitting in front of her was visibly agitated. Umm Muhammad asked what was the matter. "I'm a dead man," he replied. "I'll be hung because I've got a revolver." Umm Muhammad quickly took his gun and hid it among her baby's wrappings. The troops removed all the men from the bus and searched them, but they ignored the women. When they resumed their journey, Umm Muhammad returned the revolver to the stranger, whose name she never learned.[19] Actions like these, of course, were not without risks: a ten-year prison sentence, for instance, was imposed on a twenty-five-year-old married woman from Beersheba found in possession of eighteen rounds of ammunition and a revolver (*Palestine Post,* December 16, 1937).[20] Umm Muhammad also reported that, despite her husband's absence from the house, she once hid two wanted fighters there for several days; old fighters recounted other similar cases (see Warnock 1990: 145). Women also exploited the permeability of cultural strictures when they dressed up wanted rebels in female clothing and harbored them in women's quarters.[21] Such actions manipulated prevailing norms, which limited male entry into women's domestic space to relatives, for the sake of the national struggle.

When British troops descended on villages hunting suspects, women also protected identities of hidden rebels by participating in the conspiracy of silence (Sayigh 1987: 28). Had women informed on them, the *thuwwâr* would not have eluded capture time and time again. Rural women also reportedly refused to identify the dead bodies of rebels that the army presented them, for to do so would have invited more collective punishment (Peteet 1991: 51).[22]

Counterrevolution in the Revolution

The British military was not the only force opposing women's resistance. Women also came under pressure from within their community, especially in 1938, when a concerted campaign of intimidation was launched against urban women activists. According to women's movement veterans interviewed by Sayigh (1987), this venture was carried out by a "reactionary current" in the mosques and was orchestrated by the British; its targets were women who wore Western-style attire and engaged in political work outside the home without male escorts. No doubt they were the kind of women pictured in Walid Khalidi's *Before Their Diaspora* (1984: 222). Outfitted in "Western" dresses and high heels, they are collecting money in Jerusalem for "afflicted" Palestinian families, victims of the British war against the national insurgency.[23] The "reactionaries" regarded such deportment and attire as signs that women had succumbed to the temptations of Westernization and immorality. Their campaign included fierce attacks from mosque pulpits and street harassment from *shabâb*. According to Rafîqât al-Qassâm member Ruqayya Khûrî, young men needled Haifa female activists with slogans like this:

> Umm al-bunya, al-raqqâsa
> Bidha bomba wa rasâsa.
> [The woman who wears a hat, the dancer
> Deserves a bomb and a bullet.]

The couplet contained both a threat and an insult. *Umm al-bunya* (literally, mother of the hat) connoted a Westernized woman, while the term *raqqâsa* (dancer) implied a woman of loose morals, a virtual prostitute. In Haifa, at least, such death threats contributed to women's retirement from the field of struggle (Sayigh 1987: 27–28).

Sayigh's female informants, loyal nationalists, attributed these campaigns of moral censure and physical threats solely to Islamic ultraconservatives and British conspirators. But nationalist and feminist accounts of the period largely ignore evidence that similar "reactionary" discourses and practices emanated from within the *nationalist* camp. Prior to the revolt, in September 1931, the national leadership of the day, the Arab Executive, convened a general assembly in Nablus that was mainly attended by moderate nationalists but included radicals like 'Izzat Darwaza. Among the assembly's resolutions was one calling on "ladies . . . to abstain from wearing European dresses" (Taggar 1986: 340). And in June 1936 the popular poet and singer Nûh Ibrâhîm attempted to recruit urban women to the struggle with a chant that contrasted the frivolous Westernized habits of city women to their peasant sisters' "traditional" actions in support of the rebellion: "And you, the Arab woman, march in step with your sisters the warriors [*mujâhidât*] of the villages. Stop using your make-up, stop going to the cinema and other kinds of entertainment. Rise to the level of your sisters who carry water jugs on their heads, joining the warriors [*mujâhidîn*], singing and cheering them and so easing their death."[24] Even the AWC was divided over the correct approach to women's dress, between those who wanted to signify their emancipation by wearing "modern" clothing and those who opposed any move that might alienate them from the masses. This sartorial dispute reflected a deeper cleavage between progressive and conservative women activists (Sayigh 1989: 156).

The rebel movement must have built on such "nationalist" sentiments when it mounted its own drive against Western female apparel, a move that was in all likelihood also connected to the "reactionary" venture. The sartorial restrictions on urban women were imposed concurrently and sometimes conjointly with the drive, launched by the rebels in September 1938, for urban men to doff the *tarbûsh* and don the peasant *kûfîya*. In Jaffa, for instance, a rebel communiqué—aimed at the middle and upper classes—ordered women to veil (Porath 1977: 268). In other locales rebel orders forbade Arab women to follow European fashions, visit hairdressers, or engage in the sale of commodities.[25] A communiqué issued on October 6, 1938, by the highly respected commander, 'Abd al-Rahîm al-Hâjj Muhammad, explicitly connected the struggles over men and women's fashion:

> It has reached the attention of the Central Command that some effeminates [*mukhannathîn*][26] who resemble men are going around in the streets bare-headed, forgetting what we previously announced about the requirement to wear the *kûfîya* and the *'iqâl*. It also came to our attention that some women eager to imitate Western [*afranjî*] dress are neglecting the order to veil. To all these persons we address this warning, reminding them of the penalties awaiting them if they continue in their recklessness. ('Awda 1984: 123)

A London *Times* report (September 5, 1938: 11) likewise testifies to the connections between the rebel chiefs' imposition of the *hatta* in Jerusalem and their order to wear the *mandîl* or *hijâb* (head kerchief):

> The Arab rebels' ban on the tarbush has been completely successful, even with old effendis and Arab Government servants wearing hats. Now Christian

women are required to abandon the European hat and adopt the old-fashioned mandila, covering their hair. Today [September 4] church-going women had their hats torn off by boys, and destroyed. This change of modes at the behest of rebel chiefs, while partly due to intimidation, at least suggests that they have some backing among the people in general.

A subsequent *Times* account (October 5, 1938: 16) states that "Christian women have now fallen into line and abandoned their European hats for the kerchief of the East [the *mandîl* or *hijâb*]." A photograph of a group of Christian Palestinian women, probably dating from this period, testifies to the change: although they are still garbed in "European" dresses and high heels, their hair is wrapped in black scarves (*manâdîl*), which, according to Graham-Brown, symbolize their "allegiance to the nationalist movement" (1980: 167). My conjecture is that such efforts to force urban women to dress "modestly" and to abandon their "eagerness to imitate Western dress" contributed to the retirement of women activists (both Christian and Muslim) from nationalist work.

The rebels appear to have aimed these sartorial commands principally at urban women and not at their rural sisters, who did not wear Western dress or go to hairdressers, who normally covered their heads with scarves, and for whom veiling would have been impractical (although the command not to sell commodities, mentioned above, was probably directed at lower-class urban women.) But fragmentary evidence suggests that some similar pressures were exerted on village women. A bulletin issued in July 1938 by a commander in the Nablus district forbade peasant women to take their vegetables to sell in Nablus—a customary practice for rural women—and ordered their husbands to perform this task instead. Violators would be assessed a fine of five pounds. The following day village men rather than women brought vegetables into the city for market. Another manifesto from the same period ordered all women in the Nablus area to cover themselves heavily and not to travel about with light or transparent veils.[27] The intelligence agent relaying this information does not tell us whether the latter order was followed. I have discovered no evidence to indicate whether or not village women quit the national struggle in response to such pressures.

Revolting Memories

Rosemary Sayigh notes that women and their participation in the national struggle have been rendered virtually invisible in Palestinian histories. I would simply add that the campaigns to regulate women's behavior that were launched during the revolt by "reactionary" as well as "patriotic" men have been even better hidden. Old villagers we interviewed never mentioned such harassment of women, but since Sonia and I were not really aware of these campaigns, we never asked about them, either. The intimidation campaign is not mentioned in sympathetic Western or Arab accounts of the Palestinian women's movement, except by Sayigh (1987), who discusses its reactionary-colonialist dimensions but neglects its nationalist side.[28]

Focusing on gender as a primary category of analysis here (see Scott 1988) allows us to see additional contradictions within the national movement and complicates further our presentation of the "popular" memory of revolt. Gender problematizes, for instance, the signifier of the *kûfîya,* whose popular and insurrectionary dimension I emphasized in chapter 1 and which I have attempted to deploy as a "dialectical image" in order to disrupt the official nationalist narrative of progress. But this image of popular rupture, we discover, has a shadowy underside and is decidedly masculinist. So although the *kûfîya* was an important feature of a rebel campaign to democratize the national struggle, it was equally tied to efforts to limit women's behaviors, under the guise of preserving their honor, opposing Westernization, and asserting traditional Islamic-national values. Yet this move to control women by imposing the veil and *mandîl* also had its "popular" dimension, inasmuch as, like the *kûfîya* campaign, it principally targeted the middle and upper classes (including nationalist activists) and may have expressed—albeit in a sexist way—class antagonisms. The *hijâb* campaign had sectarian overtones, as well, since it appears to have been aimed especially at urban Christian women, who tended to be somewhat better off, and more socially "liberal," than Muslim women.[29]

Yet having raised the issue of sectarian divisions, we should add that the radical shaykh 'Izz al-Dîn al-Qassâm was involved in educating, organizing, and mobilizing women. This fact adds a gendered dimension to the popular and much-contested image of Qassâm and complicates our notions of Islamic militancy. It also raises a feature of Qassâm's career that is never mentioned by those competing forces, secularist as well as Islamist, who claim to be Qassâm's "true" heirs.

Women who mobilized in the revolt generally did so within the framework of the preexisting gender-based division of labor. But, we might ask, did their extensions and manipulations of their "traditional" roles effectively expand the scope of women's activities, as some have suggested, or did their actions simply represent the *exception* that is positively valued during times of crisis? Muslims, for instance, are permitted to eat pork during famines, and Muslim fighters are exempted from Ramadan fasting during wartime. Such exceptional practices do not challenge the normal Islamic restrictions on the consumption of pork or the requirements to fast. Are long-standing patri-archal codes, therefore, threatened when they are not tackled head-on but are simply bent or manipulated during moments of crisis? The lesson of the revolt, at least for women, suggests that to stretch dominant codes during exceptional moments may not actually bring about changes to those codes.

Still, subtle challenges and minor cracks did appear in the gendered social fabric. These fissures might, at the very least, have served and still serve as dialectical images during moments of rupture. Take the photograph, from 1937 or 1938, that is found in Graham-Brown's *Images of Women;* it shows a group of young women in Nablus, collecting donations for the nationalist cause—doing "women's work" in the public sphere (1988: 233). What is re-markable about the photo is that these young women's heads are not covered by the *mandîl* but by the *kûfîya,* the headdress of rural *men* and the insignia of the *mujâhidîn*.[30] We shall see such cross-dressing, gender-bending images sur-face again fifty years later, during the intifada.

Interlude

Women returned to everyday forms of accommodation and resistance to British rule and Zionist colonization after the revolt was crushed in 1939. The AWC survived the revolt and the disaster of 1948, but its membership was scattered, and in the West Bank and Gaza Strip it became preoccupied with relief and charity work. Between 1948 and 1967 some West Bank women activists were involved in underground parties (Communist, Ba'thist, and Arab National Movement) that ignored women's issues but provided political experience that proved useful in the confrontations with the Israeli occupation (Jad 1990: 128). "Ordinary" Palestinian women meanwhile fo-cused on survival strategies and on sustaining and transmitting the Palestinian identity in this difficult period (Giacaman and Odeh 1988: 58; Sayigh 1989: 157; Sayigh 1979).

But social changes did not necessarily come to a halt once the West Bank came under the politically repressive and socially conservative rule of the Hashemite monarchy. According to Fadwa Tuqan, the 1948 *nakba* paradoxi-cally prompted a social shake-up in ultraconservative Nablus: by 1950, she says, women had removed the veil and started to attend movies in mixed company and to participate in mixed-gender family visits (Tuqan 1990: 24–25; Warnock 1990: 37). Tuqan describes these transformations as micro-logical processes, the results not of organized movements but of subtle everyday struggles that were visible perhaps only to the female observer:

Before the final lifting of the veil, Nablus women had succeeded in changing their outer covering, by stages, over a period of thirty years. In the twenties they got rid of the full black flowing skirt, substituting a black or brown coat or one of some other sombre colour. At the beginning of the forties they got rid of the triangular bolero-like cover that was worn on the head and came down over the shoulders to the waist, concealing the shape of the upper half of the body, and behind which the woman would fold her hands over her breast, so the men could not see her fingers. In the middle forties the transparent black kerchief became more transparent, revealing the face under it, and in the middle fifties the black veil was finally lifted, allowing the God-given beauty of their faces to speak modestly for itself.

The evolution of the veil in Nablus was slow compared to Jerusalem, Haifa and Jaffa. The path our development took was neither easy nor smooth. Nablus remained a bigoted city.(1990: 114)

Yet it should be underscored that this is an elite narrative of progress. Meanwhile, in a kind of counterpoint, peasant women's dress turned *more* modest as a result of contact with and pressure from urban standards. Peasants' short-sleeved dresses, with slit fronts and no undergarments, were replaced by long-sleeved dresses with closed fronts and the new phenomenon of trouserlike underclothes (Hammami 1994, citing Weir 1989).

Committee Work

Fast forward to the intifada. If historiography largely ignores women's role in the 1936 revolt, many contemporary observers have seen the uprising as a moment of unprecedented women's participation in the national struggle (see Giacaman and Johnson 1989). This time around it was not elite aristocrats but educated middle-class members of the women's committees (many related or married to male activists from the same class) who played the leadership role. These committees were founded during the late seventies as alternatives to the "charitable" groups that had been the predominant organized form of women's activity until then;[31] they were affiliated with the four main political tendencies of the national movement in the West Bank (Fath, Communist, Democratic Front for the Liberation of Palestine [DFLP], and PFLP). Prior to the intifada, the committees surveyed the conditions of women workers; campaigned for women's rights to equal pay and maternity leave; participated in trade union activity; established literacy projects, job training and health education programs, nurseries and kindergartens; and established branches in many villages and camps. The committees had established a framework for organizing and activating women during the intifada (Giacaman and Johnson 1989; Rishmawi 1988: 90).

Several factors combined to permit women to play their enlarged role during the intifada's first phase. First, a political vacuum was created when large numbers of male activists were jailed. Second, a public structure was established in which women could be active—the popular committees and especially the neighborhood committees, the latter largely created by women. Finally, the neighborhood committee movement received the full and active endorsement of the intifada leadership (Usher 1992: 38). Women's committee activists were key actors in the popular and neighborhood committees, which ran communities' day-to-day affairs and organized food distribution and security. It is estimated that at their peak, forty-five thousand such popular committees were active in the Occupied Territories (Corbin 1990a). Women involved in committee work frequently participated in mixed-gender activities and occupied leadership positions (Giacaman and Johnson 1989: 162, 164; Vitullo 1988b: 11). Moreover, a great deal of women's political action in the early days was spontaneous, and more concentrated in refugee camps and villages than in urban areas, a reflection of the uprising's extensive mass base.[32] This grassroots upsurge spawned a membership boom in the existing women's committees and led to the creation of new branches.[33] Committees tried to manage the influx by decentralizing organizational structures,[34] so a new cadre emerged in villages and camps that, unlike the movement's heads, was often not highly educated or middle class (Augustin 1990: 3).

Much of the activity in the intifada's first phase (as during the revolt) involved the extension of women's normal domestic roles rather than the adoption of novel ones (Giacaman and Johnson 1989). For instance, the notion that a woman must defend her family, nurture its members, and organize mutual aid among kin was enlarged to encompass the entire national community, which was recoded as the family. Thus a mother would confront soldiers mistreating or arresting any young Palestinian man, whom she would regard as her son. Mundane activities like visiting the sick and wounded or attending martyrs' funerals were transformed into organized political activities and demonstrations of solidarity. Women were also central to the intifada's campaign for self-reliance and increased local and home production, which aimed at loosening the chains of Palestinian dependency on the Israeli economy. This effort, in particular the cooperative movement, involved an augmentation of rural women's normal work as small farmers, gardeners, food processors, and marketers. Cooperatives mobilized considerable female labor, especially in villages, in the tasks of food processing (yogurt, fruit juices, jams, pickles) and sewing (Warnock 1990: 115). In addition women, who constituted the majority of preuniversity teachers, performed the bulk of the alternative teaching that allowed children to continue their educations after the authorities closed the schools. All these "normal" female activities were now invested with the nationalist aura (Jad 1990: 134).[35]

Other shifts were seemingly more dramatic. Giacaman and Johnson argue that women broke the cultural "barrier of shame" that frowned upon free movement (1989: 162). For instance, women (and children) smuggled food, medicines, and provisions into besieged communities, particularly refugee camps, that were under curfew (Dayan-Herzbrun 1989: 250). Single women distributed the illegal leaflets produced by the UNLU, ensured that shop-keepers charged fair food prices and observed strikes, and enforced the boy-cott of Israeli-manufactured goods (Hiltermann 1990c: 34). Women also participated in confrontations with soldiers, although usually by breaking and carrying stones or standing guard for the mainly male stone-throwers (Hudson 1990: 65–71). By March 1988, women-organized demonstrations in towns and villages were numbering about 115 per week (Jad 1990: 133). When traditional gender-coded work was extended and redefined as nation-alist it, too, could widen the scope for female activity. Visits to families of martyrs and wounded frequently entailed long-distance outings, and progres-sives in the cooperative movement worked to get women out of their homes and into community-based projects that provided independent incomes (Augustin 1990: 13–16, 20).[36] Political awareness also increased, reflecting higher educational levels for women and the committees' "consciousness raising" work (Bennis 1990: 31). The abandonment of the practice of the *mahr,* or "bride-price," although prompted by financial hardships, was regard-ed as a progressive development because it allowed people to marry at a younger age. In addition, young women reportedly wrested more control over marriage choices from their parents (Warnock 1990: 63). And during the intifada's first year, women constituted one out of every seven Palestini-ans injured from live ammunition, beatings, or tear gas (Vitullo 1989a: 13).

Even this early period of ferment and hope had its limits. For one, women neither gained greater prominence in the leadership of established national institutions nor won representation in the intifada's underground leadership, the UNLU. Furthermore, only one UNLU communiqué issued during the uprising's first year mentioned women, and this statement—"congratu-lations to the mother of the martyr"—portrayed women as sacrificers for the nation, not as active agents (Giacaman and Johnson 1989: 165). The Pal-estinian Declaration of Independence, announced at the November 1988 Palestine National Council (PNC) meeting, was likewise mixed regarding the question of women: while it did call for gender equality, it referred to "woman" in traditional reproductive terms, as "the maker of the generations" (Warnock 1990: 188). The dominant forms of expressive culture continued to depict women as the carriers of tradition but not as political actors. Women's committees, moreover, were still divided along the same lines as the national political movement, and their projects were concerned as much with expanding the constituency and increasing the relative power of their separate political factions as with mobilizing women (Giacaman 1989: 18–19).[37] In any case, the committees had to scale back many projects dealing with women's specific needs—kindergartens, literacy, and health—in order to cope with the pressing demands of nationalist work. In summer 1989 the committees did manage to establish the Higher Women's Council (HWC). Composed of representatives from the four committees and independents, the HWC's purposes were to (1) coordinate activities among the groups, (2) take initiatives on legal issues concerning women and formulate a women's agenda, and (3) increase the influence and independence of the women's movement within the national struggle. But even the leftist organizations remained divided over whether the HWC should function independently of the national movement or simply serve as its women's arm (Augustin 1990: 8).

Counterrevolution in the Revolution Redivivus

It was a struggle over style—an uncanny repetition of 1938—that played a major role in bringing an end to the initial hopeful phase of the intifada for women. In spring 1988 the Muslim Brotherhood renamed itself Hamâs (an acronym for the Islamic Resistance Movement) and began transforming itself from an antinationalist organization that avoided confrontation with the Israeli occupation (as it had done throughout the eighties) into a nationalist movement. Hamâs kicked off this effort with a campaign to force women in the Gaza Strip to don the *hijâb* (headscarf), claiming this was their nationalist and Islamic duty. As Rema Hammami explains, the Islamist movement was able to make its inroads over the question of respect for martyrs. In local culture, it is considered a sign of respect for the deceased to cover one's head. The Islamists expanded this notion to argue that the entire nation was in permanent mourning for the martyrs (who were dying every day), so women should wear the *hijâb* continuously. Going bareheaded (for women) was thereby recoded as "frivolous" and even antinationalist in this atmosphere of perpetual funereality (Hammami 1994). Hamâs's spring 1988 drive began with graffiti calling on women to wear the *hijâb;* soon *shabâb* in the streets of the Gaza Strip were aiming the uprising's sacred stones at bareheaded Arab women. By summer 1989 the Islamists had intimidated virtually every woman in Gaza, even militant secular leftists, into adopting the "Islamic" headcovering that was now reinvested as "nationalist." Hamâs militants harassed "immodestly" dressed women in West Bank towns as well, but they were unable to impose their will because the women's movement was much stronger there (Hammami 1990; Augustin 1990: 24; Usher 1992: 39).[38] The UNLU (which did not include Hamâs) did not respond to the antiwomen onslaught until a year and a half after it began. It finally did so after two activist young women covering their heads with kûfîyât rather than hujub were physically attacked in August 1989. These militants insisted that their political committee respond; their persistence finally induced the UNLU to issue a communiqué condemning harassment of women (Hammami 1991: 80).

Both the UNLU's and the Higher Women's Council's statements on the hijâb campaign, however, essentially blamed the attacks on the occupation forces and collaborators, recalling activists' explanations for the antiwomen campaigns during the thawra. The UNLU and the HWC did not attempt to confront the Islamist trend head-on or to criticize "traditional" norms, for fear of "splitting" the national movement (Hammami 1990: 28; Augustin 1990: 24–25). Moreover, "neither the Unified Leadership nor the Higher Women's Council acknowledged the extent to which nationalist forces bought into the hijab campaign" (Hammami 1990: 28). According to Rita Giacaman, the national leadership understood the Islamist effort only in terms of factional politics, not in terms of its wider social and cultural implications (Usher 1992: 38). The UNLU statement only lessened pressures on Gaza women momentarily, for Hamâs renewed its campaign in February 1990. Having successfully imposed the hijâb, Hamâs initiated efforts to compel women to wear the Islamic jilbâb (full-length dress or coat) and to regulate women's behavior in general.[39] Calls issued from the mosques warning women not to "mix" with men in public spaces, and further attacks were mounted on women activists (Hammami 1991: 81). Some women in Gaza, however, subtly manifested their resistance to Hamâs's efforts by embroidering their hujub with the distinctive secular-nationalist checkered pattern of the kûfîya.

Although the hijâb was not forced upon West Bank women, more women did adopt the "Islamic" headscarf, and others, either out of choice or fear, began dressing more modestly and worrying about how their public activities were being judged. Thus the Islamist campaign contributed to a general decline of women's activism. By 1990, moreover, the neighborhood and popular committee movement, the chief structure for women's activity, had collapsed under the weight of Israeli repression. The military authorities banned popular and neighborhood committees at the end of 1988, and started laying automatic ten-year prison sentences on those convicted of belonging to committees, demolishing rooms of committee members' homes, and harassing owners of garden shops and people growing vegetables on home plots as part of the self-sufficiency campaign.[40]

As the popular committee structure crumbled, political activity was transformed, as well. Increasingly this came to mean acts of resistance (often armed) that were mounted by clandestine groups of young men (*shabâb*) and therefore excluded most sectors of the population, including women (Hammami 1991: 76). Mass participation in the intifada came to entail little more than strike observance. The daily commercial shutdowns commencing at noon (and eventually later), as well as scheduled daylong strikes that marked national commemorations and unscheduled ones called to protest specific acts of repression, degenerated into empty symbolic acts. Merchants, workers, and consumers continued to observe them, both because of pressure from the *shabâb* and because these were often the only visible means of asserting that the struggle continued. In addition, such strikes punished local Palestinian economic interests more than Israeli ones, and meanwhile the boycott of Israeli products had fizzled (see Legrain 1993).

The disintegration and demise of women's activism was also helped along by factors "internal" to the national movement. One such factor was the "intifada culture," which established a climate that enjoined serious behavior and frowned upon frivolity. Hamâs was able to work on this predominant sensibility to garner support for its *hijâb* campaign. Intifada culture meant, for instance, that families in Gaza were no longer allowed to go to the beach, that music and dance performances were actively discouraged, and that weddings and other community festivities were reduced to their bare bones. Although this policy of joyless austerity cut down on the social and cultural activities of all segments of society, its impact on women was particularly harsh (Hammami 1991: 77). Since wedding celebrations and the like were the sole social outlets for many women, the banning or limiting of such events only increased women's social isolation.

Among other negative "internal" factors was the prevailing public atmosphere of chaos and instability. This was fostered in part by the campaign against collaborators (discussed further in a later section). It was also the product of widespread (and well-founded) rumors that army interrogators sexually abused detained female activists and reports of women and girls being tricked into "compromising" behavior by security agents working at dress shops, photo shops, and hairdressing salons (Hammami 1994; Black and Morris 1991: 472–73).[41] The climate of uncertainty and fear prompted patriarchal families, anxious to protect their "honor," to reassert their control over female members and to pressure them to retire from the public arena ('Abd al-Jawad 1991: 63–64). A related setback was the increased incidence of childhood marriage for women and a decline in women's average marriage age from twenty-one to seventeen (Tawfiq 1990)—a sharp reversal of a fifty-year trend toward later marriage.[42] One reason for the falling marriage age was that some families decided to marry off daughters who had graduated from high school rather than send them to university, since the prolonged closure of institutions of higher learning eliminated the option of postsecondary education (Corbin 1990b: 10). Other families, especially in villages, married their teenaged daughters off rather than finance their secondary education, which now seemed wasteful since jobs for educated *men* were so scarce (Vitullo 1993). Such trends simply added to nationalist burdens already weighing on women. Nationalist discourse, vigorously pronatalist ever since the occupation, urged women to help win the demographic struggle with Israeli Jews by bearing numerous children. Lowered marriage age and nationalist natalism combined to produce the Occupied Territories' highest population growth rate ever in 1990: 4.3 percent for the West Bank and 5.2 percent in Gaza (Vitullo 1993).[43] For a long time, women had already assumed extra domestic labor because so many men were in prison (see Sayigh 1984: 24). To these tasks the uprising had added the burdens of the home economy movement. It was women who took up the national chore of ensuring that their families consumed "local" rather than Israeli products (Hudson 1990: 59). The self-sufficiency campaign, which proved an economic failure, ultimately ghettoized women in their prescribed social roles and removed them from the public arena (Usher 1992: 41).

Some of the contradictions in women's work are summed up in another women's committee project. At Kafr Na'ma, a village west of Ramallah, the local women's working committee opened a sewing workshop as part of the self-sufficiency drive. But to make a profit, the women produced shirts for the Israeli market through a subcontract with a Tel Aviv firm. Questioned about this paradox, the head of the committee explained that although the intifada leadership had called for a boycott of Israeli goods, it permitted subcontracting in the garment industry, one of the main employers of women workers in the Occupied Territories (Hiltermann 1991a: 58). Although such work did provide women incomes, it incorporated them at the lowest rungs of the global factory. Because they are considered to "belong" to the domestic sphere and to be responsible for housework and childcare, women are expected to be satisfied with such ill-paid and insecure jobs in the subcontracting end of the garment industry (see Mitter 1986; Moors 1989b).

Thus gendered nationalist discourses and practices worked together in an unlikely manner with the forces of Israeli repression and Islamist conservatism to magnify women's load and ultimately dash the high hopes raised by the intifada. Nationalist discourses constrained women within prescribed roles, as ostensible keepers of national custom and as symbols of the tradition and authenticity that had to be protected against Western influence. Their prescribed positions meshed well with a widespread sensibility that the continuity of the family, one of the few Palestinian institutions thought to have survived the dislocations of the occupation, depended on keeping women isolated from foreign and especially Israeli contact (see Rockwell 1985: 131). Here nationalist notions conjoined with Islamist ones, which centered on establishing appropriate (modest, cloistered, male-dependent) social behavior for women (Hammami 1994). Thus men in Gaza, when asked why they wouldn't allow women more freedoms, responded, "What is left for us? We don't have land, homes or identity—at least let's have our honour" (Cossali and Robson 1986: 38).

Women of the *Thawra,* Women of the Intifada

It is in part because the memory of women's role in the revolt has not been kept alive, except in very superficial ways, either in popular or official Palestinian culture, that women's mobilization in the intifada could appear to be something new and exceptional, another example of the nation's progress.[44] Therefore the very significant parallels between women's activities in the *thawra* of the 1930s and the intifada of the 1980s have not been recognized. But we have seen that at both moments of crisis women were mobilized in large part through the politicization and expansion of their usual domestic, auxiliary roles—as the mother, the homemaker, the nurturer, the keeper of tradition. In both insurrections, women provided the necessary economic base through their increased domestic work. In both cases, women left the home to enforce pricing, boycotts, and strikes; to organize demonstrations; smuggle supplies; confront soldiers; and so on. In the intifada and the revolt, the urgency of the national struggle activated women while at the same time it exerted considerable pressures on women to act as supports to movements led by men and to subordinate their own interests and demands to nationalist exigencies. Women, in the *thawra* and the intifada, were able to use their domestic roles to hide much of their essential activities from the view of the forces of power (and from researchers and official memory). At the same time the very covert nature of women's activism, its confinement within normalized spheres, meant that although women contributed to the insurgencies, they had done little to truly challenge women's subordinate status once the crisis ended. Instead, their secondary status was simply confirmed and lionized as "the mother of the martyr" and "the maker of the generations." And when female activism did seem to break the bounds of acceptability, conservatives (within and without the nationalist camp) had little difficulty in driving them back to their proper place, in the name of preserving the integrity of the Palestinian nation and Islamic culture.

Yet Palestinian women in the Occupied Territories do possess new strengths, as well as vivid memories of their days of empowerment and high-profile activities. These, too, are potential "dialectical images" for future moments of rupture. Moreover, although the HWC ceased to function in 1991 because of factionalism, the women's committees still exist and have gained tremendous experience. The various committees are now taking advantage of the services of new and independent (not connected to any faction) women's research centers like Women's Affairs in Nablus and Gaza and the Women's Studies Center in Jerusalem, which are engaged in training new cadres of organic, independent women intellectuals and activists (Usher 1992: 40).[45]

I turn now to another, related parallel between revolt and intifada. Unlike the issue of women, this comparison has been publicly discussed—collaboration.

Rough Justice

The prompt execution of petty robbers and others and the disposal of
their bodies in public places does not fail to excite terror and admiration.
                              Dr. Elliot Forster, Hebron, September 1938

The (Arab) people as a whole are behind the movement. . . . They report
with little-veiled satisfaction tales of rough justice rendered by the insurgent leaders.   *U.S. Consul General at Jerusalem,* September 1938[46]

A major point of comparison between the revolt and the uprising, one that emerged after the first phase of the intifada, was the issue of collaboration. At first it was the intifada's opponents who asserted this link, but as the intifada waned, such parallels began to be drawn by forces inside the Palestinian movement, as well. The question of collaborators was partially responsible for the transformation of the memory of the 1936 revolt from an inspirational symbol for the intifada into a memento mori.

The existing network of Palestinian collaborators initially enabled the Israeli authorities to penetrate and undermine the underground movement, but by June 1988 the uprising had dealt this infrastructure a major blow. Palestinian police and tax collectors resigned en masse during the intifada's first months, and in March and April 1988, activists compelled many collaborators to recant in public and turn in their weapons (Tamari 1990a: 40–41; see also Nassar and Heacock 1990b: 201–2; Black and Morris 1991: 475). In October 1988, the Israel Broadcasting Authority's deputy chairperson, Shlomo Koor, suggested that the media drop the term "collaborators" in favor of "Arabs who desire peace" (*Hadashot,* October 26, 1988, cited in *al-Fajr,* October 30, 1988: 10), a proposal that recalled official designations of counterrevolutionary mercenaries as "peace bands" during the 1936–39 revolt. One "Arab desiring peace" who was gunned down in October was the notorious *mukhtâr* of Bidya, involved in illegal sales of hundreds of dunums of village lands to Israeli settlers (see chapter 5). The Israeli Council of Settlements in the Occupied Territories expressed "great sorrow" over the *mukhtâr*'s death, while the mayor of Ariel settlement described him as a personal friend and expressed regret at his passing (*al-Fajr,* October 11, 1988, 3).

The army responded to the loss of such agents (a.k.a. "moderates" and "friends of peace") by setting up "special operations" units to fight intifada militants and by enlisting new collaborators. The "special operations" units gained notoriety in the fall of 1988 for hunting down and assassinating "hardcore activists," and many Palestinians asserted that they should be properly called "death squads." By the end of 1992, the special units had carried out at least 117 cases of summary execution (*"From the Field,"* July 1993). Their efforts were supported by a new generation of collaborators, mainly recruited from among the tens of thousands of new prisoners picked up during the intifada. By midsummer 1989, bands of heavily armed Palestinian quislings were in full operation.[47] Collaborators assumed certain local bureaucratic functions (issuing permits and the like) which gave them leverage over the Palestinian population, and they assisted the security forces during interrogations, fingered wanted activists for the army's death squads, set up their own roadblocks, harassed and sometimes shot intifada activists, extorted money, and vandalized property. Typically these militia included former informers, land dealers, and petty criminals (Tamari 1990a: 41; Hiltermann 1990b: 95). According to the *Jerusalem Post,* the army hoped to use them in a replay of the 1938–39 campaigns of the "peace bands" against the *mujâhidîn.*[48]

The national movement, as well as Hamâs, struck back by killing large numbers of collaborators, most of them armed counterrevolutionaries and informers. However, they also executed some who were defined as "moral deviants," that is, drug dealers and prostitutes who were known to enjoy close ties to Israeli criminal and security networks (Vitullo 1989f; Tamari 1990a: 41). Hamâs defined collaborators somewhat expansively, to include those whose moral behavior made them and society at large susceptible to "corruption" (Hammami 1994). By early 1990 over two hundred collaborators had been killed (Tamari 1990a: 41), and in August 1989 the foreign press was reporting local Palestinian concerns about excesses and demands that better discipline be exercised. The UNLU issued a leaflet stating that measures other than killing should be used against collaborators, that execution orders could be issued only by leaders and not by local groups or individuals, and that death sentences were to be carried out only after the accused had been "warned and given a chance to repent" (Vitullo 1989f; Hiltermann 1990a: 232). By early 1990 the underground leadership had reprimanded local "strike forces" on three occasions (Tamari 1990a: 44).[49]

But Palestinians (and their supporters) naturally found it difficult to publicly acknowledge, much less criticize, abuses in the anticollaborator campaign, especially once Israeli officials launched a propaganda campaign in December 1989 that was picked up by the mainstream Western media. State sources attributed the struggle against collaborators to the endemic "intercommunal strife" so typical of Arabs and claimed that the intifada was simply "being used as a cover for . . . 'settling scores' between rival terrorist and criminal groups" and to enable "brutal gangs to terrorize the population and engage in sadism, rape, and blackmail" (Hiltermann 1990a: 229). Such assessments of the anticollaborator campaign, for example the one by Hebrew University law professor Ze'ev Falk, often equated the intifada's murderous behavior with that of the *thawra*. According to Falk:

> The record of the PLO both against Israelis and Jews as well as against Arabs is well known. During the intifada as well as during the Arab Revolt of 1936–39 the Arabs killed and wounded more Arabs than Jews and created a terror regime similar to that of Lebanon. . . . People accused of collaboration, leaders who express an independent view, laborers violating one of the continuous strikes and many other Palestinians are being attacked, wounded and killed by the henchmen of the PLO and Hamas.

For Falk the intifada, like the revolt, simply provided additional proof that the Arabs were guided by a fanatical and militarist "medieval ethos" (1989).

In 1990 the Western press repeated such claims and reported on an increasingly chaotic situation marked by waves of robberies and shakedowns under the cover of nationalism (see Williams 1990: A7). Meanwhile sympathetic sources reported that in June 1990 the number of Palestinian collaborators brought down by the "strike forces" (twelve) was higher than the casualties from army gunfire, that innocent victims were being killed, and that the leadership had again attempted to rein in the local "strike forces" whose excesses were having a negative impact (Corbin 1990a). It was explained that because of the wide-scale arrests of experienced activists (by October 1993 over one hundred thousand Palestinians—about one in five men between seventeen and thirty-five—had been imprisoned since the outbreak of the intifada [Kessel 1993]), command of the "strike forces" had passed to a younger and inexperienced cadre. "Thuggish" elements emerged who were prone to "excessive retribution" in minor cases of collaboration and who undertook "moral crusades" that involved punishing drug dealers and prostitutes who were not Israeli agents as well as women accused of promiscuity (Kuttab 1990b: 10; Hiltermann 1990a: 232; Atran 1990: 516).

More vigorous complaints about exorbitant violence were voiced in the summer and fall of 1991. In June the Fath-affiliated English-language *al-Fajr,* which up to that moment had scarcely mentioned collaborators, published a translation of Israeli journalist Roni Shakid's sympathetic portrayal of five Fath activists who were running the old city (*qasba*) of Nablus. Previous reports claimed that the underground leadership had successfully asserted its control over Nablus militants in December 1989 and that between December and May 1990 no collaborators had been killed in the city and the collection of donations had halted (Kuttab 1990a; Hiltermann 1990a: 232). But according to Shakid, matters subsequently deteriorated, prompting activists to form a new committee in fall 1990 to deal with problems like "killing collaborators, robberies, immoral acts, disputes between groups of people," and illicit solicitations of funds. In June 1991 collaborators were still being punished (usually by public flogging), but none had been executed in the old city in the previous ten months (Shakid 1991). *Al-Fajr's* publication of the article served to acknowledge the "problem" and simultaneously to reassure its readers that the national movement had dealt with it.

But if Nablus had witnessed improvements, other reports indicated that strike forces elsewhere were out of control. In July 1991, Tunis-based PLO spokesperson Bassâm Abû Sharîf used the *Jerusalem Report,* a liberal Israeli weekly founded when a right-wing publisher took over the *Jerusalem Post,* as a platform to criticize intifadists who were not adhering to established guidelines for executions. The latter's policy of overkill, Abû Sharîf argued, was "alienating the Palestinian population" (quoted by Hubbell 1991: 268–69). On July 1, English al-Fajr (p. 7) reported that between April and June there had been 61 Arab-on-Arab deaths compared with 22 killed in clashes with Israeli troops. The New York Times claimed that many if not most of the roughly 400 executions of collaborators (as of summer 1991) were un-authorized and were a great embarrassment to the Tunis leadership (Hubbell 1991: 268–69). In December, the Times reported that only 4 of the 13 Pales-tinians killed in the Occupied Territories during November 1991 were dis-patched by Israeli soldiers. While noting Israeli human rights organization B'Tselem's claims that Israeli undercover squads were increasingly responsi-ble for killing Palestinians (and so might be behind some of the deaths attrib-uted to the anticollaborator campaign), the Times also cited intifada leader Faysal al-Husaynî's admission that the charge of collaboration was sometimes used as a cover for murder by feuding families and criminal bands (Haberman 1991).

What especially interests me about these discussions is how often the intifada's critics as well as its supporters raised the 1936–39 revolt as a point of comparison. We have already seen that the Israeli army hoped its collabora-tors would perform the same services that the "peace bands" fulfilled for the British in 1938–39, and have encountered Falk's assertion that the revolt and the intifada were both "terror regimes." Likewise a New York Times report by Joel Brinkley (1990) on the killing of collaborators asserted that "many Palestinians fear that such violence will be the revolt's undoing, as happened with the Arab revolt of the 1930's." A piece by Brinkley in 1991 quotes from an editorial in the Arabic al-Fajr about the summary execution of collabora-tors. "It's time," assert Nabhân Khraysha and Sirhân al-Salayma, "to think in our own code and say in a loud voice what we think about this. We have a great experience with this, most importantly in our 1936 revolution before it ended in political assassinations." In 1938–39, Brinkley goes on to explain, the Palestinian revolt turned inward, and "then as now, Palestinians grew frustrated when they saw that their revolt was bringing them few if any political gains. As a result, many took out their frustrations on other Arabs who were suspected of aiding the enemy" (1991). Here Brinkley deploys a particular memory of the revolt that attributes its demise to infighting and uses this anamnesis to proleptically blame the intifada's certain decline on the same causes. Meanwhile, Brinkley, of course, ignores the crucial role played by the Israeli army in wearing down the intifada. Such a reading is character-istic of discourse hostile to the uprising. In a manner similar to official historiography's treatment of the 1936–39 revolt (see chapter 1), it blames the intifada's problems (and certain downfall) on internal bloodletting, and it occludes the Israeli authorities' application of intense, continuous, and varied forms of repression (including their use of collaborators).

But what is curious is that similar assessments began to emanate from within the Palestinian community. Here, too, the infighting of the 1936 revolt is proffered as a warning of what might befall the intifada (as in Khraysha and al-Salayma's editorial, representative of mainstream nationalist opinion).[50] The degree to which Palestinians viewed the anticollaboration campaign with great seriousness was indicated in May 1992, when English *al-Fajr* published its first-ever critical article on the subject (Musa 1992). The piece appeared after nineteen suspected collaborators had been killed in the previous month and after an outbreak of infighting between different political factions that caused several deaths. Open-air public meetings were held in the Gaza Strip's Jabalya camp and in Gaza city, and thousands showed up to discuss the anticollaborator efforts, factional fighting, and crime. The killing of collaborators was also criticized by the respected independent figure Haydar 'Abd al-Shâfi', then head of the Palestinian negotiating team. 'Abd al-Shâfi' wrote in *al-Quds* on May 29: "What worries the people is the increasing number of assassinations and the murkiness of their justification sometimes. What worries them is that some of the assassinations might take place for personal reasons or as a way to close accounts with people." 'Abd al-Shâfi' went on to draw comparisons between the intifada and the revolt, which was "similar to our current Intifada in its all-encompassing nature and its sacrifices. The revolution was effective for two years; then it began to deteriorate and weaken in an atmosphere of individual conflicts and disputes. It ended with nothing" (Abdul Shafi 1992).[51]

Thus the flagging of the fervor that characterized the first two years of the intifada likewise wrought a revision in the memory of the revolt. The historic insurgency that was hailed in 1988 and 1989 as a national symbol and remembered for its successes and heroic moments, the upsurge that served as a kind of "dialectical image" of rupture and discontinuity (Benjamin 1969), was subsequently reinscribed in light of the new problems and conditions. A local leader from Ya'bad explained the changed circumstances: "We must have minimal national unity. To kill 'hidden collaborators' means shaking up this unity. People ask 'why did you kill this guy? He is innocent.' That's why it is necessary to have clear evidence, to show that the person is 100 percent guilty. *In times of popular revolution, it is easy to get rid of collaborators, but when the tide turns, like now, it isn't*" (Hiltermann 1990a: 234, emphasis added). In this new conjuncture, many Palestinians began to view the revolt as a kind of memento mori, as a caution against the dangers of internal bloodletting. Previously, as we have seen in earlier chapters, such a memory of the revolt as beset with internal quarrels was firmly repressed, in official as well as popular circles, for the sake of nationalist mythmaking.

In the late intifada, then, we begin to find a franker discussion of some of the problematic issues concerning the *thawra* and more open admission of its failures and excesses. But this newfound candidness is also tendentious, for it offers an interpretation of the revolt that actively forgets that the campaigns of 1938–39 against collaborators were closely entangled with the assertion of peasant-rebel hegemony over the middle and upper classes. Although rebels' campaigns against spies and traitors were certainly characterized by excesses, they also overlapped with a kind of "subversivist" class struggle. This subaltern dimension of the revolt is not acknowledged in the late intifada's recoding of the social memory of the revolt; what is stressed instead is that the revolt was strong when it was unified. But strong under whose leadership, and to whose benefit?

"Selling Their Bodies"

This public revision of the memory of the revolt likewise ignores the meanings of past and present anticollaboration campaigns for Palestinian women. In the narratives of betrayal recounted in chapter 5, women were virtually absent as actors but did figure prominently as pretexts for revenge and execution, particularly through the discourse of "honor" (*'ard*). In Rabbâh al-'Awad's account, for instance, the policeman who felt his honor had been sullied when his wife hitched a ride with Dr. Anwar Shuqayrî denounced the doctor to the rebels. In the narratives of Abû Fâris, Ya'qûb betrays his cousins and their rebel commander Abû Fâris to the British because the cousins will not "give" him his *bint 'amm* to marry. And perhaps Ya'qûb's cousins refused to "give away" their sister because Ya'qûb's behavior would taint their own honor. Finally, among the reasons that Ya'qûb's cousins participated in his execution was that Ya'qûb had enabled British soldiers' rape of "their" women. Earlier in this chapter, we encountered a discourse of sartorial patriotism that treated women dressed in "Western" fashion as virtual traitors and described Palestinian men who failed to wear the *kûfîya* as effeminate.

In winter 1938 the Palestinian newspaper *al-Jâm'îya al-Islâmîya* described informers as "people in image and beasts in feeling; women selling their bodies, creeping worms and poisonous snakes."[52] Similarly during the intifada, the connection of women to the anticollaboration campaign rarely comes up except with regard to prostitutes executed for their ties to Israeli intelligence and organized crime.[53] Criticisms of the "excesses" in the assault on collaborators rarely mention the negative effects they have had on women's mobility or how they curtailed female participation in the intifada. Nor have such criticisms stressed how often the women executed were victims of the campaign of morality. However, a recent report by B'Tselem finds that most of the 107 women killed as "collaborators" from 1988 to 1993 were executed over issues of moral behavior rather than for actively assisting the security services (*Middle East Times,* February 14–20, 1994, p. 9). As Hammami notes (1994), such executions exemplify how successful Hamâs has been in fusing nationalist and religious notions of what constitutes "correct" female behavior. The Islamists' campaign to force women to wear the *hijâb,* moreover, was premised on a notion that for women to wear "Western" dress and go about unaccompanied was to "betray" the national-Islamic movement.

While the national movement seems primarily to have opted for a "cautionary" memory of the revolt, an "oppositional" image of the *thawra* that principally emphasizes its armed character continues to be mobilized by Hamâs and its military wing Katâ'ib al-Qassâm (the Qassâm Brigades), named after Shaykh 'Izz al-Dîn. The identification of the name al-Qassâm with Hamâs's armed actions is now so complete that the Israeli military and press routinely refer to the armed Islamist forces simply as "Qassam." As Fath and a portion of the Palestinian left (the People's [former Communist] Party and FIDA [the Yâsir 'Abd Rabbu wing of the DFLP]) pursue negotiations, Hamâs continues to invoke the memory of the armed revolt of 1936–39 in its opposition to the Declaration of Principles signed in September 1993. No doubt the force of this identification between Hamâs and Qassâm's memory prompted the ultraright organization Kach to inflict yet another desecration on Shaykh 'Izz al-Dîn al-Qassâm's grave at Balad al-Shaykh in December 1993. And Hamâs continued to use Qassâm's image to mobilize the will when it launched the recent operation (April 1994) that killed five Israeli Jewish civilians in Hadera. The man responsible for the bombing, significantly, hailed from Ya'bad village, site of the celebrated Ya'bad Forest where Qassâm met his end.[54] In the meantime, Arafat began to sound more and more like a U.S. politician, condemning "extremists" on both sides and making the violence of the occupier and occupied appear somehow equivalent.

Epilogue

Fabulous Images

I am finishing off this narrative in Cairo, not long after the February 1994 massacre in Hebron, the single worst bloodbath to date of the Israeli occupation. The other night CNN (International) broadcast a report on the shooting of four Orthodox Jewish students on the Brooklyn Bridge. CNN called the incident an instance of "Middle East terror" exploding onto the streets of New York (the chief suspect, Rashid Baz, is a Lebanese immigrant). Of course the Western media would never depict the slaughter of thirty worshippers at Hebron's Ibrâhîmîya mosque by New Yorker Baruch Goldstein as a flare-up of "Western terror" in the West Bank. Instead they frame it as another incident in the tragic "cycle of violence," forgetting (once again) Israel's systematic colonization, occupation, and expropriation of Palestinian territory. In addition, Western agencies of public meaning represent Goldstein as a "crazed" or "marginal" individual and thereby conveniently cover up the long history of Zionist discourse and practice of "transfer" and ethnic cleansing. They occlude as well the material legacy of "fanatics" like Goldstein who "create facts" (like the settlements in Hebron) that are occasionally subject to official criticism but are never undone. The Israeli state's treatment of the Palestinian population, the effects of which have been much more devastating than the actions of individuals like Goldstein, must, of course, never be termed "fanatical." Rashid Baz, on the other hand, is cast as a representative of a generalized culture of Arab–Middle Eastern terror. As of late March 1994, the hundred thousand Palestinian residents of Hebron, the victims of the massacre, had spent a month under a "protective curfew" while the city's Jewish settlers enjoyed free movement.[1] Meanwhile, commentary in the Arabic press in Egypt fails to mention that the aggressive implantation of Jewish settlements in Hebron after 1967 was partly a response to the massacre of traditional, religious, and non-Zionist Jews in 1929 by Palestinian Arabs.

Despite the bloodletting in Hebron, the Palestinian leadership has returned to negotiations with the Israeli government on the implementation of limited autonomy. Given the circumstances, it is hard to be optimistic about the prospects for the Palestinians.[2] The "peace" talks move at an infinitesimal pace, Israel stalling all the way. Settlements continue to expand, new settlement roads are built, and Palestinian youths continue to die in confrontations with the army of occupation and to be tortured in prison.[3] More recently, it has become clear that Yassir Arafat governs the "autonomous" territories as an autocrat and that his ministate practices its own serious human rights violations. Yet PLO officials talk hopefully of turning the new Palestinian state into the "Singapore of the Middle East." Meanwhile, the strongest alternative to 'Arafat's rule remains Hamas.

Feeling pessimistic about the current direction of historical "progress," I hold onto images like the *kûfîya,* perhaps if only to "vitalize" my own will. I think, as Jean Genet did, that "perhaps what I write is no use to anyone" (1989: 190). Yet I hope, like Genet, that I might be able to send "fabulous images" of the struggle "into the future, to act in the very long term, after death," to send images that might be "starting point[s] for actions" (1989: 262)—without forgetting that antiwomen campaigns were integral to the emergence of the *kûfîya* as sign of national-popular struggle. I think for a moment of the *kûfîya*'s transnational travels.

Sympathetic Echoes

Are there other possible stories?   *James Clifford*

In March 1988, about three months into the intifada, U.S. news packagers began to rub their eyes in disbelief. They had just learned to appreciate the *kûfîya*'s significance from the nightly television scenes of young Palestinians confronting Israeli soldiers when suddenly they noticed that large numbers of young U.S. urbanites were also accoutred in black-and-white checkered *kûfîyât.* CBS News (March 18) and *Time* magazine (March 21) both felt compelled to explain the transgressive arrival of this sign of Palestinian struggle in stylish downtown ensembles. *Time* quickly dispensed with the possibility that it meant political solidarity with the Palestinians, and pro-

ceeded to normalize the *kûfîya* under the category of fashion, citing statements from urban wearers, apparently chosen at random: "It's just an accesso-
ry"; "The ethnic type of look is in right now"; "The idea that it's political is
ridiculous"; and "What did you say it was called again?" (Cocks 1988).

I would suggest a more subversive genealogy. The *hatta* probably first
materialized in the United States in a significant way during the late sixties
and early seventies, when activists from the "anti-imperialist" section of the
antiwar movement began to wear *kûfîyât* in conscious solidarity with the
Palestinian struggle. *Hattât* began to appear (virtually unremarked) at antiwar
demonstrations amid the other more numerous and visible signs of international comradeship, such as NLF ("Viet Cong") flags and posters of Che
Guevara. (The expression of Palestinian sympathies, however, was virtually
banned by the movement leadership and was never heard at major events or
official forums.) Foucault (1989) suggests that those heady moments, when
masses of activists imagined that the entire world was in the throes of coordinated and interrelated revolutionary struggle, have been largely forgotten
because of the mass media's successful recoding of Western popular memory. The media, Foucault argues, was able to reestablish a "geographical *cordon
sanitaire*" around popular consciousness and thereby to prevent third-world
struggles from giving off further sympathetic echoes.

Although after the sixties such echoes were certainly muted, Foucault goes
too far in suggesting that hegemonic forces were able to erect a *total* "geographical *cordon sanitaire*" around Western popular consciousness and to re-
program memory so successfully that people could no longer imagine that
struggle could be successful. Memory was certainly not completely reformed
in the United States, where international sympathies lived on, notably in
Central American solidarity groups and in the antinuclear and antiapartheid
movements. There one encountered signs of solidarity with the Palestinian
struggle and the occasional *kûfîya*. But the question of Palestine was still kept
off the mainstream progressive agenda. The nuclear freeze campaign, for
instance, mounted its most massive demonstration on New York City's streets
in June 1982, at precisely the moment that Israeli forces were raining death
(with "conventional weapons") upon Palestinians and Lebanese residents of
Lebanon. The freeze movement uttered not a word in protest. Solidarity with
the Palestinians was more spontaneously alive, if not very visible to outsiders, in the African American community. I remember one network news
report on the 1982 Overton riots in Florida, in which an African American
elected official, asked by a reporter to describe the situation, replied, "Man,
it's just like the West Bank out there!" Around the same time, the Occupied

Territories were witnessing massive protests. The official's spontaneous identification of his community with the Palestinians and of the Florida police with the Israeli occupiers is one that is hard to imagine coming so naturally to other lips. *Kûfiyât,* I am told, were also widely sold and worn in African American urban communities, especially New York City.

It was the winter of 1983–84 when the *kûfiya* crossed over into the apparently apolitical domain of urban street style, where CBS News and *Time* noticed its presence four years later. Cultural Studies work on youth subcultures suggests that, like other style items, the *kûfiya* was deployed to incite shock, to mount oblique challenges to hegemony, to display social contradictions at the level of signs, and to decompose and reassemble identities and boundaries (Silverman 1986: 150–51; Hebdige 1979). And as Walter Benjamin suggested, the *kûfiya* could be seen as one of those objects produced in the industrial world that functions as a "dream image of the collective." Through such objects from the past that have an afterlife in the present, says Benjamin, the collective unconscious communicates across the generations (Buck-Morss 1983: 214–15). Yet the *kûfiya*'s long-distance travels would urge Cultural Studies to revise its notions about identities, boundaries, and histories, blinkered as they are by Western nation-state ideology. The *kûfiya*'s uses suggest that subcultural groups sometimes not only playfully reconfigure and reinvest Western histories and culture, but also corrode Eurocentric identities. Its transnational travels also suggest that jolts of recognition and transgression sometimes shoot across national and cultural boundaries, even the divide separating the (Arab) East from the West.

Let me offer one possible interpretation for these clandestine communications. The *hatta* infiltrated the U.S. style subculture not long after the 1982 Israeli invasion of Beirut and in the midst of the great terrorism panic. To put on the *kûfiya* at that moment was to engage in staged sartorial treason. But because an amorphous, politically indirect, and ironic "postpunk" style subculture embraced the *kûfiya,* rather than a "spectacular" subculture like the punks or skinheads, the impact was muted. To wear the *kûfiya* as a scarf was a mild sort of provocation, an ironic embrace of a forbidden image. It was donned as not so much an overt gesture of "romantic alignment" (Hebdige 1979) with the Palestinian cause as an oblique challenge to the orchestrated hysteria and vilification surrounding all things Palestinian, Arab, and Muslim. The *kûfiya*'s presence in bo-ho U.S.A. problematized official representations of the Palestinian terrorist by playfully adopting those signs of dangerous otherness. This forcing of the Arab *kûfiya* into a sartorial discourse of cutups and reassemblages that was largely "Western" also involved a recognition—however inarticulate and unconscious—of the linkages between U.S. and Palestinian cultures and histories.[4]

That the *kûfîya* was on hand for use as a vehicle of stylish critique was because various political groups—Arab American, African American, and Palestinian solidarity committees—were engaged in selling it. (See, for instance, advertisements in the pages of the now defunct *New York Guardian* during the early eighties. By winter 1986, however, it seemed that street vendors on every corner of New York City were hawking *kûfîyât*.) Stylish *kûfîya* wearers of the mid-eighties were thus also connected to high moments (like the sixties) of internationalism and of utopian desires for a global collectivity, but they reappropriated and refashioned that radical tradition for conjunctural purposes rather than indulging in nostalgia. Their aim was not to declare political affinity but to mount an ironic critique of official representations of the "crisis" over "terrorism."

Certainly as it circulated through the urban style scene between 1983 and 1987, the *kûfîya* was partially cannibalized by the recycling postmodern machine, and its history was to some degree erased. Some U.S. friends tell me they bought a *kûfîya* just because it "looked cool" and was the perfect complement to their all-black outfits. Yet the *hatta* retained a hint of danger, since it was sold chiefly by street vendors and never in the fashion boutiques.[5] Unlike the sartorial styles of the spectacular subcultures like the punks or mods, styles that were overt challenges to the established order but were nonetheless rather quickly tamed and incorporated (Hebdige 1979), the *kûfîya* resisted recuperation, banalization, commodification, and domestication because it was affiliated to an ongoing, and dangerous, political struggle. You never found a *kûfîya* in the Gap or Comme des Garçons, but you could purchase an Authentic Israeli Paratrooper Briefcase at Banana Republic. Even if the *kûfîya* merely was a "quote" within a stylish ensemble, the citation carried the odor of gunpowder.

In the early days of the intifada and again during the Gulf War of 1991, the *hatta* was briefly reinvested with undisguised oppositional meanings. That short period when thousands mobilized in the streets immediately before and during the Gulf War in fact marked the first time that U.S. progressives really took up the Palestine question. (It is worth recording that two days before the war started, the Seattle antiwar coalition I worked with brought out twenty thousand people in the streets, the biggest demonstration that city had witnessed since the Vietnam War.) The *kûfîya*'s visible adoption by many anti–Gulf War activists signified solidarity with Palestinians living under military occupation. Although Saddam Hussein had demagogically raised the "linkage" issue (our organization opposed the Iraqi occupation of Kuwait *and* the U.S.-led coalition's war against Iraq), a large section of the antiwar movement agreed that true Middle East peace could only be achieved with the end to Israel's occupation of the West Bank and Gaza Strip. Despite the fact that the *kûfîya* was also worn by "our" Arab allies in the coalition, the Kuwaitis and Saudis, prowar forces immediately took its presence in the antiwar movement as a treasonous sign of identification with the Arab-terrorist-Palestinian-Muslim enemy. Unlike the early days of the intifada, when in the absence of significant public expressions of affinity with the Palestinians it was somewhat difficult to "read" the *kûfîya*'s meaning on U.S. streets, during the Gulf War of 1991 its implications became obvious. Arab friends in New York reported that they stopped wearing *hattât* for fear of violence during the moment of hyperpatriotic enthusiasm generated by Operation Desert Storm. Some female coworkers in the Seattle peace coalition were harassed for their *kûfîyât*. And one night in mid-February 1991, while walking with a *hatta* pulled over my head to protect against the Pacific Northwest drizzle, a group of teenaged boys shouted "Nuke Iraq!" at me.

I want to suggest that the *kûfîya*'s U.S. uses were embedded in a continuum of style politics and that they varied according to the particular conjuncture. The range of uses includes (1) political solidarity or "romantic alignment" with the Palestinian struggle; (2) a critique of official U.S. policy; (3) a "citation" that evoked danger and violence; (4) an embracing of the "ethnic," the exotic, or the different. To comprehend these various meanings requires us to think U.S. and Palestinian histories together and to see them as connected not through equivalence but through difference and dislocation, attraction and repulsion, as bound together by networks of economy, migration, information, exploitation, and violence. To understand these relations requires the abandonment of Eurovision and the embracing of the kind of multiple vision or multiple consciousness practiced by the old Palestinian revolt veterans I met, who were able to keep their eyes on the transnational, the national, and the local, without resting too long in one spot. They seem to urge us to refashion dream images into dialectical images that can "interrupt the context into which [they] are inserted" and "counteract illusion," images that can defamiliarize the familiar and create similarities between the dissimilar (Walter Benjamin, cited in Buck-Morss 1989: 67). But we must go even further than Benjamin and mobilize *transnational* dialectical images in order to enable transculturation and the dissolution of arbitrary Eurocentric categories like "the West" and "culture." We must adopt a persistent bifocality, to bring such transnational linkages, repressed connections, and subterranean channels to consciousness, to make explicit the histories and the political-economic conditions that permit these journeys and connections to take place, and to disrupt official efforts to erect and maintain a cultural-geographical *cordon sanitaire.*

Global Flows

Consider more images from Los Angeles, site of the April 1992 "intifada," where city government is deploying what Mike Davis calls a "West Bank" strategy of collective punishment in its battle with the "terrorists" (gang members) of South Central: suing landlords, evicting tenants, and bulldozing houses suspected of being "drug nuisances," in imitation of former HUD secretary Jack Kemp's national guidelines allowing housing authorities to expel *"families* of those *arrested* (not necessarily convicted) for drug dealing" from public housing (Davis 1990: 284).[6] City government and media frequently link black gangs to Islamic "jihad" and narcoterrorism; during the 1992 disorders, a sheriff's department intelligence report claimed that "Muslims" were organizing the gangs "to assault and take over a police station" (Davis 1993: 34). Although the leaders of the Crips and Bloods organized a truce in spring 1992, city politicians have boycotted gang organizers "with the same contempt with which Israel treats the PLO on the West Bank" (Davis 1993: 36)—or at least Israel did, before the "historic handshake" of September 1993. At the same time, Davis maintains, the organization of residential security in the affluent hillside and valley districts of L.A. is undergoing "Israelization." The LAPD seems headed toward outright legitimation of white vigilantism, and some public figures suggest that the city should go further and, like Israel in the Occupied Territories, fill public space with armed auxiliaries (Davis 1993: 32). Perhaps the appropriate term for L.A.'s trajectory is "Hebronization."

My filmmaker-activist-academic friend Joan Mandell knows an Egyptian who works in Los Angeles as a journalist, is active in the Palestine solidarity movement, and is a practicing Muslim. When the L.A. uprising erupted, his radio station assigned him to cover South Central. Apprehensive because his skin is fair, he asked his African American friends at the mosque for advice. Just put a *kúfíya* on the dashboard of your car, they told him, and the brothers in South Central will know you're cool!

I recall other images: during one television news report on the historic Israeli-Palestinian negotiations at Madrid in the fall of 1991, the camera lingered for some time over the figure of Palestinian negotiator Sa'ib Erakat and the *kûfîya* that was so elegantly draped over his shoulders, like a holy icon. Here it seemed to signify the arrival of the Palestinian nation (and the PLO) as a legitimate international player. That same week a fleeting and more illegitimate image of the *kûfîya* flickered by on a U.S. national television news report on environmental apartheid. The camera momentarily showed a young white man with a red *kûfîya*-scarf, part of a multiracial crowd protesting the construction of an incinerator to burn toxic waste in a poor and mainly black and Puerto Rican area of the Bronx. But this *kûfîya*, a reminder of secret communications between the Palestinian and the U.S. "street," was too subversive, or too unfathomable, for the network camera to zoom in on.

Back at the Front Lines

While Palestinian negotiators and leaders simultaneously mobilized and muted the *kûfîya*'s image, it remained caught up in the deadly reality of the Occupied Territories. Youthful intifada activists who wrap their faces in *hat-tât* to hide their identities when confronting Israeli soldiers are known as the *al-mulaththamîn*, the masked ones. In summer 1989 the Israeli army widened its shooting policy and declared that anyone so "masked" could be shot on sight (Vitullo 1989b). Many men have since been shot dead for being "masked" in a *kûfîya*, including some wrapped up for the "traditional" purpose of keeping out the winter cold or rain (Vitullo 1989d; Rabbani 1990). When the "masked" *shabâb* started to be shot, West Bank women who had worn the *kûfîya* as a sign of their nationalism abandoned it for the less dangerous "Bethlehem scarf."

But others have also fallen in the campaign against the *mulaththamîn*. In December 1992, three Israeli border policeman and a paratrooper were wounded when two different Israeli "special" undercover units operating in a village near Jinîn opened fire on each other. Both the soldier and the policemen were dressed as Arabs (including *kûfîyât*). This was the second known such mishap (La Guardia 1992). More recently the Israeli army was reportedly having trouble recruiting men for its "special units" because of their growing reputation as "death squads."

That it keeps going on like this . . .

Notes

Introduction

1. See Plascov (1982) for a general account of Palestinian "border" or "frontier" villages.

2. Among the various efforts to conquer the ignorance about the essential connections between Arab and European civilizations, see Alcalay (1993), Menocal (1987), and the various fiction and nonfiction works of Juan Goytisolo.

3. A fine description of this revolutionary moment is presented by Sayigh (1979: 156–77).

4. Shortly after Andrews's assassination, the assistant district commissioner in Galilee, Kenneth Blackburne, wrote his mother, "I don't want you to get worried about me—because I am not the same as Andrews. The Arabs have always mistrusted him and been determined to get him—he was mixed up in all sorts of queer transactions with Jews—and the Arabs knew it. He also knew too much about the Arabs and so they feared him. I have found all sorts of things among his papers—any of which would be sufficient to rouse the Arabs" (September 28, 1937, Blackburne Papers, box 5, file 1).

5. This account is adapted from Swedenburg (1988: 190–94).

6. Minute by Sir John Shuckburgh on press announcement regarding proposed reinforcements to Palestine, September 10, 1938, CO 733/372/3.

7. By contrast the Palestinian struggle was greeted with great sympathy in the colonies and former colonies; British policy in Palestine was hotly criticized by, among others, Eamon De Valera and Gandhi.

8. Other major anticolonial peasant-popular struggles during the 1930s, such as those in Vietnam, El Salvador, and Nicaragua, have likewise received minimal attention when compared with that granted the war in Spain. Meanwhile the Republicans of Spain rarely come under critical scrutiny for their fierce anti-Arab racism: the Communist La Pasionara, for instance, spoke of "Savage Moorish hordes, drunk with sensuality, who pour forth to wreak horrendous violations of our daughters and our wives." (see Goytisolo 1992: 220–22).

9. See Doumani (1990), Graham-Brown (1980, 1982), Sayigh (1979), and Tamari (1982).

10. Important work in the field of popular memory and national pasts includes Anderson

(1983), Bhabha (1990), Bommes and Wright (1982), Connerton (1989), Fentress and Wickham (1992), Popular Memory Group (1982), Samuel and Thompson (1990), and Wright (1985).

11. Although the subject is beyond the scope of this work, I would nonetheless argue that Israel's strategic role in U.S. neoimperialist policies in the Middle East is a more significant factor explaining the close United States–Israel relationship than the vastly overrated factor of "Jewish influence."

12. A recent example of the importance of the transnational-English dimension of the debate is the recent joint publishing arrangement between Institute for Palestine Studies—now based in Washington, D.C.—and Columbia University Press (for example, McCarthy [1990] and Muslih [1988]).

13. It is important to emphasize that Derrida, who argues that we cannot help continuing to produce truths, is frequently misinterpreted on this score. Spivak asserts similarly that antiessentialism is not a politicoethical position.

1 / Popular Memory and the Palestinian National Past

1. On memories of Qassâm, see Swedenburg 1987. Useful studies of Qassâm include Maswari-Gault (1991: 16–42), Hammûda (1985), Khalaf (1982), Khilla (1974: 375–83), Porath (1977: 132–39, 142), Qâsim (1984), Sanbar (1988), and Schleiffer (1979).

2. This amounted to 13 percent of all U.S. foreign aid given between 1949 and 1991. The figures are U.S. Senator Robert Byrd's (Neff 1992: 16). This figure does not include the indirect subsidies in the form of tax-exempt donations. It should be noted that the bulk of this assistance was given *after* Israel's occupation of Arab territories in 1967, as a kind of reward for Israel's military prowess.

3. An example is the mass slaughter the United States inflicted upon the people of Korea. An estimated three million Koreans died in the Korean War, two-thirds of them civilians (see Cumings 1986: 409). Francis Jennings writes, "The conquerors of America glorified the devastation they wrought in visions of righteousness, and their descendants have been reluctant to peer through the aura" (1975: 6).

4. But see the critiques of postcoloniality by Frankenberg and Mani (in press), McClintock (1992), and Shohat (1992).

5. On the specificities of Zionism as a colonial movement, see Rodinson (1973) and particularly Shafir (1989).

6. This is not to deny Palestinian nationalism's close connections to the development of nationalism elsewhere in the Mashriq, the eastern Arab world (see Muslih 1988, especially page 87), but rather to stress Palestinian Arab nationalism's particular relationship to Zionism.

7. This analysis resembles Arturo Escobar's description of political struggles in Latin America, which oscillate, he asserts, between two logics and forms of politics: (1) the logic of "popular" struggles (against oligarchies, imperialism) in a relatively *unified* political space and (2) the logic of "democratic" struggles in a plural space (1992: 40).

8. "The Terror" (n.d.), CZA S25/10.499.

9. The village of Balad al-Shaykh was partially evacuated in January 1948, after a string of incidents in late December 1947. An Irgun bombing, condemned as "irresponsible" by the Haganah, killed 6 Palestinian workers and wounded another 42 at the gates of the Haifa oil refinery. Palestinian workers inside the refinery went on a rampage against Jewish co-workers, killing 41 of them. A Palmach force retaliated with an attack on Balad al-Shaykh, which left 60 Palestinian men, women, and children dead (Khalidi 1992: 153–54; Morris 1987: 41–42, 156).

10. The Union of Construction and General Workers at Ya'bad launched a campaign to

erect a monument to Qassâm in 1985, but to my knowledge it has still not succeeded, because of cash shortages and constant harassment from the authorities.

11. The phrase is the famous formulation of British Zionist novelist Israel Zangwill (1864–1926), who defined Zionism as "a people [the Jews] without a land returning to a land [Palestine] without a people" (Kimmerling 1983: 9).

12. The figure is Simha Flapan's (1987: 216). Morris puts the numbers at between 600,000 and 760,000 (1987: 298), Khalidi at 727,700 to 758,300 (1992: 582), and Sanbar at between 836,000 and 840,000 (1984: 202).

13. This figure comes from the most comprehensive study of destroyed Arab villages to date, organized by the Institute for Palestine Studies (IPS) and based in large part on field research (Khalidi 1992). Many earlier estimates are somewhat lower, in part because they leave out small hamlets. Jiryis estimates 374 (1976: 79); Shahak, 385 (1975); and Morris, 369 (1987: x–xi, xiv–xvii). Morris, however, admits that his figure omits "a dozen or so very small or satellite villages and small bedouin tribes or sub-tribes" (1987: viii). The IPS village study does not examine destruction of Palestinian and "mixed" cities and towns like Ramla, Lydda, Haifa, Safad, and Majdal, and also leaves out the encampments of Bedouin nomads and agriculturalists of the Negev (Khalidi 1992: xviii, xx).

14. Ben-Gurion ordered the destruction of "abandoned" Palestinian villages in June 1948, only one month after the declaration of Israeli independence. The early demolition work was implemented by the semiofficial Transfer Committee, headed by Josef Weitz (Morris 1990: 89–144).

15. The JNF is also active in "redeeming national land" for Jews only in the Occupied Territories, but through a subsidiary company, Himnotah, which is registered abroad to avoid criticism on the part of world Jewry (Shohat 1985: 4).

16. Forty-four percent of the Palestinian population of the West Bank and 70 percent of the Gaza Strip are refugees from across the 1948 armistice line; one-quarter of all Israeli-Palestinians are "internal refugees" (McDowall 1989: 126, 211).

17. By 1994 there were 115,000 Jews living in about 140 settlements in the West Bank, in addition to the 130,000 Jewish residents of annexed East Jerusalem.

18. The Israeli Ministry of Tourism brochure for Acre observes that its "Arab citizens," mainly residents of the old city, add "their own colour and customs to the present day scene." Of particular interest for tourists is the "typically busy and colourful Oriental 'Souk' (market)" (*Akko* 1983). While tourist agencies are emphasizing the exotic hues the Arabs add to Acre's social fabric, other state bodies are working to remove Arab residents from the city (see chapter 2).

19. Tel Hai was a Zionist settlement established during the 1914–18 war, outside the boundaries of Palestine in what became French-mandated Syria. It was overrun by Arabs from a nearby community in 1920. The destroyed settlement and its leader, Joseph Trumpeldor, who fell in battle there, were almost immediately turned into symbols of bravery and of the refusal to retreat from land that had been settled for the Zionist movement (see Shapira 1992: 98–109).

20. I take Arnon-Ohanna (1981), Bauer (1966), Elpeleg (1978), and Lachman (1982) as examples of dominant Israeli historiography. Yehoshuah Porath's invaluable two-volume history of the Palestinian Arab national movement during the mandate period (1974, 1977) is the best example of the liberal Israeli historiographical trend. Significantly, Israeli authorities prevented the Arab Studies Society in East Jerusalem from publishing an Arabic translation of Porath's work.

21. Other representative descriptions of Arabs from the Zionist press include the following: "highway robbers," "treacherous murderers," "barbarian, savage, shedders of blood," "bloodthirsty savages, who perpetrate their deeds in darkness, and all their courage is from ambush." These descriptions are cited by Shapira, who notes that they were "repeated endlessly" (1992: 238).

22. A minority opinion held that the insurrection was a struggle of Palestinian peasants against the elite, but advocates of this view nonetheless had no positive views about the Palestinian peasantry (Haim 1983: 127).

23. By September 1939, the mandate government had authorized 20,000 Jewish policemen, supernumaries, and settlement guards to carry arms; this figure does not include armed members of the Haganah underground (Teveth 1985: 187). In addition, Zionist Jews (including Haganah members like Moshe Dayan) did combat with Palestinian rebels as members of the Special Night Squads (SNS), an unofficial counterinsurgency force sponsored by the British military and organized and commanded by British colonel Orde Wingate, a Christian Zionist who enjoyed reading from the Bible naked. The stated task of the night squads was to guard the strategically critical Iraq Petroleum Company (IPC) pipeline that pumped oil from Iraq to Haifa. But the real work of the SNS, as Wingate's biographer Leonard Mosley makes crystal clear, was "going out and killing Arabs" (1965: 61). For chilling details of Wingate's deadly methods, see Mosley (1955: 58, 64–65) and Harris to Nichols, September 5, 1938, AIR 23/765.

24. Scott Atran defines the *hamûla* (plural, *hamâ'il*) as a patronymic group that is not genealogically integrated but in which membership is expressed in a patrilineal idiom (1986: 28).

25. Such claims are still recycled by propagandists like Joan Peters (1984) and Leon Uris (1984). According to liberal Israeli scholar Yehoyada Haim, the Nazis supplied neither money nor arms to the revolt, while Italy furnished no weapons and probably gave no financial support (1983: 37). Porath cites evidence that Italian money did reach the revolt, although in what amounts is not clear (1977: 188). According to British intelligence, the Mufti's men did try to obtain monetary assistance for the revolt from the Comintern via Communists based in Beirut and Damascus. The Comintern declined, fearing such an action might prejudice Soviet relations with Britain (Police Periodical Appreciation Summary no. 1, Enclosure, Wauchope to Secretary of State for Colonies, February 3, 1938, CO 733/359/10).

26. Ian Black argues convincingly that the *havlaga* policy was instituted primarily out of a desire "to prevent the [British] government [from] presenting the disturbances . . . as a clash *between* Jews and Arabs, and the wish, for obvious reasons for the events to be seen unequivocally as an Arab attack upon Jews." Thus the policy of restraint was a matter of Zionist-British relations, and its moral justification "must be seen as a self-serving, buttressing of the Zionist's [*sic*] image of themselves" (Black 1986: 366).

27. In fact, Arab attacks on Jews in Hebron took place in 1929, when the national movement was still focused on fighting Jews rather than the British, who were then regarded by many Arab leaders as an impartial arbiter. By the time of the 1936–39 revolt, no Jewish community was left in Hebron. No Arab attack on Jews during the revolt was as bloody as the massacres committed at Hebron (64 killed, 54 wounded), Safad, and Jerusalem in 1929. The most deadly rebel assault, and only true massacre, was on the "mixed" town of Tiberias on October 2, 1938, in which 19 Jews (including 3 women and 10 children) were killed.

28. Lest it be protested that mainstream Israeli historiography has changed dramatically since the intifada, let me cite a more recent example: Anita Shapira's *Land and Power,* published by the prestigious Oxford University Press (1992). Shapira asserts that "the tactics utilized by the organizers of the Arab revolt were those of terror: ambushes that injured the weak and defenseless. There were relatively few attacks against the British army" (1992: 229). Likewise she terms Shaykh 'Izz al-Din al-Qassâm "a famous Arab terrorist" (1992: 106).

29. See Passerini (1979) on the significance of gaps and silences in social memory, especially pp. 90–92.

30. The term *mujâhidîn* means warriors or freedom fighters. The elderly used *mujâhid* and *thâ'ir* (pl. *thuuwâr*) interchangeably to refer to the rebels of 1936–39, while the more secular younger generation generally favored the term *thâ'ir,* presumably because of the religious connotations of *jihâd* in the term *mujâhid.*

31. British government sources estimated 1,779 Arab attacks on the British police and army, 309 attacks on Jews, and 1,324 cases of "firing" on Jewish quarters and colonies between June 1936 and April 1939 (Sanbar 1984: 52–53). For rebel communiqués reporting attacks on Jewish colonies, see 'Awda (1984).

32. IOL L/P&S/12/3343, Coll. 26/2.

33. This effort on the part of the PLO leadership "outside" to build its base "inside" was also partially motivated by the loss of its last important mass base in the Arab countries when it was expelled from Lebanon in 1982.

34. Representative Palestinian histories examined here include 'Allûsh (1978), Frangi (1983), al-Hût (1981), Kayyali (1978), Khilla (1974), Yâsîn (1975), and Zu'aytir (1955).

35. See, for instance, Nuwayhid (1981) and al-Hût (1981), who deal primarily with the notable class.

36. Yâsîn's study (1959), based on interviews with actual *thuwwâr,* is useful in that it provides the names of many fighters, commanders, and battles, but it is otherwise highly unreliable. His estimates of the British and Jewish casualties inflicted by the rebels, for instance, are absurdly inflated. Recently the memoirs of Bahjat Abû Gharbîya, a rebel who was active in the city of Jerusalem, have been published (Abû Gharbîya 1993).

37. In addition, dozens of histories of destroyed and existing Palestinian villages and towns, often amateur and privately printed, were published in the 1980s (Doumani 1992: 17); see, for instance, Hudîb (1985) and Abû Ghûsh (n.d.).

38. See the journal *Al-turâth wa-al-mujtama',* published by the Society for the Preservation of the Family, as well as 'Alqam (1982); al-Ashhab (1983); Khalîlî (1977, 1979); al-Salhût and Shahâda (1982) and al-Sarîsî (1980). A recent study of Palestinian folktales in English is provided by Muhawi and Kanaana (1989).

39. See Parmentier (1984) and Swedenburg (1990) for further discussion.

40. The Sursuqs sold tens of thousands of dunums (four dunums equals one acre) in the Esdraelon plain in the 1920s, while the Tayâns sold the Wâdî Hawârith lands (30,000 dunums or 7,500 acres) near Hadera in 1929. See Stein (1984) on land sales in general and Adler (Cohen) (1988) on Wâdî Hawârith.

41. Stein suggests that members of both families were involved in transfers (1984: 231–32, 236–37). The mention of these notables in particular may have been motivated by local politics, since one could equally have cited other notable Tûlkarm families (see Stein 1984: 229, 232, 234).

42. For a review of rural conditions, see Asad (1975: 13–21), Stein (1984: 142–46), and Swedenburg (1988: 181–85).

43. One also gets this impression from Walid Khalidi's *Before Their Diaspora: A Photographic History of the Palestinians, 1876–1948* (1984).

44. This is not to deny the mandate government's role in causing economic misery among the peasantry. For instance, as Talal Asad explains, the government set rural property taxes at a fixed percentage, based on the net productivity of the soil (that is, minus the cost of production), meaning that capital-intensive Jewish agricultural enterprises paid lower taxes because of their higher "labor costs." Regressive indirect taxes added to peasants' financial burden. The weight of taxation accordingly fell most heavily upon the *fallâhîn,* whose contributions therefore financed Jewish industrial and agricultural development and defrayed the costs of Britain's defense of the "Jewish national home" (Asad 1975: 15).

45. Archival evidence confirms that the British and Zionists did employ such tactics (see Porath 1977: 246, 249, 253; Black and Morris 1991: 9–16).

46. The Ottoman *'ulamâ'* dissuaded Sultan Mahmud II from outfitting his army with peaked Western hats, since a peak "would prevent soldiers from touching the ground with their foreheads during prayer" (Mortimer 1982: 94). The Eastern fez, by contrast, was rimless.

47. The uniforms of the rebels of 1936–39 bear a distinct resemblance to those of the Arab Revolt: compare photos in Khalidi (1984), page 46, to those on pages 208–9, 214, 219, 221.

48. Elliot Forster, a British physician residing in Hebron, noted that the order took effect in about a week and gave "a great feeling of solidarity to all the Arabs, and perhaps not least, . . . a convincing practical demonstration of the power of the rebels over the people" (September 7, 1938, Forster Diary). According to the U.S. consul general at Jerusalem, by early September not one in one hundred—including municipal councillors, wealthy merchants, government clerks, chauffeurs, and porters, although excluding religious dignitaries—had failed to adopt the "national headdress." The consul also reports that a U.S. merchant reported that within a week of the order, twenty thousand *kûfîyât* were sold in Jerusalem and perhaps three times as many were shipped to the provinces (letter to Secretary of State, September 6, NA, 867N.01/1147). A September 1938 photograph (Khalidi 1984: 226) of a group of Palestinian men being arrested in Jerusalem shows virtually all, even those in suit and tie, sporting *hattât*. A photo of Friday prayers at Jerusalem's al-Aqsa mosque, dated September 16, 1938, is a sea of white *kûfîyât* and, the photographer notes, "not a tarbush [is] in sight" (Graham-Brown 1980: 169).

49. Communiqué signed by 'Ârif 'Abd al-Râziq, September 4, 1938, CZA S/25/4960.

50. Memo, enclosed in Consul General Jerusalem to Secretary of State, September 19, 1938, NA 867 N.4016/64. Also see Morton (1957: 53); *Times* (London), September 8, 1938, 11, and December 28, 1938, 11.

51. *Manchester Guardian* (September 5, 1938, 9) reports the shooting of two Arab men in Haifa for wearing tarbushes.

52. A report on the high commissioner's meeting with a seven-man delegation from the Nashâshîbî-led National Defense Party in May 1939 saw fit to note that "all members of the deputation wore the tarbush, except ['Abd al-Fattâh Darwîsh]" (Colonial Office correspondence to High Commissioner regarding Annual Report, 1939, ISA, box 2, X/1/39). See also the *Times* (London), December 3, 1938, 12.

53. Published on December 13, 1938, and found in CO 733/386/22.

54. See CO 733/372/4; Kayyali (1978: 214); Khilla (1974: 457); and Porath (1977: 267–69).

55. See also Bethell, who claims that Palestinians of *all* classes were imprisoned by rebels for failure to don the *kûfîya* (1979: 53).

56. Record of a Conversation with General Montgomery, January 12, 1939, Scrivenor Papers, MSS Brit. Emp. 377.

57. MacMichael to MacDonald, February 27, 1939, CO 733/398/1 (part 1). In 1939, the British-dominated Egyptian government permitted some wanted rebels from the Hebron area to take refuge in Egypt, on condition that they didn't wear the *kûfîya*, that they put on the *tarbûsh*, and that they didn't discuss politics (Hudîb 1985: 90).

58. Although Sirhân notes that rebels forced *tarbûsh* wearers to don the *hatta*, elsewhere he discounts class difference within Palestinian society. He maintains, for instance, that there was little to distinguish a rich man's clothing from a poor man's other than the quality of fabric (1989: 640, 643). While Khilla (1974: 457) is exceptional in that he associates the *kûfîya* campaign with the flight from the country of wealthy Palestinians, land dealers, and agents for the British and the Zionists, he does not discuss the broader issue of class antagonisms within Palestinian society. That is, Khilla sees the *kûfîya* campaign as directed basically against traitors, not the upper classes.

59. I owe this information to Sulaymân Mansûr, who learned it from veterans of the Jordanian army. Although young leftist militants in the West Bank have tended to favor red-and-white *kûfîyât* (to distinguish themselves as "reds"), most people in the territories still associate red-and-white *hattât* with the Jordanian army.

60. In Safad nationalists sang a similar chant (al-'Askarî n.d.: 90):
Ashlah ashlah ha-al-tarbûsh

Wa albus albus al-hatta
Hayk 'allamitna al-thawra
[Take off, take off that *tarbûsh*
And put on, put on the *hatta*
That's what the revolt teaches us.]

2 / Scenes of Erasure

1. *Palestine Post,* November 24 and 25, 1937. Shaykh Farhân's execution sparked massive outrage in the Arab community.

2. An example is 'Alî Musâlam Dahdulân of Samû', sentenced to death for carrying ammunition (High Commissioner to Secretary of State for Colonies, August 23, 1938, CO 733/379/11).

3. We were unable to understand the rest of the description of the incident, written in Hebrew.

4. Beginning in the late twenties, Labor Zionists also routinely labeled the Irgun as fascists (Shapira 1992: 248).

5. After a subsequent bomb explosion (August 26, 1938) killed thirty-three Arabs in Jaffa, rioting erupted there, and for several days the city witnessed sporadic sniping, arson, and attacks on foreign institutions. Eventually the unrest became organized, and on the night of September 6 the rebels took over the city. On September 7, the district commissioner left town for a few days, the Jaffa police station was stormed, and fourteen firearms and ammunition were seized (Jerusalem Consul General Wadsworth to Secretary of State, September 19, 1938, NA 867N.4016/64). Right-wing Jews planted a series of bombs throughout the country on February 27, 1939, to protest British government policy in the joint negotiations then going on in London. The results of this "anti-British" campaign were predictable: thirty-eight Arabs killed and forty-four injured (see MacMichael to MacDonald, March 24, 1939, CO 733/398/1 [part 1]).

6. There is now finally an informative guidebook to Israel and the Occupied Territories that tells the Palestinian side of the story (Eber and O'Sullivan 1992).

7. The depiction of the Nazi mass murders as a specifically anti-Jewish phenomenon also necessarily leaves other victims (such as homosexuals or Communists) out of the story. The Romanies or Gypsies, for instance, of whom between five hundred thousand and one million were slaughtered by the Nazis, continue to struggle for recognition as holocaust victims (Sonneman 1992).

8. Such imagery also pervades Israeli literature and cinema (see Shohat 1989: 69–71). While official Israeli propagandists are usually content to assert that the Mufti was a "Nazi collaborator," Joan Peters claims he was a "staunch friend of Hitler and coordinator with Germany in the 'final solution' to the 'Jewish problem' [and] was personally responsible for the concentration camp slaughter of hundreds of thousands of Jews if not more" (1984: 363). According to Yigal Allon, the Mufti "was largely responsible for the murder of the Jewish population of Bosnia" (1970: 80). Palestinian historian Philip Mattar argues that there is no "hard evidence of the Mufti's participation in atrocities beyond his attempts to stop the Jewish immigration to Palestine that he saw as leading to displacement or eviction of his own people" (1988: 107). But although the Mufti's crimes have been exaggerated out of all proportion, I am not sure he is as totally innocent as Mattar would lead us to believe.

9. The phrase, from Yitzhak (Isaac) Lamdan's poem "Masada," rapidly became a Zionist dictum after its publication in Palestine in 1927.

10. Yadin was head architect of the Haganah's "Plan D," the essence of which was "the

clearing of hostile and potentially hostile forces from the interior of the prospective territory of the Jewish State, establishing territorial continuity between the major concentrations of Jewish population, and securing the Jewish State's future borders" in anticipation of the Arab invasion. The Haganah regarded most Palestinian villages as actively or potentially hostile. Activated in April-May 1948, Plan D stated that some hostile villages were to be destroyed by "burning, demolition and mining of the ruins . . . especially . . . villages that we are unable to permanently control" (Morris 1987: 62–63). Also see Khalidi (1959).

11. Thus Eastern European immigrants to Israel have "changed their last names to Sabra Hebrew ones—names of biblical rebels, or biblical flowers, bushes and trees, or biblical manly virtues" (Lavie 1992: 87). And of course the term Sabra, the name given to those born in Eretz Israel, means cactus.

12. For evidence that Jewish colonists' blindness toward the Arab presence continued into the 1930s, see Shapira (1992: 273–74).

13. For photographs of settler guards in hybridized Arab-Cossack uniforms, including *kûfîyât,* see Allon (1970: 10, 22, 23, 25, 26, 30).

14. The Israeli tendency to view Arabs as noble savages and as "remnants of [the Jews'] dignified Biblical forefathers" has persisted regarding the Bedouin of the Sinai Peninsula (see Lavie 1990: 8).

15. Robinson's collaborator was Eli Smith, a U.S. Congregationalist missionary based in Beirut, who spoke Arabic fluently and who served as Robinson's guide and interpreter (Broshi 1987: 18–19). After completing his work with Robinson, Smith began his famous work of translating the Bible into Arabic.

16. George Adam Smith, who relied heavily on Robinson, claims that "the Arabs stayed [in the Holy Land] for nearly five hundred years [until the Crusades], obliterating the past, distorting familiar and famous names" ([1894] 1966: 265).

17. See Said (1979: 79–81) for additional anti-Arab statements by British surveyors and archaeologists.

18. "As far as [George Adam Smith] was concerned, the history of Palestine stopped in A.D. 634 with the Arab conquest, and did not resume until Napoleon's invasion in 1798, except for the brief interlude of the Crusades. Thirteen centuries of continuous settlement by an Arabized Palestinian population are barely mentioned [by Smith], and then only to stress the inferiority and irrationality of the Orient as compared to the Occident" (Doumani 1992: 25).

19. The introduction to a 1937 volume on the renaming project states: "And the [following] generations will . . . see how we tried to *link* the times in which we are living with those times which preceded them by thousands of years, when we renewed the settlements and their names . . . names, each single one of which, and all together, express *our right* and our link to this country" (Y. A. Arikha, *The Redeeming of Names,* Jerusalem: Jewish National Fund [in Hebrew], quoted in Kimmerling 1983: 209).

20. Today an industrial plant in this socialist kibbutz produces armored vehicles equipped with water cannons. These vehicles, tested in the Occupied Territories, were designed for dispersing demonstrations in South Africa, but in the late eighties Beit Alpha decided to stop exporting the vehicles to such "sinister regimes"; they now go to France, Thailand, Singapore, South Korea, Sri Lanka, China, and England (Bleifuss 1988; Miskin 1993: 42).

21. Since 1967, the Wailing Wall in Jerusalem has also been used for these swearing-in ceremonies, coincident with the extreme right's efforts to replace the Muslim Dome of the Rock with the rebuilt Temple.

22. Yadin, in contrast, concluded, on the basis of finding a Zealot ritual immersion bath and synagogue at Masada, that the Zealots lived by religious codes and that, contrary to the religious

Jewish views prevalent from the first to the nineteenth centuries, they were not "terrorists" but "proper" Jews (Paine 1991: 21).

23. Bowerstock also observes that biblical archaeology's long stranglehold over the whole field of Israel/Palestine has hindered serious study of the Arab history of Rome and Byzantium until recently (1988: 184).

24. Symptomatic of this tendency to interpret and structure the data to show that Arabs and Jews have been at loggerheads since time immemorial is the fact that the documents of Babatha were still unpublished twenty-five years after Yigael Yadin discovered them. What little *is* known about Babatha, a Jewish woman who fled to the desert during the Bar Kochba rebellion (A.D. 131–35), makes clear that Arab-Jewish relations were harmonious in the area south of the Dead Sea (Bowerstock 1988: 188–89).

25. We will be able to evaluate the extent and significance of this liberalization more fully from Nadia Abu El-Haj's forthcoming dissertation (Department of Cultural Anthropology, Duke University) on Israeli archaeology (see Abu El-Haj 1992).

26. According to Ezra Cohen of the Israel Travel Advisory Service in New Jersey, which has brought thousands of North American Jews to Masada, "The Jews on Masada were surrounded by 15,000 Roman soldiers and they gave up—by committing suicide. Today, Israel is surrounded by 190 million Arabs, and we are determined not to repeat the story of Masada—we must fight for and keep the country of Israel" (*Jerusalem Report,* August 12, 1993, 15).

27. An example is Avneri (1982: 37–61), who makes extensive use of Western travelers as sources.

28. The British mandate authorities declared the forests around Ya'bad a reserve area in 1926. Officials report that villagers who owned land bordering on the forest reserve steadily encroached upon and cultivated forest land, especially during times of "disturbances." Increased felling of trees occurred in 1934, reportedly in response to a demand for charcoal in Damascus ("Yabad Forest Reserve," ISA 2/AF/17/3/41).

29. A report by Israeli ecologists argued that overgrazing was not in fact a significant problem in the areas of the Negev from which Bedouin were being evicted (Maddrell 1990: 13).

30. Zionist mythmakers frequently cite the disparaging and ill-informed comments about Palestine contained in Mark Twain's travelogue *Innocents Abroad* (1869) as evidence that the country was "empty" in the late 1860s (see Fisk 1990: 21–22). Melville's *Clarel* (1876) is also adduced as evidence.

31. For scholarly versions of the same story, see Sachar (1958: 265) and Avneri (1982).

32. Between late November 1947 and the end of August 1949, 133 new Jewish settlements were established, almost all on Arab-owned lands. In April 1949, the director of the Jewish Agency's Immigration Absorption Department reported that out of 190,000 immigrants arriving in Israel since its creation, 110,000 had settled in abandoned Arab homes (Morris 1987: 179, 195).

33. See Collins and Lapierre's *O Jerusalem!* (1973) for a popular account of this struggle in which Yigael Yadin played a major role. Although some of the Haganah's hardest-fought battles in 1947–48 pitted them against Palestinian irregulars in the Latrûn area before the Arab armies intervened, official Israeli histories represent the "War of Independence" as simply a conflict with the invading armies of five Arab states. Benvenisti writes, "The earlier, tougher, and vicious phase of communal rioting, shooting in the streets, flights of civilians, occupation of Arab neighborhoods, towns, and villages, pillage, and other incidents [Benvenisti leaves out massacres] typical of civil [*sic*] war were erased from the Israeli collective memory." Once Palestinians were expelled they could be dismissed as mere "refugees" or infiltrators. Benvenisti notes, "we [Israelis] wanted to forget that phase [of the 1947–48 war] because it reminded us that there was a Palestinian community with which we shared our cities and our land, a community that

bitterly fought for what it believed had been its national objectives but which had been utterly defeated" (1986a: 90).

34. For a critical eyewitness account by an Israeli soldier who participated in the expulsion, see Kenan (1975).

35. Lûbyâ's residents fled their village on July 16 and 17, 1948, in the wake of the fall of Nazareth and before an IDF attack (Morris 1987: 203; Nazzal 1978: 80–83).

36. Al-Mazra'a, the only West Galilee coastal village not evacuated by its inhabitants during the 1948 war, became the "collection point for all the Arab 'remainders' of Western Galilee" (Morris 1987: 125). According to Morris, the inhabitants of al-Ghâbisîya were expelled in May 1948 and February 1949 (1987: xv, 241); Nazzal asserts that most of the villagers fled after the fall of Acre on May 19, 1948.

37. According to Khalidi, Akzib (meaning "trickster") was a Canaanite town that was settled as early as the eighteenth century B.C. The account in Khalidi (1992: 35–37) makes no mention of historical Jewish residence at the site; this absence tends to be true of the book as a whole.

38. The mansion, according to Khalidi (1992: 37), was owned by the village *mukhtâr,* Husayn 'Ataya.

39. Julie Peteet, personal communication, August 20, 1991.

40. These representations of Palestinians at historical sites are consistent with what Israeli Jewish children learn at school and in children's literature. A study of children's books directed by Adir Cohen of Haifa University concluded that "the image of Arabs in Hebrew children's literature is totally stereotypic. The Arab is described as primitive, wearing a kefiya, with a scar on his face, a low forehead, narrow evil eyes, a thin beard, with a murderous expression on his face. His surroundings are also stereotyped—the Arab village is usually infectious, with exposed sewage, even the Arab dog is leprous, with his tail between his legs" (*Davar,* October 11, 1985, 18; translation in *Israleft* 271 [November 1, 1985]: 4).

41. In *Ma'ariv,* August 11, 1972; cited by Kimmerling (1983: 183).

42. The film was directed by PeÅ Holmquist, Joan Mandell, and Pierre Björklund. My thanks to Joan Mandell for providing me with a transcript.

43. The memory of Acre Prison is also perpetuated by a famous poem about the "red martyrs" by nationalist classicist poet Ibrahim Tawqân, but the song (in vernacular) has a wider popular purchase.

44. After a blaze, widely blamed on Arabs, destroyed much of Mount Carmel National Park in September 1989, the head of the Nature Reserves Authority stated that the fire "gives me a bitter feeling towards the Arabs. . . . It shows our struggle is against barbarism—they say it's their land, but look how they treat it" (Derfner 1989). There are close parallels with Labor Zionist leader Berl Katznelson's reactions to rebels' destruction of trees planted by Jewish colonists during the 1936–39 revolt: "The destruction of plant life . . . is instructive regarding the nature of the destroyer and his dark urges; it teaches us more than bloodshed" (quoted in Shapira 1992: 230).

45. A former resident has written a history of the village, entitled *'Imwâs Which Will Never Be Obliterated from Memory* (Abû Ghûsh n.d.). The account states that 'Imwâs's inhabitants were mainly descendants of settlers from Abû Ghûsh, a nearby, historic village that commanded the Jaffa-Jerusalem road during the Ottoman era. The book does not mention that Abû Ghûsh, located inside the pre-1967 borders of Israel, is notorious for aiding neighboring kibbutz Kiryat Anavim during the 1936–39 revolt and for assisting the Zionists again during the 1947–48 war (see Morris 1990: 192). Thus this strategically located village was spared demolition in 1948.

46. By March 31, 1993, the total number of trees destroyed by Israeli forces in the Occupied Territories had reached 161,056 (*Human Rights Update* 6 [4–6]: 47). Since the Israeli and Pales-

tinian leadership signed their agreement in September 1993, the expansion of Israeli settlements has resulted in the uprooting of 5,540 fruit trees (Palestine Human Rights Information Center press release, January 24, 1994).

3 / Popular Nationalism

1. See the account in Porath (1977: 141).

2. In his study of Palestinian folktales (*hikâyât*), folklorist al-Sârîsî says that tales depicting conflicts between peasants usually concerned either land (*ard*) or women and their honor (*'ard*) (1980: 137).

3. For discussions of honor in Palestinian society, see Warnock (1990: 22–24) and Peteet (1991: 59, 187).

4. Such a connection is likewise drawn by refugees from 'Ayn Hawd, who trace the founding of their village to Abû al-Hayjâ', one of Salâh al-Dîn's commanders (Kanâ'ana and al-Ka'abî 1987: 7–9).

5. Shortly after Qâwûqjî's arrival in Palestine, according to a report by the British military commander, "rebel tactics improved and the bands showed signs of effective leadership and organization" (Peirse Report, October 15, 1936, CO 733/317/1). The fact that Qâwûqjî was commander of the Arab Liberation Army in the 1948 war added retrospective allure to his local reputation as a commander in 1936.

6. According to Porath's tabulation, of the sixty-one townsmen who held offices in the rebel movement, seven were Husaynîs. By his account, townsmen furnished only 30 percent of the revolt's officers (1977: 261).

7. For a similar claim, see Muhsin (1986: 170). But Muhsin's assertions about 'Abd al-Qâdir's populism are called into question by the fact that the fighters Muhsin interviewed generally referred to 'Abd al-Qâdir by the aristocratic designation *bak* (bey). Porath reports that 'Abd al-Qâdir declined to join the rebel collective leadership composed of the leading regional commanders (the "Bureau of the Arab Revolt in Palestine") when it was established in fall 1938 because, as the scion of nobility, he did not want to submit to the discipline of mere peasant commanders (Porath 1977: 245).

8. British archival sources seem to buttress al-Mizra'âwî's claims. Ramallah district commissioner Pirie-Gordon considered "Shaykh Abdel Fattah" the only "nationalist" leader in the Ramallah area, and he asserted that other regional commanders, by contrast, belonged to the "robber" variety. Pirie-Gordon states that, unlike 'Umar al-Nûbânî, Abd al-Fattâh used regular fighters rather than "casual labour" from the villages (Pirie-Gordon to O'Connor, January 5, 1939, O'Connor Papers, 5/1/2; Pirie-Gordon to Keith-Roach, January 28, 1939, O'Connor papers, 5/2/2). Porath classifies 'Abd al-Fattâh al-Mizra'âwî as a "Band Commander" (1977: 398), that is, someone whose responsibilities extended beyond a single village. He incorrectly identifies Muhammad 'Umar al-Nûbânî as Muhammad al-'Amir al-Nûbânî (1977: 399). For a hagiographic treatment of al-Nûbânî, see 'Awda (1988: 140–46).

9. A report by the British CID (Central Intelligence Division) claims that after quitting Palestine for Syria in September 1937, Dâ'ûd Husaynî "actively assisted in the organization and direction of terrorist organizations. He is an arms smuggler and on a number of occasions has entered Palestine with armed bands, and is believed to have been implicated in the [murder] of the late Hassan Sidky Dajani" (Thompson, Chief Secretary's Office, Jerusalem, to Colonial Office, April 14, 1939, CO 733/314/21). Dajani's killing is discussed later in the chapter.

10. 'Abd al-Rahîm is reported to have repeated on a number of occasions, "I don't fight for al-Husaynî but I fight for Palestine" ('Awda 1988: 99).

11. MacMichael to Shuckburgh (enclosure), October 19, 1938, CO 733/359/10. 'Abd al-

Rahîm was also reportedly unlike 'Ârif 'Abd al-Râziq, who was said to have been willing both to undertake political assassinations on behalf of Hajj Amin and to forward money collected inside Palestine to Damascus headquarters (Lesch 1973: 261). The single "biography" of 'Abd al-Rahîm—mainly a collection of rebel communiqués—says almost nothing of such conflicts ('Awda 1984).

12. Thanks to 'Âdil Manâ' of Birzeit University's History Department for discussing these points with me.

13. Curiously, Al-Haj employs the Hebrew name Shefar-A'm in his book rather than the Arabic designation Shafâ' 'Amr.

14. In the late 1930s, Shafâ' 'Amr had a population of 1,500 Christians (Greek Catholic and Protestants), 950 Sunni Muslims, and 550 Druze, as well as a reputation for "harboring gangsters [that is, rebels]" (Reports on various villages [1938?], Scrivenor Papers, MSS Brit. Emp. s. 377). Yâsîn (1967: 132–33) provides a list of names of fighters from Shafâ' 'Amr (which does not include Sâlih Khnayfus), as well as an account of some operations they were involved in.

15. MacMichael to MacDonald, December 29, 1938, CO 733/398/1 (part 1). See also Kanâ'ana and al-Ka'abî for more on tensions between Druze and Muslim villagers in the Carmel region, both before and during the revolt (1987: 20–21, 47).

16. British diplomats also worked hard to discourage rebel efforts to recruit Syrian Druze, many of whom had fought in Palestine under Qâwûqjî's command in 1936, to enter the battle in Palestine during the later stages of the revolt (MacKereth, British Consul–Damascus, to MacMichael, February 3, 1939, CO 733/408/8).

17. Syrian Druze leader Sultân al-Atrash, whose visage adorned Sâlih Khnayfus's diwân, opposed Shakîb Wahhâb's participation in the 1948 war (Teveth 1972: 133) and militated against Druze participation in the 1936–39 revolt (Porath 1977: 272).

18. Porath discovered only seven persons with criminal records among the 282 rebel officers about whom he was able to find information (1977: 264). Based on the testimony of several men we interviewed who served jail time prior to the revolt, usually for crimes of "blood," I would estimate that a higher percentage of everyday fighters had prison records than did rebel leaders. Standard Palestinian histories by and large fail to mention the criminal records or reputations of any leading commanders.

19. 'Abd al-Râziq's criminal record is discussed in Porath (1977: 347 n. 158) and Maswari-Gault (1991: 63).

20. Sirhân describes Abû Kabârî in his Encyclopedia of Palestinian Folklore (1989: 12) as one of the "leaders of the Palestinian rebels [quwwâd al-thuwwâr] who fought against British colonialism and Zionist aggression." He says Abû Kabârî came from Baytâ and was remembered as being active in 1930, that is, before the revolt and before the emergence of fighters known as thuwwâr. Sirhân makes no reference to his being a bandit. Abû Kabârî may have been remembered locally because the story of his escape from Nablus prison was recounted by the colloquial poet Muhârib Dîb. Sirhân recorded Dîb's narrative in 1965 (1989: 12–16). Sirhân's nationalist encyclopedia mentions no other Palestinian bandits.

21. This claim was an attempt to discredit the struggle of the dispossessed peasants of Wâdî Hawârith by tainting it with brigandage, as well as to cast aspersions on the national movement by claiming its leaders were criminals. The most reliable study of the Wâdî Hawârith struggles (Adler [Cohen] 1988) makes no mention of Abû Jilda's involvement.

22. The related issue of smuggling has also been similarly recoded. It appears that 'araq, hashish, and tobacco were often smuggled into Palestine along with rifles and ammunition (see Intelligence Summary, Headquarters, Transjordan Frontier Force, October 12, 1929, CO 733/154/14; Bowden 1977). Former rebels talked only about the traffic in arms, not about contraband liquor or drugs.

23. I do not recall interviewees distinguishing between Arabic-speaking Jews (Sephardim)

and Ashkenazim, but I was not then as sensitized to this issue as I have become since reading the work of Shohat, Alcalay, Swirski, and Lavie. For examples of the integration of Sephardi Jews into Arab-Palestinian life before 1948, see Alcalay (1993: 134–35) and Shohat 1988 (10–11). One of the consequences of the 1936 revolt was that it hardened lines separating Jew from Arab. Arab attacks on the old non-Zionist Jewish-Arab communities, for instance at Safad and Jaffa, were particularly tragic, since everyday relations between Jews of Arab origin and other Arabs had been quite civil.

24. CID report, May 28, 1937, IOL, L/P&S/12/3343, Coll. 26/2.

25. According to Israel Shahak, the intifada prompted Israeli Jews to draw similar correlations. "Very many people in Israel," he asserts, "are now comparing the occupation during the intifada to the treatment Jews received from the Nazi regime in the early days from 1933 to 1939. . . . The lesson that can be drawn from the Holocaust . . . is that the second stage of Holocaust, the extermination, was caused by the people who were silent, who didn't protest enough during the first stage" (quoted by Seager 1989b: 15).

26. See also Brenner (1983) and Shahak (1988).

27. Wauchope to Cunliffe-Lister, March 6, 1935, CO 733/272/12.

28. In his discussion of land sales, Muslih names only the Lebanese Sursuqs as landlords in Palestine who forced their tenant farmers to live in wretched conditions (Muslih 1988: 43).

29. The bulk of sales were in the coastal plain, the Esdraelon Valley (Marj Ibn 'Amr), and the Jordan Valley.

30. Other sources claim that 'Abd al-Rahîm was wanted by police for a fraudulent land sale to a Jew (see Porath 1977: 347 n. 158; Maswari-Gault 1991: 64). This assertion was never mentioned by Abû Shâhir or anyone else who talked about 'Abd al-Rahîm al-Hajj Muhammad.

31. On attacks organized against both 'Abd al-Râziq and 'Abd al-Rahîm by a "third factor" (either Zionist or English), see Porath (1977: 246, 249). According to Porath, the disputes between 'Abd al-Râziq and 'Abd al-Rahîm were quite sharp, much more so than most of our interviewees acknowledged.

32. As reported in the official history of the Haganah, which holds 'Abd al-Râziq's men responsible for killing Hasan Sidqî Dajânî (Khalifa 1989: 166).

33. Nuwayhid (1981: 179) simply states that Hasan Sidqî Dajânî was killed "unjustly" (*zulman*).

34. Palestine Police veteran Edward Horne claims that his colleagues had a rather high opinion of 'Abd al-Râziq's military abilities. The commander was something of a legend for his reputed ability to disappear into thin air after two days' chase in the hills (1982: 225). According to Horne, the army spent thousands of hours and pounds sterling trying to catch him, and the police used to take bets about whether he would be captured. According to Horne, 'Ârif stood "head and shoulders above the others, because of his daring, his cheek and absolute scorn for those who tried to trap him by the conventional rules of warfare. In an age when most of the gang leaders are forgotten, Aref, with his 'Now you see me, now you don't' technique of fighting, will long remain one of the army's problem heroes, and will never be forgotten while a single Palestine Policeman of that time is still living" (1982: 230). It is curious that no rebels we interviewed in Palestine remembered 'Ârif in so praiseworthy a fashion.

35. My friends' lack of knowledge about the commanders of the revolt also testifies to significant gaps in the educational curriculum, in part due to Israeli occupation policies.

36. For instance, the "nationalist bandits" like Abû Jilda; the Green Hand Gang led by Abû Tâfish, which operated briefly in the Safad region after the uprising and massacres of 1929 (Kayyali 1978: 156; Lachman 1982: 56); the armed attacks on Hadera and Petakh Tikva in 1921 (Porath 1974: 130, 132); and the military attack against a British unit in Samakh by over two thousand armed Bedouins from the Hawrân (Syria) and the Baysân Valley in 1920 (Muslih 1988: 150).

37. These incidents are mentioned only by Schleiffer (1979: 65).

4 / Memory as Resistance

1. One of the worst atrocities occurred at Halhûl in May 1939, when 10 men kept in an open-air pen and denied water while the army carried out arms searches died of heat prostration (May 8, 1939; May 13, 1939; May 25, 1939, Forster Diary; MacMichael to MacDonald, September 22, 1939, CO 733/75872/91; Parkinson to Wauchope, May 18, 1939, CO 733/413/3; Abû Fâris 1990: 136–39). Bethell appears to accept the public claim of High Commissioner MacMichael that the deaths at Halhûl were the result of "unfortunate circumstances"—abnormally hot weather and the low resistance of the older men—and therefore could not be considered an atrocity (1979: 68).

2. Enclosure, dated May 5, 1939, NA 867N.4016/86.

3. MacMichael to MacDonald, March 24, 1939, CO 733/398/1 (part 1).

4. The incident is also noted in a communication from General Haining to General Montgomery requesting a report on whether a government school and sixty houses were burned at Kafr Yâsîf (Haining to Montgomery, n.d., 5/1/2, O'Connor Papers).

5. "To Every Arab of a Living Conscience," June 1939, CO 733/406/75872/12.

6. See MacKereth to MacMichael, May 1, 1939, CO 733/408/8); MacKereth to Halifax, October 28, 1939, CO 733/408/4; MacKereth to MacMichael, May 31, 1939, CO 733/408/8; MacMichael to MacDonald, August 12, 1939, CO 733/408/8; MacDonald to Sandeman, July 21, 1939, CO 733/406/12. Accusations of rebel financial corruption were aired in a pamphlet printed in Arabic by Opposition leader Fakhrî Nashâshîbî. Translated excerpts appeared in the English-language Zionist daily, the *Palestine Post,* on January 6, 1939. At the time of publication, Fakhrî Nashâshîbî was on the payroll of Pinhas Rutenberg, head of the Palestine Electric Company (Black 1986: 401).

7. Haifa's *sûq* and Arab quarter had a reputation among the British as a center of crime. According to Douglas Duff, half the murders of northern Palestine were carried out in the thirties by Haifa "desperadoes" who were hired by Nablus and Jerusalem effendis, and the numbers of prostitutes, homosexuals (whom Duff considered criminals), thieves, hired assassins, and dope merchants had increased greatly by the late 1930s (1938: 288–89). Although Duff sensationalizes, he points to a seamy side of urban life in Haifa that is generally absent from Palestinian accounts.

8. Interviewees did not discuss Qassâm's role in the early Palestinian workers' movement, a subject likewise barely touched on in Palestinian historiography. There are intriguing clues, however. For instance, when members of the fraternal committee of railway workers in Haifa received official permission in 1925 to found the first Palestinian Arab trade union, the Palestinian Arab Workers Society (*jama'îya al-'ummâl al-'arabîya al-Filastînîya*), it was 'Izz al-Dîn al-Qassâm who penned the union's first communiqué (Shabîb 1990: 22). When "Hawrani" (that is, migrant) wood transporters at Haifa went out on strike against low wages and long hours in January 1935, they turned to the "Moslem Youth Organization" (the Young Men's Muslim Association, of which Qassâm was president) for help (*Davar,* January 22, 1935, cited in CZA S25/10.49). Haifa workers were also highly involved in Qassâmite-organized celebrations of the Prophet's birthday. According to Hammûda, on one occasion thousands of workers marched in a procession organized by Qassâm's followers and raised slogans invoking the early Islamic conquests (1985: 63).

9. Support for this view of the collective nature of the Qassamite organization is found in Tegart Papers, box 1, file 3C.

10. The Quraysh, the tribe of the Prophet Muhammad, constituted the merchant elite of the city of Mecca. When Muhammad began to preach, the Quraysh opposed the Prophet and his message, forcing him and the Muslim community to go into exile in Medina in A.D. 622. The

Quraysh converted only when the Muslims conquered Mecca in A.D. 632. The statement here refers to the time when the Quraysh and the Muslim community were at loggerheads.

11. On *makhâtír's* involvement in land sales, see Memorandum of February 20, 1935; Minutes from meeting of District Officers, February 27, 1935; District Commissioner (DC) Jerusalem District to Chief Secretary, March 18, 1935; Minute (n.d., January 1935); all in ISA 23/254/18/20/20. On village registers, see Tegart and Petrie Report, January 24, 1938, CO 733/379/10; Wauchope to Ormsby-Gore, February 7, 1938, CO 733/379/10. On village occupation, see Note, Tegart Papers, box 2, file 4.

12. See, for instance, the report in the *Times* (London; December 28, 1938: 11–12), entitled "Kidnappers in Palestine. The Terrorists' Technique: Tortures in the Hills."

13. MacMichael to MacDonald, February 27, 1939, CO 733/398/1 (part 1).

14. February 20, 1939, ISA 112/2713/N/83; MacDonald to MacMichael, February 13, 1939, CO 733/398/14; MacMichael to MacDonald, February 17, 1939, CO 733/398/14.

15. See Firestone (1975); Graham-Brown (1982: 142).

16. The account of one of these men, Bahjat Abû Gharbîya, has recently been published (Abû Gharbîya 1993).

17. On the secret military activity of the Tûlkarm scouts, see the reports of "Najib" to the Zionist Executive, CZA S/25/3875.

18. Porath's appendix mistakenly identifies Sâlih 'Ayyûsh as Sâlih 'Abbûsh (1977: 390). The source of the error is probably Yâsîn (1959: 49).

19. Harris to Newall, February 13, 1939, AIR 23/766.

20. Roach to Hall, July 28, 1936, CO 733/316/9.

21. Another example of rebels' ability: on the night of April 15–16, 1938, the British military mounted a major operation to surround 'Abd al-Rahîm al-Hâjj Muhammad's band at Dayr al-Ghusûn. The band managed to slip through the cordon and was reported to have gone toward Kafr Râ'î. On April 16, a new cordon was established in the Bala'-Dayr al-Ghusûn area, but 'Abd al-Rahîm and forty men managed to escape through it. By April 17 and 18, the army had no idea where 'Abd al-Rahîm was (Haining Report, July 4, 1938, CO 733/379/3).

22. 'Attîya 'Awad was a Qassâmite chief who operated in the Haifa-Jinîn area and was killed in battle in March 1938.

23. Air Vice Marshall Peirse report, June 1936, CO 733/317/1.

24. According to Maswari-Gault, Qâwûqjî's forces were saved from destruction at the battle of Jaba' (September 24, 1936) by the *faza'* of local peasants, who impeded the British army and helped Qâwûqjî's force retreat under cover of nightfall (1991: 77).

25. Simson writes of the dangers of the Jerusalem-Nablus road, a site of many engagements: "When deep in a valley the mouth of any highwayman or rebel must water freely with such a wealth of choice spots for an ambush. The hills are steep and all along their sides, in horizontal lines, run steps of rock the height of a man, while under them or in among the clefts of larger cliffs are caves. It requires an athlete to pursue a bandit in that land, with the eyes of a hawk and the nose of a dog to see or find where the quarry has vanished into the earth" (1937: 146–47).

26. I. Ben Zvi, General Council (Vaad Leumi) of the Jewish Community in Palestine to Tegart, October 7, 1938, Tegart Papers, box 2, file 4.

27. Skayk (1981: 125–26) reports a similar incident on May 14, 1938, in which both men and women went out to sabotage track on the orders of 'Abd al-Rahîm al-Hâjj Muhammad.

28. Report of Incidents of Sabotage on the Railways and at Railway Stations, Central Manager, Palestine Railways, Chief Secretary, October 17, 1938, ISA R/9/38.

29. By 1938, the British forces occasionally employed women searchers when they made sweeps of villages "as a deterrent against rebels disguising themselves as women, as has happened

on several occasions" ("Hostile Propaganda in Palestine, Its Origin, and Progress in 1938," Haining report, December 1, 1938, CO 733/387/638/9).

30. Statement of Mustafa Khalil Hindawieh, March 3, 1938, Tegart Papers, box 1, file 3C.

31. Popular activity in the towns is likewise not given much credit. In Safad, for instance, much of the revolt activity, such as raising money, collecting supplies, and sending intelligence to the rebel bands, was carried out by various societies and clubs such as the Islamic Sports Club, the Boy Scouts, and the Society for Scientific Awakening (al-'Askarî n.d.: 88–89). The "intimidation" necessary to maintain the six-month commercial strike at Safad was mainly carried out by social marginals: boy boot polishers, shepherds, vegetable vendors, schoolchildren, and car drivers (May 4, 1936, Blackburne Papers, MSS Brit. Emp. s. 460, box 2).

32. A British observer remarked: "Practically no search carried out by troops is not accompanied by wounding (and often killing) of defenceless villagers, smashing up of property, mixing of grain (which naturally makes all of it useless) and, worst of all, extensive robbery and looting" (Letter by Aubrey Lees, n.d. [late 1938?], CO 733/371/4).

33. MacMichael to MacDonald, December 29, 1938, CO 733/398/1.

34. Sanbar also emphasizes the importance of clan organization for the prosecution of the revolt and the movement's ability to remain clandestine (1984: 53–56).

35. See DC Galilee to Chief Secretary, April 15, 1940; Shaw, CID to Ruhi Bey Nashashibi, March 20, 1940, and March 19, 1940; all in ISA box 2, O/73/40. The commander at Majd al-Krûm, Abû Faris, was connected to Father Ya'qûb, the Greek Orthodox priest at al-Râma, whom other commanders suspected of being a British collaborator (see chapter 5).

36. Notices were posted in mosques in the Jaffa area on September 22, 1938, prohibiting the initiation of legal proceedings before government courts. The district commissioner for the south reported that during that period, any Arab might be summoned to a rebel court, and his or her attendance was required (Report on Southern District for September 1938 by R. E. H. Crosbie, DC, October 8, 1938, Lloyd-Phillips Papers, file 1.)

37. January 16, 1938, CO 733/398/1 (part 1).

38. Haining Report, November 30, 1938, CO 733/379/3.

39. MacMichael to MacDonald, December 29, 1938, CO 733/398/1 (part 1).

40. November 15, 1938, Forster Diary. Another report of whipping as a punishment is found in the *Palestine Post,* March 25, 1938.

41. Entries from August to November 1938, Forster Diary.

42. Hudîb also reports an example of a police officer who passed information secretly to the rebel forces in the Hebron area (1985: 84); see also Simson (1937: 63–64).

5 / (Un)popular Memories: Accommodation and Collaboration

1. The problem with Scott's conception is his view that subservience *always* turns out to be a sham, meaning that the subaltern is always (at least mentally) resisting, no matter what actions he or she might take (see Scott 1985).

2. During the six-month general strike of 1936 the Arab stevedores went out on strike and shut down the important port of Jaffa. The British thereupon granted the Jewish community permission to open a new harbor at Tel Aviv. Soon Tel Aviv harbor rivaled that of Jaffa, which previously had enjoyed the monopoly on port traffic. The Yishuv's relative independence of the Arab economy therefore increased while the lot of Arab harbormen declined precipitously.

3. British sources occasionally mentioned that beliefs in such British machinations existed among Palestinian peasants in the thirties, but in forms that were damaging to British control. The district commissioner of the Galilee district reported in August 1938 on a widespread con-

viction among *fallâhîn* and effendis that the British government must have been encouraging a general revolt because it was impossible to imagine that the British Empire was unable to control a small country like Palestine. The latitude the British authorities showed in Iraq by permitting the press and government to express public support for the Palestine struggle was cited as an example. In this instance, the belief made "gang" leaders (that is, band commanders) even more daring in carrying out their operations (Blackburne Report on Galilee and Acre District for August 1938, Blackburne Papers, MSS Brit. Emp. s. 460/3[2]).

4. At the same time, the PFLP was calling Arafat a traitor for dealing with King Hussein—who was responsible for the Black September massacres of Palestinians in 1970—and was implicating Abû 'Ammâr in a U.S.-Jordanian-Egyptian-Israeli conspiracy.

5. According to Robert Fisk, conspiracy thinking was all-pervasive among Lebanese, as well as Palestinians in Lebanon, after the 1975–76 civil war (Fisk 1990: 78). Jean Makdisi, on the other hand, asserts that "the Plot" referred to by Fisk "expresses something quite real: the feeling of helplessness of the Lebanese and the Palestinians in deciding their own destiny in the face of great outside opposition" (Makdisi 1991: 140). Not to mention that, between 1976 and 1982, *seventeen* foreign intelligence services were "financially" active in Lebanon (Nasr 1990: 6).

6. In chapter 4 we also saw how some interviewees deployed the plot as a critical tool; for instance, when claiming that national leaders were also party to the British conspiracy.

7. According to former Palestine police officer Edward Horne, who identifies our interlocutor as "Ja'aladi," Sa'dî Jallâl was a "famed drill instructor" for the Palestine Mobile Police Striking Force (established in 1940) and was "a useful man to have when trouble was brewing as no one wanted to cross his path and be on the receiving end of his tongue. He was very popular with his British colleagues" (1982: 501).

8. Another villager we met who served the English by working in the police force during the rebellion believed that his imperial masters were responsible for the assassination of King 'Abdallah.

9. This is a common narrateme in recollections of the pre-1948 generation.

10. See Budeiri (1979: 134). Imîl Habîbî confirmed in conversation that the Palestine Communist Party had cooperated with 'Abd al-Râziq. It is difficult to reconcile this "progressive" communiqué, however, with another circular reputedly signed by 'Ârif 'Abd al-Râziq, dated March 14, 1939. Entitled "Warning to the Jewish People," it reads (in translation): "We have sworn before Almighty God that our work shall be completed and that it shall not be stopped until we have gained victory and until we are able to hand down our trust to posterity purified of the filth of Jewish Communism. . . . Just one move from you and I shall order general mobilization of Palestine's youth. And when these forces march on your colonies then you shall have a taste of war and shall know . . . that we are the descendants of those who vanquished you at Khaibar, Qinqa', and Nabq en Naddeir [Jewish communities in the Hijaz defeated by the Prophet Muhammad]. . . . Ho, then, and start war! Then you shall know the Arabs whom God preferred over you" (Wadsworth, Jerusalem Consul General to Secretary of State, March 22, 1939, NA 867N.01/1513).

11. The claims are made in Bar Zohar and Haber's sensationalist biography of "terrorist" Hasan Salâma, a leading Fath military commander whose father (also named Hasan Salâma) was a commander in the Lydda district during the 1936–39 revolt and an underling of 'Abd al-Râziq. Photographs of 'Abd al-Râziq as a rebel show him sporting a pencil-thin mustache.

12. However, Schölch shows that Palestinian agricultural exports were expanding between 1856 and 1882, prior to the beginning of Jewish settlement (1982). In their field-crop cultivation, moreover, the early Jewish settlers followed basically the same agriculture practices as their Arab neighbors (Shafir 1989: 53). Moshe Dayan's father Shmuel, for instance, learned how to plow from an Arab when he worked as a farmhand at Yavniel (Teveth 1972: 7). This is not to say,

however, that Jewish (as well as German Templar) settlers did not bring agricultural innovations to the area (see Shafir 1989: 29).

13. According to British intelligence, in spring 1938 Hâjj Amîn was already receiving complaints from notables about "atrocities" in villages. The AHC issued pamphlets deploring attacks on villagers, and rebel headquarters at Damascus circulated instructions to commanders that no executions of traitors were to be carried out without warrants of authorization (Police Periodical Appreciation Summary no. 3/38, May 28, 1938, in High Commissioner to Secretary of State for Colonies, May 31, 1938, CO 733/359/10).

14. For instance, Nasr Eddin Nashashibi (1990: 87) supports Fakhrî Nashâshîbî's dismissal of allegations that he was a British agent and a founder of "peace bands" to fight the Arab rebellion. The claim that Fakhrî didn't organize "peace bands" is sheer fantasy (see Porath 1977: 254–56; Wilson Papers). As for Fakhrî's being a British agent, the U.S. consul general at Jerusalem reported in November 1938 that "neutral circles" believed Fakhrî was paid by the Jewish Agency to publish an article in the Palestine Post attacking the Mufti. The consul had learned from reliable sources that since the article's publication, Fakhrî's servants had been paid three months back wages (Wadsworth, Review of the Palestinian Press, November 28, 1938, NA 867N.01/415). Fakhrî's source of funds was Pinhas Rutenberg, head of the Palestine Electric Company (Black 1986: 401). The account of rebel misdeeds by Ihsân al-Nimr, a historian from a notable Nablus clan, is equally self-serving in its whitewashing of the actions of the notable class (1975: 6–14).

15. In addition to the "peace bands" discussed below, Fakhrî 'Abd al-Hâdî and the Irshayds organized peace bands in the Jinîn district, the Nashâshîbîs in the Ramallah-Jerusalem-Hebron area, and Sulaymân Tawqân and Ahmad Shak'a in the Nablus district. There were also various smaller "peace bands." On peace bands in general, see Porath (1977: 254–56); on the Ramallah district, the Wilson Papers; on the Hebron district, the Forster Diaries and O'Connor Papers (5/1/2).

16. Al-Nahr and Umm al-Faraj are among the 418 Palestinian villages destroyed after 1948.

17. The incident referred to is probably the one on October 17, 1937, related in Battershill to Ormsby-Gore, October 20, 1937, CO 733/332/10. The report states that "a large Arab party" raided the al-Dâharîya police station and stole five rifles and some ammunition. The next day, a collective fine of two thousand pounds and a punitive police post—at the villagers' expense—were imposed on the village.

18. In modern usage, al-umma simply means the nation; this usage is adapted from the religious term, umma Muhammad, Muhammad's community or the community of Muslims.

19. Shaykh Rabbâh claimed to have been the commander responsible for the area between Tarshîha and Majd al-Krûm. Porath only lists him as a "peace band" commander (1977: 391), while Yâsîn mentions a "Rabbâh" from al-Ghâbisîya whom he calls simply a band commander (qâ'id fasîl), meaning someone whose authority encompassed only one or a few villages (1959: 49).

20. Al-'Amqâ was a village near Kuwaykât, attacked and evacuated by Israeli forces in July 1948 and now the site of a Jewish settlement bearing the same name (Khalidi 1992: 4–5).

21. Although Shuqayrî repudiated this declaration, his soapbox oratory and many of his ideas about Israel were massively criticized in progressive Arab and Palestinian circles after the 1967 war. Shuqayrî was removed from his office of PLO chair in 1968. Palestinian militants hailed the 1970 PLO program calling for a democratic secular state for Jews, Christians, and Muslims in all of Palestine as a vast improvement over Shuqayrî's backward proposals regarding the future of Jews in a Palestinian state (Hirst 1977: 290–92).

22. The accounts that do mention the killing (Nuwayhid 1981: 159; al-Shuqayrî 1969: 188) merely state that Anwar was killed "wrongly" (zulman).

23. See extracts from Champion's fortnightly report, Galilee and Acre District, for period ending June 30, 1939, CO 733/406/12.

24. Curiously, no one, including Rabbâh al-'Awad, mentioned rebel qâ'id Abû Mahmûd

(Muhammad al-Ghizlân, a Qassâmite), who British sources name as the culprit in the killing of Anwar al-Shuqayrî (extracts from Champion's fortnightly report, Galilee and Acre District, for period ending June 30, 1939, CO 733/406/12).

25. Shaykh As'ad was concurrently organizing Arab "moderates" who collaborated with police in clearing Acre of "terrorists" (extracts from Champion's fortnightly report, Galilee and Acre District, for period ending June 30, 1939, CO 733/406/12).

26. Although both Shuqayrî and Nuwayhid mention the killing of Anwar al-Shuqayrî (see note 23), they say nothing about Shaykh As'ad and his family's response, which involved the organization of counterrevolutionary activity.

27. Prominent Qassâmite rebel commanders were in fact known for their lower-class backgrounds; many belonged to the Haifa lumpen proletariat.

28. See also Monthly Report by Andrews on Galilee District, July 1937, enclosure in Wauchope to Parkinson, August 5, 1937, CO 733/351/8.

29. See "Disturbance of Peace in Rameh Village," DC Galilee to Chief Secretary, April 15, 1940; Shaw, CID to Ruhi Bey Nashashibi, March 20, 1940, and March 19, 1940; all in ISA box 2, O/73/40.

30. There are documented cases of Arabs who acted publicly in support of the British but privately aided the rebels. For instance, Opposition figure Hâfiz Hamdallah of 'Anabtâ reportedly used his connections with the British to hide wanted rebels and permit them to escape during an army sweep of the Tûlkarm area (July 27, 1938, CZA S/25/4960).

6 / Memory Recoded: Intifada/*Thawra*

1. I do not devote much attention here to the grassroots nature of the intifada, which is extensively covered in Lockman and Beinin (1989), Nassar and Heacock (1990a), and Bennis (1990).

2. But see the comments of liberal Israeli scholar Yehoshuah Porath, who, like some of the Palestinian scholars cited earlier, states that the 1936–39 revolt was basically a peasant and not a popular uprising, whereas the intifada had managed to unite all social strata and groups (Morris 1988).

3. May 24, 1936, and May 25, 1936, Blackburne Papers, MSS Brit. Emp. s. 460/2(3); Wauchope to Thomas, May 25, 1936, CO 733/310/2. The comment about the "bad girl" is attributed to a Dr. Battgate.

4. The importance of stones in the revolt is also suggested by an edict Nablus district commissioner Hugh Foot issued against throwing rocks at vehicles. Foot warned that not only would the boys who threw stones be punished, but their fathers and guardians, as well (*Palestine Post,* October 12, 1937). In April 1936 the Collective Punishment Ordinance was invoked to impose punitive posts on several villages in the north (including Balad al-Shaykh) that were implicated in stones being thrown at passing cars (Wauchope to Thomas, May 4, 1936, CO 733/310/1).

5. The AWC's aims are contained in Young to Parkinson, April 14, 1932, CO 733/221/9 and Mogannam (1937: 70–73). Between 150 and 200 women attended the founding congress.

6. Enclosure, Rex vs. Auni Abdul Hadi and seventeen others, Wauchope to Cunliffe-Lister, April 5, 1934, CO 733/258/1.

7. Wauchope to Cunliffe-Lister, October 23, 1933, CO 733/239/5 (part 1).

8. CID report, August 18, 1936, IOL 1/P&S/12/3343, Coll. 26/2; MacMichael to MacDonald, September 28, 1938, CO 733/372/9; Shahuda Duzdar to British High Commissioner, June 19, 1938, CO 733/398/15.

9. Arab women organized demonstrations in Bethlehem and Haifa on June 3, 1936 (Jerusalem Consul General [Morris] to Secretary of State, June 6, 1936, NA 867N.00/310;

Morris to Secretary of State, June 13, 1936, NA 867N.00/315), and in April 1938 (*Palestine Post,* April 24, 25, and 26, 1938) to protest internments at Acre Detention Center and in Haifa. Nazareth schoolgirls reportedly organized strikes in spring 1936 (May 11, 1936, Blackburne Papers, MSS Brit. Emp. s. 460/2[2]).

10. Thanks to Ellen Fleischmann (personal communication, December 29, 1993) for information about this split, which has been kept well hidden. Peteet (who does not mention it) conjectures that the cooperation of elite women from contending factions was useful to the male leadership because it kept open otherwise-closed channels of communication (1991: 49). Sayigh, who has also stressed the unity of the women's movement (1987: 29), more recently stated her belief that the women's movement veterans she interviewed during the eighties exaggerated the degree of women's unity during the thirties, primarily in reaction to the factionalism then prevailing in the women's movement in the diaspora. Sayigh notes that Wadî' Khartabîl (of Lebanese origin) was selected as a compromise choice for chair of the Tûlkarm branch of the AWC rather than one of the Palestinian candidates from rival notable families, even though she was a newly arrived bride (personal communication).

11. April 23, 1938, Scrivenor papers, MSS Brit. Emp. s. 378; Wauchope to Ormsby-Gore, June 6, 1936, CO 733/310/3; Fitzgerald to MacDonald, October 8, 1938, CO 733/372/11; *Palestine Post,* April 24, 25, and 26, 1938.

12. Creasy to Margaret Ashby, April 14, 1939, CO 733/398/15. Ashby, the president of the International Alliance of Women for Suffrage and Equal Citizenship (IAWSEC), formally protested the detention to the colonial secretary on behalf of international feminists (Ashby to MacDonald, March 27, 1939, CO 733/398/15). At the time, the central international issue for the European-dominated feminist movement was "peace," by which it meant disarmament. The IAWSEC thereby lent indirect support to the international status quo and colonialism. But for Arab feminists like Huda Sha'râwî—the IAWSEC's fourth vice-president and active participant in the organization since 1923—"peace" in Palestine meant national independence (Hatem 1989: 62).

13. Qassâm also set up literacy classes for women around the same time.

14. Rosemary Sayigh tells us about a virtually unknown woman courier for the revolt named Fâtima 'Araqîl. A key figure in the rebel movement in western Galilee, 'Araqîl used her job as a keeper in a Turkish bath to relay messages between mountain and urban *thuwwâr* via her women clients (1992: 5).

15. The prestige of purdah and veiling, however, was also imposed on (and enjoyed by) rural women from large landowning families that could afford to dispense with female family labor outside the home (Moors 1989a: 199).

16. For an analysis of women's economic and social position in a village during the mandate based on Hilma Granqvist's ethnographies, see Moors (1989a: 196–201); see also Sayigh (1979: 16).

17. The most famous of these was Fâtima Ghazzâl, who died in battle near Lydda on June 26, 1936 (Peteet 1991: 55); a photograph that shows her bearing a rifle is reproduced in Bendt and Downing (1982: 46). Another woman fighter is mentioned in a report on rebel leader Abû Ibrâhîm's recruiting efforts in the Acre district: "A favorite theme is a story of a follower of Abu Durra who was killed and whose wife then took his rifle and ammunition and joined the 'jihad.' The moral is that in Jenin women are fighting while in Acre the men are reluctant to carry a rifle. This propaganda is having a disturbing effect" (Report on Galilee and Acre District for August 1938, Blackburne Papers, MSS Brit. Emp. s. 460/3[2]). Our interviewees mentioned two cases of women fighters but did not remember their names.

18. See also May 19, 1939, Forster Diary; Peteet (1991: 55).

19. Similar stories are found in Wilson Papers; R. H. Haining, "Hostile Propaganda in Pales-

tine," December 1, 1938, CO 733/387/63819; Simson (1937: 227); and *Palestine Post,* January 12, 1939.

20. The case was later reviewed and the woman was released and bound over, due to the "special circumstances of the case and because of [the] satisfactory record of [the] Beersheba district where she lives" (Wauchope to Ormsby-Gore, December 20, 1937, CO 733/332/10). For other examples of women sentenced to between one and ten years in jail for possessing arms or ammunition, see *Times* (London), February 22, 1938; and the *Palestine Post,* October 23, 1936; February 22, 1938; and January 12, 1939.

21. Faysal 'Abd al-Râziq told us that Commander 'Ârif 'Abd al-Râziq "was like the son of any of the villages [around al-Tayyiba]. There were times, in the beginning of the revolt, when 'Ârif was protected by women, wore women's clothes, was in women's houses, and was in the women's sections of the mosques." Also see R. H. Haining, "Hostile Propaganda in Palestine," December 1, 1938, CO 733/387/6389.

22. Peasant women also organized spontaneous demonstrations. Yâsîn tells us that in January 1938 the army arrested all the men of al-Mujaydil after the IPC pipeline—a frequent rebel target—was cut near the village. The women of al-Mujaydil proceeded to Nazareth, six kilometers away, and women of the town joined them in a demonstration in front of the district offices. The government backed down and released most of the men (1959: 92). Another demonstration involving women occurred along the Nablus-Tûlkarm road after nationalist leader Salîm 'Abd al-Rahmân of Tûlkarm was arrested in May 1936 (Shabe Khalidi to Bowman, May 26, 1936, Bowman Papers, box 2, file 3/66–70).

23. The city-dwelling contributors in the photo sport suits, ties, and *kûfîyât,* indicating that it dates from after September 1938.

24. Translated by Maswari-Gault (1991: 60) from Yuval Arnon-Ohanna, *Falahim Bamered Ha'aravi Be'eretz Yisrael, 1936–39,* pp. 44–47 (Tel Aviv: Papirus, Tel Aviv University, 1982). The original verse was in rhymed couplets; no doubt something is lost in the process of its translation from Arabic to Hebrew to English.

25. Draft Dispatch from High Commissioner to the Secretary of State for Colonies, November 24, 1938, CZA S/25/22761. My thanks to Ellen Fleischmann for sharing this reference with me.

26. The term also means "bisexual" and "impotent."

27. July 21, 1938, CZA S/25/4960. The document identifies the commander in question as Marzawi; no doubt this is 'Abd al-Hamîd Mirdâwî, from the village of Mirdâ (Porath 1977: 398).

28. Young also discusses such rebel actions (1992: 148), citing my earlier and very tentative conclusions (Swedenburg 1989b).

29. The sectarian tensions of the revolt's second period were mentioned in chapter 3; see also Porath (1977: 269–71).

30. The photo originally appeared in *Al-mar'a al-'arabîya wa qadîya Filastîn* (The Arab woman and the Palestine question), Proceedings of a conference of Eastern women, Cairo, October 15–18, 1938, Cairo, 1938.

31. See Sihâm Barghûtî's revealing account of activist women's efforts leading up to the formation of the women's committees, in Najjar (1992: 126–27).

32. The role of lower-class women of the camps and villages during the intifada, especially their actions outside the women's committee framework, remains seriously understudied; most research has thus far focused on "organized" activity.

33. The Union of Palestinian Working Women's Committees (Communist) estimated that its membership rose from a few hundred before the intifada to five thousand by July 1989; the Women's Committee for Social Work (Fath) reported that forty new committees were established between December 1987 and April 1989 (Augustin 1990: 2). The women's committee in

'Arrâba village expanded from twenty to over one hundred members during the same period (Hiltermann 1990d: 34).

34. In the leftist committees, Leninist principles of "democratic centralism" were not questioned but were undermined as regional and local groups gained more autonomy. Only the Fath women's committee decided not to decentralize (Augustin 1990: 3).

35. For an analysis of intifada "legends," in which women appear as heroines mainly by playing either the role of the nationalist "mother" or that of the simple peasant woman whose naive statements reveal a profound truth, see Kanaana (1992).

36. The DFLP's Federation of Women's Action Committees in particular promoted work outside the home, while Fath's Women's Committee for Social Work sponsored home work (Augustin 1990: 15–16).

37. The women's movement in the Occupied Territories was nevertheless more unified and independent of the directives of political organizations than was the Palestinian women's movement in the diaspora (Sayigh 1989: 166–68).

38. In Ramallah, the local Hamâs organization tried unsuccessfully to ban women from wearing tights.

39. Wearing "traditional" dress, however, did not necessarily signify political conservativism. Some activist women from conservative areas in the West Bank chose to put on modest Islamic dress when leaving home to do organizing work (see Gluck 1991: 210; Bennis 1990: 33; Hammami 1994). The issue, as Hammami emphasizes, is one of compulsion. It should also be stressed that women sympathetic to Hamâs were not simply ciphers; they, too, confronted Israeli soldiers. The issue of how Islamist groups mobilized women deserves further study.

40. See Corbin (1990a); *al-Fajr,* September 4, 1989, 2; Najjar (1992: 116); and Lewis (1988). Some have claimed that the popular and neighborhood committees were also weakened by factional infighting.

41. For more information on the sexual abuse of Palestinian women prisoners, see the publications of the Women's Organization for Political Prisoners (WOFPP), P.O. Box 31811, Tel Aviv, Israel.

42. Moors found that between 1928 and 1967 half of all brides in al-Balad village were under 16 and one-quarter were under 14, whereas between 1967 and 1981, only 10 percent were under 16 and none were under 14 (1989a: 208). Some of the intifada decline in the marriage age, however, may be accounted for by the abolition of the *mahr,* mentioned above.

43. That is greater than the annual growth rate for the Middle East as a whole, which at 3 percent is the second highest among the major cultural regions of the world. Egypt's annual growth rate has recently dropped to 1.9 percent. The women's movement, meanwhile, urges women to have no more than four or five children, while older nationalist women see ten as the optimal figure for winning the demographic war (Gluck 1991: 216).

44. Al-Azharî's comparison of the revolt and the intifada makes virtually no mention of women's part in the 1936 rebellion, while it claims that their participation was one of the intifada's "surprises" and signified the "maturity" of Palestinian women (1989: 10).

45. See Giacaman and Johnson (1994) for an assessment of the women's movement's prospects in the wake of the September 1993 peace agreement.

46. Consul General at Jerusalem (Wadsworth) to Secretary of State, (extract), September 6, 1938, in U.S. Department of State (1955: 944).

47. According to B'Tselem, the network of collaborators now numbers five thousand persons (*al-Hayât,* January 10, 1994, 5).

48. *Jerusalem Post,* May 5, 1989, cited by Tamari (1990a: 41).

49. Vitullo (1989g) reported in December 1989 that inhabitants of Nablus were expressing "mixed feelings" about the Fath-affiliated Black Panthers and the PFLP-associated Red Eagles,

both said to have killed a number of collaborators in the city, and had criticized them for "lack of discipline and respect for political leadership."

50. Such comparisons were also raised earlier, but in order to cast a positive light on the intifada. A report by Joel Greenberg in the *Jerusalem Post* quotes a Palestinian activist from Tûl-karm, who says, "The one thing we fear is a repetition of the mistakes of 1936." He adds, how-ever, that whereas in 1936–39 people were killed in political or family feuds, today they are tar-geted for serving Israeli authorities (Greenberg 1989).

51. The Israeli human rights organization B'Tselem recently published a report that esti-mates that between 1988 and 1993, somewhere between 750 and 950 Palestinians were executed as collaborators. B'Tselem reckons that more than half of these were not true collaborators with the Israeli authorities (*al-Hayât,* January 10, 1994, 5). As a point of comparison, it should be noted that, according to official French government estimates, about ten thousand French col-laborators with the Nazis were summarily dispatched before and after liberation.

52. Maswari-Gault (1991: 89), citing Arnon-Ohanna (see note 24), p. 84.

53. There were also some reports of excesses in this regard; for instance, the strike force leader in Tûlkarm refugee camp, who received forty lashes for sexually molesting a woman false-ly accused of collaboration (Hiltermann 1990a: 232).

54. Hamâs also imitates Qassâm in that its leadership in Gaza lives in the popular quarters, whereas the mainstream Fath leadership resides in villas in bourgeois quarters.

Epilogue / Fabulous Images

1. Palestine Human Rights Information Center, press release, March 22, 1994.

2. See the ongoing criticism of the "peace process" since the Oslo Agreement by Edward Said and Noam Chomsky (published variously in the *Nation, Z Magazine,* and *Al-Ahram Weekly*).

3. On the Israeli army's continued use of torture, see Amnesty International's March 1994 report, entitled "Israel and the Occupied Territories: Torture and Ill-Treatment of Political Detainees"; continuing reports on the expansion of settlements and settlement roads are being issued by the Land and Water Establishment, Anata-Shu'fat Crossway, P. O. Box 20873, East Jerusalem, via Israel (email: lawe@baraka.gn.apc.org).

4. Further investigation should be made of the relation of the *kûfîya* to U.S. youths' adop-tion of Mayan-Guatemalan wear, Rastafarian fashion, and, more recently, World Music. I would argue that the Palestinian *hatta* was always more politically charged and controversial than these other third-world items. It should be noted, too, that the *kûfîya* was the single "ethnic" item embraced by postpunk style circles, which otherwise vigorously rejected third-world "ethnic" apparel as a sign of "hippieness."

5. To my knowledge, virtually the only shops selling the *kûfîya* were "ethnic" ones owned by South Asian immigrants, whose political sensibilities regarding Palestine/Israel often diverge from hegemonic U.S. views.

6. According to Davis (1992: 8), these guidelines were almost certain to be continued by the Clinton administration; I do not know if this has in fact been the case.

Bibliography

Archives

Central Zionist Archives (CZA), Jerusalem
India Office Library (IOL), London
Israel State Archives (ISA), Jerusalem
Liddell Hart Centre for Military Archives, Kings' College, London
   General Sir Richard N. O'Connor Papers
Middle East Centre, Private Papers Collection, Saint Antony's College, Oxford
   Ernest Bowman Papers
   Dr. Elliot Forster Diary
   Ivan Lloyd-Phillips Papers
   Sir Charles Tegart Papers
   Miss H. M. Wilson Papers
National Archives (NA), Washington, D.C.
Public Records Office, London
   Air Ministry (AIR)
   Colonial Office (CO)
Rhodes House, Oxford
   Sir Kenneth William Blackburne Papers
   Sir Thomas Scrivenor Papers

Interviews

Interviews conducted by Karen Buckley in Damascus, 1986
Interviews conducted by Sonia Nimr in the West Bank, 1984
Interviews conducted by Ted Swedenburg, West Bank, 1984–85 and 1993
Interviews conducted by Ted Swedenburg and Sonia Nimr, West Bank, Gaza Strip and Israel,
   1984–85

235

Unpublished Works

Abu El-Haj, Nadia (1992). "Excavating the City: The Struggle over History in Contemporary Jerusalem." Paper presented at the American Anthropological Association Annual Meeting, San Francisco, December.

Augustin, Ebba (1990). "Changes in Structure and Politics of the West Bank Women's Movement during the Intifada." Paper presented at the Middle East Studies Association Annual Meeting, San Antonio, November.

Broshi, Magen (1991). "Archaeology and Archaeological Museums in Israel: Reflections on Problems of National Identity." Photocopy.

Buckley, Karen (1987). "Palestinian Popular Memory and Palestinian History: Identity Formation and Preservation in Exile." Master's thesis, Department of Anthropology, University of Texas.

Clark, Susan Elaine (1992). "The Prison at Akka: Palestinian Resistance and Oral Poetry." University of Indiana. Photocopy.

Doumani, Beshara (1990). "Merchants, Socioeconomic Change, and the State in Ottoman Palestine: Jabal Nablus 1800–1860." Ph.D. dissertation, Department of History, Georgetown University.

Hajjar, Lisa (1992). "Druze Translators in the Military Courts: A Case Study of Israeli State-Sponsored Identity Construction." Paper presented at the American Anthropological Association Annual Meeting, San Francisco, December.

Hammami, Rema (1994). "Between Heaven and Earth: Transformations in Religiosity and Labor among Southern Palestinian Peasant and Refugee Women, 1920–1993." Ph.D. dissertation, Department of Anthropology, Temple University.

Hudson, Leila (1990). "The Palestinian Intifada: Culture of History and the Practice of Ideology." Department of Anthropology, University of Michigan. Photocopy.

Kanaana, Sharif (1992). "The Role of Women in Intifadah Legends." Paper presented at the Discourse and Palestine Conference, University of Amsterdam, April 9–11.

Koptiuch, Kristin (1989). "A Poetics of Petty Commodity Production: Traditional Egyptian Craftsmen in the Postmodern Market." Ph.D. dissertation, Department of Anthropology, University of Texas at Austin.

Lesch, Ann Mosely (1973). "The Frustration of a Nationalist Movement: Palestine Arab Politics, 1917–1939." Ph.D. dissertation, Department of Political Science, Columbia University.

Maswari-Gault, Meira (1991). "The Palestinian Peasant Revolt in the 1930s." Master's essay, Board of History, University of California–Santa Cruz.

Paine, Robert (1991). "Masada between History and Memory." Paper presented to the Canadian Historical Association, June.

Parmentier, Barbara (1984). "Toward a Geography of Home: Palestinian Literature and the Sense of Place." Master's thesis, Department of Geography, University of Texas at Austin.

Swedenburg, Ted (1989b). "Palestinian Women in the 1936–39 Revolt: Implications for the Intifada." Paper presented at the Marxism Now: Tradition and Difference Conference, University of Massachusetts, Amherst, December.

Torstrick, Rebecca Lee (1993). "Raising and Rupturing Boundaries: The Politics of Identity in Acre, Israel." Ph.D. dissertation, Department of Anthropology, Washington University.

Wood, Davida (1991). "Human Rights and the Martyr's Wedding: Palestinian Discourses on Violent Death in the Intifada." Department of Anthropology, Princeton University.

Official Publications

Palestine Royal Commission (1937). *Memoranda Prepared by the Government of Palestine.* Colonial no. 133. London: His Majesty's Stationery Office.
U.S. Department of State (1955). *Foreign Relations of the United States: Diplomatic Papers, 1938.* Vol. 2. Washington, D.C.: Government Printing Office.

Books and Articles

Abboushi, W. F. (1977). "The Road to Rebellion: Arab Palestine in the 1930's." *Journal of Palestine Studies* 6 (3): 23–46.
'Abd al-Jawâd, Islâh (1991). "Ila ayna tattijihu al-'alaqât al-ijtimâ'îya dâkhil al-'âi'la al-Filastînîya?" (Where are social relations inside the Palestinian family headed?). In Women's Studies Committee/Bisan Center, *The Intifada and Some Women's Social Issues* (Ramallah: Bisan Center for Research and Development, 1991), 57–65.
Abdel Fattah, Awad (1984). "The Forced Concentration of the Naqab Beduin." *Al-Fajr,* February 1, pp. 8–9.
——— (1985). "Ain Karim: From Palestinian Village to Chic Israeli Suburb." *Al-Fajr,* March 1.
——— (1988). "Arabs Protest Acre's Deputy Mayor's Call for Their 'Transfer' from City." *Al-Fajr,* December 12, p. 6.
Abdul Shafi, Haidar (1992). "Intifada Flaws or a Crisis of National Movement?" *Al-Fajr,* June 1, p. 5. Translated from *al-Quds,* May 29, 1992.
Aboudi, Sami (1985). "Hisham's Palace: Umayyad Legacy in Palestine." *Al-Fajr,* March 22, p. 16.
Abou-el-haj, Rifaat (1982). "The Social Uses of the Past: Recent Arab Historiography of Ottoman Rule." *International Journal of Middle East Studies* 14 (2): 185–201.
Abu Aker, Khaled (1990). "Gulf Crisis Threatens Olive Season." *Al-Fajr,* October 8, p. 3.
Abû Fâris, Muhammad 'Abd al-Qâdir (1990). *Shuhadâ' Filastîn* (Martyrs of Palestine). Amman: Dâr al-Farqân.
Abû Gharbîya, Bahjat (1993). *Fî khidamm al-nidâl al-'arabî al-Filastînî: mudhakkarât al-munâdil Bahjat Abû Gharbîya, 1916–1949* (In the midst of the Palestinian Arab struggle: The memoirs of freedom fighter Bahjat Abû Gharbîya). Beirut: Institute for Palestine Studies.
Abû Ghûsh, 'Abd al-Majd (n.d.). *'Imwâs al-latî lan tumhî min al-dhâkira abadan* ('Imwas, which will never be obliterated from memory). Jerusalem: Baysân li-al-taba' wa-al-nashr.
Adler (Cohen), Raya (1988). "The Tenants of Wadi Hawarith: Another View of the Land Question in Palestine." *International Journal of Middle East Studies* 20 (2): 197–220.
Akko (1983). Jerusalem: Israel Ministry of Tourism.
Alcalay, Ammiel (1993). *After Jews and Arabs: Remaking Levantine Culture.* Minneapolis: University of Minnesota Press.
Allon, Yigal (1970). *Shield of David: The Story of Israel's Armed Forces.* New York: Random House.
'Allûsh, Nâjî (1978). *Al-haraka al-watanîya al-Filastînîya 'amâm al-yahûd wa-al-sahyûnîya 1882–1948* (The Palestinian national movement in the face of the Jews and Zionism, 1882–1948). 2nd printing. Beirut: Dâr al-Talî'a.
'Alqam, Nabil (1982). *Madkhal li-dirâsât al-fûlklûr* (Introduction to folklore studies). Al-Bîra: Jam'îya in'âsh al-'usra.
Anderson, Benedict (1983). *Imagined Communities.* London: Verso.
Anderson, Perry (1977). "The Antinomies of Antonio Gramsci." *New Left Review* 100:5–78.
Antonius, George (1965). *The Arab Awakening.* New York: Capricorn Books.

Antonius, Soraya (1983). "Fighting on Two Fronts: Conversations with Palestinian Women." In *Third World—Second Sex,* compiled by Miranda Davies, 63–77. London: Zed Books.

Arnon-Ohanna, Yuval (1981). "The Bands in the Palestinian Arab Revolt, 1936–39: Structure and Organization." *Asian and African Studies* 15:229–47.

Asad, Talal (1975). "Anthropological Texts and Ideological Problems: An Analysis of Cohen on Arab Villages in Israel." *Review of Middle East Studies* 1:1–40. London: Ithaca Press.

al-Ashhab, Rushdi (1983). *Al-hikayât wa-al-asâtîr al-sha'bîya fî mantiqa al-Khalîl* (Folktales and legends in the Hebron District). Jerusalem: Jam'îya al-dirâsât al-'arabîya.

Ashrawi, Hanan Mikhail (1978). "The Contemporary Palestinian Poetry of Occupation." *Journal of Palestine Studies* 7 (3): 77–101.

al-'Askarî, Yasâr (n.d.). *Qissa madînat Safad* (The story of the city of Safad). Amman: Al-munazamât al-'arabîya li-al-turbîya wa-al-thaqâfa wa-al-'ulûm.

Athamneh, Khalil (1990). "Terms from the Occupation Dictionary." *Al-Fajr,* July 30, p. 5. Translated from *al-Ittihâd.*

Atran, Scott (1986). "*Hamula* Organisation and *Masha'a* Tenure in Palestine." *Man* 21 (2): 271–95.

——— (1990). "Stones against the Iron Fist, Terror within the Nation: Alternating Structures of Violence and Cultural Identity in the Israeli-Palestinian Conflict." *Politics and Society* 18 (4): 481–526.

Avneri, Arieh (1982). *The Claim of Dispossession: Jewish Land-Settlement and the Arabs, 1878–1948.* Efal, Israel: Yad Tabenkin/New York: Herzl Press.

Avneri, Uri (1983). "Remembering Zakaria." *Al-Fajr,* July 1, p. 7. Translated from *HaOlam Hazeh,* June 15.

'Awda, Ziyâd (1984). *'Abd al-Rahîm al-Hâjj Muhammad: Batal . . . wa thawra* ('Abd al-Rahîm al-Hâjj Muhammad: Hero . . . and revolt). Amman: Al-wikâla al-'arabîya li-al-tawzî' wa-al-nashr.

——— (1988). *Min ruwwâd al-nidâl fî Filastîn 1929–1948* (Pioneers of the struggle in Palestine). Vol. 2. Amman: Dâr al-jalîl li-al-nashr.

al-Azharî, Muhammad Khâlid (1989). "Thawra 1936 wa intifâda 1987 (ru'ya muqârina)" (1936 revolt and 1987 intifada: A comparative look). *Shu'ûn Filastînîya* 199:3–26.

Barthes, Roland (1970). "Historical Discourse." In *Structuralism: A Reader,* edited by Michael Lane, 145–55. London: Cape.

——— (1977). *Image-Music-Text.* New York: Hill and Wang.

Bar Zohar, Michael, and Eitan Haber (1983). *In Search of the Red Prince.* New York: William Morrow.

Bashir, Sulayman (1980). *Communism in the Arab East.* London: Ithaca Press.

Bauer, Yehuda (1966). "The Arab Revolt of 1936." *New Outlook* 9 (6): 49–57; 9 (7): 21–28.

Bell, J. Bowyer (1977). *Terror out of Zion.* New York: St. Martin's Press.

Bendt, Ingela, and Jim Downing (1982). *We Shall Return: Women of Palestine.* London: Zed Press.

Benjamin, Walter (1969). "Theses on the Philosophy of History." In *Illuminations,* edited by Hannah Arendt, translated by Harry Zohn, 253–64. New York: Schocken Books.

——— (1971). *One Way Street and Other Writings.* London: New Left Books.

——— (1983–84). "Theoretic of Knowledge; Theory of Progress." *Philosophical Forum* 15 (1–2): 1–40.

Benjelloun-Ollivier, Nadia (1983). "Israel-Palestine: Le nombre et l'espace." *Hérodote* 29/30:83–94.

Bennis, Phyllis (1990). *From Stones to Statehood: The Palestinian Uprising.* New York: Olive Branch Press.

Benvenisti, Meron (1983). *Israeli Censorship of Arab Publications: A Survey.* New York: Fund for Free Expression.

———— (1984). *The West Bank Data Project: A Survey of Israel's Policies.* Washington, D.C.: American Enterprise Institute.

———— (1986a). *Conflicts and Contradictions.* New York: Villard Books.

———— (1986b). *1986 Report: Demographic, Economic, Legal, Social and Political Developments in the West Bank.* Boulder, Colo.: Westview Press.

Benziman, Uzi (1989). "The Weapon of Stupidity." *Al-Fajr,* November 13, p. 10. Translated from *Ha'aretz,* November 2, 1989.

Bethell, Nicholas William (1979). *The Palestine Triangle.* London: Deutsch.

Bhabha, Homi (1986). "The Other Question: Difference, Discrimination, and the Discourse of Colonialism." In *Literature, Politics, and Theory,* edited by Francis Barker et al., 148–72. London: Methuen.

————, ed. (1990). *Nation and Narration.* London: Routledge.

Black, Ian (1986). *Zionism and the Arabs, 1936–1939.* New York: Garland.

Black, Ian, and Benny Morris (1991). *Israel's Secret Wars: The Untold History of Israeli Intelligence.* London: Hamish Hamilton.

Bleifuss, Joel (1988). "An Eye for an Eye, a Bullet for a Stone." *In These Times,* January 13–19, pp. 4–5.

Bommes, Michael, and Patrick Wright (1982). "Charms of Residence." In *Making Histories,* edited by Richard Johnson et al., pp. 253–301. Minneapolis: University of Minnesota Press.

Bowerstock, G. W. (1988). "Palestine: Ancient History and Modern Politics." In *Blaming the Victims,* edited by Christopher Hitchens and Edward Said, 181–91. London: Verso.

Bowman, Glen (1985). "Time for Churches to Link Up with Palestinian Churches." *Al-Fajr,* July 12, pp. 7, 15.

———— (1992). "The Politics of Tour Guiding: Israeli and Palestinian Guides in Israel and Occupied Territories." In *Tourism and the Less Developed Countries,* edited by David Harrison, 121–34. London: Belhoven Press.

Brenner, Lenni (1983). *Zionism in the Age of Dictators.* Highland Park, N.J.: Lawrence Hill.

Brinkley, Joel (1988). "Troops Kill a Palestinian as General Strike Ushers in Seventh Month of Uprising." *New York Times,* June 10.

———— (1990). "As Palestinian Revolt Continues, Violence Declines." *New York Times,* May 4, A4.

———— (1991). "Uprising by Palestinians Seems to Lose Impetus." *New York Times,* June 12.

Broshi, Magen (1987). "Religion, Ideology, and Politics and Their Impact on Palestinian Archaeology." *Israel Museum Journal* 6:17–32.

Brown, Ken (1989). " 'Transfer' and the Discourse of Racism." *Middle East Report* 19 (2): 21–22, 47.

Bruner, Edward M., and Phyllis Gorfain (1984). "Dialogic Narration and the Paradoxes of Masada." In *Text, Play, and Story: The Construction and Reconstruction of Self and Society,* edited by Edward M. Bruner, 56–79. Washington, D.C.: American Ethnological Society.

Bryan, C. D. B. (1993). "This Side of Paradise" (review of Calvin Trillin's *Remembering Denny).* *Nation,* June 7, 784–88.

Buck-Morss, Susan (1983). "Walter Benjamin's *Passagenwerk."* *New German Critique* 29:211–40.

———— (1989). *The Dialectics of Seeing: Walter Benjamin and the Arcades Project.* Cambridge: MIT Press.

Budeiri, Musa (1979). *The Palestine Communist Party, 1919–1948.* London: Ithaca Press.

Canaan, Tewfik (1927). *Mohammedan Saints and Sanctuaries.* London: Luzac.

Cantarow, Ellen (1989). "Beita." In *Intifada,* edited by Zachary Lockman and Joel Beinin, 81–96. Boston: South End Press.

Charney, Marc D. (1988). "The Battleground from the Jordan to the Sea." *New York Times,* February 28, E3.

Chatterjee, Partha (1986). *Nationalist Thought and the Colonial World—a Derivative Discourse.* Minneapolis: University of Minnesota Press.

Clifford, James (1986). "On Ethnographic Allegory." In *Writing Culture,* edited by George Marcus and James Clifford, 98–121. Berkeley: University of California Press.

Clines, Francis X. (1988). "An Emotional Defense in Nazi Trial in Israel." *New York Times,* February 18.

Cockburn, Alexander (1988). "Beat the Devil." *Nation,* November 21, 520–21.

——— (1989). "Beat the Devil." *Nation,* February 6, 150–51.

——— (1990). "Beat the Devil." *Nation,* January 8 and 15, 42–43.

Cocks, Jay (1988). "Scarves and Minds." *Time,* March 21, 72.

Collins, Larry, and Dominique Lapierre (1973). *O Jerusalem!* New York: Pocket Books.

Conder, Claude R. (1878). *Tent Work in Palestine.* 2 vols. New York: Appleton.

Connerton, Paul (1989). *How Societies Remember.* Cambridge: Cambridge University Press.

Corbin, Neil (1990a). "Israel Seeks to Alter Its Trigger-Happy Image." *New York Guardian,* August 15, p. 14.

——— (1990b). "Statehood Hope Receding on Intifada's Third Anniversary." *New York Guardian,* December 12, pp. 10–11.

Cossali, Paul, and Clive Robson (1986). *Stateless in Gaza.* London: Zed Books.

Cumings, Bruce (1986). "Reckoning with the Korean War." *Nation,* October 25, 393, 406–9.

Daqqaq, Ibrahim (1983). "Back to Square One: A Study in the Re-emergence of the Palestinian Identity in the West Bank, 1967–1980." In *Palestinians over the Green Line,* edited by Alexander Schölch, 64–101. London: Ithaca Press.

Davis, Mike (1990). *City of Quartz.* London: Verso.

——— (1992). *Beyond Blade Runner: Urban Control: The Ecology of Fear.* Open Magazine Pamphlet Series, no. 23. Westfield, N.J.: Open Media.

——— (1993). "Who Killed Los Angeles? Part Two: The Verdict Is Given." *New Left Review* 199:29–54.

Davis, Uri, and Norton Mezvinsky, eds. (1975). *Documents from Israel, 1967–1973.* London: Ithaca Press.

Dayan-Herzbrun, Sonia (1989). "Femmes dans l'intifada: Le combat politique des Palestiniennes." *Peuples méditerranéens* 48/49:241–56.

de Certeau, Michel (1980). "Writing vs. Time: History and Anthropology in the Works of Lafitau." *Yale French Studies* 59:37–64.

——— (1986). *Heterologies.* Minneapolis: University of Minnesota Press.

Derfner, Larry (1989). "After Mt. Carmel Blaze, Nature Authority Chief Urges: Teach Arabs to Care for the Land." *Jerusalem Post,* September 22, p. 2.

Derrida, Jacques (1978). *Of Grammatology.* Translated by Gayatri Chakravorty Spivak. Baltimore, Md.: Johns Hopkins University Press.

Dirlik, John (1991). "Canada Park Built on Ruins of Palestinian Villages." *Al-Fajr,* October 21, p. 5.

Dominguez, Virginia (1989). *People as Subject, People as Object: Selfhood and Peoplehood in Contemporary Israel.* Madison: University of Wisconsin Press.

Doumani, Beshara (1992). "Rediscovering Ottoman Palestine: Writing Palestinians into History." *Journal of Palestine Studies* 21 (2): 5–28.

Duff, Douglas V. (1938). *Poor Knight's Saddle.* London: Herbert Jenkins.

Eagleton, Terry (1981). *Walter Benjamin; or, Towards a Revolutionary Criticism.* London: Verso.

Eber, Shirley, and Kevin O'Sullivan (1992). *Israel and the Occupied Territories: The Rough Guide.* London: Rough Guides. Originally published by Harrap Columbus, 1989.

Eisenzweig, Uri (1981). "An Imaginary Territory? The Problematic of Space in Zionist Discourse." *Dialectical Anthropology* 5 (4): 121–30.

Elon, Amos (1983). *The Israelis: Founders and Sons.* Harmondsworth: Penguin Books.

Elpeleg, Tsvi (1978). "The 1936–39 Disturbances: Riot or Rebellion?" *Wiener Library Bulletin* 29:40–51.

Escobar, Arturo (1992). "Imagining a Post-Development Era? Critical Thought, Development and Social Movements." *Social Text* 31/32:20–56.

Evron, Boaz (1981). "The Holocaust: Learning the Wrong Lessons." *Journal of Palestine Studies* 10 (3): 16–26. Translated from *ETON* 77 (May–June 1980).

Fabian, Johannes (1983). *Time and the Other: How Anthropology Makes Its Object.* New York: Columbia University Press.

Facts about Israel (1961). Jerusalem: Information Division, Ministry for Foreign Affairs.

Falah, Ghazi (1989). "Israeli State Policy toward Bedouin Sedentarization in the Negev." *Journal of Palestine Studies* 18 (2): 70–91.

Falk, Ze'ev (1989). "No Case for Israel to Answer." *Jerusalem Post,* September 10, p. 4.

Fanon, Frantz (1965). *A Dying Colonialism.* Translated by Haakon Chevalier. New York: Grove Press.

Fentress, James, and Chris Wickham (1992). *Social Memory.* Oxford: Blackwell.

Firestone, Ya'akov (1975). "Crop-sharing Economics in Mandatory Palestine." Part 1: *Middle Eastern Studies* 11 (1): 3–23; part 2: *Middle Eastern Studies* 11 (2): 175–94.

Fisk, Robert (1990). *Pity the Nation.* New York: Atheneum.

Flapan, Simha (1987). *The Birth of Israel: Myths and Realities.* New York: Pantheon.

Foucault, Michel (1979). *Discipline and Punish: The Birth of the Prison.* Translated by Alan Sheridan. New York: Vintage Books.

——— (1989). "Film and Popular Memory." In *Foucault Live,* 89–106. New York: Semiotext(e). Translation of "Anti-Retro: Entretien avec Michel Foucault," *Cahiers du Cinema* 251–52 (1973): 5–15.

Foucher, Michel (1983). "Israel-Palestine: Quelles frontières?" *Hérodote* 29/30:95–134.

Frangi, Abdallah (1983). *The PLO and Palestine.* Translated by Paul Knight. London: Zed Books.

Frankenberg, Ruth, and Lata Mani (n.d.). "Crosscurrents, Crosstalk: Race, 'Postcoloniality' and the Politics of Location." In *Displacement, Diaspora, and Geographies of Identity,* edited by Smadar Lavie and Ted Swedenburg. Durham, N.C.: Duke University Press. In press.

Freud, Sigmund (1959). "A Child Is Being Beaten." In *Collected Papers: Authorized Translation under the Supervision of Joan Rivière,* vol. 2, 172–201. London: Hogarth Press.

——— (1967). *Moses and Monotheism.* Translated by Katherine Jones. New York: Vintage Books.

Friedman, Thomas (1987). "Putting Hammers into Jewish Hands." *New York Times,* n.d., F16.

Frow, John (1985). "Discourse and Power." *Economy and Society* 14 (2): 193–214.

Fûrânî, Fathî (1984). *Difâ'a 'an al-judhûr* (Defending the roots). Nazareth: Al-matba' al-sha'bîya.

Genet, Jean (1986). *Un Captif amoureux.* Paris: Gallimard.

——— (1989). *Prisoner of Love.* Translated by Barbara Bray. London: Picador.

al-Ghazali, Said (1986). "Bir Zeit Center Revives the Memory of Ein Houd." *Al-Fajr,* February 28, p. 11.

Giacaman, Rita (1989). "Health as a Social Construction: The Debate in the Occupied Territories." *Middle East Report* 19 (6): 16–19.

Giacaman, Rita, and Penny Johnson (1989). "Palestinian Women: Building Barricades and Breaking Barriers." In *Intifada,* edited by Zachary Lockman and Joel Beinin, 155–69. Boston: South End Press.

———— (1994). "Searching for Strategies: The Palestinian Women's Movement in the New Era." *Middle East Report* 186:22–25.

Giacaman, Rita, and Muna Odeh (1988). "Palestinian Women's Movement in the Israeli-Occupied West Bank and Gaza Strip." Translated by Nahed El Gamal. In *Women of the Arab World,* edited by Nahid Toubia, 56–68. London: Zed Books.

Glock, Albert E. (1985). "Tradition and Change in Two Archaeologies." *American Antiquity* 50 (2): 464–77.

Glover, Yerach (1986). "Were You There, or Was It a Dream? Militaristic Aspects of Israeli Society in Modern Hebrew Literature." *Social Text* 13/14:24–48.

Gluck, Sherna Berger (1991). "Advocacy Oral History: Palestinian Women in Resistance." In *Women's Words: The Feminist Practice of Oral History,* edited by Sherna Berger Gluck and Daphne Patai, 205–19. New York: Routledge.

Goering, Kurt (1979). "Israel and the Bedouin of the Negev." *Journal of Palestine Studies* 9 (1): 3–20.

Goldring, Beth (1991). "In West Bank Village, Daily Life is Bleak." *New York Guardian,* June 26, p. 12.

Goytisolo, Juan (1992). *Saracen Chronicles: A Selection of Literary Essays.* Translated by Helen Lane. London: Quartet Books.

Graham-Brown, Sarah (1980). *Palestinians and Their Society, 1880–1946: A Photographic Essay.* London: Quartet Books.

———— (1982). "The Political Economy of the Jabal Nablus, 1920–48." In *Studies in the Economic and Social History of Palestine in the Nineteenth and Twentieth Centuries,* edited by Roger Owen, 88–176. Carbondale: Southern Illinois University Press.

———— (1983). "The Economic Consequences of the Occupation." In *Occupation: Israel over Palestine,* edited by Naseer Aruri, 167–222. Belmont, Mass.: Association of Arab-American University Graduates.

———— (1984). *Education, Repression and Liberation: Palestinians.* London: World University Service.

———— (1988). *Images of Women: The Portrayal of Women in Photography of the Middle East, 1860–1950.* New York: Columbia University Press.

Gramsci, Antonio (1971). *Selections from the Prison Notebooks.* Edited and translated by Quintin Hoare and Geoffrey Nowell Smith. New York: International Publishers.

———— (1985). *Selections from Cultural Writings.* Edited by David Forgacs and Geoffrey Nowell Smith. Translated by William Boelhower. London: Lawrence and Wishart.

Greenberg, Joel (1989). "The Plight of the 'Collaborator.' " *Jerusalem Post,* May 5, p. 4.

Gresh, Alain (1985). *The P.L.O.: The Struggle Within.* Translated by A. M. Berrett. London: Zed Books.

Guha, Ranajit (1982). "On Some Aspects of the Historiography of Colonial India." In *Subaltern Studies I: Writings on South Asian History and Society,* edited by Ranajit Guha, 1–8. Delhi: Oxford University Press.

———— (1983). *Elementary Aspects of Peasant Insurgency in Colonial India.* Delhi: Oxford University Press.

———— (1989). "Dominance without Hegemony and Its Historiography." In *Subaltern Studies VI: Writings on South Asian History and Society,* edited by Ranajit Guha, 210–309. Delhi: Oxford University Press.

Haberman, Clyde (1991). "After Four Years, Intifada Still Smolders." *New York Times,* December 9, A6.

Hadîb, Mûsâ 'Abd al-Salâm (1985). *Qarya al-Dawâyima* (The village of al-Dawâyima). Amman: Dâr al-jalîl li-al-nashr.

Haim, Yehoyada (1983). *Abandonment of Illusions: Zionist Political Attitudes toward Palestinian Arab Nationalism, 1936–1939.* Boulder, Colo.: Westview Press.

Al-Haj, Majid (1987). *Social Change and Family Processes: Arab Communities in Shefar-A'm.* Boulder, Colo.: Westview Press.

Hall, Stuart (1979). "Culture, the Media and the 'Ideological Effect.'" In *Mass Communication and Society,* edited by James Curran et al., 315–48. Beverly Hills, Calif.: Sage.

——— (1980). "Race, Articulation and Societies Structured in Dominance." In *Sociological Theories: Race and Colonialism,* 305–45. Paris: UNESCO Press.

Hall, Stuart, Bob Lumley, and Gregor McLennan (1977). "Politics and Ideology: Gramsci." *Working Papers in Cultural Studies* 10:45–76.

Hamilton, Masha (1987). "Islam's Past Neglected during Digs." *Austin American-Statesman,* December 6, H-1.

Hammami, Rema (1990). "Women, the Hijab and the Intifada." *Middle East Report* 20 (3/4): 24–28.

——— (1991). "Women's Political Participation in the Intifada: A Critical Overview." In Women's Studies Committee/Bisan Center (1991), 73–84.

Hammûda, Samîh (1985). *Al-wa'î wa-al-thawra* (Consciousness and revolt). Jerusalem: Jam'îya al-dirâsât al-'arabîya.

Hart, Alan (1984). *Arafat: Terrorist or Peacemaker?* London: Sidgwick and Jackson.

Harvard Student Agencies (1984). *Let's Go: The Budget Guide to Israel and Egypt (Including Jordan).* New York: St. Martin's Press.

Hassassian, Manuel (1988). "Comparing 1936 to 1988." *Al-Fajr,* April 24, p. 16.

Hatem, Mervat (1989). "Egyptian Upper- and Middle-Class Women's Early Nationalist Discourses on National Liberation and Peace in Palestine (1922–1944)." *Women and Politics* 9 (3): 49–70.

Hebdige, Dick (1979). *Subcultures: The Meaning of Style.* London: Methuen.

Hentoff, Nat (1986a). "The Olive Trees of Qatanna." *Village Voice,* December 23, 46.

——— (1986b). "The Peasants' Gift to Martin Luther King." *Village Voice,* December 30.

——— (1988). "Who Is a Jew? What Is a Jewish State?" *Village Voice,* December 20, 44.

Hiltermann, Joost R. (1990a). "The Enemy inside the *Intifada.*" *Nation,* September 10, 229–30, 232, 234.

——— (1990b). "Israel's Strategy to Break the Uprising." *Journal of Palestine Studies* 19 (2): 87–98.

——— (1990c). "Sustaining Movement, Creating Space: Trade Unions and Women's Committees." *Middle East Report* 20 (3/4): 32–36.

——— (1990d). "Work and Action: The Role of the Working Class in the Uprising." In *Intifada,* edited by Jamal R. Nassar and Roger Heacock, 143–57. New York: Praeger.

——— (1991a). "Between a Rock and Iraq." *Mother Jones,* January/February, 54, 56–58.

——— (1991b). *Behind the Intifada: Labor and Women's Movements in the Occupied Territories.* Princeton, N.J.: Princeton University Press.

Hirst, David (1977). *The Gun and the Olive Branch.* London: Faber and Faber.

Hitchens, Christopher (1989). "Minority Report." *Nation,* August 7 and 14, 159.

Hitchens, Christopher, and Edward Said, eds. (1988). *Blaming the Victims.* London: Verso.

Hodgson, Marshall (1974). *The Venture of Islam.* Vol. 3, *The Gunpowder Empires and Modern Times.* Chicago: University of Chicago Press.

Horne, Edward (1982). *A Job Well Done.* Leigh-on-Sea, Essex: Palestine Police Old Comrades Benevolent Association.

Hubbell, Stephen (1991). "The P.L.O. Grapples with New Realities." *Nation,* September 9, 267–69.

al-Hudhud, Rawda al-Farakh (1976). *Fî ahrâj Ya'bad: Al-shaykh 'Izz al-Dîn al-Qassâm* (In the forests of Ya'bad: Al-Shaykh 'Izz al-Dîn al-Qassâm). Amman: Manshûrât râbita al-kuttâb al-Urdunnîyîn.

——— (1983). *Sâ'im fî sijn 'Akkâ: Farhân al-Sa'dî* (Fasting in 'Akkâ Prison: Farhân al-Sa'dî). Amman: Manshûrât râbita al-kuttâb al-Urdunnîyîn.

Hudîb, Mûsa 'Abd al-Salâm (1985). *Qariya al-Duwayma* (The village of al-Duwayma). Amman: Dâr al-Jalîl li-al-nashr.

al-Hût, Bayân Nuwayhid (1981). *Al-qiyâdât wa-al-mu'assasât al-sîyâsîya fî Filastîn 1917–1948* (The leadership and the political societies in Palestine, 1917–1948). Beirut: Institute for Palestine Studies.

Ibrâhîm, Hanna (1979). *Rîha al-watan* (The smell of the nation). Acre: Dâr al-aswâr.

Jad, Islah (1990). "From Salons to the Popular Committees: Palestinian Women, 1919–1989." In *Intifada,* ed. Nassar and Heacock, 125–42. New York: Praeger.

Jameson, Fredric (1984). "Postmodernism; or, The Cultural Logic of Late Capitalism." *New Left Review* 146:53–92.

——— (1988). "Cognitive Mapping." In *Marxism and the Interpretation of Culture,* edited by Cary Nelson and Lawrence Grossbeg, 347–57. Urbana: University of Illinois Press.

Jennings, Francis (1975). *The Invasion of America.* Chapel Hill: University of North Carolina Press.

Jiryis, Sabri (1976). *The Arabs in Israel.* Translated by Aneid Bushnaq. New York: Monthly Review Press.

Johnson, Richard, Gregor McLennan, Bill Schwarz, and David Suttow, eds. (1982). *Making Histories: Studies in History Writing and Politics.* Minneapolis: University of Minnesota Press.

Kanâ'ana, Sharîf, and Bassâm al-Ka'abî (1987). *Al-qura al-Filastînîya al-mudammara. Ruqm 1: 'Ayn Hawd.* (The destroyed Palestinian villages. No. 1: 'Ayn Hawd). Bîr Zayt: Markaz al-wathâ'iq wa-al-abhâth, Jâmi'at Bîr Zayt.

Kanafani, Ghassan (n.d.). *The 1936–39 Revolt in Palestine.* N.p.: Committee for a Democratic Palestine.

Katz, Eliyahu (1988). "Moledet's Success: Thanks to Public Anxiety about the Intifada." *Al-Fajr,* November 6, p. 11. Translated from *Yediot Ahronot,* November 2, 1988.

Kayyali, A. W. (1978). *Palestine: A Modern History.* London: Croom Helm.

Kenan, Amos (1975). "Report on the Razing of Villages and the Expulsion of Refugees." In *Documents from Israel, 1967–1973,* edited by Uri Davis and Norton Mezvinsky, 148–51. London: Ithaca Press. Originally published in Amos Kenan, *Israel—a Wasted Victory,* Tel Aviv: Amikmam, 1970.

Kessel, Jerrold (1993). "Longest Held Palestinian Prisoner Freed." *Manchester Guardian,* October 20, 1993.

Khalaf, 'Alî Husayn (1982). "Tajriba 'Izz al-Dîn al-Qassâm al-Sûrîya 1882–1920" ('Izz al-Dîn al-Qassâm's Syrian experience, 1882–1920). *Shu'ûn Filastînîya* 124:17–35.

Khalaf, Issa (1991). *Politics in Palestine: Arab Factionalism and Social Disintegration, 1939–1948.* Albany: State University of New York Press.

Khaled, Leila (1973). *My People Shall Live: The Autobiography of a Revolutionary.* London: Hodder and Stoughton.

Khalidi, Rashid (1988). "Palestinian Peasant Resistance to Zionism before World War I." In *Blaming the Victims,* edited by Christopher Hitchens and Edward Said, 207–33. London: Verso.

Khalidi, Walid (1959). "Why Did the Palestinians Leave?" *Middle East Forum* 35 (7): 25–28.

——— (1984). *Before Their Diaspora: A Photographic History of the Palestinians, 1876–1948.* Washington, D.C.: Institute for Palestine Studies.

——— (1992). *All That Remains: The Palestinian Village Occupied and Depopulated by Israel in 1948.* Washington, D.C.: Institute for Palestine Studies.

————, ed. (1971). *From Haven to Conquest.* Beirut: Institute for Palestine Studies.

Khalifa, Ahmad, trans. (1989). *Al-thawra al-ʿarabîya al-kubra fî Filastîn, 1936–1939 (al-riwâya al-isrâ'îlîya al-rasmîya)* (The great Arab revolt in Palestine, 1936–1939 [An official Israeli account]). Beirut: Institute for Palestine Studies; Kuwait: University of Kuwait. Translation of Yehuda Slutski (1964), *Sefer Toldot ha-Haganah* (The History of the Haganah). Vol. 2. Tel Aviv: 'Am 'Oved.

Khalili, Ali (1980). "Palestinian Folklore." *Al-Fajr,* May 11.

al-Khalîlî, ʿAlî (1977). *Al-turâth al-Filastînî wa-al-tabaqât* (Palestinian heritage and social classes). Jerusalem: Manshûrât Salâh al-Dîn.

———— (1979). *Al-batal al-Filastînî fî al-hikâyât al-shaʿbîya* (The Palestinian hero in popular narratives). Jerusalem: Mu'assasa Ibn Rushd li-al-nashr.

Khilla, Kâmil Mahmûd (1974). *Filastîn wa-al-intidâb al-Barîtânî 1922–1933* (Palestine under the British Mandate, 1922–1933). Beirut: PLO Research Center.

Kifner, John (1988a). "Palestinian Leadership: Diffuse and Decentralized." *New York Times,* April 3, sec. 4, 1.

———— (1988b). "Israelis Recall 16,450 Who Died in War." *New York Times,* April 21, p. 3.

Kimmerling, Baruch (1983). *Zionism and Territory: The Socio-Territorial Dimensions of Zionist Politics.* Berkeley: Institute of International Studies, University of California.

Kuttab, Daoud (1990a). "The Need for a Rethink." *Middle East International,* August 3, pp. 9–11.

———— (1990b). "Reining in the Activists." *Middle East International,* January 19, p. 10.

Lachman, Shai (1982). "Arab Rebellion and Terrorism in Palestine, 1929–39: The Case of Sheikh Izz al-Din al-Qassam and His Movement." In *Zionism and Arabism in Palestine and Israel,* edited by Elie Kedourie and Sylvia G. Haim, 52–99. London: Frank Cass.

Laclau, Ernesto (1977). *Politics and Ideology in Marxist Theory.* London: New Left Books.

La Guardia, Anton (1992). "Four Hurt in Israeli Undercover Mix-up." *Daily Telegraph* (London), December 9, 12.

Lavie, Smadar (1990). *The Poetics of Military Occupation: Mzeina Allegories of Bedouin Identity under Israeli and Egyptian Rule.* Berkeley: University of California Press.

———— (1992). "Blow-Ups in the Borderzones: Third World Israeli Authors' Gropings for Home." *New Formations* 18:84–106.

Layoun, Mary N. (1988). "Fictional Formations and Deformations of National Culture." *South Atlantic Quarterly* 87 (1): 53–73.

Legrain, Jean-François (1993). "De la faiblesse de l'OLP, de la sincérité d'Israël." *Le Monde,* September 10.

Lewis, Anthony (1988). "Through a Glass Darkly." *New York Times,* June 26, E27.

Livneh, Micha, and Zeʿev Meshel (n.d.). *Masada.* Jerusalem: National Parks Authority.

Lockman, Zachary, and Joel Beinin, eds. (1989). *Intifada: The Palestinian Uprising against Israeli Occupation.* Boston: South End Press.

Lustick, Ian (1980). *Arabs in the Jewish State.* Austin: University of Texas Press.

Maddrell, Penny (1990). *Beduin of the Negev.* Minority Rights Group Report no. 81. London: Minority Rights Group.

Makdisi, Jean Said (1991). "Lebanon Agonistes." *Transition* 53:133–42.

Mandel, Neville (1976). *The Arabs and Zionism before World War I.* Berkeley: University of California Press.

Marcus, Greil (1989). *Lipstick Traces: A Secret History of the Twentieth Century.* Cambridge: Harvard University Press.

Margalit, Dan (1978). "The Green Squad." *Journal of Palestine Studies* 7 (3): 143–45. Translated from *Ha'aretz,* September 30, 1978.

Marzorati, Gerald (1988). "An Arab Voice in Israel: Novelist Anton Shammas Talks about the Other Israelis." *New York Times Magazine,* September 18, 54, 100–101, 106, 108–9.

Matar, Ibrahim (1983). "From Palestinian to Israeli: Jerusalem 1948–1982." *Journal of Palestine Studies* 12 (4): 57–63.

Mattar, Philip (1988). *The Mufti of Jerusalem.* New York: Columbia University Press.

McDowall, David (1989). *Palestine and Israel: The Uprising and Beyond.* Berkeley: University of California Press.

McKay, Fiona (1989). "Ain Hawd vs. Ein Hod: Deprivation vs. Prosperity." *Al-Fajr,* March 27, p. 9.

McMickle, John (1989). "Shakespeare and Israeli Authors among Books Banned in Areas." *Al-Fajr,* November 6, p. 15.

Menocal, Maria Rosa (1987). *The Arabic Role in Medieval Literary History.* Philadelphia: University of Pennsylvania Press.

Mies, Maria (1986). *Patriarchy and Accumulation on a World Scale: Women in the International Division of Labor.* London: Zed Books.

Miskin, Al (1993). "Mediations: Another Time, Another Deportation." *Middle East Report* 182:41–42.

Mitter, Swasti (1986). *Common Fate, Common Bond: Women in the Global Economy.* London: Pluto Press.

Mogannam, Matiel E. T. (1937). *The Arab Woman and the Palestine Problem.* London: Herbert Joseph.

Moors, Annelies (1989a). "Gender Hierarchy in a Palestinian Village: The Case of Al-Balad." In *The Rural Middle East,* edited by Kathy and Pandeli Glavanis, 195–209. London: Birzeit University and Zed Books.

——— (1989b). *Restructuring and Gender: Garment Production in Nablus.* MERA Occasional Paper no. 3. Amsterdam: Middle East Research Associates.

Morris, Benny (1987). *The Birth of the Palestinian Refugee Problem, 1947–1949.* New York: Cambridge University Press.

——— (1988). "A United Uprising" (interview with Yehoshuah Porath). *Jerusalem Post Magazine,* March 4, p. 7.

——— (1990). *1948 and After: Israel and the Palestinians.* Oxford: Clarendon Press.

Mortimer, Edward (1982). *Faith and Power.* New York: Vintage.

Morton, Geoffrey (1957). *Just the Job: Some Experiences of a Colonial Policeman.* London: Hodder and Stoughton.

Mosley, Leonard (1955). *Gideon Goes to War.* New York: Scribner.

Mouffe, Chantal (1981). "Hegemony and the Integral State in Gramsci: Towards a New Concept of Politics." In *Silver Linings,* edited by George Bridges and Rosalind Brunt, pp. 167–87. London: Lawrence and Wishart.

Muhawi, Ibrahim, and Sharif Kanaana (1989). *Speak, Bird, Speak: Palestinian Arab Folktales.* Berkeley: University of California Press.

Muhsin, 'Isa Khalîl (1986). *Filastîn al-umm wa ibnuhâ al-barr: 'Abd al-Qâdir al-Husaynî* (Mother Palestine and her righteous son: 'Abd al-Qâdir al-Husaynî). Amman: Dâr al-jalîl li-al-nashr.

Musa, Imad (1992). "Palestinians Address Flip Side of Intifada." *Al-Fajr,* May 25, pp. 1, 15.

Muslih, Muhammad (1988). *The Origins of Palestinian Nationalism.* New York: Columbia University Press.

al-Muzayyin, 'Abd al-Rahmân (1981). *Al-azyâ' al-sha'bîya al-Filastînîya* (Palestinian popular costume). Beirut: Manshûrât Filastîn al-muhtalla.

Nairn, Tom (1981). *The Break-Up of Britain,* 2nd ed. London: Verso.

Najjar, Orayb, with Kitty Warnock (1992). *Portraits of Palestinian Women.* Salt Lake City: University of Utah Press.

Naqâra, Hanna (1985). *Muhâmî al-'ard wa-al-sha'b* (Lawyer for the land and the people). Acre: Dâr al-aswâr.

Nashashibi, Nasr Eddin (1990). *Jerusalem's Other Voice: Ragheb Nashashibi and Moderation in Palestinian Politics, 1920–1948.* Exeter: Ithaca Press.

Nasr, Salim (1990). "Lebanon's War: Is the End in Sight?" *Middle East Report* 20 (1): 4–8.

Nassar, Jamal R., and Roger Heacock, eds. (1990a). *Intifada: Palestine at the Crossroads.* New York: Praeger.

——— (1990b). "The Future in Light of the Past." In *Intifada: Palestine at the Crossroads,* edited by Jamal R. Nassar and Roger Heacock, 309–15. New York: Praeger.

Nazzal, Nafez (1978). *The Palestinian Exodus from Galilee, 1948.* Beirut: Institute for Palestine Studies.

Neff, Donald (1992). "Israel's Dependence on the U.S.: The Full Extent of the Special Relationship." *Middle East International,* May 1, pp. 16–17.

al-Nimr, Ihsân (1975). *Ta'rîkh Jabal Nâblus wa-al-Balqâ'* (The history of Nablus Mountain and al-Balqâ'). Vol 4. Nablus: Matba'a jam'îya 'ummâl al-matâba' al-ta'âwanîya.

Nuwayhid, 'Ajâj ([1961] 1981). *Rijâl min Filastîn: Mâ bayn bidâya al-qarn hata 'âm 1948.* (Men from Palestine: From the beginning of the century until 1948). Beirut: Manshûrât Filastîn al-muhtalla.

Owen, Roger, ed. (1982). *Studies in the Economic and Social History of Palestine in the Nineteenth and Twentieth Centuries.* Carbondale: Southern Illinois University Press.

Passerini, Luisa (1979). "Work Ideology and Consensus under Italian Fascism." *History Workshop* 8:82–108.

——— (1983). "Memory." *History Workshop* 15:195–96.

Pêcheux, Michel, and C. Fuch (1982). "Language, Ideology and Discourse Analysis: An Overview." *Praxis* 6:3–20.

Peneff, Jean (1990). "Myths in Life Stories." In *The Myths We Live By,* edited by Raphael Samuel and Paul Thompson, 49–60. New York: Routledge.

Penley, Constance (1984). " 'A Certain Refusal of Difference': Feminism and Film Theory." In *Art after Modernism: Rethinking Representation,* edited by Brian Wallis, 375–89. New York: New Museum of Contemporary Art.

Pesa, Flavia (1985). "The Image of Woman in Palestinian Literature." *Al-Fajr,* March 15, p. 11.

Peteet, Julie (1986). "No Going Back? Women and the Palestinian Movement." *Middle East Report* 16 (1): 20–24.

——— (1991). *Gender in Crisis: Women and the Palestinian Resistance Movement.* New York: Columbia University Press.

Peters, Joan (1984). *From Time Immemorial.* New York: Harper and Row.

Plascov, Avi (1982). "The Palestinians of Jordan's Border." In *Studies in the Economic and Social History of Palestine in the Nineteenth and Twentieth Centuries,* edited by Roger Owen, 203–41. Carbondale: Southern Illinois University Press.

Pomerantz, Marsha (1984). "Chaotic Revival." *Jerusalem Post Friday Magazine,* March 16, pp. 6–7.

Popular Memory Group (1982). "Popular Memory: Theory, Politics, Method." In *Making Histories,* edited by Richard Johnson et al., 205–52. Minneapolis: University of Minnesota Press.

Porath, Yehoshua (1974). *The Emergence of the Palestinian Arab National Movement, 1918–29.* London: Frank Cass.

——— (1977). *The Palestinian Arab National Movement: From Riots to Rebellion.* London: Frank Cass.

Poulantzas, Nicos (1980). *State, Power, Socialism.* Translated by Patrick Camiller. London: New Left Books.

Qâsim, 'Abd al-Sittâr (1984). *Al-shaykh al-mujâhid 'Izz al-Dîn al-Qassâm* (The rebel shaykh 'Izz al-Dîn al-Qassâm). Beirut: Dâr al-'umma li-al-nashr.

al-Qâsim, Nabîh (1976). *Wâqi' al-durûz fî Isrâ'îl* (The reality of the Druze in Israel). Jerusalem: Dâr al-'atyâm al-islâmîya al-sinâ'îya.

Rabbani, Mouin (1990). "Killed for Wearing a Mask." *New York Guardian,* May 13, p. 13.

Rapaport, Herman (1984). "Vietnam: The Thousand Plateaus." In *The Sixties without Apology,* edited by Sohnya Sayres et al., 137–47. Minneapolis: University of Minnesota Press.

Ress, Mary Judith (1991). "Will North Impose 'Eco-fascism' on South?" *New York Guardian,* July 3, p. 18.

Rishmawi, Mona (1988). "The Legal Status of Palestinian Women in the Occupied Territories." Translated be Nahed El Gamal. In *Women of the Arab World,* edited by Nahid Toubia, 79–92. London: Zed Books.

Rockwell, Susan (1985). "Palestinian Women Workers in the Israeli-Occupied Gaza Strip." *Journal of Palestine Studies* 54:114–36.

Rodinson, Maxime (1973). *Israel: A Colonial Settler State?* Translated by David Thorstad. New York: Monad Press.

Rose, Jacqueline (1986). *Sexuality in the Field of Vision.* London: Verso.

Rosen, Ruli (1991). "Us and You." *Al-Fajr,* October 7, pp. 10, 15. Translated from *Kol Ha'ir,* September 20, 1991.

Sachar, Howard Morley (1958). *The Course of Modern Jewish History.* New York: Dell.

Said, Edward (1978). *Orientalism.* New York: Random House.

——— (1980). *The Question of Palestine.* New York: Vintage Books.

——— (1984). "Permission to Narrate." *Journal of Palestine Studies* 51:27–48.

——— (1986). *After the Last Sky.* New York: Pantheon.

——— (1988). "Identity, Negation and Violence." *New Left Review* 171:46–60.

——— (1989). "Intifada and Independence." In *Intifada,* edited by Zachary Lockman and Joel Beinin, 5–22. Boston: South End Press.

Saleh, Samir Abdallah (1990). "The Effects of Israeli Occupation on the Economy of the West Bank and Gaza Strip." In Nassar and Heacock (1990a), 37–51.

al-Salhût, Jamîl, and Muhammad Sâlih Shahâda (1982). *Suwar min al-'adab al-sha'bîya al-Filastînîya* (Pictures from Palestinian popular literature). Vol. 1. Jerusalem: Manshûrât al-ruwwâd.

Samuel, Raphael, and Paul Thompson, eds. (1990). *The Myths We Live By.* New York: Routledge.

Sanbar, Elias (1984). *Palestine 1948. L'Expulsion.* Washington, D.C.: Institut d'études Palestiniennes.

——— (1988). " 'Izz al-Dîn Qassâm, un homme d'unanimité. Remarques preliminaires à une recherche sur le mouvement de Shaykh 'Izz al-Dîn Qassâm." In *Studia Palestina: Studies in Honour of Constantine K. Zurayk,* edited by Hisham Nashabe, 52–68. Beirut: Institute for Palestine Studies.

al-Sârîsî, 'Umar 'Abd al-Rahmân (1980). *Al-hikâya al-sha'bîya fî al-mujtama' al-Filastînî* (The popular tale in Palestinian society). Beirut: Al-mu'assasa al-'arabîya li-al-dirâsât wa-al-nashr.

Sayigh, Rosemary (1979). *From Peasants to Revolutionaries.* London: Zed Press.

——— (1983). "Women in Struggle—Palestine." *Third World Quarterly* 5 (4): 880–86.

——— (1984). "Looking across the Mediterranean." *MERIP Reports* 124:22–26.

——— (1987). "Femmes palestiniennes: Une histoire en quête d'historiens." *Revue d'études Palestiniennes* 23:13–33.

——— (1989). "Palestinian Women: Triple Burden, Single Struggle." In *Khamsin, Palestine: Profile of an Occupation,* 153–77. London: Zed Books.

——— (1992). "Introduction. Palestinian Women: A Case of Neglect." In Orayb Najjar, *Portraits of Palestinian Women,* 1–26. Salt Lake City: University of Utah Press.

Schenker, Hillel (1988). "Violence in Occupied Territories Signals More Tragedy on Horizon." *In These Times,* January 13–19, p. 11.

Schleiffer, Abdallah (1979). "The Life and Thought of 'Izz al-Din al-Qassam." *Islamic Quarterly* 23 (2): 61–81.

Schölch, Alexander (1982). "European Penetration and the Economic Development of Palestine, 1856–1882". In *Studies in the Economic and Social History of Palestine in the Nineteenth and Twentieth Centuries,* edited by Roger Owen, 10–87. Carbondale: Southern Illinois University Press.

Scott, James (1985). *Weapons of the Weak.* New Haven, Conn.: Yale University Press.

Scott, Joan (1988). *Gender and the Politics of History.* New York: Columbia University Press.

—— (1992). "Experience." In Judith Butler and Joan Scott, *Feminists Theorize the Political,* 22–40. New York: Routledge.

Seager, Moe (1989). "Israelis Who Stand Up for Peace." *New York Guardian,* December 6, pp. 1, 15.

Seger, Karen, ed. (1981). *Portrait of a Palestinian Village: The Photographs of Hilma Granqvist.* London: Third World Centre for Research and Publishing.

Segev, Tom (1986). *1949: The First Israelis.* New York: Free Press.

Shabîb, Sâmih (1990). "Al-haraka al-sha'bîya al-Filastînîya fî 'ahd al-intidâb al-Barîtânî" (The popular Palestinian movement during the British mandate era). *Shu'ûn Filastînîya* 205:19–39.

Shafir, Gershon (1989). *Land, Labor and the Origins of the Israeli-Palestinian Conflict, 1882–1914.* Cambridge: Cambridge University Press.

Shahak, Israel (1975). "Arab Villages Destroyed in Israel." In *Documents from Israel, 1967–73,* edited by Uri Davis and Norton Mezvinsky, 43–55. London: Ithaca Press.

—— (1988). "Yitzhak Shamir's Ideological Heritage." *Middle East International* (November 18): 16–17.

Shakid, Roni (1991). "Who Is Really in Control in Nablus?" *Al-Fajr,* June 3, pp. 10, 15. Translated from unidentified Israeli newspaper, probably *Yediot Aharanot.*

Shammas, Anton (1988). "The Morning After." *New York Review of Books,* September 29, 47–51.

Shapira, Anita (1992). *Land and Power: The Zionist Resort to Force, 1881–1948.* New York: Oxford University Press.

Sharpe, Jennifer (1993). *Allegories of Empire.* Minneapolis: University of Minnesota Press.

Shehadeh, Raja (1982). *The Third Way.* London: Quartet Books.

Shohat, Ella (1988). "Sephardim in Israel: Zionism from the Standpoint of Its Jewish Victims." *Social Text* 19/20:1–36.

—— (1989). *Israeli Cinema: East/West and the Politics of Representation.* Austin: University of Texas Press.

—— (1992). "Notes on the Post-Colonial." *Social Text* 31/32:9–113.

Shohat, Orit (1985). "A Sad but Inevitable Comparison." *Israleft* 270, October 15, p. 5. Translated from *Ha'aretz* supplement, September 27, 1985.

al-Shuqayrî, Ahmad (1969). *Arba'ûn 'âman fî al-hayâ al-'arabîya wa-al-duwalîya* (Forty years in Arab and international life). Beirut: Dar al-nahâr wa-al-nashr.

Siddiq, Muhammad (1984). *Man Is a Cause: Political Consciousness and the Fiction of Ghassan Kanafani.* Seattle: University of Washington Press.

Silberman, Neil Asher (1989). *Between Past and Present: Archaeology, Ideology and Nationalism in the Modern Middle East.* New York: Anchor Books.

—— (1990). "Lure of the Holy Land." *Archaeology* (November/December): 29–34.

Simson, H. J. (1937). *British Rule and Rebellion.* Edinburgh and London: Blackwood .

Sirhân, Nimr (1989). *Mawsû' al-fûlklûr al-Filastînî* (Encyclopedia of Palestinian folklore). 3 vols. Amman: Al-Dustûr.

Skayk, Ibrâhîm Khalîl (1981). *Ghazza 'abr al-ta'rîkh (al-jiza' al-râbi'): Taht al-intidâb al-Barîtânî* (Gaza throughout history, vol. 4: Under the British mandate). N.p.

Smith, George Adam ([1894] 1966). *The Historical Geography of the Holy Land.* 30th ed. London: Fontana.

Sonneman, Toby (1992). "Burned in the Holocaust." *New York Times,* May 2, p. 17.

Spivak, Gayatri Chakravorty (1985). "The Rani of Sirmur." In *Europe and Its Others,* edited by Francis Barker et al., vol. 1, 128–51. Colchester: University of Essex.

——— (1987). *In Other Worlds.* New York: Methuen.

——— (1990). *The Post-Colonial Critic: Interviews, Strategies, Dialogues.* Edited by Sarah Harasym. New York: Routledge.

Stein, Kenneth (1984). *The Land Question in Palestine, 1917–1939.* Chapel Hill: University of North Carolina Press.

Swedenburg, Ted (1987) "Al-Qassam Remembered." *Alif: Journal of Comparative Poetics* 7:9–24.

——— (1988). "The Role of the Palestinian Peasantry in the Great Revolt (1936–39)." In *Islam, Politics, and Social Movements,* edited by Edmund Burke III and Ira Lapidus, 169–203. Berkeley: University of California Press.

——— (1989a). "Occupational Hazards: Palestine Ethnography." *Cultural Anthropology* 4 (3): 265–72.

——— (1990). "The Palestinian Peasant as National Signifier." *Anthropological Quarterly* 63 (1): 18–30.

Taggar, Yehuda (1986). *The Mufti of Jerusalem and Palestine Arab Politics, 1930–1937.* New York: Garland. Reprint of Ph.D. thesis, University of London, 1973.

Tal, Yarih (1991). "What Was Published Abroad: In the Beginning Members of the Unit Disguised as Journalists and then as Arabs." *Al-Fajr,* July 1, p. 10. Translated from unidentified Israeli newspaper.

Tamari, Salim (1981). "Building Other Peoples' Homes: The Palestinian Peasant's Household and Work in Israel." *Journal of Palestine Studies* 12 (1): 31–66.

——— (1982). "Factionalism and Class Formation in Recent Palestinian History." In *Studies in the Economic and Social History of Palestine in the Nineteenth and Twentieth Centuries,* edited by Roger Owen, 177–202. Carbondale: Southern Illinois University Press.

——— (1990a). "Eyeless in Judea: Israel's Strategy of Collaborators and Forgeries." *Middle East Report* 164/165 (May–August): 39–44.

——— (1990b). "The Revolt of the Petite Bourgeoisie: Urban Merchants and the Palestinian Uprising." In *Intifada,* edited by Jamal R. Nassar and Roger Heacock, 159–73. New York: Praeger.

Taraki, Lisa (1990). "The Development of Political Consciousness among Palestinians in the Occupied Territories, 1967–1987." In *Intifada,* edited by Jamal R. Nassar and Roger Heacock, 53–71. New York: Praeger.

Taussig, Michael (1987). *Colonialism, Shamanism, and the Wild Man: A Study in Terror and Healing.* Chicago: University of Chicago Press.

——— (1992). *The Nervous System.* New York: Routledge.

Tawfiq, Basem (1990). "Openness and Frankness Dominate Discussion on Women's Role." *Al-Fajr,* December 24, pp. 8–9.

Teveth, Shabtai (1972). *Moshe Dayan.* London: Weidenfeld and Nicolson.

——— (1985). *Ben-Gurion and the Palestinian Arabs.* Oxford: Oxford University Press.

Thompson, Paul (1977). "Oral History in Israel." *Oral History* 5 (1): 35–39.

Torney, Kate (1991). "Israeli Army Launches Campaign to Recruit Arabs." *Al-Fajr,* August 12, p. 3.

Toubia, Nahid, ed. (1988). *Women of the Arab World: The Coming Challenge.* London: Zed Books.

Tuqan, Fadwa (1990). *A Mountainous Journey.* Translated by Olive Kenny. Saint Paul, Minn.: Graywolf Press.

Uris, Leon (1984). *The Haj.* New York: Doubleday.

Usher, Graham (1992). "Palestinian Women, the *Intifada* and the State of Independence: An Interview with Rita Giacaman." *Race and Class* 34 (3): 31–43.

Vitullo, Anita (1988a). "Israeli Bullet, but Palestinians Pay." *New York Guardian,* April 20, pp. 1, 12.

——— (1988b). "West Bank Lives Shaped by War." *New York Guardian,* June 1, pp. 10–11.

——— (1989a). "Women Rise Up for Palestine." *New York Guardian,* March 8, pp. 1, 13.

——— (1989b). "Israelis Expel Activists, Flouting the UN." *New York Guardian,* September 13, p. 16.

——— (1989c). "Attacks on Collaborators Have Israel Worried." *New York Guardian,* September 27, p. 14.

——— (1989d). "Palestinians Gain Strength through Two-Year Struggle." *New York Guardian,* December 20, p. 12.

——— (1993). "Palestinian Women: Several Steps Back." In *For Palestine,* edited by Jay Murphy, 105–11. New York: Writers and Readers.

Ware, Vron (1992). *Beyond the Pale: White Women, Racism and History.* London: Verso.

Warnock, Kitty (1990). *Land before Honour: Palestinian Women in the Occupied Territories.* New York: Monthly Review Press.

Weir, Shelagh (1989). *Palestinian Costume.* Austin: University of Texas Press.

White, Hayden (1981). "The Value of Narrativity in the Representation of Reality." In *On Narrative,* edited by W. J. T. Mitchell, 1–23. Chicago: University of Chicago Press.

Williams, Daniel (1990). "Palestinian Intifada: Hints of Failure amid Growing Discontent." *Los Angeles Times,* July 22, A1, A7–8.

Williams, Raymond (1977). *Marxism and Literature.* Oxford: Oxford University Press.

Winkelhane, Gerd (1988). "Le Costume damascène a la fin de la période ottomane: Tradition et occidentalisation." In *Mémoire de soie: Costumes et parures de Palestine et de Jordanie,* 134–40. Paris: Institut du Monde Arabe-EDIFRA.

Women's Studies Committee/Bisan Center (1991). *The Intifada and Some Women's Social Issues.* Ramallah: Bisan Center for Research and Development.

Wood, Chris (1988). "Where Will the Revolt End?" *Maclean's,* April 18, pp. 20–24.

Wright, Patrick (1985). *On Living in an Old Country: The National Past in Contemporary Britain.* London: Verso.

Yadin, Yigael (n.d.). Preface to Micha Livneh and Ze'ev Meshel, *Masada.* Jerusalem: National Parks Authority.

——— (1966). *Masada: Herod's Fortress and the Zealots' Last Stand.* New York: Random House.

Yâsîn, 'Abd al-Qâdir (1975). *Kifâh al-sha'b al-Filastînî qabl al-'âm 1948* (The struggle of the Palestinian people before 1948). Beirut: PLO Research Center.

Yâsîn, Subhî (1959). *Al-thawra al-'arabîya al-kubra fî Filastîn, 1936–1939* (The great Arab revolt in Palestine, 1936–1939). Cairo: Dar al-kâtib al-'arabî.

——— (1967). *Harb al-'asabât fî Filastîn* (The war of the bands in Palestine). Cairo: Al-mu'assasa al-Misrîya al-'âma li-al-ta'lîf wa-al-nashr.

Yehoshuah, Abraham B. (1970). *Three Days and a Child.* Translated by Miriam Arad. Garden City, N.Y.: Doubleday.

Young, Elise G. (1992). *Keepers of the History: Women and the Israeli-Palestinian Conflict.* New York: Teachers College Press.

Zu'aytir, Akram (1955). *Al-qadîya al-Filastînîya* (The Palestine question). Cairo: Dar al-Ma'ârif.

——— (1980). *Al-haraka al-watanîya al-Filastînîya 1935–1939: Yawmiyât Akram Zu'aytir* (The Palestinian National Movement, 1935–1939: The diaries of Akram Zu'aytir). Beirut: Mu'assasat al-dirâsât al-Filastînîya.

Newspapers and Newsletters

Al-Fajr (English, Jerusalem), 1980–92.
"From the Field" (A Monthly Report on Selected Human Rights Issues, Palestine Human Rights Information Center, Jerusalem), 1993.
New York Guardian, 1987–91.
Al-Hayât (London), 1992–94.
Human Rights Update (Palestine Human Rights Information Center, Jerusalem), 1993.
Israleft Bi-Weekly News Service (Jerusalem), 1984–85.
Jerusalem Post (Jerusalem), 1984–85, 1988–90.
Palestine Post (Jerusalem), 1935–39.
Times (London), 1936–39.

Index

Ted Swedenburg is assistant professor of anthropology at the University of Arkansas. He lived in Lebanon between 1964 and 1976, and he received his undergraduate degree from the American University of Beirut and Ph.D. in 1988 at the University of Texas at Austin. He previously taught at the University of Washington. He is coeditor of *Displacement, Diaspora, and Geographies of Identity,* and has contributed articles to *Cultural Anthropology, Diaspora, Cultural Studies,* and *New Formations.*